Days
to
Remember

Arved Ojamaa Ashby, MD.

Days to Remember is a new title for a compilation of two books,
Capful of Wind printed in 1999
and Wind at My Back printed in 2001 in Tallinn, Estonia.

Cover Image: The background of the cover of *Days to Remember* is a watercolor by Dr. Jim Michael painted for Dr. Arved Ojamaa Ashby. Pictured is the old downtown Sheboygan Clinic building on Eighth Street. We see the corner office of Dr. Ashby's. In the painting you see through the corner window a lady disrobing behind a screen, and at the next window Dr. Ashby dictating the patient's history.

The soldier at the top of the Civil War statue, standing tall across the street in Fountain Park, has a direct view through the clinic window of the undressing lady. The demure soldier covers his eyes so as not to be a Peeping Tom.

ISBN — 978-1507607831
Printed by Sheboygan County Historical Research Center, 2015,
schrc.org
arvedoa@gmail. com

CAPFUL

of

WIND

Arved Ojamaa Ashby, M.D.

Introduction

This is the story of a first generation immigrant to the United States of America. I landed at Ellis Island on the 23rd of August, 1951 at the age of 29. A cardboard suitcase carried all my worldly possessions, just a few personal belongings and one hundred dollars in an unsolicited loan from the Lutheran World Relief Organization.

I also carried an identification certificate stating my name and birth date. This paradoxical document listed Estonia as my place of birth, but the next line answering the question of citizenship - carried the German word "*staatenlos*", meaning without a country. The Soviet Union had occupied Estonia during the Second World War, and claimed it as her own territory. The annexation, however, was not recognized by Western powers. This left me, officially and personally, *heimatlos* as well as *staatenlos*.

So I arrived in America with no homeland to my name and no employable trade or profession, and my high school English was far from fluent. I had studied medicine in post-war Germany and in the process had become fluent in German. None of this counted for a hill of beans in the unemployment office in Fresno, California, my destination in the United States. But, I considered myself lucky to have escaped the Russian occupation and deportation to Siberia as an "enemy of the Revolution," the fates and avenues to death suffered by so many of my friends and classmates.

I found work at the Kingsbury Cotton Oil Company in Kingsbury, California. I was fortunate to be admitted to the University of California Medical School in San Francisco in fall 1952. I graduated with the M.D. degree on the 23rd of June, 1955, just three years after arriving at Ellis Island

Now retired, I can lean back with a feeling of satisfaction. I was able to fulfill my goal, and I must say - against all odds. I found hope and opportunity free for the taking. To make things go your way, all you need add is ambition and endurance. If there is such a thing as luck, it will seek you out as an added blessing, but don't count on it. The word "impossible" should have no place in your endeavor; leave it behind as an unknown to be looked up in the dictionary.

Writing is terra incognita to me. Up until now my only expository prose was confined to medical histories. In this field, where malpractice lawyers might be looking for derogatory or unprofessional remarks, one was not free to practice a literary talent. I still admire the wit of Doctor Burnell Eckhardt, an internist who once wrote the following consultation note about one of our patients, "I can't find anything wrong with Molly between her medulla oblongata and sphincter anii." Now there is literary value in this sentence, and he managed to cover all the lady's organ systems as well, quite an accomplishment. This pearl dates back to the early 1960s. I don't know a doctor today who would be brave and creative enough to exhibit literary skill in writing medical histories.

I am my own "patient" now and free to write my own "history." The whole story is about life in the old country, and my struggle to make it through the war years. It is written for my two sons and not for the public at large. It is not a novel. The persons, places and names are not imagined. To animate some experiences I have added dialogue, which itself is not true word for word, but the circumstances surrounding it are not fictitious. The sentimentality or lack thereof might not coincide with present-day sophistication, but I shall write about things jus the way I felt about them back then, in the second quarter of the twentieth century.

I remember the morning of August 1951 when our old military transport ship, the General Blatchford, reached New York harbor. I was pressed against the ship's railing by the crowd of immigrants behind me. My eyes were fixed on the blurred horizon when suddenly the morning fog lifted, and the Statue of Liberty appeared majestically out of the mist. The harbor was bustling with ships. Their horns filled the air like a cacophonous symphony for the skyscrapers, their windows ablaze in the morning sun.

Arved Ojamaa Ashby, M.D. in his office.

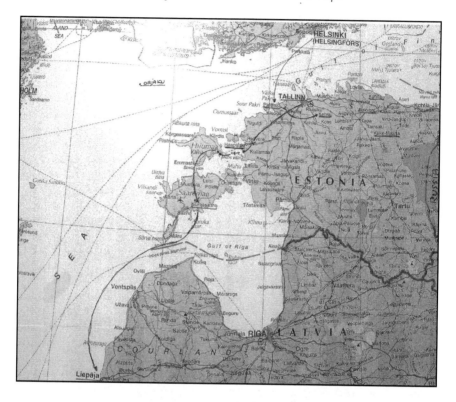

When returning from Finnish Army, leaving Helsinki in August 1944 to Estonian to the city of Paldiski.

From Paldiski to military camp in Kehra.

From Kehra 48 hour leave to Tallinn.

From Tallinn by train to Haapsalu, but deparked before reaching the city, on foot to village of Rannaküla at the sea.

From Rannaküla by small boat to a small Island Härjarahu, from Härjarahu by the same boat to Orjaku in Hiiu Island.

From Orjaku by military truck to Saaremaa island to city of Haapsalu

From Haapsalu by a German boat with civilian evacuees to Germany, first night anchored overnight in a Latvian harbor town, Lepäja.

From there to Danzig, Germany.

Chapter 1

My Father

My father's name was Juljus.

He was born on the 24th of June, 1886 in the Estonian village of Kunda, on the Finnish Sea. He once told me about his great grandfather, a Finnish fisherman, who was caught in a storm that drove him to the Estonian side of the sea. The man didn't return to his homeland, but settled in the same village. My father was born there three generations later. Whether the fishing was better on Estonian shores or the girls prettier, we can only suspect. Nothing more is known about him or his family. My father had told about his great uncle, blind in his old age, but still sought after as a musician for old-time weddings. A wooden barrel, used for collecting rainwater, was turned upside-down and the old man was lifted to the top, or so the story goes. He sat there and fiddled for hours.

My father never said much about his own father. Their relationship was less than cordial. His real mother died of "brain fever" when Juljus was only seven years old. The new stepmother had more cruelty than affection for the young boy. "Just wait until your father gets home" was a phrase she repeated often.

Meager food and physical punishments were as common as rain in the fall or snow in winter. At the age of 14 he was expelled from school for breaking his writing slate over the skull of a classmate who had made derogatory remarks about his clothing. However, this time the corporal punishment did not materialize. He was brave enough to resist. The incident ended with a resounding victory or loss, depending on how one looks at it. He was kicked out of the house and his stepmother threw his few belongings after him through the open window.

Juljus was big for his age and found work in a local cement factory. The fact that he had neither lunch bucket nor lunch did not go unnoticed by his coworkers who shared their own meager supplies of salt herring and bread. The water to wash it down was entirely free for the taking.

When two weeks went by and his first paycheck arrived, he considered himself a rich man. He had never seen that much money in his entire life, and all of it was his to keep!

It did not take long to save enough to buy himself a new suit, shoes and other accessories. He even bought a chain to decorate the front of his waist coat, no watch at the end of it, but no matter. All dressed up, he paraded past the old homestead, walking back and forth. He whistled a happy tune, his hands placed elegantly in his pockets, straw hat pushed back on his head and his coat unbuttoned which allowed the watch chain to gleam in the sun.

It did not take long for his stepmother to notice him and yell to the others in the house, "Come out and look . . . It must be our Juljus!" His father and half-brothers and sisters rushed to the porch with open mouths, studying him from head to toe. But, Juljus paid no attention and just kept on going past the house, oblivious to the onlookers. He later admitted that this was the most rewarding moment in his young life, seeing jealousy in his stepmother's face, where he had previously seen only rejection and contempt.

He also saved enough to make a down payment on an accordion, and taught himself to play. Before long he could play all the popular tunes of the day and became a sought-after musician for weddings and Saturday night dances. The money he earned helped pay for the instrument.

It was the turn of the century. On Saturday nights he used to walk down the village street in the summer nights full of light and yearnings, carrying his accordion on top of his head and playing. The young girls would open their windows and call his name. Music in those days was a rare commodity. Not only that, a man who could walk and play at the same time was greatly admired.

Estonia was then just a small province in the Russian Czar's empire and my father had to serve in the Russian military as a foot soldier. There was no glory in this since many shops and restaurants carried signs saying, "Out of Bounds to Dogs and Soldiers." Such signs really didn't matter much to him since he served his time in the Siberian wilderness. Worst of all, he had to leave his accordion behind. But his music was not to be stopped. In Siberia he built himself a string instrument called the *simmel* and learned to play Russian tunes he had learned from his singing comrades. Then he was asked to play at the officers' barracks. This gave him privileged status, at times excused him from guard duty, and helped him promoted to corporal.

At the onset of the First World War his unit was transferred to the Western Front to fight Kaiser Wilhelm's elite Prussian troops. The chances of surviving this ordeal were pretty slim, so when the military was looking for shoemakers and shoe repairmen, he registered himself as experienced in this field, even though he had never so much as run a needle through a piece of leather. He was not sent to the front lines but was left behind to fix GIs' shoes. His inexperience showed, but being handy with tools and a quick learner, he managed to hang on. The officer in charge liked his music-making and the Russian tunes he had learned in Siberia came in handy. In those days, there were no radios or gramophones. The only way to make music was to sing or play an instrument, and my father could do both.

He learned his new trade within a year, and could now make any kind of shoes from scratch. Even officers came to him to have their feet measured for high-class footwear. I can personally testify to his shoe-making ability as he made a pair for my confirmation in the summer of 1943. I had the distinction of being the only graduate with a new pair of shoes since this was war time and no shoes could be bought. It really didn't matter that the shoes were light brown and my suit black; he had no black leather, but craftsmanship aplenty.

My father was in the Russian Imperial Army making shoes and playing his *simmel* until the Bolshevik Revolution in 1917. The entire Russian front then collapsed and soldiers deserted. If any of the officers tried to stop them, they were shot. Czar Nicholas the Second and his family were arrested, taken to Siberia, and later executed. By the time my father deserted with his simmel, there was not much left of the Czar's armies. It took him a couple of weeks of traveling in freight trains to get back home.

On Sunday, February 24, 1918 he married my future mother, Ida Aman. She was born on December 6, 1888. Their wedding date and the year became an important date in Estonian history. That very same Sunday, Estonia had declared itself independent from Russia. It must have been a very courageous step since Estonia had barely one million inhabitants while Russia was more than a hundred times bigger in population and territory. The Russians' new Bolshevik government was not willing to give up the Estonian province which Peter the Great had called "The Window to the West" before taking it from Sweden (Peace Treaty of Nystad, 1721).

Estonia's War of Independence (1918-1920) followed the first world war and ended with an Estonian victory (Peace Treaty of Tartu, 1920) and freedom from communist Russia, which relinquished all claims on Estonia "voluntarily and forever,"

Estonia and Russia have nothing in common. Estonians are Finno-Ugric in language and ancestry while the Russians are Slavic. By their language and ethnic characteristics, the Estonians are closely related to the Finns. The Russians have darker skin and hair and their language is glottal, full of different sounding s's and z's.

During the Estonian War of Independence, my father fought at the front and played his simmel and composed songs when he wasn't caught in the heat of battle. I remember him sitting at the open window in the summer evenings when I was still a young boy, playing and singing his wartime songs.

> "Mets mühab, pilved jooksvad ruttu,
> Kaugelt kuulda lahingut -
> Oh ütle, sõber, kelle peale mõtled,
> Oh ütle sõber sa . . ."

> ("The wind murmurs in the trees,
> The clouds rushing in the sky
> Listening to the sound of distant battle
> Tell me, my friend, what are you thinking of,
> Tell me, my friend, what is on your mind. . . ")

For his services in the War of Independence, the Estonian government awarded him a plot of black, fertile soil in Kullenga. There were no hills, trees or houses in the vicinity. The land was flat as a pancake since it was located in the delta of an ancient river called *Abaja* (an archaic Estonian word, meaning "the mouth of the river").

The river must have been extinct for centuries, but in its youth, it had carried top soil from distant fields and deposited it on our land. Some springs the rapidly melting snow would bring the dead river to life again, retracing its old boundaries far and wide. Our house and farm buildings were on higher ground, so we never flooded out, but at times we lived on an island for days on end. The rushing water filled the pond behind the barn and then it vanished for a year or two - the black soil consuming its passing supply.

My parents started tilling this land in 1920.

They had limited resources, and farming their Abaja was a back-breaking struggle, long hours of never-ending toil. There was not enough money to hire a farm hand or a maid. My father had to till the land and build the barn. My mother's work was repetitious and never-ending; she cleaned the house, did the laundry by hand and prepared and served the meals. Not much importance was given to the job of milking the cows or feeding the pigs. At the end of the day my father could gaze with some pride at the land he had plowed under with his two horses, named Miira and Maara. My mother, on the other hand, had nothing to show for her efforts; there was only a new load of laundry and dishes waiting. Seasonal work, such as raking hay, spreading manure, or pickling potatoes was an extra workload. Of course, one had to add in the pregnancies, childbirths and care of the children as God-given rights.

So far I have spoken about my father and how he would sit at the kitchen table and tell stories of his past. My mother was busy preparing the food and settling the table. At times she stopped whatever she was doing and said, "Oh, those were the old days. They are gone for good." She would then try to reassure me with, "I'm sure our son will never have to face the hard times we did."

Her statement would deter my father's reminiscence. But he was not talking about "hard times." To my understanding he never seemed to have had any.

Chapter 2

The Early Years

I was born on August 8, 1922 in our small farm house in the village of Kullenga, Assamalla County, the second child and the first boy to Juljus and Ida Bachblum (later Ojamaa). I cannot tell how much I weighed; it was not the custom to weigh newborns. I must have been a vigorous baby. As the story goes I showed off the power of my vocal cords with the very first breath.

The house I was born in was an old cabin-like structure with a thatched roof. It consisted of two rooms of equal size. The first room was the kitchen, the dining room, and the family room, all in one. It had a wood-burning stove for cooking. Attached to it was a clay oven for baking bread and heating the house. A small window, shaded outside by the nettle bushes and burdock leaves, let in dull light. The wooden floor boards covered a vegetable and potato cellar underneath. The room behind the kitchen was both bedroom and guest room. It had a large wooden bed with a straw mattress covered with home-woven linen sheets, blanket and pillows. Pushed against the wall was the cradle. Through the only window draped with white muslin curtains, the soft daylight fell into a heavy round table covered with a lace doily. The only decoration in the room was a clay vase with painted birds. In it were a few dried-out flowers.

We had no well.

The drinking and cooking water had to be brought in by horse in a wooden barrel from the community well. It had to be hand-cranked, bucket by bucket, from a depth of some 20 feet. It took the same number of buckets to fill the barrel, a supply that would fulfill our water needs for a week. The farm animals got their water from a large pond behind the barn.

My first childhood recollection is a strange one.

I must have been two and a half years old and we were still living in the old house, where the flies were fierce in the summer. It was customary to fight them with "Fly Killer", a five-inch square piece of cardboard, marked with a skull and crossbones and saturated with sugar and some kind of poison. Fly killers were widely used and could be purchased for a few pennies each at the nearby farm store. It was kept on a dinner plate in the middle of the kitchen table, where the flies would gather in swarms. They just loved the sweet dish without knowing the consequences. Apparently, I wasn't aware of it either. Left alone for a moment, I crawled up to the table and ate the whole thing. But the "Fly Killer" was soon found to be missing, and I became the immediate suspect. The timeliness of this discovery, and milk as an antidote, saved the day and lengthened my life for many decades to come. It immunized me against the future hardships and misfortunes in the distant and not-so-distant future. If fly killer could not kill me, nothing would!

Anyway, my mother discontinued its use, and we learned to live harmoniously together flies and all.

I cannot remember having any toys.

It was not customary to give small children presents. Not even for birthdays or holidays. The city and its toys were far away and money to buy them was hard to come by. The local general store carried only essentials such as sugar, herring in a barrel, tobacco and booze. There might have been some hard candy somewhere for young men to purchase before calling on their sweethearts. The grown-ups would entertain children by cutting dolls from old newspapers. Once, when left alone in the house, I did some cutting myself. Instead of paper, I used the lower ends of the living room curtains. Luckily, we had just the one window, so the damage was not too great. I don't remember the consequences, but I can still picture myself sitting alone on the floor just under the window, in the early evening dusk, cutting away with a pair of large scissors.

For Christmas we had a tree decorated with candles, cookies and wads of cotton. I was three years old when I had my first Christmas present from a faraway land called America (from American Red Cross). The small, smooth, glittering and colorful balls, called marbles were heavenly wonders for a small boy. I could sit next to the Christmas tree and roll them on the floor in front of me for hours on end. At night I kept them under my pillow. At half-wake moments I reached for them, feeling renewed happiness in their presence. America was a land I thought of with great admiration - the Land of the Marvelous Marbles.

Wherever there is happiness, one can also find sorrow. In a child's life they alternate like days of sun and days of rain.

The first grief I can remember took place the following summer. I had seen pictures of children running with colorful things like soap-bubbles tied to a string. I was familiar with soap bubbles, but I didn't know how one could tie them to a string without breaking. Then I learned about balloons, unbreakable soap bubbles, with as many colors as the rainbow. From then on I could not get balloons off my mind. My mother was tired of listening to my tedious inquiries. My father promised to bring me one on his next trip to Rakvere, the nearest town.

When the day to go to the city finally arrived, and my father took off with his horse and buggy, my last minute reminder went unanswered. I knew he did not like to be reminded, but just the same, he might forget my balloon! It was the longest day of my life. "Go out and play" was my mother's only answer to my inquiries. Besides, I was getting in her way in the kitchen. My sister, Asta, almost four years older than I, just stuck out her tongue, meaning get lost!

Toward evening, I saw my father's horse and buggy approaching along the dirt road. My heart sank. There was no balloon in sight.

"Where is the balloon?," I inquired.

"Just wait," he said, beating his dusty hat against his pants. "First I have to take care of the horse."

When he finally stepped into the house and opened his wallet, he took out something that looked like a wrinkled old rag. But when it was blown up and tied to a string, it became a gorgeous red balloon!

I took hold of the string and ran out of the house.

The balloon followed me, floating over my head, the red against the blue sky while the setting sun streaked it with rays of gold. It was the happiest moment in my young life, perhaps even happier than the day with Christmas marbles. I did not believe there was anything more tantalizing in the whole world than my own red balloon! I continued to run along the fresh-cut field of rye. Then the balloon hit some stubble on the ground and just disappeared leaving only a piece of red rag at the other end of the string.

My happiness with the balloon was short-lived, but the sorrow that followed stayed with me.

To lift my spirits my father decided to give me a short horseback ride. He hoisted me on the back of our old horse Maara and handed me the bridle. He kept a firm grip on my ankle while he guided the horse to the pond. I was holding the bridle real tight while my father's grip must have relaxed for a moment. Then disaster struck. The horse reached down for a drink pulling on the bridle and making me somersault along his neck and into the muddy pond. The screams that followed frightened the man and the beast. The commotion brought my mother to the scene. I was still sitting in the shallow water and bawling. She did not find my predicament entertaining nor worth any sympathy. I was thrown in the wooden bathtub for a thorough scrub and then given a set of dry clothes. By then I had quit bawling and was trying to tell her there was nothing to it, but my mother would not budge. Future horseback rides would be out of the question.

After every summer comes winter, and in Estonia it seemed to last forever. It brought its usual ailments for the children, measles, mumps and scarlet fever, to mention a few. These were thought unavoidable and a part of growing up. Of course, the coughs, colds, runny noses and earaches were usually ignored. The only known and effective treatment was applying goose grease to the bottom of the feet and holding them next to a fire.

In the winter of 1927, my sister came down with scarlet fever. The country doctor had to be brought in by horse and sleigh from miles away.

Doctor Anderson was a good-natured man, patient and reassuring. When he examined my sister, he even did not seem to mind my studying his medicine bag. When he was finished, he reassured my parent and gave them some pills for my sister to take and a whole load of instructions. After that he turned to me. Remembering my eagerness to get in his way, he asked me my age. I was then four and a half years old. My parents wanted to impress the doctor by telling him that I could read at my early age. The doctor, well aware that the eight year old children were still studying the alphabet in first grade, asked for a demonstration. My sister's school book was brought out and I read him the story about the wolf who got trapped in a covered-up sinkhole. Doctor Anderson was visibly impressed and asked the usual question about what I wanted to be when I grew up.

"A doctor", was my firm answer.

This had been my first encounter with a physician, and my admiration knew no bounds. I still remember his hearty laugh as he slapped his thighs. "Be sure you don't intend to settle in Väike-Maarj or you'll put me out of business!"

This episode with its good laugh, lifted everyone's spirits. A kid living in a log house with a back yard full of weeds in summer and snowbanks up to the roof in winter, wanted to be a doctor? What an imagination and foolishness! My parents would have been happy if I had said fireman or policeman. The doctor laughed knowingly. The odds of my dying of diphtheria or polio or scarlet fever were great before I'd even have a second chance to think of becoming a doctor. However, my sister recovered from her illness, and I did not even get sick that winter.

When I was seven years old, we moved into a new house with many windows. Entering the hallway, to the left there was the pantry and straight ahead our all-around kitchen with three large windows. The door to the right led to the family room and the bedroom. One had to go through the bedroom to the large parlor with four windows, and this led, in turn, to the balcony, enclosed with colored glass windows on all sides. It was a different world for all of us, and a far cry from the two-room log cabin.

We even had our own well.

No more heaving the heavy bucket from the community well and pouring it through a funnel into a barrel. This tedious and time consuming work was entirely eliminated. What a blessing! Now all you had to do was pump the handle, and the water just ran into the bucket under your very eyes. It was so easy even children could do it! What a luxury! It made it convenient to water the farm animals in winter. All you had to do was pump, and the water ran through a hollowed tree trunk directly to the barn. No more need to carry it, bucket by bucket, from the frozen pond, where the path was all ice from previously spilled water with its danger of falling.

We thought we now had everything we could think of, and what we did not have, we did not miss.

We didn't have indoor plumbing, but we had a roomy outhouse. We didn't have electricity, but we had kerosene lamps giving soft, yellow light that was easy on the eyes. We didn't have a telephone, but we didn't know anybody who had one, so there was no one to call. We didn't have a car, but then we didn't have any friends in far-away places to visit. The horse and carriage took us where we needed to go, and a recently-acquired bicycle was an extra help in quick transportation. Burglar alarms were unknown then, but so were burglars.

There must have been many more conveniences in the world at the time, but we couldn't miss what we didn't know about.

Life was easygoing and worry-free.

Lilac bushes were planted to the south side of the house leading to the dirt road. Spruce and pine trees to the north shaded us from the winter winds and snowdrifts. The jasmine bushes under the pantry window gave off a sweet fragrance, and rows of red poppies could be seen through the living room windows.

The swallows made their nests under the barn eves, diving deeply over the freshly cut hayfields predicting rain. The meadow larks seemed to be stuck in one spot in the sky where they'd sing. Beyond the immediate farm buildings were endless fields. The distant woods were just blue-green streaks on the horizon.

When summer thunderstorms filled the open sky, they seemed menacing and exciting. I spent my early years in solitude.

My sister had no interest in my wanderings or in the games I invented. My toys were primitive pocketknife carvings of cows and horses with minimal resemblance to the real thing, but the power of a child's imagination mad them look real.

Summer splendors find many ways to entertain a lonely boy. On sunny days I walked barefoot along the narrow path while the wheat fields closed over my head, waving in the wind and blossoming. The pollen filled the sky like fine powder, and the sun threw only faint shadows. The warm dust on the foot-path felt soothing between my toes.

When the heat of midday had passed and the sun was low on the horizon, I sat at our pond behind the cattails, where the water spiders went gliding along the mirror-like surface. Small green frogs jumped from one lily pad to another, and the minnows flashed in the dark water. Or I went to the old log house, where a ladder led to the hayloft. I climbcd to the upper end of the ladder and sat on the last rung from where I could see all the way to the main road and hear the horses' hooves on the pavement and the rumbling of wagon wheels, late travelers were on their way home. The wild chamomile growing in the backyard was velvety soft. I felt tired, let my face rest on the cool grass and slept until my mother found me. She took my hand and led me into the dark house. Half asleep, I drank a mug of milk, still warm from the cow's udder. Then she washed my sunburned hands and feet with a cool cloth and put me to bed.

The sounds of crickets filled my room through open windows as I slept dreamless into the night.

Chapter 3

The Social Life in Kullenga

There was not much social life for grown-ups in Kullenga in the 1920s and 30s. People got together for weddings and funerals, confirmations and anniversaries. Alcohol was used freely on those occasions, but daily cocktails were unheard of. It was generally believed that getting drunk a few times a year were better for your health than having just one glass of booze every day.

The government had a monopoly on brewing and selling alcohol. The brand commonly sold contained 40% ethyl alcohol and 60% *aqua distillata*. It came in two sizes, a quart size was called *The President* and a smaller bottle, the size of a pint, *The Peasant*. There might have been different brands sold in the cities, but in the local liquor and farm store, owned and operated by my uncle, Aleksander Aman, this was the only brand sold.

However, an organization in Kullenga called the Kullenga Voluntary Fire Department added much color to local social life. I would be doing an injustice to the volunteers who so courageously did so much beyond their call of duty, if I didn't recount their accomplishments in greater detail.

The firehouse was nothing special; just an old stone building on a small hill in the middle of the village. To be honest, Kullenga was not even a village, just a settlement at the road crossing. It had its liquor and farm store, the creamery, the blacksmith's place and, of course, the firehouse.

Well, it was not really a firehouse either, rather a drying house for wheat and rye. That was its original purpose when it was built some hundred years ago. It had its own bell tower and was roomy enough to store the fire engine and the rest of the paraphernalia. Monthly fire drills, held only in summer, ended usually with members resting on the grassy hillside and passing around a bottle of booze.

Now if a fire happened to break out somewhere in winter, you were on your own. The firehouse was snowed in or the wheels of the fire wagon would get stuck in the first snow drift. If the fire happened to break out in summer, the outlook was improved. Help was, so to speak, just around the corner.

One day, in the month of May, Karsi's house caught fire. The messenger from the site of the calamity had to bicycle to the fire house, climb the tower, and ring the bell which was audible for miles. Then, the designated farmers, hearing the alarm, rushed with their horses to the fire station. When all were present, the horses were harnessed to the fire engine. The entire team would then gallop off in a cloud of dust, brass bell ringing, to the distant smoke and flames. By the time they arrived, alas, the chimney with bread-baking oven was the only structure standing, still hot from the blaze.

The firemen, sporting their brass helmets, rushed into action. They hand-pumped the fire engine, guiding the steady stream of water to cool the chimney, the bread-baking oven and the surrounding hot ashes. When things were cool enough, they completed their duties by toppling the chimney.

The victorious team then returned to rest on the green hillside at the firehouse. The horses grazed on fresh grass while the firemen passed around a bottle of government brew supplied by my uncle as a public relations gesture, free of charge.

The most festive event each summer was the local Fireman's Parade, followed by a competitive exhibit and then a social gathering in the evening.

The parade was held in a meadow not far from the fire station. To use the main road would have blocked traffic, which consisted mainly of horse-drawn vehicles. The shiny instruments and bugle-blowing would have driven even the most docile farm horse wild, driving it into the ditch with its driver and wagon. Or a passing truck would have whirled up a heavy cloud of dust, choking the horn blowers and making their instruments inoperable.

Thanks to the firemen's foresight, a meadow was selected for the festivities and then mowed, the area marked with ribbons and flags. To enjoy the show, the public circled around the perimeter of the field.

Blowing brass instruments and marching at the same time with the sun burning down on their backs made the men mighty thirsty. They all came prepared for such an emergency by carrying government brew in their pocket and taking a good swig whenever the need rose. After the parade, a competitive fire drill followed. The team that pumped up the highest waterspout in so many minutes was declared the winner.

When the official part of the program was over, the folks gathered at the school house in Assamalla, sat at long tables set for hearty food and drink, listened to speeches and applauded the winning team.

The fire chief distributed the awards. By this time, he was somewhat disabled from the elements, his speech not entirely coherent. However, this was hardly noticed by the guests, as they had their own thirsts to attend to, and no one paid much attention to the speaker. It soon became obvious that the chief needed help. The 60% *aqua distillata* had not entirely evaporated through perspiration, while the kidneys had separated it from the ethyl alcohol and needed relief. One of the fire-fighter's apprentices was trained in first aid. He made the proper diagnosis, and guided the fire chief to some nearby bushes.

It was nearly dawn when everyone's hunger and thirst was fully met. Homeward bound, the fighting men tried to keep up with their wives, dragging their musical instruments through the dew-wet grass. One hoped they went back refreshed and ready to face the weeks and months of backbreaking labor on their farms. Only the young folks stayed behind for dancing and romancing until the wee hours of the morning.

My father was not a volunteer fireman. His accordion-playing days had passed. On occasion he still brought out his *simmel*, placed it on the open windowsill and played and sang to the wheat and rye fields, reminiscing about the days when he was walking down the old village road in Kunda carrying his accordion on his head and playing.

One of the most memorable events of that summer was an excursion to the Finnish Sea. It was organized by the local Society of Country Housewives. One could be a member of the society only if married to a farmer. Those women were tough, physically and mentally. They were proud of their social superiority and did not associate with women lacking the same status. City ladies had their neuroses and hysterias, while the farmers' wives believed themselves immune to such afflictions.

An open truck was hired and fitted with wooden benches and freshly-cut young birch trees were placed in each corner for decoration. I remember the excitement of riding the very first time in a truck, up high, speeding down the road. Everyone was in a festive mood. The birch branches waved in the wind as the women sang in high voices:

> Noorus onilus aeg,
> Noorus ei tule iial tagasi. . .
>
> Youth is a wonderful time,
> Youth shall never return. . .

It was my first trip to the sea. The landscape circled as the nearby trees and houses rushed toward us. Distant scenery hurried in the opposite direction. The telephone posts seemed to rise up when approached and lie down again when passed. Only the clouds above our heads seemed to stay the same in their unhurried drift toward the distant sea, and the world below seemed to circle like a carousel.

Our destination was Võsu beach at the Finnish Sea. It took well over an hour to reach our journey's end some 30 miles away. We traveled the winding road through nameless villages, chased by countless packs of dogs. The truck's horn scared the daylights out of stray chickens, scattering them in all directions, their feathers flying. Local folks ran out of their houses to see what the commotion was all about; dogs barking, chickens screaming, horn blowing, dust flying, and a bunch of folks in a truck waving and singing of youth that shall never return.

They all smiled at us and waved. The young boys waved with their caps, secretly wishing to be part of the crowd, which seemed to promise excitement and adventure. We were happy with the attention we received and the commotion we created.

Soon the dust settled. The dogs gave up their chase. The chickens returned to the road, and folks went back to their houses, happy and sad in this fair Sunday morning, full of sunshine and white clouds.

This was the very first time I saw the sea. Its great blueness filled the horizon. The rhythmic roar of the rushing waves, the smell of rotten seaweed and the taste of the salty mist were overpowering, not spoiled by previous photos or movie images. Light yellow sand was washed by the waves, inrushing and then receding, some breaking into foam even before reaching the shore.

And here were birds with slender, pointed wings, diving and rising against the haze where the sky became part of the sea. Their cry blended with the roar of the waves and became one. The shadows of the clouds ran across the beaches making the sand look white and sea green. And there were boats, low in the water, their hulls at times hidden behind the rolling waves, others further out toward the open sea had white triangular sails, heading out to distant lands.

Chapter 4

School Days

My seventh birthday was on August 8, 1929 and Monday, September 2 was my first day at Assamalla Elementary School. I was one year younger than the rest of my schoolmates, and also the smallest kid in class. My godmother Priida, a professional seamstress, sewed me a brand-new outfit for school with bows and buttons, making me look like Little Nell on some nineteenth century Christmas card. Priida and my mother seemed pleased with the results and I, of course, didn't know any better. I sure stood out like a sore thumb from the rest of the fellows in my class.

I also made a fool of myself the very first day.

This happened because of my mother and her repeated warnings, "Be sure to greet the teacher properly!" The only proper greeting I knew was handshake. When the teacher, a young and handsome man, entered the classroom, everybody just stood in the corner bowing and bobbing. With a "proper" greeting in mind, I walked straight to the teacher, who was standing in the middle of the room, to shake his hand. The rest of the first grade seemed frozen to the ground. The teacher, Mr. Traks, gave my hand a good shake. Then he lifted me well over his head with a hearty laugh.

After he put me down again, he said, "Now, children, let's be seated." Then he looked around and asked, "Where is Koida?"

A well-dressed girl stepped out from the crowd.

"Well, Koida, you sit at the very first desk." Then he looked down at me, as I was still standing next to him. He asked for my name. "Well, Arved, you take your seat just behind Koida and the rest of you children, sit wherever you like in these first two rows." Rows further back were for second and third year students.

All the girls in my class had sunburned faces and blond hair that was cut at mid-neck level. They moved clumsily and stumbled frequently and looked down at their hands when sitting at their desk. Only Koida was different. I was sure that my handshake had gained me the privilege of sitting behind her. I learned later that she was our county secretary's only daughter. She had light brown hair, reaching to her shoulders. Her face was radiantly pale with large brown eyes, and all of her movements were slow and graceful.

She looked at me just once, over her shoulder and with a faint smile that filled me with an odd sense of happiness which I had experienced only once before. That was in the previous year on a late fall afternoon with hard frost, but no promise of snow. Three girls on their way home from school came to skate on our pond. They had slender legs covered with black woven stockings. Their short skirts caught in the breeze as they were sliding on the ice, unaware that my melancholy loneliness was replaced by a feeling of content.

Nothing very interesting happened my first school year. I was involved in one fight, which I lost. I don't remember what caused it, but I remember how Sylvia, a foxy little girl with sharp fingernails pinned me down at my own desk. I didn't get much sympathy at home when they learned that a skinny little squealer had given me the scratched-up face.

The opportunity to regain my self-esteem arrived the following week. It happened during a lunch break, when Sylvia was standing on a stool and cleaning the blackboard. I "accidentally" elbowed her chair. She lost her balance and her tail-end hit the hardwood floor. You should have heard her howl. The front of the room was crowded at the time. Sylvia was facing the blackboard, and nobody seemed to know how the misfortune had happened. Her screaming brought the teacher out investigate. Sylvia was still bawling, and couldn't give any answers. Koida, who was sitting next to the blackboard and witnessed the event, told the teacher that Sylvia just fell off the chair. When I took my seat after the lunch break, Koida gave me an over-her-shoulder knowing smile.

I found the rest of the school year boring. Most of my classmates were just learning to spell and add numbers up to ten. The teacher tested my reading only once, and then just ignored me. He must have finally gotten tired of looking at my raised hand, and came up with a tricky question, "How much is 2 x 25?"

I was the only one with my hand up.

"OK, Arved, what is the answer?"

I stood up, looked around the class, and said in a firm voice, "Fifty."

After that I kept my hand down.

I had demonstrated my superior knowledge to the entire class, including Koida. Maybe it was just my imagination, but after that it seemed that Koida started to glance over her shoulder more often than before.

Christmas of 1929 took place when I was in the first grade. Soft snow fell, making the drab gray fields spotless white. For our Christmas program out classroom desks were in storage, replaced by long benches for parents and guests to sit on. In one corner stood the Christmas tree decorated with candy canes and live candles.

The teacher played the harmonium as we sang Yuletide songs. Then, my turn came to recite a Christmas poem while standing by myself at a small podium next to the Christmas tree. Alas, after two lines of text I became mesmerized by the flickering lights of the candles as reflected in the window while the soft snow still fell. The hush from the audience woke me from my daydreams, and I started bravely from the beginning,

> Tulid meil, Joulud, Joulukesed
> Lurnise teega kaunid puhakesed . . .

> When Christ arrived for Christmas
> On a holy day with snowy roads. . .

I repeated it for the third time and stopped. I could not remember the rest, and after a short pause the teacher rescued me from the podium. I received even more applause than the Christmas Choir, but I knew my first public appearance had been a bust. I worried about being in the teacher's doghouse.

Not to worry. The teacher told my mother that the recital, the way it went, was more entertaining than if I had finished the entire poem. I was still happy to redeem myself the next Mother's Day by giving a short speech the teacher had composed. I remembered all my lines and presented them fluently and with childlike passion. What a glorious feeling, repeatedly bowing to long applause. The mothers must have remembered my previous blooper and were happy with my present success.

That is all I remember from my first grade at school.

I did not learn much, and I did not make any friends. The only one I missed during summer recess was Koida.

I had nothing to ready over the following summer until my Aunt Leene saw my predicament. She'd take me along to the public library on Sundays, the only day it was open. The so-called "Assamalla Public Library" was no big deal, just a couple of bookcases with locked glass doors, located in our old school building. There were no books intended for children, but the young lady librarian always found something suitable for me, such as Jules Verne's *Mysterious Island* and Daniel Defoe's

Robinson Crusoe. When I returned each book the following Sunday, she always asked how I like it. We even talked about Captain Nemo of the *Nautilus* and Captain Harding, the engineer and inventor who made it possible to survive on an uninhabited island. We also talked about Robinson Crusoe and his friend Friday. And let's not forget Robert Louis Stevenson's *Treasure Island*.

These books opened new worlds of mystery and adventure. I could read for hours, stretched out on the living room rag carpet, the book resting on the floor between my elbows and my hands supporting my face. My mother also liked to read novels, but the only time she had for reading was in late winter evenings when the rest of the family was safe in bed. Even then, my father complained about "ruining the eyes" and "wasting the kerosene" if he happened to wake up in the middle of the night and notice the light in the living room.

I attended Assamalla Elementary School for another year, then transferred to Lasila Boarding School, about four miles from my home in Kullenga. This school had all six grades the law required one to attend. If you turned 16 and had not finished your six grades, you were dismissed; the government would not waste any more money trying to educate you. The sixteen-year limit allowed you to repeat two grades, if you were dumb enough to need it. Nobody was promoted to the next grade unless all the required subjects were completed with at least a passing grade. There were no favors given or exceptions made. Of course, if you were fourteen and still sitting in the third or the fourth grade, you were free to go and plow your father's field or haul manure. Nobody cared if you believed that the north pole was damned cold and the south pole hot like hell. It was up to you if you wanted to stick around for another two years, but at the age of sixteen you were out!

The little Assamalla schoolhouse was painted red with white windowsills and had flower beds decorating both sides of the path to the front door, while Lasila Elementary School was located in a towered mansion once owned by a German landowner. Its high arching windows overlooked a park with ancient oak and maple trees. The rooms were decorated with fading gold-leaf tapestries and painted ornamental high ceilings. It was a boarding school which supplied meals and sleeping quarters for the students who lived further than walking distance. For the students who lived nearby, it was just a regular school.

I was the youngest student and the only third grader as a boarder. The boys all slept in a single room with two dozen beds. The girls occupied two smaller rooms.

The day started at seven o'clock. We made our own beds, then washed our faces with ice-cold water under a long row of taps in an unheated basement, then dressed in a hurry. The 7:30am breakfast that consisted of some kind of porridge and milk, was served at the long dining-room table. Classes started at eight and lasted until noon with ten-minute breaks. Lunch was from twelve to one, with classes again until three in the afternoon. Then there was no assignment until five in the evening. During free time one could take a nap, play ball in the park or pester the girls. But, in the evening from five to eight, students had to sit in the classroom and do homework. No conversation or socializing was permitted. The only sounds were the hiss of the kerosene lamp hanging from the ceiling and the ticking of the large clock over the blackboard.

Supper was served after eight. The students had to cover the tables, bring up food from the kitchen, clear the tables after the meal, and do the dishes. The janitor's wife did the cooking. Groceries were brought in fresh every day by parents taking turns, bread, milk, eggs, potatoes and other basic foodstuffs. Everyone had to have his own sugar, butter or jam. These personal supplies were kept in the dining room cupboards in designated sections. The cupboards were inspected at times by Mr. Phillips, the headmaster. If your designated area had leftover rancid butter or moldy bread, you were in trouble, meaning extra kitchen duty.

After supper one had some free time again. You could sing or play games, chase the girls in the park, or just sit in a group and tell tales. At ten o'clock everybody had to be in bed, and the kerosene lamps were put out.

On Saturdays the classes lasted until noon and then everybody was excused until Monday morning. Either you walked home, or your parents came to pick you up for a bath, clean clothes or other personal needs. When the weather was nice, I usually walked home, and had a ride back to school on Sunday afternoon by horse and buggy or sleigh depending on the season.

During winter if there was heavy snow, most of the students stayed at school. Meals were served as on regular school days and there was plenty of free time to spend as one chose. I liked to sit at one of the tall windows overlooking the park, watching the low-flying clouds and listening to the wind swooshing in the trees.

I enjoyed school and the companionship of my classmates. I did not miss the long winter evenings in the isolated farmhouse. There was always something happening or something to do in the mansion. Most memorable were the scrimmages between "boarders" and the "home gang". On the dark fall evenings it was hazardous to go outside. You took the chance of being roughed up by the "home gang." It so happened that my bench-mate in third grade was Aleks Gruber, a rather quiet chap. He was not a boarder and had fresh home-baked cookies with him every day. He also had trouble with math. I had no cookies but I knew math. Bartering was the logical solution. He shared his cookies with me, and I helped him with his math. A rewarding relationship, *manus manum lavat.*

It took me a while to notice another bonus. Alek's older brother was a husky fellow and leader of the "home gang". Alek must have mentioned other useful relationship to him, since his gang members never bothered me. Fortunately, I was easy to recognize, even in the dark, as the smallest kid among the boarders. From then on, when the great bullies of the "home gang" met me outside, they acted like buddy-buddies and even asked in a friendly way how I was doing. If it had been Harald Rüütel, or Valter Kirss, or Endel Kukk, the biggest boarders from the upper classes, they would have been in trouble. These scrimmages were pretty much limited to fall evenings, and ended sometimes with an occasional black eye or aching bottom.

Schoolwork was easy. I didn't spend much time studying and my grades fell a bit lower than a B average. I spent time reading books from the school library. I counted among my friends Karl May's storybook heroes such as the great Indian chief Winnetou and his friend, the hunter and mountain man Old Shatterhand. Their adventures in the Wild West were fascinating and I even cried when I read the last volume of the series called *The Death of Winnetou.* I really got emotionally involved and in my ignorance believed it to be true. I learned much later that the story was written by a German author who had never been further west than the Elbe river, and had never seen a live or dead Indian in his entire life.

That three years I spent in Lasila Elementary School were full of happy memories. I made friends I did not have before. Living with a group of older boys gave me a more mature outlook, and I learned to communicate at their level. There seemed to be so much to do and never enough time to do it all and whatever I was doing at a particular moment seemed to be fun.

Everyone had a little booklet where his schoolmates wrote small notes or poems as mementos. I still remember the poetic entry dreamed up by my classmate Elmar Pauts:

> Kui taevas koogipilves
> Ja klimpe sadamas.
> Siis Arved kodu oues,
> On klimpe korjamas. . .

When the sky is covered with pancake clouds,
And it is raining dumplings.
Then Arved in his backyard,
Is busy picking them. . .

Chapter 5

Starting High School

I left Lasila Elementary School after the fifth grade to become a first grader at Väike-Maarja High School, six miles from home.

The high school curriculum took five years and if you wanted to enter the university, there was an additional three years "Gymnasium" before you could take the entry examinations.

The curriculum in high school was standard for all students, and included five years of English and three years of German. Physics, chemistry, algebra, trigonometry and calculus were all obligatory before graduation. No elective subjects were offered.

While elementary school was tuition-free and obligatory, high school, of course was not, and carried a tuition fee of about 60 crowns per year per student or about $30 in 1935 currency. There were no scholarships or foundations to help the needy. Tuition payments were due at the beginning of the school year and again after Christmas. If the tuition was not received, the student wasn't allowed to attend, in other words, was expelled. Of course, lodging and meals were an extra expense, as were textbooks and other school supplies.

While Lasila Elementary School was in a rural area, Väike-Maarja was a small old town with its institutions of learning. The town landmark was a 500-year old stone church with a high bell tower inhabited by bats. The church itself was hidden among age-old oak and lime trees and surrounded by ancient graves, their marble faces partially covered with moss.

It was the smallest town in Estonia to have its own high school with rigid rules. Half its students were from the surrounding areas, the rest from different sections across the countryside. The parents of the "outsiders" were usually upper-class city dwellers who wanted their children in an institution with limited opportunities for mischief. For instance, there was this stringent rule; students were not permitted outside in the evenings between five and eight, the hours set aside for study. The teachers were taking their evening walks during those hours along the main street, which was the only paved street in town. They could drop in for an unannounced visit; you had better be home studying!

From eight to ten in the evening one could go for a walk to rest the brain and get some exercise in the fresh air. Walking was a popular pastime and the town's main street became crowded with promenading students, usually strolling four or five abreast, row after row, talking, laughing or running from one group to another all the way past the graveyard, where the pavement ended. Then, it was time to turn around and walk back to town. At this hour there were hardly any horse-drawn or motorized vehicles on the road. The town with its main street belonged to the students, the future intelligentsia of a young country.

I had my eleventh birthday in the fall of 1933. My sister Asta had turned fifteen, and we both entered the first grade at Väike-Maarja High School. Being of the opposite sex, we had some difficulty finding an apartment to share. Mrs. Rosenberg had an apartment with two rooms and a kitchen. One of the rooms was spacious and was occupied by five upper-class female students. The smaller room was still vacant and became living quarters for me, my sister, and her 16-year old girl-friend, Linda Laumann. It sounds like an unheard of arrangement by today's standards, but there were no Miss Manners columns to dis-suade us, and the landlady was happy with the added income. The five teenage girls from the other room seemed delighted to have a young gentleman in their midst. Mrs. Rosenberg put a folding screen by Linda's bed to safeguard her privacy. So things worked out just fine, and everybody was happy with this arrangement.

It was the first time I had lived in a house with electricity. What a convenience! Just push a little red button on the wall and the entire room lit up with a snap of the fingers. The town had its own electric generator, attended by an old man who shared the shack with the con-traption and its booming monotonous sound. Whenever the gadget missed a beat or two, it woke up the attendant, who would do some adjustments to restore the regular rhythm and the town, after a minute or two of flickering lights, would return to full power. At times the old man would get drunk and sleep soundly through the needed adjust-ment. Then the motor would die, and the whole town bathed in dark-ness. The sheriff on duty would bicycle or run across town to the shack and wake up the attendant to get the generator going again. Some might call these blackouts inconvenient, but most of us thought it a small flaw in advanced technology and nothing to get excited about. The town had no electric gadgets that I knew of apart from lights, and the outhouse had only natural light over daylight hours.

The school did have a movie projector, and the science teacher, Mr. Pervik, a huge and shy bachelor, showed the occasional silent movie. If there was a romantic scene with prolonged kissing, Mr. Pervik placed his large thumb in front of the lens to forestall moral decay in the students. The audience sat in darkness for a minute or two, and it was generally agreed that this kind of "power failure" was more annoying than the other.

We did not have plumbing in our rented apartment so the water for drinking and cooking and bathing had to be cranked up, bucket by bucket, from an open well. Our landlady had a dachshund that disappeared quite unexpectedly one day. A week later our roommate, Alma Pedari went to get a bucket of water. She was amazed how heavy the water bucket was that morning, but Alma was not a city girl and had enough stamina to crank it up. What she saw made here scream and loose her grip on the handle. The bucket with the dead dog plummeted back to the bottom of the well. The landlady was mad at Alma for letting the handle go. It took the plumber a whole day and maybe a hundred buckets of water to "rescue" the dead dog from the deep well. What an unnecessary expense for the landlady! Alma with the other girls gagged and acted silly, knowing that they had been drinking and cooking and washing their faces and armpits for a week with t-h-a-t.

There was another incident involving Alma's jar of milk, which like other edibles was kept in the hallway closet. The closet had no windows and the flies did not like dark places, making it the safest place to store foodstuffs. It took Alma about a week to reach the bottom of her one gallon jar of milk where she discovered a drowned mouse. Retching and gagging were again the order of the day.

Being a high school student gave us a feeling of importance. So did the privilege of wearing the green high school cap with its white stripes. Our first classroom was a sunny second-floor corner room with large windows, providing an open view of distant farmlands and the nearby houses. The class adviser was the art teacher, Miss Jänes. She was a large-boned woman in her late thirties with a peaceful face and quiet manners. She never seemed to be upset or angry at anybody, and her class consisting of twelve boys and twelve girls, overflowed with childish enthusiasm. Every subject had a different teacher, all well disposed and able to present their subjects in a most interesting manner. The geography teacher was Mr. Pervik, the silent movie projectionist I mentioned earlier. One day Maimo Saar, a dimple-faced, dark haired girl who was on duty, announced absentmindedly at the onset of his class, "Nobody is absent today." She must have thought we had English class, giving this pronouncement in English instead of Estonian. To Maimo's great embarrassment, Mr. Pervik with a big smile wrote in the class day -book that a student going by the name of Nobody, was not present that day. Then he told a story on how to reinforce one's memory. At bedtime your mother was not sure whether she had closed the damper, and she asked you to check. You found it closed. The next morning your father, finding the house chillier than usual, asked about the damper. You and your mother could reassure him it had been closed. You *remembered* it for sure, because you *double-checked*. A fine story.

When teaching us about variations in the length of daylight and the length of the glow after sunset in relationship to geographic latitude, he told about his personal experience in southern France, where it gets dark very quickly after sunset, in contrast to our country, where the after-glow last for hours. Mr. Pervik got lost one evening and fell into a drainage ditch. From that day on everybody remembered not to go for a late walk in southern France or you might get all wet in a drainage ditch like Mr. Pervik, who did not know any better.

One of our new subjects in first grade was English taught by Mrs. Neemre. She was a perfectionist in a friendly way, coming to every student's desk to see that we pronounced the "th" properly by placing the tongue between the teeth and inhaling through our mouths. We were asked to practice this frequently in our free time. After that lesson, it was not unusual to see a green-capped pre-teen high school student walking down the street, tongue between his teeth, hissing like a snake.

Miss Jüriado was a dark-haired, short and slender woman in her late twenties. She was always serious, but when she smiled it was so sincere that everybody just had to smile along. She taught ancient history.

I still remember her story about the Pelopponesian Wars, the Spartans attacked the Messenia. The Messenian king consulted the oracle, and Apollo asked him to sacrifice a virgin of royal race. The king put to death his own daughter, but still lost the war. The way Miss Jüriado told the story, she and the entire class was misty-eyed. We all felt so bad about the fate of the poor princess and losing the war, circa 700 B.C. (We were not sophisticated enough to question the moral status of the king's daughter.)

Our German teacher, Miss Behrens, was in her 40s. Her body was shaped like an hourglass except that her lower "bulge" seemed more voluminous than the upper. Her long graying hair was twisted into a bun, held together with pins on the back of her head. She liked chocolate and cigarettes, and her breath was an uncanny combination of these two. She was a romantic and emotional spinster who could burst into tears when a roughneck like Endel Saar used a foul word in conversation with his desk-mate. Bashful about never having mastered Estonian, she used only here native German after the first six months. At times she liked to read short stories in front of the class, and she did this with a compassionate voice and clear diction. Somehow, I remember one of her stories concerning an enchanted village named Kermelshausen. It emerged but once every 200 years and then only for a few hours before midnight. Once a young man went for a walk in an unfamiliar forest in late evening and found himself suddenly in a strange village full of friendly people, where he met a lovely girl named Gertrude. They spent a few hours together, fell deeply in love, and promised to remain forever faithful to each other. Then the Guild House clock struck the midnight hour and the young man found himself quite alone in the dark forest. Oddly enough, I still remember the young man's lovelorn words at the end of the story, "Lebewohl! Sagte er leise und die grossen hellen Tranen waren in seinen Augen[1]. . .

. . . As they were in the eyes of Miss Behrens. She was truly a fine lady.

My favorite teacher was Miss Helmi Eller who taught Estonian grammar and world literature. She was in her middle thirties, slender, with a small face and hands. She never raised her voice, which stayed just a few decibels about a whisper with a perfect articulation. When she spoke, her left hand was always holding an open book while she animated her talk with delicate movement of the fingers of her right hand held a neck-level, never raising it above her chin and never hiding her face or her lips. Her smile was sophisticated and bashful at the same time, accompanied by slight movements of her head and a shine in her eyes that lasted no longer than her smile.

There was little entertainment as this was before television. The town did not have a movie theater and nobody I knew owned a radio. School plays and poetry readings were popular entertainments, well attended by the town folks as well as the students.

In my fourth year, Väike-Maarja High School celebrated its 25th anniversary by producing the four-act play, *Pal tänava poised* (The Boys of Pal Street) as translated from the work of a Hungarian playwright. I was Boka, the leader of the Pal Street boys' gang. Miss Eller spent countless hours trying to make the play commendable. Then a professional producer from the capital city was brought in as a consultant for the last week of rehearsals. The school spared no expense in making its silver anniversary a memorable one.

It was May 12, 1938. The main hall of the club house across from the high school was filled to capacity, and the play was a great success. After the final curtain call, Miss Eller ran to me, took hold of my shoulders and said, "Arved Ojamaa, I just love you!" Her emotional outburst was more than ample payment for the long hours of rehearsal and the time spent memorizing my part. It sounds sentimental, but our mutual admiration lasted for decades.

My story would not be complete without a chapter called, "The Algebra Lesson." This chapter shows the way some teachers used to teach their subject in high school some 60 years ago, I found the story in my old diary which my sister saved for over half a century before she was able to return it to me for safe-keeping.

The episode carries the date, Friday, January 12, 1938. The following story and its dialogue are accurate, and include the name of the teacher and the names of my classmates.

> Our teacher in Algebra is nobody other than the high school principal himself, Kurt Hugo Lipp, a rotund man of medium height with a wrinkled forehead and a sullen face. Here he comes with a beat-up late nineteenth century Algebra text-book in his right hand, and the fingers of his left hand are in his upper waistcoat pocket, holding his gold watch between his fingers for frequent consultation.
>
> The whole class stands up. With a sweeping gesture he gives us permission to take our seats again. He writes a short note in the class day-book and stands up to write an Algebra exercise on the blackboard. After that, he takes the seat again at his desk and starts studying his little black notebook, snufflingly. The whole class is dead silent, holding their breath and wondering where the lightning will strike.
>
> "Viks!"
>
> Tiiu Viks is his first victim.
>
> Tiiu throws both her pigtails behind her shoulders and steps to the blackboard. Her father is the Lutheran minister in the local parish. She is the tallest, perhaps the most beautiful girl in our class. Aino Meos or Hilja Toos might not agree with me, but Tiiu has gorgeous golden hair in two long and thick pigtails that reach down below her waist. Treial's or Sein's pigtails are not even close in comparison.
>
> Tiiu remains motionless, holding the chalk in her right hand and eyeing the blackboard. The headmaster keeps leafing through his small notebook, oblivious to the class. He suddenly revives and notices that nothing has been added to the Algebra puzzle. There is some irony and cynicism in his voice, "We have admired your pigtails long enough. Return to your seat with a big F." He scribbles something into his notebook.
>
> "Mäesalu!"
>
> Tiiu's deskmate is a small, round-faced and large-eyed girl, Laine Müesalu. Algebra is also her hour of suffering.

Laine behaves differently at the blackboard. While Tiiu kept her back towards the class and her eyes on the board, Laine keeps looking continuously over her shoulder towards the class.

When the headmaster notices this, he jumps up from his chair, his face full of pretended fear, "What! . . . Are you ready to bolt? God forbid . . . not that!

Then calming down, he explains, "Horses usually bolt when they look over their shoulders, and I am very much afraid of bolting."

Laine has not altered the assignment on the blackboard in any way and is asked to return to her seat.

"Poor Laine, how could you know it, being so tiny!"

The next "guest" to step to the blackboard is nobody else but Rähni. He is the tallest in the entire school. When he goes for a walk with his girlfriend, he usually walks in the ditch to be face-to-face with her. He has a prominent chin and a head full of wavy hair. He combs and adjusts his locks at least a hundred times each day.

Rähni goes to work quickly.

The blackboard is too low for him, but stooping and bending his knees, he works diligently with the Xs and Ys at times placing them in a most awkward position. The headmaster turns around in his chair, inspects the blackboard and announces, "That is wrong."

To see Rähni's entire creation, he reaches out with his hand. "Step more aside. . . More!. . . What is wrong with it? You mean you do not see? Now tell, me Rähni, how many ways could one solve this problem?"

Rähni frowns and stretches his neck like someone whose collar is too tight.

"Taul."

The girl in the back row jumps up from her desk and starts talking fast, but then stops abruptly.

"She is a little mixed up! Kruusamäe!"

"Two ways", is Kruusamäe's firm answer.

"Let me see, how many ways I can alter your grade!" and he starts turning the pages of his little book.

"Lillep."

"Many ways."

"Listen! How many ways have you lost your marbles?"

"Metsamaa."

The headmaster does not even let him answer. "What happened to you? Your hair is all messed up, clothes unkempt. Oh yes," says the headmaster, noticing that Metsamaa's mouth is wide open and ready with the answer.

But meanwhile Metsamaa's mouth has closed.

"Come to the blackboard." And he goes there, too.

"How much is 64 squared?" The answer is on the blackboard, but Metsamaa does not notice it and starts calculating using his head.

"Don't search for anything in your head. The way it looks, there might be something else besides 64 squared, hiding there."

The class bursts out laughing. The headmaster's mood has improved. He is obviously enjoying his own wit.

Metsamaa used this moment to slip quietly back to his seat, leaving Rähni to face the fireworks alone.

Meanwhile the headmaster has become serious again, inquiring, "Tell me Rahni, where were you last Saturday?"

"At the funeral," is his somber answer.

"I have information, however that your shoes were in the repair shop."

Rähni is trying to explain that he was at the funeral and yet his shoes were also worn out, making it impossible to attend school that day.

The bell rings. The long hour of suffering is over. The headmaster grabs his beat-up textbook and leaves as the class stands up.

Rähni takes out a large comb and starts to rearrange his handsome locks.

(Here my old notes end.)

---

[1] Farewell, he whispered, and big luminous tears were in his eyes.

Chapter 6

BEFORE THE STORM

It happened in the summer of 1937. Mr. and Mrs. Kihlefeldt, an elderly and childless couple, owned and operated the only bookstore in Väike-Maarja.

She was a large woman, somewhat neurotic, with frequent migraine headaches. I had been one of her customers since my first grade in high school. Whenever they had a sale on books, she gave me additional discount on already discounted books. Her husband Mr. Kihlefeldt was a skinny and small man who barely reached his wife's shoulders. He was a serious businessman, keeping the inventory and ordering all textbooks for the high school each year. Their living quarters were behind the store on the first floor. The house also had a second floor furnished apartment-unoccupied, since an noise from upstairs might trigger one of Mrs. Kihlefeldt's migraine attacks.

The bookstore was almost deserted that summer, when Mr. Kihlefeldt had his next book sale. I had bicycled twelve miles round trip to find some bargains. Mrs. Kihlefeldt was standing behind the counter and greeted me with her pleasant smile. From conversations she learned that I had not secured a place to live for the coming school year. It was mainly due to my dislike of noisy boarding houses. My sister had transferred to an all-girl school in Oru, at the Finnish sea, just next to the Estonian president's summer palace. The newly-opened school taught young ladies etiquette, and possibly how to also collar a husband.

When I explained my housing predicament to Mrs. Kihlefeldt, she just stood there looking out the window to the empty marketplace for a while, then excused herself and went the next room to converse with her husband. After a few minutes they both came out and she announced in her quiet voice that they would be happy to rent to me one of their upstairs rooms with the kitchen, for the entire school year. "My husband and I know you are a young man who loves books and hopefully doesn't have any noisy friends." They both started to smile before I realized that I had been smiling from ear to ear, listening to their offer.

Well, that was the way I secured my private lodgings for the rest of my school years in Vaike-Maarja. I had never had a room for myself, not to mention one with a private entrance. There was even a doorbell ringing upstairs if I had visitors - another first in my life, and a luxury no other student could claim.

And the view from my second floor window was unique. It looked

41

down a short dead-end street leading to the ancient stone church partially hidden in a grove of old oak and chestnut trees. Whenever the church bells started to ring the frightened bats flew out of the tower and started circle gracefully around it to the beat of the bells like black-clad ballet dancers, while a cluster of shadowy crows left the treetops and flew past my window. Then there was nothing but the clear sound of the bells with their changing moods — jubilation to sorrow, happiness to despair, spreading over the land for centuries, as far as the eye could see.

On my evening walks I met my new classmate. His name was Mihkel Holm and he had recently transferred from another school. He always seemed to be in a bad mood with his frowning face. No wonder they called him, "Mihkel the Terrible." He was above average height with a lean body and a face with high cheekbones. He never wore a hat or the school cap. His long brown hair reached back to his collar, and tended to slip across his face. He had the habit of whisking it back with the fingers of his right hand, and it had become an involuntary movement whenever he was feeling excited, arrogant or nervous. His father was a farmer like mine, and I could feel his heavy calluses when we shook hands. Their farm was large by acreage, but had sandy soil and rocky ground. It was a struggle to make ends meet. He lived just across the street, in a boarding house run by a woman with a homely face and ugly temper.

During our evening walks he shed his pretentious cynicism, became friendly, talkative, even funny. He was preoccupied with Nietzsche's *Also sprach Zarathustra*, a book he quoted sections of in German.

I can recall only bits of his recitals on Nietzsche's *Ubermensch* and such pronouncements as "God is dead" and "the greatest fulfillment in life can only be achieved by living dangerously." I, of course, had read the same book myself, but can only recall the exhortation "*Wenn du zur Weibe gehst, vergiss die Peitsche nicht,*"[2] This kind of philosophy is outdated now due to the advent of women's lib.

At times, Mihkel was like a man possessed, spreading his hands over his head and exclaiming, "Who are we? Who are we?" followed by his own rebuttal, "We are the rising intelligentsia."

Mihkel was also deeply in love with Endla, a blue-eyed girl from the upper Gymnasium class. The odd thing about all this, or maybe not so unusual when it comes to adolescent love, was that he had not even spoken to her, would do anything but confess his admiration to her. No, he could not do that. It would be humiliating to Endla and cheapen his love towards her. He reminded me of Don Quixote also with his platonic love, fighting windmills for Dulcinea, a peasant girl he had never met. But I did not get tired of his monologues no could I predict what he might do next.

I still remember an incident involving aspirin. In those days aspirin was sold in glass vials of twelve. Everybody knew the dose for aspirin was two tablets, but when Mihkel saw the full vial at my desk he wondered what would happen if he took all of them at once.

"It might kill you," was my opinion. "Let's find out," he said, and swallowed the entire vial. Of course, it is dangerous to consume aspirin in large doses, but the only thing what happened to him was that he fell asleep for two hours, resting his head at my desk and snoring.

On one of our winter evenings our walk led us to the end of town and its old graveyard. Without the shelter of the trees the wind caught us, blowing sharp snow-crystals in our face. The sky was cloudless and bursting with stars. The moon was full, shedding blue light on the open fields. The snow-drifts swirled like wandering ghosts. Mihkel had neither hat nor gloves and had outgrown his coat by a couple of years. I turned my back to the wind and started a slow walk toward the shelter of the trees. Mihkel, on the other hand, was unwilling to return and ignored the biting wind. He just stood there, the full moonlight throwing his faint shadow on the snow-covered road.

"How far is it to your home from here?' Mihkel asked.

"Oh, about six miles. Why?"

"I will walk from here to your place to tell them 'good evening', and will turn around and walk back the same night," he said.

I was astounded, "Why would you do such a thing like that? Do you know how cold it is? Must be well below freezing."

"I want to find out whether I can do it, that's all."

He pulled up his collar, stuck his hands in his side pockets and started to walk away from town.

"You might freeze to death!" I yelled after him.

"I might!" was all he said as he continued to walk into the blue light and drifting snow.

I stood for a while in the middle of the road, puzzled about his sudden decision. What was one of his Nietzsche quotations, "The only fulfillment in life is to live dangerously," I wasn't sure Nietzsche had this kind of danger in mind, but it helped me to understand his actions. His breakneck attitude impressed me, but I never felt like competing. Today this kind of behavior might seem abnormal, but when one is only 16 it calls for admiration.

You might wonder what happened to him. Not much. He arrived at my parents' home after midnight, half frozen. They would not let him leave and he did not insist. My father brought him back the next day, which was Sunday, with the horse and sleigh. Mihkel did not have much to say, and appeared to be depressed. He had completed only half his objective and quietly admitted having "the weaknesses of his flesh and falling short in willpower."

When the next school year started, I asked Kihlefeldt's permission to have Mihkel as my roommate.

The following years in high school were filled with study and fun. Knowledge was considered king, and the payoff was passing the entry exams to the Gymnasium.

There was only one valedictorian in the Väike-Maarja Gymnasium, but none in my graduating class. The feared headmaster, Kurt Hugo Lipp, was working behind the scenes to see if I could qualify for the honors. There were two obstructions. A 'C' in music, which I truly deserved as I couldn't hold a tune and had only a minimal understanding of the basics. Mr. Neemre, the music teacher, was willing to give me a better grade if I wouldn't embarrass him by applying for admission to the conservatory or taking up a career as an opera singer.

The other obstacle for me was German. Miss Behrens was willing to give me a better grade if I would agree to take another exam in her subject. Well, who knew, it could even demote my grade, and I gracefully declined. Why the headmaster had taken up this battle without asking me how I felt about it. Was it because he had given me an "A" in algebra, thinking his subject was the beginning and the end of the sciences. Few years back when there was the beginning and the end of the sciences. Few years back when there was an algebra puzzle on the board and the entire class could not find the answer, he had the bad habit of saying, "Ok, Ojamaa, you tell them!" But there were times when Ojamaa couldn't come up with the answer. And there lay the crux of the matter. My negative answer would have offended the arrogance. I started out bravely, in what I thought was the right direction. He must have gotten the message and he interrupted me with a stretched-out "Y-e-e-s-s", giving me a casual hint, a hidden clue, to put me on the right track, thereby saving his vanity and my embarrassment. It is true in algebra one can play with the numbers and letters. Together they could give the answers to tricky questions and solve problems which the numbers along would not do. One had to know the rules of the game. You just couldn't pile them all together like in alphabet soup and "hope for the best."

Most girls in our class loved algebra like they loved the plague.

Hilja Toos was one of them.

She was a good looking girl who sat in front of me in class. Whenever I became bored I poke her ribs gently with my pencil and was rewarded with an over-the-shoulder smile. At times Hilja used home-grown "recipes" to produce some of the most remarkable algebraic soups in history. She showed me one of her test results, a fat red "0".

Anyway, according to the headmaster's request I received an "honorable mention" at the graduation ceremonies. Saage Vello was the smartest fellow in our class. He had polio in his childhood and walked with a noticeable limp. The Gymnastics' teacher would not be able to make his body whole; he was even stretching the issue when he gave him a "C", and that unfortunately disqualified Vello from valedictorian honors.

Shortly after graduation, we had to take the entrance exams to the Gymnasium. I felt uncomfortable with the result; the would-be-valedictorian was a close third in the final tabulations. Saage Vello and Lydia Vaiksalu had higher scores.

Well, I considered third place not too "pushy", but still distinguished enough when I glanced at the row of classmates' names below the #3 slot.

———————

There was an extra honor for students in the Gymnasium. A wavy, white band was added to the top of the school cap, making a visible earned distinction. Every high school kid was envious of our superior standing and dreamed of someday having the respected wavy white line in his or her cap sometimes in the future. They were well aware that it took willpower, sweat, and brains to earn one!

The Gymnasium classes were small, less than 30 students in each. We were now only three years from the entrance exams to the prestigious University of Tartu, the only institution of higher learning in Estonia, established by the Swedish King Gustav II Adolph in the year 1632.

There was no time for school plays anymore. Miss Eller had left to teach elsewhere and her replacement was a plump female in her late twenties. She had neither the charm nor the enthusiasm of Miss Eller. Our high math and trigonometry teacher was Mr. Steinberg, a tall and talented young man with glasses so thick one could not see his eyes behind them. He was all business but still had a quiet sense of humor without the mean theatrics of Kurt Hugo Lipp. I had a friendly relationship with him. Once he showed me how to multiply any number below ten by nine, by using one's own ten fingers. For instance, to calculate 7 x 9, all one need do is bend the 7th finger and you have the answer before your very eyes. The number of fingers to the left of your bent fingers would give you the tens and the number of fingers to the right, the single digits. In this case 6 and 3 means 63.

One of our new subjects was Latin. The old Latin teacher, Mr. Kristoffel had retired. His replacement was still doing his doctorate in classic languages in Tartu and had to commute to Väike-Maarja by train. Because of his tight schedule we had to have Latin classes every Tuesday evening from six to eight and again for two hours on Wednesday.

I remember his first Tuesday class. There was an eerie feeling in waiting in the empty schoolhouse. Our class was the only one in session. We could hear echoing footsteps before we glimpsed a man, portly and bald, coming down the hallway. Endel Saar, one of our defiant classmates, saw him first and shouted, "Here comes our Fatty Freddy!" I do not remember his real name, but from then on the entire school called our new Latin teacher Fat Fred.

He entered the class without saying a word or introducing himself or the subject he intended to teach. He threw the books he was carrying on the teacher's desk and turned to face the blackboard. The setting sun through the second-floor window made his bald head shine red and pink. He grabbed the chalk and wrote on the blackboard, "Terra, terrae, terram, terra. . . " And this is all I can remember of Latin and its teacher.

On the lighter side of high school life were the social hours. The headmaster had professional dance teacher from Tallinn for two weeks to teach the latest dances to any of the students who were interested. We learned dances like the foxtrot, tango, English waltz, and one called the Lambeth Walk. Aino Abel, a minister's daughter, was my dance partner. We were both sixteen and danced well together. I still remember her as a teenager with the soft look in her eyes and her vibrant body next to mine. We danced to music supplied by the dance teacher's gramophone.

But our own performing, "Heli Neli" (Melody Four) provided music for school dances. The group consisted of Villem Märks on piano and three others from our class. I recall two of them. One was nearsighted and curly-haired Elmar Toom. Another was very talented chap, Ants Viidalepp. They sang into megaphones. Songs like "Tango Nocturno", "Oh sole mio..." and "The Isle of Capri" were the tunes of the day. There were no microphones or loudspeakers back then.

So far I haven't mentioned a course that was required in high school only of male students, two hours each week, in "Military Theory and Practice" we studied military science, weaponry and offensive and defensive tactics. At the end of the fourth high school year the mandatory two-week Reserve Officers Training Course was added. The military garrison from Rakvere supplied one officer with the rank of captain and a number of drill sergeants who were very much in charge. School was out and we were no longer students, but members of an Estonian paramilitary force. All high school rules and regulations went out the window. We did not wear uniforms, just our old clothes. We went through military drills and carried rifles, crawled through the bushes and hid behind tree stumps. We read military maps using a compass, and tested our marksmanship at the rifle range. But most of all, we marched in columns, singing, and I mean singing, singing loud. The drill sergeant was never satisfied, " I can't hear a thing! Are you men or mice? Louder. . . louder!"

And we sang. Let the lungs burst! We sang loud and foul. The dirtier, the better,
> "Käi p. . . , uhke ratsanik, las lilled õitseda . . . "
> Kiss my a . . proud hussar. And let the flowers bloom.

At our next lunch break, I overheard the commanding officer's praise to our drill sergeant, "My compliments, sergeant. Your unit can sing, and I mean really sing."

---

[2] When you go to your woman, do not forget the whip.

Chapter 7

The Year of Discontent

It was the summer of 1940.

After the end of the school year and two weeks of military training, I returned home to face hard work at the farm. At the age of seventeen everything seems like fun. After endless hours of studying and never-ending exams, it felt good to rest the brain and flex the muscles instead.

There was a war going on somewhere in Europe.

Poland was already conquered and divided up between Hitler and Stalin. The paper mentioned something about Nazi troops marching into a faraway city called Paris. We knew no one, apart from Mr. Pervik, who had ever been there. It was just a spot in the school atlas, which nobody rushed to get off the bookshelf. We were interested only in what was happening in our own back yard within radius 10 to 15 miles. Anything beyond that was of no concern to us. The local paper had big headlines about a fellow named Alfred Peitak from Kadrina who had shot his uncle and taken wagonloads of wheat to sell a the market in Rakvere, but was caught by the police before he got that far. Peitak remained the topic of conversation for weeks and not much heed was given to war stories as reported by the Virumaa News (Virumaa was the name of the province). The prices of butter and pork were up, earning extra cash for the farmers. When my father had his fiftieth birthday party, the farm folks, who had been invited to the feast brought him an expensive, but off kilter present, a porcelain dinner service for twelve. To my knowledge it was never used for its designated purpose, or for any other purpose, except the gold-rimmed soup serving bowl with its painted lid. It became a safe-deposit box, a place to hold surpluses of our legal tender.

The young stalks of rye were already knee-high, with scattered warted bunias and cornflowers tall enough to bend in the summer breeze. Fields of silver-toned clover displayed color and sweet aroma in early hours of the morning, but with the midday-sun, their crown became hidden among the leaves and the field changed to dark green. In the backyard, behind the stacks of firewood, burdock leaves were big enough to shine shoes with or to be used as a soaped-down washcloth for an evening bath. A heavy wooden log served as a footing for the washbasin. I remember the old log well since it served more than one purpose. Chopping wood or cutting off the heads of defiant roosters or unproductive chickens. The end of the old tree stump was stained dark brown from spilled blood, and was scattered with chicken feathers that the ax had buried into the log at times of slaughter.

It was also time to harness the horses and mow the hay. The white clover was the first to go. When dried, it became prickly and lost all its color and aroma. The hay from the meadows where primrose, heather and bent grass were dominant, remained feather-soft and its fragrance was rejuvenated when raked into haystacks. One could dive onto it and be rewarded with a generous bounce and a flowery smell.

About the time when the green barley awns started to grow out of their sheaths and the cuckoo-birds stopped their calls for the season, the Virumaa News reported an agreement between the governments of Estonia and the neighboring Soviet Union, whereby a certain number of Red Army units would be stationed at the Baltic seacoast in Estonian territory using it for their military base to safeguard the western border from invasion. There were no further comments on which country the Russians were concerned about. Stalin and Hitler had signed a mutual peace treaty the previous. The only country on the other side of the Baltic Sea was Sweden. Were the Swedes really planning on invading Russia?

Soon the shabby Russian troops arrived. Their convoys traveled with a constant rumble along the main road from east to west. Columns of boxy old trucks stirred up clouds of dust which settled on nearby trees and houses leaving the roadside landscape gray and lifeless. Nobody waved at the passing convoys. The soldiers in them looked gloomy, their uniforms dirty and their faces hostile and tired.

When one of their trucks broke down next to the Kadila-Porkuni road crossing, it became the center of attention. People gathered on both sides of the road to watch the Russians as they ran around the disabled vehicle, gesticulating and swearing in their native tongue. Every third word sounded the same, "yobtvolu mat. . . yobtvoiu mat". When it was translated into Estonian (mother f.....r), the women covered their faces and laughed while the men just laughed.

The Russian soldiers wore long brown-green uniform shirts which hand outside their pants and appeared to be extra-large in size. The soldiers folded their shirts behind them to compensate for the generous width, creating something like a rumpled tail that reached down to the back of their knees. It was held in place by a wide canvas or leather belt. Hand-movements tended to unfold the shirts making it necessary to "tighten the tail" every couple of minutes. Their caps were black from dirt and sweat and carried a red tin star. They all reeked for moldy cheese and dead fish. The officer in charge wore the kind of loose shirt and pants but instead of a regular cap, he wore a hat with its brim pinned up and a horn at the top, much like a swollen thumb. He had two red stripes on his collar, indicating the rank of lieutenant.

No Russians were stationed in Kullenga, so there were no immediate changes. People were still cheerful during the day, but at night, when the rain showers beat against the dark windows, the continuous rumble of Russian convoys on the road made our hearts ache. But there was no escape. One had to face the unknown future alone.

But changes were coming.

We lost our independence and became a land under Soviet rule practically overnight. The population of our country was 1,100,000. We had a military of 16,000 and were occupied by 25,000 Soviet troops. The first Russian troops arrived on Estonian soil June 17, 1940. The elected Estonian government was dismissed by a Revolutionary Committee, which was set up in Moscow and imported along with Russian tanks. President Päts, and the Chief of the Estonian Armed Forces, General Laidoner, were arrested along with government ministers. Their whereabouts remained unknown. Newspapers and radio were censored and spread only communist propaganda.

Mock elections were held a month later and by then only the communist candidates were on the ballot. The polls were watched by agents. Each voter was required to bring along an issued passport for stamping. This helped later on in identifying every non-voter as an "enemy of the people".

If you were in a nursing home or hospital, not to worry. Agents would find you with their portable ballot box and show you where to mark an X, at the same time keeping an eye on you and your ballot so that nothing was changed or added. In case you were blind or senile and didn't know what was up, or maybe even thinking that Nicholas the Second was still the Czar, then the agent marked the ballot for you and dropped it into the black box he carried. A most helpful service, never offered before.

The election had been preceded by another "wrinkle." At the very beginning any party could set up their own candidate. This was just a clever way of bringing opposition leaders out of the woodwork. The non-communist candidates disappeared from the ballots before election, perhaps even from the living. Some of them were later found among 1,741 bodies in a mass grave, executed within the first two months of occupation.

After balloting our local paper, now renamed *Red Virumaa*, was jubilant. "The will of the Estonian people has spoken. For the first time in the history of our land, 98.6% per cent of the population has voted and only communist candidates were elected to the new government. What a glorious day for the entire nation."

The new government convened on 21 July, 1940. A delegation traveled to Moscow, requesting that Estonia be admitted as a new republic into the Soviet Union. The request was unanimously accepted on my 18th birthday, August 8. The members of the Russian plenum stood up and applauded each other.

The folks back home said, "They sold us out." Many drowned their sorrow in alcohol, the custom practiced after the death of a dear friend or a close relative.

"They have buried the entire nation," they said.

Even more foul-smelling Russian troops arrived. They occupied the parsonages, clubhouses and sometimes even the churches. Stories of their odd behavior circulated. For instance, tales of troops using the attics of the buildings where they were stationed as outhouses. This wasn't too bad in the winter since the excrement froze. But with the spring thaw, it all melted and started to run, covering the outer walls of buildings and polluting the neighborhood with an indescribable stink. There were also stories about Russian officers having trouble using the wash basins; they were too low, and to get fresh water you had to pull repeatedly on a handle at the end of a chain.

The Russians could not understand how Estonian stores and markets could have such a huge variety of goods compared to Russia where one had to stand in line for hours on end and needed to work the better part of a year before one could afford a pair of shoddy boots.

The shops full of merchandise and no lines to wait in? Impossible!

"Just another con-game set up by the capitalists to fool the Soviet citizens." The political commissaries were smart enough to see through the phony market arrangements, and ready to ferret out any anti-Soviet thinking! It was the duty of KGB to offer this explanation to comrade soldiers, regular military officers and their families. "It is only smoke and mirrors," they said, "a false exhibit". Truth be told, capitalist countries are far behind our glorious Motherland. Our achievements are admired and envied throughout the world. Let's give three "hurrahs" to Comrade Stalin!

Meanwhile, back in the farm, the long hot days of summer had passed. The weather had been beautiful with a good harvest. The fall had arrived, with low-flying clouds and an early nightfall, chilly evenings with long shadows resting in the cool grass. The smell of hay from the meadows reminded us of things past. If you get to be my age, just recollecting happiness gone-by is painful enough; the sufferings endured will lighten the burden.

In the fall of 1940, I began my senior year at Väike-Maarja Gymnasium. It was always exciting to return to school after the summer break, to meet old classmates or greet the new students who had transferred from other schools.

This year everybody appeared and behaved differently. We were now a communist country. Town officials had been replaced by unknown faces. The local police force was disbanded and replaced by a militia with red armbands.

Our high school janitor was now the Chief of Police, sorry, the Chief of Militia.

The teachers were the same except for headmaster Lipp. The rambunctious algebra teacher had fled to Germany, probably knowing better than anyone else what was coming. His replacement was Edward Kansa, the previous headmaster of Tapa High school, now demoted to Väike-Maarja. He was a tall slender man with gray hair and mild manners. He had the unpleasant duty of setting up new obligatory courses like "History of the Bolshevik Revolution", "Lenin's Life and Teachings," etc.

The teachers, forced to teach these subjects, lacked the usual devotion and the students had no enthusiasm to learn. We were all just going through the motions of studying "The Great Bolshevik Revolution," and parroted the expected answers back to the teachers who did not seem to care.

It was odd. We, the students, had to give answers we did not believe in, to teachers who knew they were wrong. But all of us had to accept it as the truth. Everything was now red.

The Russian rainbow was only one color - red. Their army was called the Invincible Red Army. Their flag was red. All the banners hanging overhead were red, claiming the eventual victory of communism and announcing, "He who doesn't work, doesn't eat!" There were so-called "Red Corners" in each school and public building.

Only sailboats, with their sails colored red by the setting sun, were banned to prevent anyone from fleeing the "Red Paradise."

Each classroom had four large pictures hanging on the wall, lined up in a neat row. Marx, Engels, Lenin and Stalin from left to right in that order.

In this Kafkaesque world, certain words lost their meaning or meant quite the opposite of what they meant before. For instance, the communists used the word "freedom" to mean suppression. Democracy meant tyranny. What they called free elections were really con games.

Specific words or combinations of words were unofficially classified as: a) most dangerous, b) dangerous, c) possibly dangerous, etc. Be sure, comrade student, for your own good, watch your language.

Some colors or combinations of colors were dangerous, a small blue-black-white pin on your lapel could earn you free transportation to Siberia with the kind of accommodations capitalist countries use to transport their cows and pigs.

Let me describe the so-called "Red Corner" in our school building. In the main hall one area was designated as the "Red Corner." It was decorated with the blood-red Soviet flag, with its sickle and hammer insignia.

A sample of intruding thought circulated underground way back then: "The sickle is there to cut your throat and the hammer to hit on your head." The apparently innocent words used in this particular combination would be classified as (a) extremely dangerous. If you used these words in the morning, in this sequence and at a volume at which person X, who was at least semi-fluent in the Estonian language, could hear you, you wouldn't be around to brush your teeth that night. Guaranteed!

Let's look at the possibilities in a little more detail: a) person X is an informer. No need to explain here how your words would make you a "goner," b) person X is not an informer, but person Y is. He heard what you said to X and X did not report it. So person X becomes a co-conspirator and would be as bad off as you, c) person X is not an informer, but he is not sure whether Y heard your statement or whether he is an informer. To save his own skin, X becomes an informer.

———

Sorry for the little digression. We were discussing "The Red Corner" in Väike-Maarja High School, newly established in 1940, the fall semester. The table under the flag was covered with red velvet on top of which there sat a large bust of Stalin. Next to the table was a bookcase with volumes covering the history and ideology of communism plus a few pictures of the Russian Revolution of 1917, such as Lenin making a speech to comrade workers and the like. A bulletin board listed communist youth meetings and newspaper clippings on Stalin's new "Five Year Plan," A couch and chairs offered comfort for the reader, or, if you preferred, you could just sit there and admire the bust of the "Great Leader." Nobody was actually forced to lounge there, and I must admit, it was the loneliest corner in the entire school building.

We had to learn new songs. Those from the capitalist era were considered trash or just plain counter-revolutionary. Oh well, if you wanted to sing a song that had been composed a hundred years earlier, you would be wise to sing it to yourself at your own place and on your own time.

But, the new songs, the songs full of revolutionary spirit and praise for your new Fatherland and new freedom, those were now in our repertoire. The music teacher was still Mr. Neemre. He was now to be addressed as Comrade Neemre or Comrade Teacher. Words like mister, mrs., sir, lady or madam, these were bourgeois terms, again, counter-revolutionary, and their use was precluded.

The only freedom song I still remember went like this:

> Suur ja lai on kodumaa me oma,
> Kus nii vabalt hingata voib rind.

> Immense is this homeland of ours,
> Where our breath is full and free. . .

The word "free" choked us. In no time we were singing, "immense are these prison camps of ours..."

Comrade Neemre looked worried. He'd say, "Please, why are you doing this to me?" You se, he was in the position of person X, obligated to report incidents to the authorities, which he obviously did not intend to do. But, by failing to report, he was placing himself in danger. If one of his students, maybe the one who was singing the new version the loudest, happened to by Y, the informer, when Comrade Neemre would be in hot water. So, it could even be dangerous to teach the punks the new songs about their new-found freedoms!

I cannot leave this song business yet! We had learned about teaching communist dogma and how the students rejected it by building conscious "antibodies", if you will, to the spoken words. "One just doesn't believe the stuff." But songs have two ingredients the melody and the words. One might actually like the melody, which, in itself, is innocent enough and you might start humming it. But, the libretto will flow into your subconscious mind even without vocalizing it. You had secured the front door against reds propaganda, but left the back door unattended. It could corrupt your brain and your ability to think independently. This chain of events is called insidious indoctrination.

So much for the "good news."

The "bad news" concerned my roommate, Mihkel Holm. He had abandoned his "Rising Intelligentsia" idea and had become a full-blooded Communist during the summer break. The *Übermensch* was now the builder of the "workers' paradise." The only thing he kept from Nietzsche as the phrase, "Der Gott ist tot." How could it happen? How could a young romantic utopian man become a communist overnight? Since we now lived in the same room, heated arguments were common. He believed in the "new world order" of true communism which hadn't materialized yet. But, we were well on our way to a time and system where *"everybody gives his full efforts to society and in return will be rewarded according to his needs."*

I did not buy any of it.

"Fair enough, but who will determine what my full effort shall be? Let's say I work hard, but my next door neighbor, Ivan, had to much vodka last night and when he shows up late and insists that this is his 'full effort'. Who could tell otherwise? *'I shall be rewarded according to my needs?'* Who will decide for each individual what his or her needs are? The comrades in the government? That would create a bureaucracy the likes of which the world has never seen before.

"What about the fat-cats who drive 30 miles to Narva Jõesuu to have breakfast at the beach, living off the blood and sweat of the working class? Communism will bring salvation and justice to the workers."

"Why do the workers need salvation," I'd say. "Salvation from what? I could personally tell you about the thousands of workers in the Kunda Cement Factory where I spent my last summer vacation as one of my aunts is married to a common laborer there. They all have small apartments. Food is plentiful. The milkmen and the bakers and greengrocers rolled by in their wagons every morning, hawking their wares. In fact, I can even remember the words of the baker, walking behind his horse-drawn wagon:

"...Prouad...saiad...leivad...sepikud...magushapud...peened...leivad...pro uad..." ("...Ladies...white bread...rye bread...barley bread...buns and rolls...ladies...")

Their wives slept late and didn't even have to go to the market! But, now they ain't "ladies" no more. They're comrades. All that bourgeois baking will be eliminated. The baker will be calling out now: "Comrades...breads...comrades.....breads"

But wait, the worst is yet to come: the baker is now called a capitalist. He had been living *off the blood and sweat of the working class* (now a standard slogan repeated over and over again, ad nauseum.) Well, his horse and wagon and his bakery will be confiscated (their word is *nationalized*), and comrade housewife, you'd better get off your duff early in the morning and line up for a loaf of rye bread at the state-owned Bakery Combine. I was getting hot under the collar and wouldn't let Mihkel interrupt me.

"The farmers are now called kulaks and capitalists. As you know, there are no big landowners in our country. You and I had to works some days up to 16 hours during our summer recess. But your friends will fix that, too. They'll 'nationalize' your land and nobody will care if the hay is gathered before the rainy season sets in. If the cows don't eat the stuff, so what? They ain't your cows no more. If the snow comes and buries half of the potato crop, so what? Those ain't your potatoes either."

Of course, my views were considered counter-revolutionary. I was well aware that expressing such views in public would have serious consequences, but I was arguing with my friend and classmate in the privacy of our room. True, these arguments were fruitless, and we tried to avoid them, but hidden hostility remained.

Another classmate of mine, comrade Arnold Saarik, was already a well-established communist and was active in the local political arena. He was from the city of Narva and not a country hick like Mihkel and I. He was tall, with an emaciated body, and an ascetic face with a narrow chin. His mouth seemed to reach almost to his large ears, or was it the other way around? His light colored hair, for some reason, grew straight up and was cut flat at the top to the length of two or three inches. He was also a poet and a writer of some distinction. His charm and oratory had carried him to the position of local Communist Part Secretary. He was attending school sporadically and no teacher had the courage to ask about his whereabouts. In class he kept his old friendly manner. He did not seem to pay any attention to Mihkel at school, but I was sure they were communicating with each other and he must have been well aware of my views on communism.

I tried to avoid him, but after a few weeks we met face-to-face in our evening walk. (Mihkel and I did not take our walks together any more. He seemed to be out most evenings.) To my surprise, Saarik extended his hand with a friendly smile, "Well, how is your counter-revolutionary spirit tonight?"

"So what? How are your friends at the KGB?"

He ignored my hostile answer and exhibited his old charm. "Hey listen, we used to be friends! Don't forget. I have been looking for a chance to talk to you in private."

We had not been friends in the true meaning of the word, rather we were classmates. A talented chap like him with all his charm, now a high communist official, calling a country dude a friend?

"About what? I don't believe we have much in common."

His ear-to-ear smile appeared, "Who knows! Hey, listen. Let's take a walk together and talk."

The evening dusk had settled on the sandy path of the churchyard. We were facing each other under the old oak trees, where the only witnesses were centuries-old graves of past dignitaries with their leaning marble crosses.

He told me about his patriotic accomplishments in Narva, the fake explosions and hidden megaphone interruptions during the communist mass meetings. If he had been telling me the same story today, I would rank in with Baron von Münchhausen's imaginary adventures in the 18th century. But, I was naïve and his actions sounded heroic to me. At the end of his daredevil stories, he told me about his true calling. He had become one of the leaders of a resistance movement with the goal of restoring Estonian independence. He had already organized a local cell, but he couldn't reveal names for security reasons. According to his story, he was given the task of infiltrating the communists' ruling clique as a redneck revolutionary. This task he had already accomplished. His present assignment was to obtain inside information, such as the names of citizens to be arrested, so they could be forewarned. He knew I was a true patriot, and keep the conversation absolutely confidential. He asked me to become a member of the resistance movement and to be ready for action when the time was right.

Then he added, "Be careful with your roommate Mihkel. He cannot be trusted, not even in your so-called "private conversations." Another thing, tone down your anti-communist rhetoric for your own safety!"

Before we departed he told me he had been meeting with KGB officials where the subject was to silence the opposition among high school students. He added that my name had been mentioned. Then he continued in a happier vein.

"I was sitting next to a KGB officer at that time and I placed my foot next to his shiny boots, it was a perfect match!" He then added, "The day will come when I will wear those boots!" As we will learn later, that day never came to Arnold Saarik.

I was happy to find a friend I did not even know I had and agreed to become a member of his covert organization. After a hearty handshake we departed, walking in different directions.

Back in my room, I listened to Mihkel's praise of comrade Saarik's devotion to the "right cause." He seemed surprised when I agreed with him whole heartedly.

A few weeks passed. It was a peaceful evening in autumn. I was sitting along in my room, reading Knut Hamsun's "Growth of the Soil", a story about Isak, a strong and coarse fellow with a red-iron beard who settles in the Norwegian wilderness. Since then I've read it once in German and even twice in English. Every time I pore over it, it brings back memories of that October evening in 1940.

My tranquil mood was interrupted by the doorbell. I rushed downstairs to unlock that entrance.

Two men in leather jackets were standing there. They asked for my name, "You come with us."

The evening was cool and I turned to run upstairs to get my coat. One of them grabbed my wrist, "Where you are going, you do not need a coat."

They took my arms from both sides and pulled me toward a waiting car with turned-off lights. One of the agents opened the car door and pushed me in. The other walked around the back of the car and sat next to me. The driver started the engine and turned on the headlights. He was dressed in similar fashion, wearing a leather coat and cap. It was obvious they were KGB agents.

I started to shiver. Was it fear or the coolness of the leather against my bare arms in a short-sleeved shirt?

"What's this all about", I managed to ask. There was no response. After the car had reached the main road, one said casually, "Their Päts (referring to our arrested president) fooled around with these tin-horns. We'll just bury them with their mouths full of dirt." The one did not bother to respond.

The car pulled up to our high school building. The lights were still on in the foyer. One of the agents took my arm and led me to a room on the first floor just next to our library. I recognized it as the administrator's office. I was told to sit on a solitary chair in front of the desk. A gooseneck lamp was turned to direct the light into my face. Because of that I could not see much of anything in the room, except for the outline of Stalin's face across the desk on the opposite wall.

So far I hadn't been told what I was charged with. I knew I hadn't committed any acts of violence against the new regime. True, I had been rather vocal in expressing my opinion about communism, but it was a view shared by 99% of my countrymen.

They could not arrest and shoot us all. Maybe in the long run, but not all at once. Whey then was I their first prey?

How about my room-mate Mihkel and the warning from Arnold Saarik not to trust him. Where was he spending his evenings anyhow? To my knowledge, he did not have a girlfriend or any friend beside me. He must have new friends in leather coats.

The agent stepped to the opposite side of the desk, opened his coat and unbuckled his gun belt, throwing it on the table in front of me. Then he sat down behind the desk without removing his cap or coat. He took a folder from a leather case on the table that I hadn't noticed before, opened it and read, "Under Article 93 of the Penal Code of Criminal Justice of the Soviet Union, you are accused of being the part, or a member of the party, that removed the picture of Comrade Lenin form the high school library and used it for target practice. You are also accused of drawing a gallows on the same picture and then nailing it to a telephone pole downtown."

Then he looked at me with a continuous stare. His right hand removed the gun from its holster and placed at the middle of the desk, its back barely touching the upper end of his open folder and the barrel pointing at me. The bright light hurt my eyes and the heat from it had turned my face red. I felt sweat trickling down the back of my neck and running down along the curve of my spine. The perspiration from my face made my eyes burn.

This accusation was a horse of a different color. It had serious implications. I was well aware that I had to prove my innocence and they didn't have to prove my guilt.

Then the questioning started, "Where were you last night? The night before? Last evening? Where is the handgun? What caliber? Did you do the shooting? Draw me a picture of the gallows..." The questions were shouted at me. New threats were made about being buried "six feet under."

I don't remember how long the interrogation lasted. The acute fear which had incapacitated me first had vanished. The "fight or flight" instinct, shared by all living creatures, had come to my rescue. I could not flee so I had to fight back. I moved forward in the chair and placed both of my hands at the edge of the desk. I kept perspiring, but it not seem to bother me now. When he pounded the top of the desk I pounded back from the opposite side. I had nothing to lose. I had never even heard about the "picture incident" and never fired a handgun. I leaned forward looking straight at him, "I was at home last night and the night before. Comrade Holm, you must know him, he is my roommate and can testify to that fact. I have never handled a handgun and do not know how to operate one. We had no guns at home. Comrade Holm has been there, too, and could confirm it. Ask him! What do you mean by the gallows? Do you mean a guillotine? I can draw a picture of a guillotine...."

The questions were repetitious, but my head remained clear, and I did not hesitate with my answers. I did not care. They could shoot me now if they chose.

The agent had placed his index finger on the trigger, pointing the gun between my eyes with his continuous stare. I stared back, eyeball to eyeball, without blinking as long as it took.

Suddenly, he broke eye contact, "If you did not do it, who did? Who might have done it? I want names. Give me names!"

I claimed ignorance.

"Well, it is up to you. If you do not cooperate, I will place you under arrest on grounds of obstructing an investigation to carry out justice, and being under suspicion of having committed a serious crime. The choice is yours."

Obviously, I was not a suspect anymore, and suddenly I felt very tired. I did not want to be arrested. I gave him a couple of names of my classmates, ones least likely to be involved. It was not easy to be an informer. It isn't easy to be coward.

The agent stood and picked up his belt with the gun.

"You are free to leave now, but if further evidence implicates you, we will come to get you", he said. "This conversation was private and has to remain so. If you discuss it with anybody, we shall meet again, and I can promise you, it won't be as pleasant as today's chat."

Walking through the chilly night back to my room, I felt bizarre happiness mixed with fear. Happy to be free again and breather the cool autumn air, and fear of having to face them again.

Mihkel was stretched out in his bed smoking. He did not ask where I had been. I think he knew. Maybe he was surprised that they let me go.

The late evening interrogation must have been audible throughout the school building. There were still some students and teachers present. I was told Miss Behrens, our German teacher, had been running down the hall crying, "My God, they'll shoot him!" All the citizens of German extraction had departed to Germany long ago, except Miss Behrens. I have no way of knowing whether the incident she had witnessed helped to make up her mind, I only know that two weeks later she left for Germany. The next day at school, everybody seemed to know what had happened the night before. Obviously, word gets around. How could the agent yell loud enough to be audible throughout the building and then ask me not to tell anybody?

The hidden fear from this encounter remained inside me. Whenever the phone rang, whenever a car stopped near me, whenever I heard steps behind me, I had a panic attack, it's them! They've come to get me. Even on weekends in the country when I saw somebody approaching the house by the lonely road, the thought flashed through me head, they're coming!

The students whose names I had given to the KGB all seemed to behave normally over the following weeks and I was convinced they had not been contacted. This fact, at least, gave me some relief.

Life continued with its gray days of late fall when the lights had to be turned on at 3 p.m. A foggy mist seemed to hang over the school, the town and the surrounding fields.

The teachers went through the motions of teaching, but seemed absent-minded and preoccupied. It all seemed trivial and precarious at the same time. I had given up my anti-communist rhetoric. My relationship with Mihkel had improved and there were no more political arguments. He believed that I was starting to "see the light", and I didn't care. I was sure he had supplied the KGB with information about me. Maybe he even had a feeling of guilt, who knows? We talked about daily events, even about Endla, the girl with whom he was still in platonic love. He had even engraved a large "E" in the web of his left hand with pen and ink, just between the thumb and index finger. He believed the self-inflicted wound would help to alleviate his sufferings.

After these conversations, our relationship seemed to be like it had been in the old days. Here is a contradiction. According to communist standards, love was not an accepted emotion between two sexes. No miss or misses or lady or madam, only comrades. One could love only the State, Communism and Comrade Stalin. Platonic love would be even worse, perhaps as intolerable as religion. Of course, I didn't bring up the contradiction and I would not report Mihkel's love life to the KGB. In fact, I was happy that he still had feelings such as love.

There wasn't much hope, but there was some.

Well, I could hope, but Mihkel must know. He could not "believe" because only religious people believe. The communists have nothing to do with religion. Do you think comrade Stalin uses that word? Did he ever say to his KGB henchmen, "I *believe* comrade So-and-So should be shot." Not in your life, he would just say, "Shoot the devil" and that would be the end of it.

A new decree was passed by the local authorities. Each high school student must name a local resident named as guardian. The apparent purpose was to keep an eye on you and have someone else to be co-responsible for your actions.

Mihkel and I knew a sergeant from the Estonian military, now of course, part of the Red Army. Integration had not been completed because of the language barrier and company-size Estonian units still existed. The man was a bachelor and lived across the street from us. He was a friendly fellow in his thirties. One day we got acquainted and he asked us to have a beer with him. We obliged. Drinking and smoking were the few new "freedoms" for students.

After we had had a couple of beers, an idea crossed my mind. Why not ask him to be our guardian? It would certainly look good on paper, the Guardian for Arved Ojamaa, Comrade Sergeant from the Soviet Union's Red Army. Someone would surely go over the list and it would look like a trustworthy and useful relationship. No civilian would question the loyalty of a member of the Red Army. I ordered another round of beer and came out with my suggestion. Mihkel liked the idea at once, the same guardian for him. Sergeant Rebane was appreciative, "It will be an honor, comrade students. Let's drink to that."

To fill his first obligation as guardian, he ordered the bartender to have a case of beer delivered to our residence.

As you can see, there were a few bright moments to life even way back then.

December arrived with its early darkness, but the frost was late and so was the snow. It started to fall just two days before Christmas, and continued to come down in large, soft flakes. There was no wind to speak of and the snow settled on the trees, buildings and sidewalks, making the small town look like a Christmas scene from a bygone era.

We already knew there were no holidays, and we went to school the morning of Christmas Eve. In fact, the word "Christmas" was banned for good. You would not hear that word on the radio or read it in the newspapers. It was now called the "Change of Year Festival," or in Estonian, "The Nääri Festival." (The world Nääri goes back to the 16th century, when the holidays before the New Year were called Nääri.) The authorities were successful in separating Christ from Christmas and voilá, they gave us one week off!

The class was ready for lunch break when the teachers came to the classes, all in smiles, announcing not Christmas (meaning Christ) not the holidays (meaning something holy) but one week of recess to celebrate the Nääri and the New Year.

There was pandemonium! Everybody was yelling and throwing books repeatedly on the desks. We were too conservative for hugging or kissing, but there were handshakes all round with shouts of "Merry Christmas". I turned to shake hands with Mihkel, but he had already left with his books.

On my way home, I stopped at the post office to use the public phone to call my uncle in his Kullenga liquor store to let my folks know about the recess and ask them to come and take me home. Mihkel was already stretched out on the bed smoking, "Isn't it nice to get off for a few days, I announced cheerfully, being careful not to use the forbidden words.

After he had taken a deep drag on his cigarette and blown the smoke towards the ceiling, the only thing he said was, "One week, I could use the time."

My father arrived in the early evening by horse and sleigh. I was running downstairs to meet him when the church bells started to ring. It was getting dark, but I could still make out the church tower where the bells were announcing the birth of Christ. The short road was filled with people, all going to Christmas Eve service. I had never seen such a crowd on this road before. I should know, since they had been passing my window for the previous three years.

I hadn't been to church for some time, but the sound of the bells and the crowd rushing past my doorstep made me yearn for something, so I said, "Let's go to church, Dad."

He agreed, saying, "Let me give the horse a hay stack first and cover her with a blanket."

The church was filled to capacity. We could hardly find room to stand. The 15th century church was stone-cold and during the choral singing, vapor from each breath rose toward the high arches of the cathedral ceiling, uniting into one big cloud of prayer to the Lord. By the time the sermon started the vapor had condensed and fell down on worshipers in the form of snow.

It snowed inside the church on Christmas Eve! Reverend Hiiemets read the holy scripture. I could not hear the sermon as the words echoed between the massive stone columns where the candles flickered in ancient brass holders.

I learned later that Mihkel had been sitting in the first pew, wearing an old beat-up cap. He did not stand up or remove his cap throughout the service, and busied himself by taking notes. Reverend Hiiemets was arrested the first part of the coming year and died as a martyr. Whether Mihkel's Christmas Eve notes had anything to do with it will never be known.

At home we had the old-fashioned Christmas with blood sausage, headcheese and home-brewed beer, plus a Christmas tree with live candles. We listened to a radio broadcast from Tallinn, where they were singing, "….and Nääri bells were ringing…."

It was my last Christmas at home.

Chapter 8
Life as a Fugitive

I clearly remember the sunny day of June 22, 1941.

On that day the Germans invaded Russia. There was war between the two countries and we were also involved since Estonia was now part of Russia. Hidden rejoicing could be felt throughout the land on that day. We had had Soviet occupation for one year, and it seemed like an eternity. Stalin's oppression was hard to bear and escaping from it, which had recently seemed only a pipe dream, might now become a reality. Everybody hoped and prayed for the Germans to come and kick out the comrades and commissaries and occupying Red Army and KGB.

I had spent seven school years in Väike-Maarja and could finally call myself a graduate, but as a draftee I was now required to join the "victorious" Red Army and fight for the communist cause. Not in a million years would I wear their uniform with the red star. By now you needn't ask why!

I was to join a group of "Forest Brothers" that very afternoon. I decided to take a final walk down the main street I had traveled for almost half of my young life.

As I stepped into the midday sun, Velda's farewell handkerchief was tied around my neck, still carrying a trace of her perfume and still moist from the tears of departure.

Behind Kihlefeldt's bookstore grew ancient horse chestnut trees, now past full bloom. I wondered how many springs I had walked down the same road without noticing their blossoms in the dust.

The first classmate I ran across was Vello Saage, the genius of our class. I was not jealous of his high IQ, but envied his disability. He did not need to worry about the draft. My observation was rude, and his bitterness showed when we shook hands "until we meet again." Neither of us believed our paths would again cross. To me his future appeared worry-free and bright, but nobody would have given a wooden nickel for mine.

My classmates seemed a restless bunch. Half a block down I rant into Endel Saarik.

Whatever had happened to his liberation organization, he did not say. I learned some fifty years later that he had given one of our classmates the assignment of bringing rifle ammunition was punishable by death or a trip to Siberia, depending on the circumstances. I could well imagine what would have happened if the contents of his heavy "luggage" had been discovered during his long railroad trip. Saarik must have had some connection with the resistance movement, supplying the ammunition. Was this all just a part of Saarik's game? He had used the same classmate to eavesdrop on KGB officer meetings by hiding him in a nearby closet. The classmate, Aleksander Traks, jeopardized his life believing he was doing a service for his suffering country, but unknowingly had been chasing Saarik's follies. There might have been other classmates with different "assignments" that I have no knowledge of. I only know that I did not receive any. Was it because he already considered me a "poor risk" because of my previous encounter with the KGB?

Was Saarik playing the game of double-agent, trying to impress his patriotic classmates as a freedom fighter and hoping they would come to his rescue if communism fell? During our meetings over the school year, he was always eager to discuss his patriotic feelings but failed to mention his promotions in the communist hierarchy. Who was he? What did he really believe in? And here he was again with his ear-to-ear smile, his bony hand stretched out well before we met, poised for a friendly shake.

We talked about our immediate plans. I didn't hesitate to tell him of my intention to go into hiding to escape the Russian draft. My only hope for survival was just that, a hope; the hope that the Germans would liberate us from Soviet occupation. That would mean life. The continuing Russian and communist regime in Estonia would eliminate any chance of my survival. He admitted that his involvement in communist activities had become too extensive to be forgiven. His plan was to retreat to Russia if needed and support himself with his literary talent. Being a civil servant in a communist hierarchy, he did not have to register for the draft.

Now, half a century later, I believe his feelings at the beginning of the school year were honorable. But his addiction to power was his downfall and the organization of so-called "freedom fighters" was mostly, if not all, his own pipe dream.

He wished me luck as a fugitive. His chances for survival were superior to mine, but my conscience was not burdened like his.

We shook hands again. The smile on his face could not hide the sadness in his eyes. He had directed his talent in the wrong direction, and now it was too late to change sides.

I believed we would never meet again. In this crazy world, one of us might survive. I felt some grief standing there and watching him go, bent forward, his coattails flying in the wind. I could not help but say "good luck!" We were classmates once, but now players on opposing teams.

I continued my walk toward Cat's Tail Road, past the Town Hall. The large, fenced-in yard with neighing horses and swearing farmers. The Red Army needed the horses for cannon fodder more than the farmers needed them to sow or harvest crops. The confrontation was fierce.

The farmer's horse is more than his friend, it is part of his family. They work together long hours in the field. When traveling the snow-covered winter roads, only a fool would try to lead the horse, because only the horse would know where the footing was firm under drifting snow. After a day's work, the farmer would feed his horses before he gave himself even a bite. Thus the kinship between horse and owner was strong and separation painful.

At the epicenter of this calamity of the hostile farmers and the kicking horses, was nobody else but my ex-roommate Mihkel Holm, "The Chairman of the Horse Draft." I hadn't seen him for a few days. Was he eating and sleeping with his KGB buddies?

It was a struggle to get closer to him. "Hi Mihkel," I yelled, Dosvidania! Tomorrow I will be a member of the glorious Red Army. What about you?"

He frowned without saying anything. He knew that I was making fun of him by saying good-by in Russian. We lived in different worlds without any connecting bridge. I could not stomach any longer the hostility and despair in the yard. I struggled to get out, out to the open road, but I could not get Mihkel out of my mind. Just a couple years before when graduating from high school, together we wrote in our yearbook witty notes on every classmate under the pseudonym "O + HO" (Ojamaa + Holm). There is no plus sign in this equation. I noticed he was carrying a gun-belt. If I were carrying a gun, I would be shot. It had nothing to do with being right or wrong. He had the gun and the power. He was the hero in his Red World.

But the shell game was far from over. Maybe at the end I would have the power and carry the gun.

I felt sorry for the horses, but not for Mihkel with his gun-belt.

I was glad to be out on the open road again, on my way to Cat's Tail Road to see my classmate Endel Saar. Thinking of him, I even felt like laughing as I recalled a couple of episodes from previous years. (Not the past school year, when laughs were as rare as snow in the Sahara Desert.)

Our curriculum in high school included one hour of religious teaching each week throughout our high school years. It was taught by a Lutheran minister, Reverend Abel. We were all Lutherans, so there was no question as to who would teach it. The minister had the custom of giving a short prayer at the onset of each religion class while we were still standing. Once Rev. Abel got a bit carried away, asking God to bless everyone and everybody to bless the President, the government, the school, the teachers and the students. At the end there was a moment of silence, when Endel Saar whispered, but loud enough to be heard by everybody, including the minister, "Bloody Hell! He forgot to bless the principal!" He was a trouble-maker all right, but not obnoxious. He could be witty, but could also be embarrassing at times. He used to argue with the teachers, and in general made a nuisance of himself. When our petite biology teacher, Mrs. Ruubel, called him a big hooligan for his misbehavior, Endel interpreted the word "big" to mean "tall", and she said the word hooligan with such a loving smile that Endel took it as a compliment. His face was full of pretended appreciation. He even stood up and took a bow. The class burst out laughing including the biology teacher.

I knew he was also under the military draft, but I was sure he had no interest in joining. His home was in Tartu, a far-away city. He was registered by the local draft board and wasn't permitted to leave the area. He had no knowledge of the countryside nor any place to hide. I could help him in his predicament. That was in my mind when I knocked on the door on Cat's Tail Road. Endel cam out stark naked after a short pause, and closed the door quickly behind him. Obviously he wasn't alone.

"I came to say good-by," I said. "By sunset you can call me a deserter. I am joining a bunch of fellows who are called bandits by some authorities. Are you by any chance interested in becoming an outlaw?"

"Wait a minute, I'll put my pants on," was all he said. He went back into his room without inviting me in. I could hear whispers, then hushed crying. I was sure it wasn't Endel doing the crying. After a few minutes he cam out stuffing his shirttails into his pants and throwing his jacket over his shoulder. All he said was, "Let's go!"

The sun was low on the horizon when Endel and I walked a narrow path between the cornfields toward our destination in the River Hill Woods. This really was not much of a hill, but rather a wooded mound with birch, spruce, lime trees and alder bushes. The woods ran east to west in a two-mile wide strip for a while, then merged with the forest that extended all the way to Lake Peipus and the Russian border. The name River Hill was from ancient times when the extinct River Abaja

70

still flowed alongside it. Now the hillside was covered with bent grass and dog daisies.

We reached River Hill and squatted down behind a fieldstone fence and waited. Nothing happened.

We could see some movement further back in the forest but nobody approached us as planned. Endel and I couldn't be sure the shadows back there didn't belong to the communists' Search and Destroy Battalion, which was out looking for guys like us.

Then it dawned on me that there were two of us and they were only expecting one. This itself might have mad the welcoming party suspicious.

I stood up on top of the stone fence, crisscrossed my hands over my head, and yelled out my name. Nobody took a potshot at me which was itself reassuring.

Then two men, carrying their rifles under their arms in a relaxed manner, approached us. Both appeared young with their peach-fuzzy beards and sunburned faces, typical country youngsters. We, the graduates from an institution of higher learning, could not claim any privileged status or seniority here, best to be unpretentious and reserved.

I told them who I was and introduced Saar as a fellow schoolmate and deserter who was looking for a place to hide.

One of the fuzzy-bearded fellows said good naturedly, "Welcome to the gang of outlaws."

Then both youngsters threw their rifles over their shoulders. One said, "Follow us, the captain wants to see you."

We zig-zagged through the woods. In some areas, the canopy of full -grown trees shaded the late sunlight and only ferns covered the ground, reaching almost to our waist. Then we walked along the hillside where the tops of the young birch trees were still lit by the setting sun. The grass here was lush with an abundance of wildflowers, their bittersweet fragrance mixed with the smell of decaying old leaves and cool, moist earth. This was the place to sing the line "where our breath is full and free…"

We soon reached a small clearing with aged oak trees. At its center was the summit with dry rocky ground and scattered juniper bushes. I saw a few men stretched on the ground next to their rifles. Our guides led us to a man who was sitting by himself on the ground leaning against a tree trunk.

"Instead of one, we found two," said one of our guides and without further ado retreated, their mission complete.

The man leaning against the tree trunk was obviously the leaser of the group, the one called captain. He seemed undisturbed and didn't say anything, just kept looking, apparently waiting for us to speak up first. Remembering my military etiquette, I introduced myself first and added a few words about my companion, ending my short statement with the word "captain." He stood up to shake our hands, mine first and added, "I know your father. A good man."

Then the others came up to us and told us their names with a handshake. Two of the men were heavily bearded, rough-looking characters, possibly in their forties. One told us his name was Aleks Metsnik and added, "My farm is just a stone's throw from here. You'll meet my folks when we drop over for a hearty meal. Nice meeting you."

I knew he was smiling since I could see his white teeth. The rest of his face was covered with beard. His companion just shook our hands and said, "I am his brother."

He introduced himself, "My name is Johannes Must. I am a reserve officer from the Estonian infantry. The fellows just call me captain."

"You said you are high school graduates, and I know you have had military training and target practice. Tomorrow we will supply you with Russian military rifles and ammunition; you are quite familiar with these, so I won't go into that any further.

"We don't do target practice, for obvious reasons. We don't want to attract attention to ourselves, and our ammunition is limited. We all know we are called traitors and bandits by the communist henchmen, who still hold power because of the Russian occupation. The folks call us heroes, the "Forest Brother." Any one of us who is caught will be shot, so we forget about the hero business. There are already too many dead heroes. We are not looking for action, and shoot only in self-defense. We do not take prisoners and will not surrender for obvious reasons. If it comes to that, we would rather die in battle than by firing squad."

We agreed with what the captain was telling us. It was nice to know his philosophy. I particularly like his stand on not looking for action and his statement about there being too many dead heroes in the world. We sure didn't intend to lengthen the list with our own names. Endel just nodded his head to everything and did not offer his usual arguments. I was happy about that. I didn't want to feel embarrassed that I'd brought a screwball to the camp.

The captain continued to outline his strategy, "We don't light any fires, not even for cooking, and we don't spend two nights in the same place. When we leave one area, it has to look the same as before. We do not leave anything behind and any garbage we have, we bury inconspicuously. Nobody is to leave camp without my knowledge or permission.

"We never, ever occupy or sleep in the hay shacks. We know what happened to a group like ours from the Lasila region. They were found sleeping in a hay barn and all of them were shot before they had a chance to fight.

"We are not concerned about the Russian troops traveling the main road, which runs parallel to our woods but is separated from us by open fields. They have their war to fight and have no time to waste chasing a few rednecks in the woods.

"There are, however, small platoon-size Russian KGB forces, guided by our own local reds. They have raided some areas before and they may do it again. If any unit approaches the woods, we would know about it. We will not try ambush them, but will move further east to join the new group, and so on. We fight only when we have no escape routes open, and this is a remote possibility.

We can hold out here for months and wait until the Germans come and kick out the Russians and their comrades. We know they are coming. The latest Estonian language broadcasts from Helsinki reported that one half of Lithuania is already freed, and my guess is that they will be here in four weeks at the latest."

Then the captain turned on his side, using the protruding tree roots as a pillow. He closed his eyes, pulled his hat over his face to keep out the mosquitoes and added, "Make yourselves at home."

We found an open spot behind the juniper bushes and stretched out on the green moss covering the ground. Endel used a rock for a pillow. I used my rucksack for the same purpose and pulled my jacket over my head and shoulders.

It had been a long time since I felt safe. It felt good to be away form the hassles and uncertainties in Väike-Maarja. Away from the KGB, an unpredictable and dangerous roommate, and the mysterious and two-faced Arnold Saarik. Away from the draft board, and the continuous rumble of passing troops and their wagons under my window.

Here I could pick up only the snoring that came from the next juniper bush and the hollow call of the screech owl. I slept. Restless dreams, my frequent companions over the recent past, had deserted me for the night.

In the month of June the sun rises in Estonia at four in the morning and sets only for one hour before midnight. The five hours in between are filled with twilight. During these restless nights your sleep is usually shallow, and your daydreams flow into it and become one with your night-dreams, and you can't tell them apart.

They consist of memories of those evenings that had followed a day's work in the farm, images of washing yourself behind the wood-pile in the backyard, pouring hot water from the bucket to the washba-sin and using the hard soap your mother had made in the spring by boil-ing tallow in a black kettle.

Or they contain recollections of holding the sweaty palm of a young girl next to the wooden swing in the clearing, with the trees catching the lights of dusk. Higher and higher went the swing, the girls shrieking with laughter and their dresses hanging for a moment weightless in the air, exposing their sunburned legs above their knees, their hot breath burning the side of your face. There is no one night with one dream but a multitude of clippings, the moments of being awake spliced with longing and imagined moments crossbred with reality.

That's what those carefree nights in June were all about, sleeping as a fugitive in the woods in the middle of the war.

At six in the morning we broke camp to find a sunny spot in the clearing to get the chill out of our bones and to relieve our stiffness from sleeping on the ground.

There was no fog at our campsite because of the elevation, but it still blanketed the valley below, including the road with its troop movement. We could hear the muted rumble of the vehicles and the footsteps of the men; the world was still at war. For me, it was the first full day of peace and serenity. The expected time of leisure was a godsend. My life had been filled with preparation for final exams. The anxiety of living amidst pressuring circumstances. Every hour had seemed jam-packed with obligations and no orderly plan of action. I was running like a de-capitated chicken, without direction and sometimes without purpose.

The campsite had a clearing where we could dry our dew-dampened clothes. There was enough breakfast in my rucksack to share with my friend and classmate. We learned all the other members of our group were from local farms that dotted the perimeter of the nearby woods. They had all known each other before. This was, of course, an excellent arrangement for safety and food supplies. Everyone seemed friendly, if still reserved towards us.

In the afternoon, long after the fog had cleared from the valley be-low, we moved to a new location on the northern side of the slope. We had a good view of Kullenga-Kadila road, which crossed the woods west of us. It was not long before our outpost reported a truck ap-proaching along the road not traveled by motorized vehicles during the war. The captain studied it with his binoculars. There was some anxiety until the captain studied it with his binoculars. There was some anxiety until the captain announced, "Don't get excited. I was expecting this truck. It means another young man will join our distinguished group and bring along some supplies."

The captain sent out delegates to meet the newcomer. We all realized how unusual this mode of transportation was for a future outlaw. Somebody else, using the binoculars, could read the sign on the side door,

Baumann's Sausage
Rakvere

I looked at Endel and he looked at me. Could it be that our classmate Karly Baumann, whose father had a meat packing and sausage plant in Rakvere about ten miles away, was joining us? He was known as a carefree chap. The owner of a good singing voice, he had an unlimited collection of bawdy songs.

Sure enough, we recognize him by his walk: the back slightly humped, his long arms swinging like a windmill, the chin long and his sad eyes turned toward the ground in front of him, as though he were studying his shoes. Both of the guides were carrying good-sized sacks on their backs and Karl, in the middle, carried nothing. He was just bringing himself, and most likely, his repertoire of uninhibited songs.

In no time, Karl was everybody's friend. Some people talk, using their hands to stress the point they are trying to make, but usually not raising them higher that their face. Karl was different. He raised them well over his head, talking fast and laughing in between without any particular reason, while slapping the backs of those ominous looking brothers with full beards. He was already telling everybody how he got out of town by hiding under canvas, behind sausage crates, while the driver made deliveries to country stores. He was also passing around some Krakow sausages, which could keep for weeks without refrigeration. The whole afternoon just slipped by. We sat in the shade, ate his sausage, and listened to the latest news from the city.

When dinner-time came around, it was the turn of Metsnik's womenfolk to feed us. The place was not far, maybe one mile to the west across the Kullenga-Kadila road, which was entirely deserted because of the war.

The Metsnik's farm buildings were just outside the woods but we waited at the edge of the forest and did not go into the house. Soon a group of women came toward us carrying a bucket of soup, a basket full of sandwiches and some dishes and cutlery. They all seemed to be dressed up and in a festive mood.

We just sat in a circle and let the girls, in their late teens, serve us.

They had to bend deep to place the soup bowls in front of us, showing hints of their concealed bosoms and sunburned legs under their short skirts. They circled merrily at the center of the ring. The men were as eager to look at the girls as they were happy to tease about with their semi-hidden beauty. Metsnik and his wife went into the barn to "check the hay supplies". After a short time they came out perspiring, it must have been hot in there!

The evening found us stretched out on the southern hillside. The leaves of the birch trees that hung over us had turned dark green and purple from the late rays of the setting sun. The smiling eyes of the young girls were still fresh in our memory when Karl started his melancholy song,

> Oora maja ukse taga
> nutab emmekene.
> Tahab oma tütart näha,
> Kes on litsiks läinud tal...
>
> Behind the whorehouse-
> The mother was crying
> She wanted to see her daughter
> Who was a harlot now...

There was not much we missed in those summer days in July, 1941. The days became weeks. Life continued a semi-peaceful existence consisting of eating and sleeping and making our rounds to nearby farms for regular liberation of the Baltic States. Latvia was already freed from the Russians. There were battles now at the southern Estonian border. It appeared that the Germans might arrive within two weeks. The Metsnik brothers had become restless, including some of the fuzzy-bearded youngsters. Their trigger fingers had become itchy and they wanted a piece of the action. It seemed shameful for brave men to sleep in the woods for weeks on end and let the womenfolk feed them. If someone would ask later, "What did you do when the Russians were here?" it would be shameful to say something like, "Well, I was saving my ass by hiding in the woods."

We, the outsiders including Karl, did not participate in these discussions. The captain appeared reluctant to instigate any combat. "You youngsters, I have the responsibility of bringing you back to your mothers safe and sound. Any small piece of hostile action we might come up with wouldn't count for anything in this big war, but it might mean your mother would find your name on a list of dead heroes."

His stand was grudgingly accepted by the valiant warriors, for the time being. A few days later when the sound of cannon fire reached us, a new wave of action was proposed. Meanwhile there was a new development, making a hostile action possible with minimal risk.

The Kadila-Kullenga road, which until recently had been deserted, started to show traffic in the form of single passenger cars. The local communist bigwigs from the southern regions were trying to reach the main military road north of us, which led directly east and to Russia. But there was a small catch to the route. They had to travel through the partisan-infested woods for a few miles to get to the designated road.

According to the Metsnik brothers' report, these cars carried only male passengers, no women or children. This fact was also confirmed by the captain's own observations. It was generally agreed that the local communists were the true enemies. They had assembled the lists of deportees, and had given the names of dissidents to the Russian KGB. They had organized the raids to capture partisans, some of whom belonged to the so-called Destruction Battalion, whose duty was to burn down villages and towns after the troops had retreated. The Russian soldiers were draftees, and would have preferred to stay at home and not fight in a land where they were hated. We had no bone to pick with them so long as they were heading east, back to Mother Russia.

No true Estonian had a passenger car at his disposal at a time like this. They were only kept by bigwigs, and it was now an open season for revenge. They were called traitors here, but they would be comrades and heroes as soon as they reached Moscow. Go and get them, we thought. It would be like shooting fish in a barrel.

No opposing voice was heard. Our group was resolved to ambush a car to show our patriotism and individual bravery.

That same afternoon our "devil's dozen" was well camouflaged at the northern side, where the road made a sharp bend and the approaching vehicle would be almost facing us. We were told to concentrate the fire on passengers and avoid the engine and gas tank.

We waited almost an hour before our outpost gave the signal of an approaching car. We were all well hidden in a thicket at the side of the road, with only a few inches of gun barrels sticking out through the green leaves, ready to fire. A small gray passenger car was approaching, and I could see two men sitting in the front. When the car was about 50 yards from us, the captain gave the order to fire. Shots from thirteen barrels answered the command. I could see the front window shattering. The car veered off the road and tipped over, the wheels spinning in the air.

I had never witnessed a killing before. Now I was one of the executioners myself, a member of the firing squad. When I saw this little car approaching us along the yellow wood-lined road, it appeared so picturesque that my shot went well above the target. It was more a reflex than a willed action.

One of the Metsnik brothers ran to the car and pulled open the door of the upside-down vehicle. Two bodies fell on the ground. Blood started dripping on the grass. I remained behind with my two classmates and the captain while the others dragged the two bodies into the bushes and turned the small car upright. Gasoline was leaking profusely, someone must have hit the tank. The car was pushed hastily into the woods and covered with tree branches. A few minutes later the road looked peaceful and deserted. We made a quick getaway, worried that the sort volley might have alerted any communist units in the vicinity.

But all remained quiet the rest of the day. We were lying low a few miles from the previous action, waiting for early darkness before we were back to the site of battle to retrieve the car and bury the bodies. Both men had their communist party membership cards and belonged to the executive committee of the neighboring county.

Metsnik wanted the car. His farm was nearby, so we pushed it to his barn and covered it with a load of hay. Then we returned to the dead men to carry them deeper into the woods to be buried. When my turn came, I grabbed the foot-end of one of the stretchers, knowing the load was lighter there. But this position forced me to look at the corpse, which moved up and down with each of our steps, his cool and bare foot rubbing against my right hand. Both of my hands were holding the stretcher and there was no way I could prevent it. As we walked, the heavy fern branches beat against my bare arms and hands and made them burn. Without warning, my grip gave way and my end of the stretcher hit the ground. As the front carrier was still moving forward, the dead man slid off the stretcher and lay on the ground, looking at me with his glass y stare.

They laughed at my weakness and rolled the dead man back onto the stretcher.

I was sweating, but then I felt cold and could not stop shivering.

The captain, noticing my distress, mad an exception and let me sleep alone in the haystack that night. I covered myself with the hay. Both of my hands still burned from the fern, the retribution for my sins, as I fell asleep.

On August 8, 1941, my 19th birthday, my father came to take me home after six weeks of hiding in the nearby woods. I was sitting next to him on our farm wagon while our young horse Noora was trotting toward the house, still half hidden behind the uncut fields of rye. A faint veil of smoke was still hanging in the air from yesterday's battle. German tanks had rolled through with sporadic firing. The sky was overcast and it smelled of rain.

Our small group of "Forest Brothers" dissolved spontaneously since everybody was now free to go home. Before we departed our captain gave each of us a "Freedom Fighter's Certificate" which gave us permission to bear arms.

We were now heroes who had placed their lives in jeopardy by defying the Russian military draft and showing armed resistance as reported in our local paper, once again called the Virumaa News. I did not feel I'd done anything heroic, except save my own neck and find an opportunity for a six week vacation in the woods, fed by friendly women in the neighborhood.

We all lived now just as we did before the Russian invasion. Fear and heartaches were forgotten. People looked up and laughed, expressing their views freely whether the subject was politics or the weather. One no longer needed to look over his shoulder before opening his mouth. I had lost all my fear of being followed or arrested. At the age of 19 I was full of hope for the future.

Al the red banners, pictures and flags disappeared. The schools and the government replaced them with pictures of President Pats and General Laidoner, both of whose whereabouts were unknown.

The schools restored their old curricula. No pictures of any foreign rulers or their flags could be seen anywhere. Our government buildings again flew our national flag of blue, black and white. No new subjects or unknown songs were forced upon us.

We volunteered to comb the woods and farm fields in our neighborhood for stray Russian soldiers. Any civilian now hiding in the woods was considered suspect and detained for identification if he wasn't recognized by local people. No blue-blooded Estonian had any reason to hide.

We found one Russian soldier, who had crawled for three days with a wounded leg, between the cornfields. He was not able to stand up to see which way to go. To our surprise, a German military ambulance, and told us he would be hospitalized. I knew for sure that if the tables were turned, the Russians would have been generous enough to put a bullet through a wounded German's brain.

While our neighborhood was safe and sound, the news from Väike-Maarja was devastating. All houses on the north side of the main road had been destroyed by fire. That included our high school, the Kihlefeldts' bookstore where I lived with Mihkel, and the house I shared earlier with five senior high school girls, the place where Alma Pedari had re-drowned the landlady's dog. These were just a few of the places I had been sentimentally attached to at one time or another.

There was more news to come. About five miles south of Väike-Maarja a group of ex-partisans found two men hiding in the woods. Their names were Mihkel Holm and Endel Saarik.

Due to a lack of handcuffs, their hands were tied in front of them and then roped to the bicycles, forcing them to jog along with their captors all the way back to Väike-Maarja. Mihkel Holm was known best for his forceful conscription of local horses. It had even been rumored that he had started the fire.

Saarik's "I can explain everything" was not listened to. After a few days of captivity they were taken to the woods, offered an opportunity to scape, then shot in the back.

Revenge is a powerful feeling. It has no restraints. It tolerates no explanation or excuse. It does not know mercy or recognize forgiveness.

Meanwhile life on the farm continued at a hurried pace. Because of the war the farm work had been neglected and we had plenty of catching up to do. First, the hay had to be mowed and when it was dry enough, gathered, loaded onto hay wagons and hauled to the barn. The rye and wheat fields, trampled in places by the retreating troops, were ready to be cut with a horse-drawn harvester and then hand-tied into sheaves and placed into shocks to be dried. Any prolonged rain would make it sprout, ruining the crop. But the weather held. While the rye was drying in the shocks we had to harvest the oats, which was used mainly to feed the horses and make their skin shine. Barley, when dried and threshed, had to be taken to the mill to supply us with flour to feed the pigs.

The cattle had to be driven home from the pasture in the evening for milking, watering and extra feeding to promote production. The milking was done by hand, strained into metal containers, kept in cold water, and delivered to the local creamery each morning.

One could not leave the flock of sheep overnight in the nearby meadow; they had to be driven to their fold next to the barn for their own protection. Times were still iffy, there were reports of people

slaughtering stolen sheep. Only the chickens could peck fearlessly behind the barn and sleep undisturbed in the chicken coop at night, until
the rooster was inn his reveille in the morning– no foxes, chicken
hawks or chicken thieves about. We could rest peacefully at night,
knowing that Morfi, our German Shepherd, would keep any prowlers
away.

Chapter 9

In The Military

The German troops had freed all of Estonia and were now on the outskirts of Leningrad. Although Estonia was again an occupied country, we felt safe. There were no restrictions in our everyday lives that we were aware of. In fact, we were hoping things would stay the way they were. Everyone was afraid the Russians would return since the German occupation as such protected our lives. Our new temporary government consisted of those previous ministers and representatives who had been in hiding and had escaped execution or deportation. They were fiercely, anti-communists and pitted against the Soviets' new kind of "democracy".

To my knowledge the Baltic States were the only ones where the German conquerors were greeted with flowers. The country folks knew nothing about the Nazis. They were probably familiar with the word, but entirely unaware of the malignant side of their actions. This was a time when everyone's concern was limited to their own families and the farms. Men who had been in hiding could now return safely to their homes.

My mother was out at the main road along with other farmers' wives, wildflowers in hand, waiting to greet the Germans, oblivious to the dangers of being caught in crossfire. The lead tank rumbled to them, then came to a full stop. The lid opened and an officer jumped out, gathered the flowers, and then took my mother by the waist (she was the lightest in the bunch) and lifted here all the way up with a friendly laugh. Then he jumped back in and closed the lid and the entire column again rumbled eastward.

During the time of Estonian independence, every healthy young man who reached the age of 18 had to serve one year in the military. Most of the Gymnasium graduates entered the service before they started their studies at Tartu University. Our newly-formed government reached an agreement with the German military authorities that the young men who had escaped the Russian draft and had not completed their military obligation by serving in the Estonian Armed Forces were asked to serve as volunteers in the German paramilitary force for a period of one year. After fulfilling the agreed to obligation, the Gymnasium graduates would have priority in entering the University of Tartu. The agreement called for service would consist of basic training followed by guard duty at the bridges, the power stations, and the government buildings. The units would wear German Wehrmacht uniforms with the Estonian coat of arms on the left sleeve. Non-commissioned and commissioned officers would be from the old Estonian military and communication would be carried out in Estonian without any political indoctrination, unlike the Red Army. The unit flags, if any, would be in the colors of their choice. There would be only one German officer assigned to each battalion as a quartermaster.

It all sounded quite promising to me. What is one year when you are only 19 and you would have had to serve it anyhow if Estonia were still an independent state? The way I figured it, at age 20 I would be eligible to enter medical school and after six years, at the age of 26, I would be a physician. Some of my classmates who had escaped from the Red Army draft, including Endel Saar, signed the agreement.

I signed up in Rakvere and was assigned to the 15th company of the 183rd Battalion. Our company consisted of 160 men, the company commander was Captain Alphonse Rebane. He was a handsome Estonian officer with the manners of a gentleman and an apparent respect for new recruits. I received the rank of private like anybody else who had no previous military training. I was in the second squad. A squad consisted of 12 to 14 men plus a squad leader, ours was a young sergeant whose name I can't recall.

Basic military training is the most monotonous physical activity known. It tries to make a caterpillar out of a column of 14 men, 28 legs and the same number of hands. Thy all have to move synchronously, as if they shared one brain. The training lasted for one month, alternating with days of target practice. After that we were pronounced ready for our assignment and were lined up for final inspection.

Captain Rebane complimented us for our enthusiasm and discipline. He also announced a change in our deployment, "Men, there has been a new development. The German military command has concluded that the original objective is superfluous since Estonia, because of its strong anti-communist sentiment, has only a marginal danger of communist sabotage. There is, however, a greater need for the same kind of duty in the communist-freed parts of Russia, just east of the Estonian border. I know the original assignment you agreed upon was serving within the boundaries of our country. But, now, men, you have two choices. First, you can sign the new contract, offering your services in the same capacity and for the same length of time, one year, in the Leningrad region, which is at our back door. The second choice, you do not sign anything and are free to go back home after you have returned all the military equipment and supplies in your possession to our quartermaster. After you have done that, you will receive a note of your release."

Then he raised his voice and announced further, "Now men. Whoever decides to come along with me is welcome. I will still be the commander of the 15th Company, your company. Let's go and see for ourselves what the Red Paradise really looks like, like one that the "comrades" have been raving about. "Company dismissed!"

That announcement was quite a surprise to all of us. To be truthful, most men who had signed up earlier for home duty were actually eager to serve in a greater capacity than walking along railroad tracks or marching back and forth over some bridges in Estonia. The new assignment seemed to excite them. Besides, none of us had ever been outside our own country. Some had left their own county for the first time when they came to Rakvere to sign up for the service. The company had accepted volunteers up to the age of 40. Men from that bunch had adventurous spirits and a fatalistic attitude and need for revenge. Some were willing to go anywhere, and most of the youngsters were them, the more daring the assignment, the better.

I believe there were only two men from our company of 160 who had resigned, and they did it for family reasons.

To be honest, the change in location for my one-year service was not my primary concern. Having guaranteed entry to our university was my only consideration.

Exactly one week after the new contract was signed, our company left Rakvere for a 60-minute ride east to the city of Narva, the old border town between Estonia and Russia.

It was a sunny day in late autumn.

The platform in the Rakvere railroad station was filled with people. Young women were distributing flowers to their departing countrymen. The feeling of patriotism, so long suppressed, had emerged with new vigor. And we who had yet to accomplish anything, were at the receiving end of their affections.

What a glorious feeling when a young girl, a stranger with love and admiration in her eyes, gives you a flower.

Sitting in my room today, I can still recall the occasion distinctly. There was the train with its freight car doors wide open, the doorways filled with young men who were singing and shouting and waving as if they were on an excursion train, headed for a late summer picnic. There wasn't a cloud in the sky, the clanking of the wheels on iron tracks, and there is a sea of white handkerchiefs, waving to the departing men. Nobody wondered even for a moment, shall I return? Will I ever return.

———————

It was a new day. We had left the city of Narva behind us and after a few miles of marching in full battle gear we reached Russian territory.

The land was flat and colorless in the late autumn. We passed villages of small log houses with thatched roofs, the window frames decorated with wood carvings. The collective farm buildings were drab, assembled from prefabricated blocks of cement showing crumbling corners and hanging doors surrounded by muddy roads and rusting farm machinery left out in the open, overgrown with weeds. There was the occasional tree here and there but none next to the buildings, no lawn or children's playground in sight. Old women in babushkas stood like statues on the roadsides with blank faces. Young teenage boys, pimple-faced and in long Russian shirts, gave us hostile looks. They were outnumbered by teenage girls in flowery dresses and when we waved at them they smiled, but did not wave back.

One day we reached our destination, a Russian village named Kiorstovo. The next day it started to snow, hiding the drab colors and making the small Russian cottages picturesque with their woodcarvings and smoking chimneys.

The peasants were friendly folks. They made room for us in their village and invited us to their homes. They all seemed to have suffered under Stalin, and talked about their hardships. There were even Estonian villagers in the neighborhood. They had lived under communism from the very beginning. They all spoke Estonian freely and showed us much hospitality.

My one year of Russian study came in handy as I could communicate freely on simple matters. The girls in the village were talkative and willing to teach. I practiced my Russian whenever I had the chance.

Our real duty was not socializing with the native girls, but securing the area behind the front lines from Russian partisans. The coastline under our jurisdiction had two abandoned Russian frigates, partly submerged. Because of the shallowness of the sea, their decks and superstructures were well above the waterline and now in the frozen grip of ice about two to three miles from the shore. Russian partisans from Leningrad used these abandoned ships as a resting station in their infiltration route behind the front lines where they would cause havoc by blowing up bridges and interrupting rail service.

One morning in December the ships were hardly visible from the shore because of low clouds and falling snow, but after careful observations one could make out a bluish haze rising from one of the semi-sunken frigates.

"Smoke!"

Our platoon leader, sergeant Vika, lowered his binoculars with a big smile, "Somebody's trying to keep himself warm and I don't think they are tourists from Leningrad! Russkies are frying fish for lunch. Let's go, boys, and break up the party!"

Our camouflaged clothing blended into the winter landscape, but we could not approach them directly from the shore. That would be suicide. They were well protected by the steel hull of the ship while we would have no place to hide on the frozen and snow covered sea. They would probably wind up using us for target practice. Our plan was to ski far out to the sea and approach them from the back side. Even if they were cautious enough to keep an eye out on that side, the snow would be blowing in their faces and binoculars and make us hard to detect. But still, one had to admit, it was quite a risky assignment. Sergeant Viks, a towering man well over six feet, just loved challenges of that nature. Without another word he broke the track in the snow and 13 of us followed him.

Soon the coastline vanished behind us and there was nothing but white emptiness, no horizon, no sky or ground. The only sound was the howling wind ripping on our clothes and the steady hiss of our skis. We followed the sergeant in a single row, stopping every ten minutes or so for him to estimate our speed and figure out our approximate position by consulting his compass and watch. After an hour of vigorous skiing we spread apart and started to ski back to the coast. We wondered whether we would ever find the ships in the empty and frozen world, but after another quarter of an hour we could make out the silhouettes of the boats, over a hundred yards in front of us. We could not detect any sign of life on this side of the boat, but smoke was still rising from the interior of one frigate. We ignored the other vessel and approached our target in a semi-circle. We freed our hands by hooking the ski-poles to our belts and held our automatic weapons ready. Amazingly, we made it to the back side of the boat unnoticed. It was a grave mistake for them not to post a look-out at that side. Their omission turned the tide much in our favor.

They were not even aware of our presence, when Sergeant Viks stepped out from the starboard side and fired a burst from his automatic weapon. Three Russians who had been keeping lookout on the wrong side, were lying dead in the snow. We could hear hurried steps from the steel deck above. Someone was running to see what all this shooting was about. He was dead before he could find out.

Our sergeant was all smiles, as though he'd won a prize at a turkey shoot. True, he had singlehandedly eliminated the enemy. Some of us who still wanted a part of the action fired volleys into the doorless opening on the deck, but there were only rusty steel and frozen sea inside the hull.

The bodies were dragged out to the frozen sea and quickly buried by the blowing and drifting snow.

"We don't want future delegations to become more alert than these dudes in case we have to call again," Sergeant Viks explained.

This was my second encounter with what the dictionary would call a hostile action. Things had happened so fast that I did not have a chance to fire a single shot but we had done some killing. I still had trouble with my terminology, in war one does not kill, he eliminates. Killing is murder and calls for punishment while elimination is valorous action and deserves reward, a medal or promotion. An ex-student and now a private first class, I felt I had passed my first "fire exam" with a good grade. It was not a question of easy elimination. We had put our lives on the line and had won fair and square. They had played their hand recklessly and lost. We had outsmarted them and they had paid for their mistake with their lives. Instead of our being covered with the blowing snow, it was them. War is a game with high stakes where no "mulligans" are given.

In mid-December we saw action again.

This time our entire company was out on foot, carrying our machine guns and rifles and ammunition on our backs. The day was cloudy with mild temperatures and wet snow. That, and the scattered hillocks with stunted birch trees and willow bushes made it impossible to use our skis. We were combining the woods many miles from our home-village.

Our company commander, Captain Rebane, was in charge of the expedition and we had left early in the morning. It was now late afternoon. We were tired of walking in a barren wasteland and our alertness was not up to par. Right after discovering a footpath in the snow we came under fire from some buildings hidden behind bushes and birch trees. Our task was to surprise them, but they surprised us.

By the time our company had surrounded the area the enemy had fled. All the log buildings were deserted. There were no weapons or ammunition left behind, just a large kettle of soup, still boiling on the stove.

By now, it was almost dark. There was no sense in trying to follow them and risk an ambush or injury from the scattered small mines hidden in the snow. The captain's pat man had stepped on one already and had lost his right foot while another soldier had a bullet in the belly.

We slept in the heated buildings overnight with our weapons ready and tight security outside.

We did not eat their soup.

When we left the next morning we set fire to the buildings believed to be the partisan headquarters, far from any habitation or roads. Our wounded man died during the night, the very first casualty in our company. We carried him on a stretcher all the way back to Kirostovo, along with the one who had lost his foot.

And then came the Christmas of 1941.

The hunters had shot a deer to supplement our generous Christmas rations. The cigarette and booze bonus was more than adequate. A large spruce was decorated with cookies and live candles and these were lit just before the company chaplain read from the Bible and Captain Rebane made a speech, praising us for serving our country away from home.

Then we feasted on roast pork with sauerkraut, blood sausage, and deer meat served with mashed potatoes and gravy, all washed down with our cook's home-brewed beer.

The villagers had lit kerosene lamps and placed them in their windows. We visited practically every home, wishing them a Merry Christmas with bottles of champagne and cognac. The women had the champagne and the men drank cognac, and this was apparently the very first time in their lives they had had anything besides vodka. No glasses were uses, everyone drank from the same bottle. There were lots of laughs when the women tried to drink the champagne from the bottle and the bubbly liquid ran over their faces and trickled down to their hidden breasts. The dance floor was cleared in the community hall. Accordion and balalaika music filled the village air and its snowy streets.

As I was returning alone to my quarters to fetch another bottle of champagne, a cottage door opened in front of me and I was asked to enter. An old lady took my hand and led me to the holiest corner in the house where a small kerosene lamp was shedding a glimmer of light on an ancient icon of Christ.

She had lost her son in the war and wanted to pray with me for my safe return. She asked me to kneel with her in front of the icon for a silent prayer. I did what she asked, and at the end she crossed herself and said, "God bless you." When I was out on the snowy road again, the distant balalaika music did not sound inviting anymore. I returned to my plank bed, but couldn't sleep, wondering how a peasant woman could pray for an enemy soldier when she lost her own son.

Then came New Year's Eve.

The day was mild with soft gray clouds. We were at the outer edge of the village, about 200 yards from a small barn, which we used for target practice with our machine gun as we tried to adjust its calibration. An old man stood behind us watching us closely, and during a pause in the action, he remarked that it was his barn we were shooting at. He did not really mind if we would only let him do some shooting himself. He claimed he hadn't had the chance to fire a gun since the First World War. "It's my barn, you know!" he said, by way of persuasion.

Sergeant Viks was in a holiday mood, saying, "Sure, go ahead, pop."

We were all having a good time. It was New Year's Eve. Let the old man shoot.

And shoot he did. His toothless mouth was all smiles, his body jerking from the back-thrust of the gun when suddenly he jumped up and shouted, "Nie streliaite...Nie streliaite...banya gorit!" Don't shoot, don't shoot! The barn is on fire."

More than 50 years have passed and I have forgotten most of my Russian, but I'll never forget the words, "Nie streliaite...Nie streliaite...banya gorit."

Well, when you come right down to it, he was the one who was doing the shooting. The banya was not on fire before. We had trouble with the calibration. He was the "hot shot" and he knew it.

He started to run toward his barn, but in no time it was engulfed in flames. He turned around and walked back slowly. We were laughing with tears in our eyes. When he reached us we saw that he was crying. Sergeant Viks knew how to fix things, he pulled out a small bottle of vodka from his back pocket and offered it to the old man to alleviate his sorrow.

The old man took the bottle and tilted it towards the sky, no need to worry about knocking out your front teeth if you don't have any. After the third swig he was all smiles. "Let the damned thing burn," he said, and handed the empty bottle back to Sergeant Viks.

He wished us all a Happy New Year, 1942.

The New Year began innocently enough.

The usual ski patrols, guard duties and infantry drill took up the daylight hours except on Sundays. Captain Rebane believed in well-disciplined units. In his opinion free time could corrupt the company's morale. The "caterpillar" walk was the order of the day again, but in the evenings the card game called "21" was the popular pastime. We couldn't buy anything with the money we had, at least not in Russia. It was good for only one thing, gambling. Many of us did not play the game, but still enjoyed watching how piles of money changed hands. The room filled with cigarette smoke and moments of tension followed by victory and jubilation or the anger of defeat.

I did not gamble much. I usually lost. I did not have the right mental makeup. I usually gave good cards away by smiling, and I could not bluff either when I had a bad hand. Tuli was a master at pretending and he usually won. Maybe I should say more about him, about Tuli and Arge, actually. They were the only members of our second squad whose names I can still remember.

Tuli's name meant "fire" in Estonian, and this fit him well. He was about 40 years old and rather short with heavy shoulders. He had a loud raspy voice and fierce temper. His bloodshot eyes came from too many late-night card games, in that order. He was number one in all three. He usually won big in poker, but when he lost, he lost everything, all the money he had won in advance. He was one of my two friends during my service in Russia. The other one was Private Arge. He was raised in an orphanage and did not have a soul in the entire world who cared whether he lived or died. He was short and skinny with a large head, a prominent Adam's apple and emaciated face. His voice was unusually deep for his small size. The calf muscles of his left leg were wasted and he walked with a slight limp. It remained a mystery how he ever passed his physical examination. All that aside, he was the most serious and sincere young man one could ever meet. He neither smoked nor drank. He gave away his cigarette and alcohol rations and never asked anything in return. This itself was unheard of, since bartering was a way of life. Money was worthless and cigarettes and booze were legal tender. You will meet both these characters, Tuli and Arge, again later on.

I remember one late afternoon in early February when I went for a walk in the village at that odd twilight hour when the sky is already dark and the snow reflects the meager light, making the outlines of buildings distinct. Kerosene lamps threw light here and there, making the ice flowers glow in the windows.

The wind blew snow in my face as the road dipped toward the sea, forcing me to raise my coat collar.

I was thinking about Tanya. Tanya and her mother. They both lived a few houses down toward the sea.

Her mother opened the door with her usual giving smile. She was in her early forties, still shapely, which was seldom seen in this part of the country. I could only guess that she wasn't from this village, but we never discussed the past. Her eyes had a glow like a person with fever when she opened the door for me. I could not tell who I like more, her or her daughter, Tanya. I could have loved both of them! Meanwhile, I had become more versed in Russian and could carry out simple conversations.

"Welcome," she said, "Tanya is in the living room. Why don't you join her?"

She closed the front door behind be. "I am so glad that you could come."

"I brought a few sugar cubes."

"Good. I'll make tea and after awhile we will drink it together, all three of us."

They must have been lonely during the long winter nights, just like me. My visits lifted us from our melancholy, and we were all content.

I sat in a low chair at the window, next to the young girl, observing her while she knit. We did not speak.

When she looked down at me and smiled, I saw she had the same fevered glow in her eyes her mother had. She turned all red if I looked at her for any length of time. In a wistful way, I found this platonic relationship entertaining. I sat there by the window with my knees crossed and my chin on my hand.

"What are you thinking of?" she asked.

"Nothing."
"You must be thinking of something."

The snow had almost covered the window pane and the shadowy dusk was creeping into the room. I could see the bird tracks in the snow.

"I was hoping."

"What?"

"To sit with you may times to come, just the way we are."

She dropped her knitting in her lap and looked down at her hands. They trembled slightly when she wiped the fallen hair from her face.

Her mother had lit the kerosene lamp and brought it in the copper samovar. Our shadows danced on the walls as the three of us sat at the table drinking tea and taking pleasure in each other's company.

On my way home I was thinking in Russian, how to ask Tanya what she was thinking when I sat there while she knit.

I didn't ask the question, because I never saw Tanya and her mother again. The next morning our company was transferred to Luban, more than 100 kilometers to the southeast of Kirostovo.

Chapter 10

In The Battle

The new landscape consisted of birch and pine woods, frozen moors and swamps, and of course, the dirt roads, now frozen and covered with snow. There were small villages scattered along the riverbank, a God-forsaken place where time had stood still for generations.

We were stationed in a village named Klubochka. The truck convoy unloaded us quickly and left in a hurry. I couldn't blame them. According to rumors, Russian Forces had broken through the front lines in this region and nobody knew where they were or how man. We did not even know where the Germans' defense line was supposed to be or whether it existed at all. A messy situation, to say the least.

Besides, this was no longer paramilitary service, the service we had agreed upon. It was front line duty and we had only light automatic weapons, rifles and machine guns, quite inadequate for the new assignment.

According to Captain Rebane, this was supposed to be a short stop-gap measure until reinforcements arrived. No Russian tanks or heavy artillery were expected, since the swamps and the river were not sufficiently frozen to carry their weight and the road crossings further east were still held by the Germans.

We were houseguests of a Russian family consisting of a mother and two grown-up daughters whose husbands were apparently fighting in the Red Army. The village, as stated, was behind the back woods and swamps and no one hade ever seen a German uniform before. The only thing they had heard about the Germans was that they burned villages and killed women and children.

One of us who spoke Russian, assured them that we didn't intend any harm. Arge gave them a package of cigarettes, our new daily ration increased because we were at the front. None of the women smoked but cigarettes were a valuable commodity for bartering for any service the old men in the village could provide, like cutting firewood or fixing a leaky roof. Arge's generosity broke the ice, so to speak, and the younger women gave us a brief smile while the old ones were still in semi-hiding.

It was noon, on February 7, 1942 when our company skied to a new position in a village called Yaglino located further east on the frozen banks of the Volhov River. The enemy was on the opposite side, and over a thousand yards from the village. Russian sharp-shooters, however, were busy taking potshots at us as our squad ran from one building to the next to take our position in the foxholes this side of the river. The sharp shooter's timing must have been off, the bullets cracked into the house corners a fraction of a second late. None of us was hit and we all laughed when playing the dangerous game called Russian Roulette.

When we reached the last building on this side of the main road I saw a German officer lying on his back in the middle of the road. He was a slender man in a well-tailored uniform. His cap was on and a camera in a leather case with the strap was still resting on his chest. His hands were in black leather gloves, the left hand resting at his side while the right was on his upper abdomen just below the camera. There was no sight of blood or wound.

At first I thought he had fainted. I stretched my neck out, well past the sheltering house corner and noticed that some snow had drifted into his earlobes and his eyebrows were covered with frost. His face was pale, probably frozen.

I was ready to dash out and pull him to shelter behind the barn when someone grabbed me from behind, "Are you nuts? Do you want to commit suicide?"

I turned and saw Private Tuli holding me by the belt.

"What's the use?" he added with his raspy voice and reassuring laugh. "He's dead, isn't he?" Just then, two bullets hit the corner of the barn. "See, you would have cashed in all your chips by now."

I looked away, but the image of the dead officer in the spotless uniform remained. It was the first dead German I had ever seen. Then I saw as clear as day, myself lying next to him, just as pale and frozen and dead.

I was suddenly overcome with panic, a seizure of terror and fear as though I was facing imminent death. I could not move or even talk in this trance-like state. When I came to, I found myself alone behind the corner of the same barn. My buddies had already crossed the road and were waving, "Come on...come on... what is the matter with you?"

To cross the road and jump over the dead officer, I was sure I could not do it. Circling around him would be time consuming, and by all accounts, fatal. I just did not know what to do. Then I notice Tuli standing next to me. He had come back to help me cross the road. "Hey buddy, let's do it together, side by side. I stay on your right, and if we are not fast enough, I'll get the first slug."

We made it across the road and never spoke about the incident. In battler or under fire, it was not fitting to exchange pleasantries, no *thank yous* or *you're welcomes*.

It was the first and last time I froze. In future circumstances that were similar, I felt only pleasant excitement.

Before nightfall, our squad was positioned along the high bank of the curving river. The village itself was uphill, and over one hundred yards behind us, separated from us by a snow covered field. The early twilight and our camouflaged garments gave us the chance to take our positions in previously dug foxholes. Somebody must have been here before and fled, leaving the empty foxholes and dead officer behind.

The holes were shallow in the frozen ground, spaced about 25 yards apart. There was no connecting trench in between, leaving us quite isolated. Earlier our squad leader had been shot in the mouth and there was no one to give us any directions. Before darkness set in, we found that our foxhole was a the lower end of a U-shaped curve, high up on the bank and the closest point to the enemy.

"It looks like we have the center seat in the first balcony!" was Arge's dry statement. We were sharing the foxhole. The cold shroud of evening haze sank across our positions. It penetrated our unlined overcoats and chilled us to the bone. The temperature must have fallen well below freezing.

It was after midnight on Sunday, February 8, 1942, when the Russians attacked. They appeared like rows upon rows of dark dots in the snow-covered valley below. Multiple flares from the village illuminated the landscape with eerie orange and blue, followed by fire from multiple machine guns and rifles that crackled like malignant laughter echoing back from the village and forest.

The Russians were coming!

They did not have any camouflaged garments or snow-shoes or skis. Because of the deep snow they had to start their approach in columns, a rather dull-witted way to attack. They thought it would be a cake-walk with minimal or no resistance. When new flares hit the river below we could see tracer bullets flashing at the approaching enemy, but nobody was shooting at the few columns just directly in front and below us. Arge and I lifted our heads until our eyes were only a few inches above the foxhole mound and started to fire salvos at them.

The Russian units in the forest responded with a murderous counter-fire aimed primarily at the village. Because of its elevation they could shoot safely over the heads of their attacking units.

The fluffy snow was up to their hips, slowing them down. After they reached the middle of the frozen river, they seemed to hesitate and then stopped to advance altogether. They did not know that a small paramilitary force of Estonians, outnumbered at least by ten-to-one, was here to greet them, and at least temporarily, change their minds. Their walk in the strategy was abandoned and they started to retreat to the sheltering forest. After an hour of two things were quiet again except for the occasional machine gun flurries.

Sunday morning arrived with clear skies. The rising sun made the snow glitter in the frozen valley below, with scattered brown flecks like dead flies on a white tablecloth. The snow to the center and front of us was free of any markings, telling us that Arge and I had scored no hits.

With daylight, the Russian sharpshooters became active again. We pulled down our white face covers and huddled together for warmth in the bottom of our foxhole. It was like lounging in a reclining chair facing the cold rays of the winter sun. After my panic attack earlier in the village, I felt calm and didn't give a damn.

"Let's have some breakfast!" I said.

Arge had half a loaf of frozen bread, and we took turns chewing it until it was down to the size of a baseball. He put it back in his side pouch, saying "Let's save it for lunch."

To urinate we used the empty zinc ammunition container and placed it a the outer edge of our foxhole. Before the fluid had time to freeze, it ran out through several bullet holes. We laughed. Our excreted urine drained into the adjacent snow while our bladders were, thank God, still intact. I turned my back again and tried to stretch out, knowing it was safer to stick out your feet rather than you head.

Arge peeked out once more at the snow covered river down below, then shouted, "Jesus Maria...look at them! There they are, coming again...in full daylight."

A platoon size group of the Russians was approaching in columns. "They must be drunk."

Then we realized that they were coming across the area where there were no "brown dots" from the previous night. This sector was not visible from the village or even from our flanks, and our bullets at night had been going over their heads, whistling Dixie. It explained their new strategy of approaching us across the virgin-clean snow.

We waited until they were a good 800 yards from us and some 200 from the forest. Resting our rifles on the frozen mound in front of us, we took careful aim. We missed them at first, but after adjusting our distance calibration we started to hit the "brown dots" quite regularly. I had no feeling of guilt or regret. The faceless "dots" were coming to kill me and I was trying to save my own skin, or at least lengthen my life by an hour or two. Besides it is easier to kill if one shoots only at dots. We concentrated our fire on the spots closest to the sheltering woods. There was plenty of time to take care of the ones still advancing. The sun was bright, the dark and now motionless blemishes stood out from the white surroundings. When it was all over we counted the dots, 45 in all. We divided the figure by two, giving ourselves 22 1/2 points apiece and then we shook hands. The high five hadn't been invented yet. Unknown to the village, the two of us had repulsed their limited attack.

At afternoon teatime we chewed the rest of our frozen bread and ate some snow. It had become overcast again and light snowfall followed, shading the Russian-infested woods, making even the village behind us look peaceful. Maybe too peaceful? This last thought startled me. Had our unit withdrawn? Nobody else but us had been firing at the previously advancing columns. How long had it been since we had heard firing from our flanks? Neither I nor Arge could tell.

I decided to investigate by crawling over the edge of our sheltering foxhole, adding "I'd better visit the neighborhood and see what's up."

Arge responded, "I don't need to remind you that curiosity killed the cat."

I crawled like a mole in the fluffy snow, very much aware of Russian sharpshooters. I reached the neighboring foxhole in one piece and found it to be half-filled with snow. It must have been uninhabited for hours. No wonder we hadn't noticed any firing from our flanks. After another 25 yards of crawling, I found what I was expecting. The next hole was just as deserted as the first.

It wouldn't make any sense to investigate the foxholes further down and it didn't make any sense to join Arge. I had to find out if our company was still occupying the village.

I continued to crawl, head down, plowing through the snow with my helmet, occasionally lifting my head to see where I was going. With my last inspection I found myself close to the village and saw the tops of familiarly shaped helmets. That made me forget the melting snow I had plowed into my collar and sleeves. Not to be shot by my countrymen, I held up one hand, moved in a circular fashion and yelled in Estonian as loud as I could, "Don't shoot, don't shoot. . .it's me!"

In a few minutes I was happily among my buddies. They kept slapping my wet back and shouting, "Where the hell have you been? Where did you come from? All of our outpost, those who were still living, were ordered back to the village at midnight, shortly before the Russian attack."

"Who said?" I inquired.

"The company messenger went around and informed all the men in the foxholes to retreat to the village. We were told that you and Arge did not respond to the call and you both were counted among the missing and presumed dead."

Obviously the messenger had been too frightened to come all the way down to the bottom of our "U." Anyway, he had reported us missing in action.

That reminded me. Arge was still out there, holding the fort by himself with a single rifle. There were no volunteers to go and get him, and after a bowl of hot soup I said, "I'll go. Just pass the word around not to shoot me. We will be back with half an hour. If an hour goes by, you may shoot at anybody your heart desires."

I crawled back along my old tracks and about ten minutes later, hope to be in hearing distance, I yelled, "Arge! Arge! Then I just listened.

"Yeah?" was the distant and somewhat annoyed answer.

"Follow my tracks. I'll be waiting for you here. We're pulling back to the village."

After about ten minutes of waiting and wondering what was taking him so long, I was happy to see him coming, plowing snow with his helmet. He didn't say a word. Besides, it wasn't the greatest time or place for conversation. Russian bullets were whistling over our heads.

We weren't shot from either side and reached the village in one piece. After some hot food and dry clothes, we were asked to see Captain Rebane.

"Welcome back alive from no-man's land," he said. We had been apparently on his "hero's list. I am happy to see you safe and sound. We have lost too many men already."

He shook hands with us. This was the first time that a commanding officer had showed this kind of familiarity with his low-ranking troops.

Late that same evening, German reinforcements arrived with tanks and artillery. We had held the line successfully for more than 24 hours and now it was up to them. Our company was ready to ski back to Klubochka, a few miles from Yaglino. Our losses had been heavy: 20 killed, and another 20 wounded. We had come with 158 men. Only 118 full-bodied men skied back to the village we had left some 36 hours earlier.

How did it happen that Arge and I survived by ourselves in the most hazardous place? There was no explanation. Why does someone fall in the bathtub and break his neck while another guy falls off a mountain and survives? Luck was with us. Or was it the old woman's prayer on Christmas Eve in the snowbound village named Kiorstovo?

Chapter 11

Blood on the Snow

After returning to Klubochka, life was not the same. The woods from Yaglino to Klubochka stretched only two or three miles and the Russian front units might show up at our gate at any time. Dangerous moments became dangerous hours and days. Nobody planned even a week into the future. Oh yes, we might look the same, laugh the usual way, eat, swear, and drink our liquor rations with the same bravado, but after going through our first front-line duty we were not "youngsters" any more.

Because we had held the front in Yaglino and were known to be good on skis, our company got a brand new assignment – reconnaissance. The woods and swamps in the Volhov region were endless, with scattered enemy units and no fixed front line. The local German Military Headquarters had to know about their location. It was up to us to find out.

We considered ourselves now an elite unit with special assignment. Our food rations were doubled. We got a pack of cigarettes every day and a bottle of whiskey every week. Chocolate was supplied for the ski-trips to give us instant energy and add endurance. We did not sleep in the trenches but in the peasants' homes they were happy to have us. With our unlimited supplies we could be quite generous toward our hosts. When a soldier's belly is full and he has cigarettes in his pocket and a bottle of booze in his ruck-sack, the rest becomes irrelevant.

One reconnaissance unit consisted of 14 men including a sergeant who was the leader. We patrolled the woods on skis, carrying light automatic weapons with two magazines of 40 bullets in each. We were camouflaged white, from our helmets to our boots and skis. We did not smoke, talk, or chew gum during an assignment. Only hand signals were used to communicate.

Two men skied 25-30 yards ahead of the rest. These two were our eyes and ears, advancing with slow and deliberate movements to save their own lives and possibly their buddies. The front men were rotated every 15 minutes. When their time was up they stopped and gave a hand signal. Then the entire unit stopped except for the two men at the front of the group. They skied up to the outposts becoming the new leaders. The old leaders waited until the entire unit had passed them, then they joined the *Spähtrupp*[3] at its very end.

We did not look for action. If we accidentally stumbled on the enemy and they opened fire on us, we were down in a flash, spraying automatic fire and disengaging in a hurry. Half of us continued to fire while the other half pulled back, and we alternated these roles until we were out in the clear. Because of our limited supply of ammunition we had to disengage quickly. They could not follow us without skis. Without white camouflage they would be an easy target. Only once did we lose both our front guards in an ambush. The next day we returned to recover their bodies. They were frozen stiff, tied to tree trunks and shot in the head. We had special light plywood boat-like structures to two them back to the village. The next day we had the burial.

The old men from the village made the caskets using boards from an abandoned barn. Each carpenter received a package of pipe tobacco for the effort. We knew they were heavily overpaid, but we also tried to keep them happy, knowing that we would need their services again in the future.

The night before a burial, a young birch was cut down to make the crosses. I was the designated calligrapher and used an iron spike, heated in an open fire until it glowed red, to engrave the names in the wood.

The bodies, frozen in a sitting position, were thawed out overnight and placed the next day in their caskets. The caskets were then lifted into a straw-covered sleigh. The women from the village gathered around, crossed themselves, and dried their tears with their babushka corners. Then the slow ride, a horse with three men and two caskets, started toward the already-dug grave site. I held onto the crosses, another held onto the caskets, and the third man drove the horse.

After the double grave had been closed, I hammered the crosses into the frozen ground and placed the men's helmets on top as the only decoration. After we had bowed our heads in silence for one minute, we rode back to the village in the twilight hour. We did not feel like talking. We just passed around the bottle of liquor supplied by the quartermaster for the occasion. The Russians had set up a battery of cannons for our "entertainment", and fired sporadically at the village. One of their shots set a nearby barn on fire, the one we stored our skis in. We were pleased with the results-no skis, no ski patrols! No such luck. The very next day a truck brought us replacements. All we had to do was adjust the bindings to fit our shoes.

One day returning from our regular ski-troop assignment we found an unwelcome visitor. A Russian cannon shell had come through the roof and ceiling. It had landed on top of my ruck-sack which was at the foot end of my straw-covered sleeping spot. It had dragged it along going through the floorboards, but by a stroke of luck it had not exploded. We could even see its tail end just inches lower than the floor. For a few packages of tobacco, the old men patched the hole in the roof with straw and hammered boards across the gap in the ceiling to keep the snow and winter cold out. We left the bomb with my ruck-sack alone, and the carpenters covered the hole with an old barn door. Hammering nails in this location was not recommended. Our squad continued to live in the same place, bomb or no bomb. Today, I would feel leery about living next to it for months to come, but back then we just forgot about it. The general census was that even the lightning never strikes at the same spot twice, and the Russian artillery could do no better. Someone even suggested that this place was now safer than any other.

There were no outhouses in the village. We just went behind the cow barn. Every day a fresh layer of fallen snow covered installments from the previous day. Since our food rations had been doubled, the snowbank was increasing at an accelerated rate.

One day, when I was in need of the "outdoor establishment", the Russians aimed their cannon-fire rather close. I found it necessary to go into the cow shed instead. The cow apparently didn't approve of my intrusion since she pushed the door open with her horns and jumped out. I ran after her, holding up my pants with one hand and trying to grab the cow with the other. We made a few circles under the kitchen window which was filled with laughing faces. Finally, I was able to grab the cow's collar and drag her back to the barn while Russian shells continued to explode around us.

This happened the very day I was promoted to corporal and had received the Iron Cross for "bravery" (according to the captain's report: "Holding out under intense enemy fire when the rest of the company had retreated more than twelve hours earlier, and singlehandedly neutralizing the attacking enemy unit). There was no mention of Arge's accomplishments, but he did not seem to mind. Well, this cross was flapping on my chest as I was circling in the snow with my tail-end exposed. Once more I had disregarded my own safety, this time to save a Russian cow from destruction. This second act of "bravery" was considered a joke and did not call for promotion or decoration.

As you can see, fun can be had even in the face of danger.

We had developed a new kind of mental mechanism that I call "Instant Selective Suppression". Tragic events were eliminated from recent memory instantaneously, while happy events were retained. Nobody could save his sanity if his brain were working in reverse. The following episode took place just a few days after my struggle with the cow.

The Russians wore sloppy boots in the winter. They were the most useful footwear for a Russian winter since they'd keep feet warm even when wet. The German military did not supply such stuff, but I had written home some time ago and asked if my father would be able to secure a pair and send them through the military mail (Feldpost). Sure enough, I received a pair of the finest felt boots, reaching above my knees. They even had leather soles and heels that would help keep my feet dry as well as warm.

Everybody admired them, and some even tried to put them on. This was not an easy task as I have small feet. But one of my distant cousins, by the name of Reismann, was able to get them on and walk around the room so I myself could admire their beauty from a distance.

Suddenly he had the urge to go "behind the barn", and wanted to try out my boots in the snow. I agreed quite reluctantly, warning him to be extra careful where he placed his feet.

He barely got out the front door when a Russian artillery shell exploded a few yards from him, followed by a second explosion on his other side. The double explosion made his body roll back and forth in the snow.

We buried him with my new boots the next day, in the ritual I've described.

I did not want to wear the dead man's boots, even if they did belong to me. You see, if I had said "no, you cannot go outside with my boots", then he would have pulled them off and gone looking for his own. He would have missed the explosions. The boots were under a kind of curse. No way would I take any chances wearing them myself.

Nobody talked about Reismann and my new boots the next day. That episode was forgotten, but they were still making fun of me, and the valor I, under enemy fire and with my pants down, had shown in saving a Russian cow.

We had lice. Everybody did. We slept on a straw-covered floor and the creatures had free-range. Since my buddies seemed to be scratching all the time I thought my lice were less aggressive than theirs, I believe the lice staked out their own territories. It would not be smart to hunt my peaceful tribe to extinction and get a new breed of aggressive ones from the neighborhood. I'm no ethologist, I admit, but I witnessed an incident that might support my theory.

It happened on one of those sunny winter days when we were out in no-mans-land on ski patrol. The Russians also had their expedition out.

It was easy to spot them in their dark outfits without skis. They had not seen us, of course, and that gave us a distinct advantage. When they were close enough, a short burst of fire from our automatic weapons took them out before they could even say *yobtvoiu mat*.

We were ready to continue our reconnaissance when Sergeant Maamees noticed that one of the Russians had on a pair of beautiful officer's pants. A few days ago he had dried his wet pants too close to the hot stove and now the seat part was disintegrating. It took only a minute or two and our sergeant was wearing the handsome pair of Russian riding pants.

We had skied less than five minute when Maamees decided to go back and retrieve his old pants. He seemed pretty annoyed as he pulled off the fine pants and reclaimed his old ones from the snowbank.

Was our sergeant getting sentimental? Was he having second thoughts about robbing a dead man of his pants? I did not believe a reasonable man like Maamees would entertain such sentimental thoughts. There was nothing said about the incident, and we couldn't ask any questions as we weren't supposed to talk when out on patrol. Why was he so eager to put them on in the first place, only to change his mind? Dress codes weren't enforced here, and he and his "bounty" pants could have been the main topic of conversation during the evening "cocktail hour".

The answer, I learned later, was a simple one. His own lice and the Russian lice went on the war-path. The new pants carried a violent breed which wasted no time in taking over new territory and starting to feast on their new host. Maamees did not like the battle taking place in his private parts so long as the Russian lice were winning. The lesson learned; if you had lice and they seemed domesticated, leave well enough alone. Any new ones might be less refined. They might even be as voracious as killer bees!

As the days, weeks and months passed toward spring, our losses mounted, our defiant spirit became depleted, and we became more superstitious and distrustful.

Pulling a queen of spades in a card game was a bad omen, and if you got her more than once in the same game, you were a marked man. I remember one of us, I can't recall his name, drew it several times in one evening. The next day he was brought back from patrol in the plywood "boat", his chest full of buckshot. When they pulled him past us, he looked at us standing in the doorway and managed to say, "Look what the queen of spades will do to you…"

Keeping a diary was a sure way to increase your chances of kicking the bucket. If you kept one, better have a package of pipe tobacco saved so that your comrades would not need to pay the carpenters. It gave us the creeps to read the dead men's diaries that were piling up on the table. Were there any volunteers to contribute a new volume to our "library"?

It also was dangerous to get new garments like boots, gloves, or pants from the warehouse. The old ones had protected you. The new ones might be bewitched. Remember Reismann and my new boots?

One night one man screamed and sat up at midnight from our straw-covered floor. We had to hold him down for awhile as he kept it up for quite a spell. When he finally came to, all he said was, "I had a bad dream". The next evening he was in a casket of weather-worn boards on the straw covered sleigh, heading toward our graveyard on the frozen meadow. Watch out for nightmares-they might become true!

The graveyard used to be a lonely place, next to the woods. But, now the best part of our company was there with their Birchwood crosses and their helmets, the chin straps frozen in ice. There were now empty spaces on the straw-covered floor where we used to sleep in close quarters. It had been reassuring to hear the men snoring at night. You knew they would not leave you in a snowbank, but would pull you out with their "snowboats" even if you gave up the ghost on the way home.

Where are they now? How many names did I burn into the birch-tree crosses?

I do not want to know. They used to watch me when the glowing iron touched the wood and bittersweet smoke curled toward the ceiling. I remember asking them: "Who will be the one to burn in my name?"

They laughed and patted my shoulder, saying: "Not you, you are the lucky one."

Someone added, "Be sure you spell my name right".

And we all laughed.

"Pretty soon the village carpenters will have enough pipe tobacco to last them a lifetime."

"Did you notice the damned barn has no boards left?"

"Maybe it's a good sign. No boards, no more caskets. No need for tobacco, and no need for the carpenters."

I will stop counting the months spent at Klubochka. I realize that one can describe gloominess only with so many words. But as you can see, one can have sprightly time under grave circumstances.

The 15th Company was withdrawn from ski-reconnaissance in April of 1942, for two simple reasons: the snow had melted, and there weren't many of us left.

I clearly remember the roll-call numbers when we lined up for the last time in the muddy street of Klubochka. Our company, originally 160-strong, had shrunk down to 44 men. My platoon of 44 men at the beginning was down to 11.

From a squad of 14 men, three of us returned: Tuli the gambler and Arge, who had been temporarily on the "heroes list" with me. And, of course, yours truly, sometimes called "the Undertaker" and sometimes "The Lucky One". It's no wonder I cannot recall many names from our old squad. They were not around long enough.

We had our own song after the Battle of Yaglino. I don't remember the tune, only words of one verse. It sounds too corny and sentimental for present-day tastes, but I will quote it just the same, in memory of my comrades, counting myself as the only one left who can still recite it:

> Jaglino, Klubotška, Luban -
> nimed mis ei unune.
> Volhov Ilmenisse voolab
> lahingverest punane...

> Yaglino, Klubochka, Luban-
> The names one cannot forget.
> Volhov flows to the Ilmen Sea,
> Tainted red with battle blood...

[3]Reconnaissance group

Chapter 12

Sun With the Shadows

We spent the summer of '42 in rest and recreation bunkers at the Finnish Sea, surrounded by stone walkways and beds of wildflowers.

On a hot day I could walk barefoot along the wet sand at the beach and feel a gusty breeze blowing in from the sea.

On a cloudy day it was good to sit on top of the sand-covered bunker where the beach grass was growing. I'd just sit there for hours watching the waves breaking on the beach and drawing crosses and circles in the sand in front of me. In the evening the steady rumble of the sea helped wash away painful memories and prepare me for a restful night.

During the day, when I was tired of the seascape I could walk through the deserted village just beyond the sand dunes, where all the houses were empty and the doors ajar, and thorn bushes crept along the walls and in through the broken windows. The footpath was overgrown with weeds, partly hiding a rusty bucket someone had left at the open well. Nobody was at home but wind. It wailed through the rafters.

We had become restless in isolation by late summer and were transferred to a city. I do not even remember its name. No wonder. Nothing extraordinary happened-just the usual daily grind. Our company was reinforced and there were so many new faces that one ran across an old fighter from Yaglino only occasionally. Even our company commander, Captain Rebane, had departed. He had become a battalion commander elsewhere. I was still corporal and the leader of the second squad. There were ten new faces in my squad and today I do not remember any of them. But Tuli and Arge were still around. As we were now behind the front, our food, cigarette, and liquor rations were down. No wonder Tuli was troubled. His cigarette and alcohol rations were inadequate and all his gambling buddies had fallen victim to the "Queen of Spades curse" and were no longer with us. At times he became agitated, could not sit in one place, and paced nervously in the room between the bunk beds.

At those moments of distress, Arge came to the rescue. All three of us found a quiet corner somewhere. Arge acted as the proprietor and bartender. He placed one shot glass in front of me and Tuli and held the bottle. According to the ground rules, he distributed his "firewater" in a three-to-one ration-one shot for me and three for Tuli, in two rounds. Then he corked his bottle and ignored Tuli's plea for "one more round

111

for the third leg".

Our one year contract was coming to an end. My forest brother, Endel Saar, and I had applied for admission to the University of Tartu, and were accepted.

Oh yes, Endel Saar was also one of the lucky survivors from the reconnaissance missions, but he did not participate in the "outdoor activities" because of his supposed "frozen toes". He confessed to me later that there was nothing wrong with his toes. Sergeant Viks was in charge of the outfit, and in the evening card games Viks was a chronic loser and Saar the winner. To keep our sergeant in the game he had to "borrow" money. Endel Saar became the banker and he set the loan's guidelines, saying "Who ever said rubles were worthless? They saved my life!"

We handed in our request to be released from military service as our contract had ended. This happened to be the time when everybody was encouraged to sign up for another year of service. The war was not progressing as planned and the German military could use all the help they could get. Extended vacations were given freely to the veterans who renewed their contracts. Many did just that, including Tuli and Arge. Endel Saar and I declined, waiting for our *Entlassung*[4].

Life in the company had become boring. Then Endel came to see me with his big smile just about one week before Christmas, showing me the release certificate he had just received. I became all excited and rushed to the company office to inquire about my status.

The staff sergeant had no information about my release. "But," and with a wicked smile he pulled out my ledger, "the captain has a new assignment, placing you in charge of an outpost with twelve men, some 20 miles from here. The responsibility consists of occupying a deserted railroad station in the forest a few miles from an isolated small village. You are to observe partisan activities in the region. You will be leaving tomorrow morning 9 A.M. sharp. Here is the list of the men you have under your command. You notify them to be ready to leave at the time specified. That's all I have for you today."

Well, how do you like that! Endel was going home for Christmas, and I was going to some God-forsaken place in the Russian forest. Was his "frozen toe syndrome" more meritorious for discharge than my unplanned "bravery" in Yaglino? Then I realized how useless this train of thought was. Besides, there wasn't a damned thing I could do about it. I would not sign the extension of my contract, and hopefully my day would yet come.

We made the abandoned railroad station in the deep forest livable by using boards from a nearby storage shack for a table to eat and play cards on, benches to sit on, and double bunks to sleep in. A kerosene lamp gave us enough light and a large oven heated with logs kept us warm. Food and liquor rations were again increased because of our outpost in the wild. Each man had to perform guard duty two hours out of 12, and the remaining 10 hours were for him to spend as he chose. What a life of leisure. How would you like to be back with your company, marching in snow each day and listening to sergeant naggings about your poorly-made bed or missing button from your coat. I was in charge of this outfit in the woods and that gave me the privilege of sleeping in a single bunk and doing no guard duty.

Christmas was coming.

Two men were sent to the village with a "ski-boat" to haul in the holiday rations our company supply truck had delivered. We cut down a spruce tree and made makeshift candles by pouring some oil into hand grenade safety caps and inserting cotton strings for wicks. We tied the contraptions to the tree branches. They burned with a bright flame when lit. There was no fear that the hand grenades would explode without the caps unless someone pulled the now-exposed strings to activate them. We stored the case of grenades in a safe place until after Christmas, when we would replace the missing caps.

Our Christmas Eve was a quiet affair. We did not try to sing any Christmas songs since none of us was blessed with the ability to carry a tune. We couldn't read from the Bible because we didn't have one. Besides, it seemed sacrilegious to do so. We observed the holidays by not playing poker. We cooked our dinner and drank liquor in moderation. The evening was still young when we stretched out in our bunk beds. One of our oldest members, a fellow with Gary Cooper's looks and fine city manners, reminisced about his bawdy encounters with city dames. His colorful and detailed description of these events truly made it a memorable evening. Even before the last flicker of our "hand grenade candles" had faded, a loud snoring from the bunks signified, if not peace on earth, then at least peace in this forlorn cabin in the wild.

It was Christmas Eve of 1942, and I was already 20 years old.

New Year's Eve was approaching and our squad members were acting strange. They had a lively discussion among themselves but seemed to change the subject when I approached. On the morning of the last day of the year I stretched out in my bunk after breakfast and was still chewing a toothpick when two men who had made the trip to the village sat next to me. They started their story about how friendly the folks were there and how many nice young girls they had seen, all beautiful. (Of course, even grannies look beautiful when you haven't seen a woman for a long time.) After these preliminaries, they came out with a suggestion that we all go down to the village for a New Year's Eve *gulanye*-meaning celebration, dance, and festivity.

"What?" I sat up in my bunk. "First, how do you know there is a *gulanye?* Second, who invited you? And third, what about our guard duty?"

I should have known-they had all the answers ready, "First, we were told there will be a *gulanye.* And second, the starosta[5] himself extended the invitation to all of us. There probably won't be any *gulanye* if we don't show up because there are no young men left in the village. As far as our guard duty is concerned, we know damned well that there was nobody here before we showed up a couple of weeks ago. We have not seen any partisans, unless you count the rabbits and squirrels, and as far as the so called 'listening post' is concerned, the only sound has been the squawking of the crows. It is New Year's Eve, and all of us have forgotten what dames look like!"

I could not come up with opposing arguments, and that settled the matter.

The last day of the end of the year was coming to a close when we reached the village. Approaching darkness gave its snowy landscape and lit cottage windows a festive appearance. The village elder took us to a large heated room which might have been the village community center. A long table was standing by the window. There were benches along the walls. The floor at one end of the room had freshly-spread straw for us to sleep in. We had taken along all our weapons, ammunition, food and liquor, and it did not take us long to get our supplies in the room with us. Three bottles of liquor with shot glasses were set at one end of the table for the guests.

Soon the villagers started to trickle in. There were young girls in short dresses and scented with *Belye nochi* (White Nights) perfume, accompanied by their mothers and a small group of elderly men led by the *starosta.*

When consuming alcohol indoors in the presence of ladies, drinking from the bottle was considered *nye kulturnaya* (having no uncouth). Well, familiar with the "culture" aspect of drinking, we had secured a couple of shot glasses and continued to fill them as the old men who had taken up positions close to our supply table took turns emptying them. A Russian youngster, apparently too young to be drafted, played the accordion.

The dance floor was soon filled with young couples. The girls, dresses swirling, had their arms well across their partners' shoulders, and our boys had their right arms stretched around their cohorts' waists to hold them close. It wasn't long before they were dancing in chin-to-forehead togetherness. Their mothers were sitting alone on the benches along the walls, keeping their eyes on their daughters, who by now had abandoned them. We brought the old ladies small glasses of liquor which they emptied with a *spasibo* (thank you). The old men had abandoned their wives as well and were congregating next to the liquor bottles.

There was no need for small talk.

In a young relationship, eyes can express feelings more tactfully than spoken words, and looks are subject to wider interpretation. The eyes of a girl give you expectation but no commitment, hope but no promise. Expectation and hope can be more substantial in a young man's imagination.

A moment of happiness, so elusive in the life of a soldier, could be found in a winter night in a God-forsaken Russian village, where 1943 slipped in unnoticed.

It was well past midnight when the party ended and the girls were escorted back to their homes. The old ladies followed their daughters at a discreet distance while the old men took some time reaching their destination since they weren't walking in a straight line. Soon the entire village was hidden in total darkness. Only stars blazed overhead, promising happier days ahead.

The magic of the lonely village and its people had cast a spell over us and we decided to spend another day or two with the friendly folks. Besides, we were invited to one of the homes for an evening get-together. The girls were all there in a joyful mood, jabbering in Russian. This was the evening when a brand new game was invented called *"kerosina nyet"* (no kerosene). This is the only game I know of that has no rules. The game had to be started unexpectedly by blowing out the kerosene lamp. Before the landlady, who was usually sitting at the end of the table and knitting, could stumble out in total darkness to find the matches, one could get a hug or a kiss from your beau.

I wanted to mention it because of its historic value. Electricity has made this game obsolete. Played for less than one week in the No Name Village, it came to an abrupt end, not because of the arrival of electricity, but because of the arrival of our company commander. I do not want to go into details of the dialogue between the4 captain and me, but as you can imagine, it was not pleasant.

We had to clear out of the village within an hour-no goodbyes-and return to our lonely post. With our next supply, a sergeant arrived to replace me. I was relieved of my duties and returned back to the 15th Company. Two days later the entire company had to line up and stand at attention. When the officers arrived, I was asked to step forward. The company sergeant major read the *Befehl*[6] from the battalion commander: "Corporal Arved Ojamaa, while in charge of the outpost near village [X], abandoned it with the soldiers under his command for more than 24 hours. In time of war this would be considered desertion, requiring the most severe punitive measures. However, taking into consideration his previous meritorious service I have relieved him of his command and hereby sentence him to ten days solitary confinement with half the regular food ration. He will retain his rank as Corporal. Company dismissed!"

I went back to my bunk and wondered when they would come to lock me up. Apart from some needling from my roommates, such as "how were the *devuskas* (the girls) at the village?" and something about "scoring", nothing else happened. On the third day I ran across the staff sergeant and asked about my imprisonment.

All he said was: "Don't push it!"

I had a most relaxing ten days. I was given no assignments, and was not told to participate in the company drill. I continued to receive my regular daily food rations. When the ten days were up, I was asked to report to the company office again. The staff sergeant was in a jovial mood and handed me an official-looking document. I unfolded the paper and glanced at the headline, *"Entlassungs Befehl"*[7]

[4]discharge
[5]village elder
[6]command
[7]Discharge order

116

Chapter 13

Home Again

I stepped out of the freight train in Rakvere station in the heart of winter, when the daylight hours were short and the nights long with swirling wind and drifting snow.

There were only strange faces hurrying by, some cast sidelong glances at a man with ill-sitting clothes and a canvas bag thrown over his shoulder. This was the same station where a sea of waving handkerchiefs sent us on our way. Where were they all now, when an old soldier was coming home, knowing that only a few would return.

They were right. I didn't look much like a soldier but more like a drifter looking for shelter in the station.

No one was there to greet me.

The trains from Russia were for military transport only and the date of my arrival had been uncertain. In her letter my mother had advised me to hire a coachman with promises of bacon and eggs. In the city there items were available only on the black market with prices very few could afford. The trouble was that I could only promise those things. The first two coachmen I approached were reluctant to make a 20-mile round trip in the winter on promises alone.

The third one I approached listened to my story and then said: "Hop in, son, I will take you home. My own son, a captain, has been a freedom fighter for some time."

I asked for his name, as I was sure I would have heard of him. "Names are not important, only the goals you boys are fighting for."

Later I learned that he was the father of Captain Karl Talpak, the most recognized name among the freedom fighters during the Russian occupation, and a national (living) hero.

It was pleasantly warm under the lambskin cover pulled up to my neck. The road was familiar but the snowy landscape made it look strange. I had never traveled it in winter until we reached Assamalla. The old schoolhouse looked just the same, still the same red paint with white window frames. And probably the same teacher, Aleksander Traks-the fellow I greeted with a handshake on my very first day at school. Koida must now be a young lady of 12, wherever she was. I remembered her soft over-the-shoulder smile, when I was in love for the first time at the age of seven.

Then came Kullenga with my uncle's Liquor and General Merchandise Store just next to the road. For some reason the sign mentioned only liquor and a new tin sign featured a large bottle with the words "Drink only Saku Beer". Behind the liquor store was the familiar fire department building, buried in the snow.

We turned left to take the road toward Kadila. There were the woods I hid out in with my forest brothers two summers earlier. Turning left again, the final stretch of the road was full of snow drifts. At times the city horses lost their footing and had to wade chest-deep in the snow toward a lonely farm house-my home. The four large windows, like two pairs of eyes, seemed to look at me in a friendly way. Smoke was rising cheerfully from the chimney.

It was good to be home, but I had difficulty adjusting to civilian life in the isolated farm house.

I even felt cagey at night, when everybody went to bed without a sentry on duty. I laughed about my silly notion, but an uncertain anxiety remained. The stillness at night seemed more menacing than the sounds of not-so-distant battle in Klubochka.

In the evening when I skied across the empty fields to pick up mail from the village, skiing alone gave me an eerie feeling. I saw in the flying snow unreal shadows skiing with me. We were scouting together again in a long row with automatic weapons thrown across our backs. Someone was looking at me over his shoulder, an unsmiling colorless face:

"Is that you, Külmoja? Oh yes, my friend, I burned your name into a cross of fresh-cut birch. It was even funny when I and Mägi, you remember him...? We were taking you to burial with the horse and sleigh when the Russians opened cannon fire on the three of us: you and Mägi and I, not counting the horse.

"And Mägi said, "Hell, wouldn't it be funny if both of us got killed trying to get you buried." We just laid low on both sides of your coffin, knowing that you would shield at least one of us, depending which side the shell landed on. Well, never mind, we got you buried, all right. On our way back we tilted the whiskey bottle toward the darkened sky and drank to your memory. I believe Mägi was trying to give you some moral support when he said he was drinking to your health! We both had a good laugh. You know Mägi: he was a funny guy, saying the wildest things at the wrong time and place."

There was no mail other than the local *Virumaa News,* and the news was not good from the Eastern Front. The entire Sixth Army of General Paulus had been surrounded by the Russians in the deep Ukrainian winter, and had surrendered. The collapse of the Soviets seemed less and less likely. What is the Russians returned? Nobody said it aloud but it was a worry in the back of everyone's mind.

It became obvious that the Germans needed help at the Eastern Front and after two months of my civilian life, general mobilization of young men was announced in the Baltic States. That of course included Estonia. The fact that I was born in the decade of the "lost generation" could not be altered. It was also announced that certain jobs were exempt from the draft, but any job taken after the declaration date was not valid for deferment.

I couldn't believe it. I had barely gotten home and in two weeks I had to face the draft board with zero chances of being deferred. I felt that I had already given more than my fair share toward defending my country, and didn't want to return to the German military. My mother suggested I have a talk with my uncle Aleksander Aman, who was running the liquor store at Kullenga. He was a shrewd businessman who over the years had learned back-door ways. He also seemed to know the right people in Rakvere, the seat of the local government and the German Draft Board.

He listened to my predicament, scratching his stubby red beard for awhile, then said, "Let' see what I can do."

He mentioned something about phone calls he'd have to make. Then he had to go to Rakvere himself to meet some people. He actually had to make more than one trip with his horse and sleigh. But before the week was up he came to see us with good news.

"Well," he said with a smile, "it has all been arranged. It will cost your dad half a hog. I need it slaughtered, cleaned and wrapped in a white clean sheet by tomorrow… and don't pick an undersize one, Juljus! Next Monday Arved has to report to the administrator of the German Military Hospital in Rakvere. He will work there as an orderly. I will bring the certificate of his employment along tomorrow after I have delivered the goods. It will be backdated to please the Draft Board. You still have to appear before the board, but this certificate will give you the deferment."

I believe my father had never been happier to slaughter one of his best hogs, half of which would be on its way to Rakvere the next day. Pork was almost unobtainable for civilians in Germany, as everything went for the war effort. The German military officers in charge would divide up the pork and send it to their families. They wouldn't care if there was one less recruit to fight the war; their own families came first!

The German military hospital occupied the Rakvere high school building. A smaller adjacent structure now served for the hospital administration. On Monday morning I met the administrator, Colonel Galt, in his office. He was a somewhat rotund officer in his early fifties with relaxed and friendly manners. The walls were bare, with no pictures of the *Führer* anywhere in sight. He seemed to be pleased with my fluent German, which would make me a more useful employee. When he found out that I had to appear before the draft board that Wednesday, he asked me to report to head nurse Hildegard on Thursday morning. He then dismissed me with a smile, saying, "Remember, young man, that you have been working for us more than a month now!"

Well, it was darned nice of him to give me three days off before I even started.

Things were looking up all right!

Before noon on Wednesday I was facing three German officers on the draft board. We were standing in line. When my turn came, I gave my name and stated that I was working in the German military hospital in Rakvere. I was holding my employment certificate in my right hand, ready to produce it when requested. One of the officers consulted the list in front of him and surprised me by using an English expression, saying "*OK*" before he added in German, *"you may go"*.

He was probably getting part of the loot. Nobody even asked to see my document.

Glory be, I was a free man indeed.

So what if I had to work in the hospital as an orderly?

Besides, I didn't mind living in the city with its movie houses and cafeterias. Thursday morning came, and I reported to head nurse Hildegard. She was a tall and skinny woman in her early forties with a sharp nose and thin lips. Her facial features seemed to indicate chronic pain or a chronic need to go to the bathroom. Perhaps this all went with her job qualifications.

She looked at me with distaste. My impression was that she had an aversion toward the natives. She rushed me through her ward while listing my duties, such as answering any call requiring the *Schieber* (bedpan) or the *Ente* (urinal). Between these "emergency" calls I was supposed to follow the German orderly, who brought in and readjusted all kinds of traction equipment I did not know anything about. I was not even familiar with the nomenclature of sticks and pulleys and ropes, and my ignorance was clear as day.

I started my job, carrying out mountains and rivers of solid and liquid waste. Whenever Hildegard saw me leaning against the wall for a moment she found me a new errand to run.

To be honest, after my first day I felt like asking the draft board to reconsider. But a good night's sleep improved my disposition and I went to work with a "wait and see" attitude. I was sure that if they gave me an assignment to set up some of the traction rigmarole, sister Hildegard would have apoplexy and the new head nurse might have more mercy on me.

Well, it didn't happen. I continued as the "administrator" of bedpan and urinal service. (That was the title by which I tried to impress my new acquaintances). I was not asked to set up any of the orthopedic "architecture", and sister Hildegard did not come down with a stroke.

But luck was again with me. The scenario even helped me coin a proverb: *"The one who likes you the least might help you the most."* My working hours were changed from days to the "graveyard shift".

I'm sure sister Hildegard had gone to the hospital administrator complaining about my inefficiency, and telling them how she didn't want me to work there. And Colonel Galt didn't want to fire me, so he switched me to the night shift. I worked from eight in the evening until six in the morning on the same orthopedic floor. My assignment remained the same with a big difference: most people sleep at night and put their bathroom needs off until the daylight hours.

As the portable toilet supplier (and cleaner), I suddenly found my workload decreased by about 80%.

Life was worth living again.

There were two night nurses on duty. They were both in their mid-20s, and I got along splendidly with both of them. I had special affection for Anne-Marie. She was a short and slender young woman with light brown hair. Her eyes, behind a pair of gold-rimmed glasses, had a soft look. Maybe it was just my imagination, but they always seemed to light up for just a second when she smiled.

The summer of 1943 was the most carefree and glorious summer.

I spent the days at the municipal pool. I looked oddly impressive with my deep tanned dace and blond hair, now sun-bleached white. Deprivation and anxiety had been my bedfellows for the last three years. Now I intended to enjoy myself, to forget the traumatic past and build up reserves for the unknown future.

The night work at the hospital was enjoyably slow as the patients were usually asleep or trying to sleep through their painful hours. The evening twilight colored the long walls of the hallway red and yellow as I wandered past the third-floor windows, looking at the semi-darkened city below.

Anne-Marie stopped for a moment when she was passing by.

"What are you looking at," she inquired.

"Can't you see what I can see?" I countered as I continued to look at the twilight falling upon the city below.

For a moment we both looked at the colors and shadows in the late evening landscape.

"Oh, du bist ein romantischer Kerl."[8]

She gave me a brief smile before leaving to answer a patient's call.

I felt lonely and yearned for something as I continued looking at the city below. Perhaps for her, because of her smile and half intimate *"du"*.

I lived in a room by myself at the edge of town, not far from the hospital. From my second floor-window I could see the nearby meadows and further out there was a pine forest. It was early summer. The footpaths were dry. I walked different trails in rolling fields covered with spring flowers in the wild. Once I ventured out to the edge of the pine forest. I changed my direction and came to a pond. Beyond it I found an old house surrounded by a large fenced-in garden: a lonely place in the green landscape.

Curiosity took me to the garden filled with beds of flowers.

An elderly woman who was attending the rosebushes came to open the gate. After I told her how much I admired her garden, she walked ahead of me recounting the flowers and how to care for them. I did not pay much attention to her words, but admired the whole scene and the friendly way of the hostess.

We do not get many visitors out here," she said, wiping her forehead with the back of her right arm. "We used to be in the nursery business for many years but we are retired now. My husband and I still tend our garden to keep us busy. The flowers make us feel young. One never feels lonely among them. In wartime, people seem to have hardly any time for us. We still have some old customers but I have not seen a young man here for ages."

Then we admired the rosebushes, just ready to burst into full glory. I decided to buy two of the red rosebuds.

"Usually they come in odd numbers!" she laughed.

She cut three of them.

"Young man, I enjoyed your visit and there is no charge. Come and see us again when you need more flowers. We will be happy to share them with you."

That same evening I gave each of the night nurses a red rose. I think they both overreacted when they showed pleasure in smelling them again and again. "We have not seen a rose since… since when? It was nice of you to think of us."

Thinking of the nursery lady's "you never feel alone with flowers," I placed the third one at my window in a glass of water.

One day, when I was walking around downtown, I met one of my class-mates. His name was Elmar Toom, the singer from our *"Heli Neli"* band. He was working as a copy editor for the *Virumaa News*. He was nearsighted and wore thick glasses. Without them he could not tell friend from foe. He probably could tell a Russian by the smell, but that wasn't good enough for the draft board.

He was unhappy with his living arrangements in the city and we agreed to become roommates. He was a most likeable fellow with a good sense of humor and leisurely manners. He had curly hair, spoke slowly as though he were weighing each word before and after he used it, and his vocabulary did not recognize such expressions as "to rush to" or "in a hurry".

We used to take our suppers together in the restaurant, since neither of us had any talent for cooking. I can clearly remember one of our evening meals of Swedish meatballs and half-done potatoes in a small cafeteria with sparse furniture. There were no other customers there but us. The evening sun cast dim light through the old linden trees. Elmar had left a large tip for the waitress, who in my opinion had no laudable qualities.

When I inquired after his generosity, he gave me a short answer, "She had a new pair of stockings on."

What powers of observation for such poor eyesight! I had the habit of not looking below the waistline unless the upper part of the anatomy called for it. In this case, I didn't even know she possessed a pair of legs.

On one of those summer afternoons a few of my new friends and I entered our favorite cafeteria for a cool drink. We barely got inside when the lady in charge ran to us all in tears, begging for help. "See that man in the uniform there?! He is drunk and threatens to wreck my place unless we serve him some liquor. But we don't have any! I told him so, but he doesn't believe me. Maybe you can do something to calm him down!"

I saw a raving man in a *Wehrmacht* uniform, knocking the ashtrays off the tables, swinging an empty soft drink bottle and swearing up a storm!

Wait a minute!

I knew him! His name was Tuli, one of the survivors from our second squad. I yelled, "Tuli!"

He looked toward us, wondering who could know him in this one-horse town.

"Don't you remember me," I said, my voice full of emotion.

As soon as he recognized me, he dropped the bottle. "Ojamaa. My buddy!!!"

The next moment we were hugging each other. He started to cry and I almost did. He lost all his hostility on the spot. We sat at the empty table he had just knocked the ashtray off of. All our sentences started with "Remember when…?"

Finally I asked him: "What made you so mad? You know the cafeterias don't serve liquor. You aren't starting trouble again?"

"Nah. I'm all right now. I am glad you came in at the right time or I would really have wrecked the place."

"I know you have a short fuse, but how did this all get started?"

"That bitch," he said, meaning the hostess and proprietor, "she told me I was drunk and wanted to kick me out. Serves her right. But I am happy that you came when you came." He added, "I got a pass because I signed the third-year contract. You know, it is hell out there. I am fighting to keep the communists out so that she can keep her ashtrays and all the crap here."

It seemed Tuli was getting hot under the collar again, so I offered the following: "Now listen to me. She was wrong. I'll tell her that myself. For my sake don't get mad again."

It was the very first time I saw him laugh. "You're the boss," he said. "Don't worry. I'm all right. In fact, I have to be off to see a dame and I am late already."

We shook hands. "See you around," he said. We never met again. But, I remember him as my friend even though he was twice my age.

The waitress started to pick up the ash trays. The hostess's face was still red, but she was smiling now. She knew she was helpless. She couldn't call the police since they had no authority to arrest a man wearing a Wehrmacht uniform. The German military police would have restrained him, but the place would have been in shambles by the time they arrived, and one couldn't replace any broken inventory during the war. Tuli, of course, would have no obligations for restitution. A soldier on leave, short of murder, had free range and no responsibility for his actions. I should say something about Tuli as a man of integrity and guts...

It happened in the winter of 1942.

We were out on ski patrol in the middle of an open field when we saw movement in the woods in front of us. They could shoot us at any moment if they so decided, and for us there was nowhere to hide. The possibility existed that this was a German unit, but they could shoot us just the same, taking us for the Russians.

Tuli saved the day, saying:, "If we wait here long enough we'll be all dead," and he skied out alone to meet either a friendly force or certain death. I do not know anyone who would have had the guts to do the same. But he was a gambler and he won the round for all of us.

I was in charge of that patrol, by the way. If it had been an enemy unit, I would not be here to tell the story. Of course, neither would Tuli, who caused all this commotion in the restaurant. I got the credit for establishing peace.

The true hero was still Tuli.

The summer was still young.

In the month of June there are no nights-the days are endless. The sun just stayed up forever, and when it set behind the Fortress Hill, the long shadows on the cobblestone streets faded into semi-darkness but the stones still radiated heat from the day.

That was the time of day and time of year I worked at the hospital with the big windows. The twilight hours were the *Kameradschaft* hours.

I had many friends among the ambulatory patients.

125

They were all from the *Ostfront,* places like Luban and Volhov, familiar places still fresh in my memory. I was the "native" and the only contact these people had with the outside world. They looked through the windows at a foreign country and yearned for their *Heimatland.* They hated the war. They pulled out pictures, and together we admired the beauty of their wives and the handsomeness of their children.

They asked me to have a drink with them. I had made more promises than I could endure. How could you say "no" when they called you *mein Freund* and you looked at their family pictures and had a share of their loneliness?

"*Mein Freund,* will you come Saturday when I get my liquor rations and have a drink with me?"

Of course, you would answer just as I did: "*Sicher, mein Freund.* It will be an honor."

Come Saturday evening, the nurses answered the calls when we were having *Kameradschaft Stunde,* singing (and drinking) together:

> Heimat, deine Sterne,
> Die strahlen mir auf einem fernen Ort.
> Was die sagen, möchte ich ja so gerne.
> In der Ferne trauma ich vom Heimatland

> Homeland with its stars,
> They shine on me from a foreign place.
> What they are saying delights me.
> From afar I dream of my native land.

At the end of the *Kameradschaft* hour I was more than tired. In the hallway stretchers were piled on top of each other. They were too inviting to resist, and I stretched myself out on them. Next thing I knew, someone was covering me up with a blanket. It was Ann-Marie pulling it up to my shoulders and as her hands were slowly sliding over my face I kissed them. She bent down with her face close to mine. I could smell her perfume when she said, *"Gute Nacht!"*

The next moment I was alone, warm under the blanket when I fell asleep.

Those Saturday nights in June are full of light. It even reaches inside you and stays with you during the winter hours. Even through the years, when you are well past the age of 20.

I do not even remember if it ever rained that summer.

On each one of my trips to the nursery, the wildflowers on each side of the path seemed plentiful: the globe flowers and golden margaritas, birds eyes, and buttercups. There were many more I could not name.

The bent blades of grass on the rolling mounds waved at me in unison when they caught a breeze, while the dog daisies shook their yellow crowns in disbelief at seeing a young man admiring their beauty in times such as these.

I had been a frequent visitor to the isolated nursery couple. I did not even know their names, and they did not ask mine. I was pleased to be addressed as the "young man", and I called her the "Rose Lady".

She liked to talk about flowers while her husband just sat in an old wicker chair and smoked his pipe. The tobacco must have been home grown. Its aroma reminded me of burning weeds. Even the peonies he was sitting next to seemed to start wilting.

On my next visit I brought him a whole package of first-class tobacco. He filled his pipe and lit it. A sweet aroma filled half the garden after his first puff.

"I'm sure my wife will even let me smoke this stuff inside the house," he said.

I had free flowers for the entire summer.

The Rose Lady refused to take any money, which was almost worthless anyway. On my weekly visits, I kept the old gardener supplied with pipe tobacco and the Rose Lady supplied me with fresh-picked flowers.

Sometimes I tried to refuse them: "The old ones still look good for another week!"

"Now listen, young man, I'd rather see you share them with the young nurses you told me about than let them die alone in my garden. Flowers are for young people to enjoy!"

It was true.

Once a week I delivered a bouquet that she had made especially for the night nurses' desk. This made me popular with them. At times I was even asked "to take a rest" after midnight, when there were only a few calls – mostly for the nurses, asking for a sleeper or medication for pain. Why should they wake me up to be the messenger?

Even when the summer nights were warm, I had to be covered with a blanket. Whenever Anne-Marie noticed I was awake, she was careful not to touch my face, but brought her head rather close to mine. I could smell again the familiar aroma from her face and neck and well-hidden breasts. Then she tucked me in like a child and said *"Gute Nacht!"*

The nurses wanted to give something to the Rose Lady. They mentioned handkerchiefs and scarves, but I thought that might seem like barter and would hurt her feelings. Then the other night nurse (I don't even remember her name) had a good suggestion: "I have a small bottle of good liqueur, which might be introduced as medicine."

I was sure I could "sell" her the medicine idea. It came from the hospital nurses. She must have arthritic pains or the occasional cold in the winter needing treatment.

When I made my next visit, I had my speech ready and was even willing to argue with her, if needed.

I started with the line: "I have some good medicine from our nurses for you. Every week they have gotten so much pleasure from your gift of flowers. This is their thank you, their show of appreciation, and I must add that this stuff is hard to come by during the war."

"I am not sick. What is it for?"

I unwrapped the bottle, which was shaped to fit in a pocket. The label had pictures of three gold coins and some fine print.

"This is the best French liqueur and a small shot glass of it will cure whatever ails you. And if nothing ails you, it is good for that too."

She laughed merrily and got out her glasses to read, but everything was in French. She put the bottle in her garden-apron pocket and held the glasses in her right hand:

"I better hide it or my man might come down with his rheumatism tonight. Give my regards to the fine lady-nurses at the hospital. It was thoughtful of them. I am sure it will become handy in a time of need."

That same evening, I delivered a large bouquet of red, purple, and violet carnations to the night nurses and was happy to report how much the liqueur was appreciated.

They were delighted, saying "We even take the old flowers to our room when the new ones arrive. They still look good for several days."

"Why not take the fresh ones with you in the morning and leave the old ones for head nurse Hildegard? Has she ever asked about the flowers and where they are coming from?"

"We told her. The only thing she said was that she's allergic to them and they make her sneeze."

We all laughed. This time they were going to take their carnations with them at the end of their shift.

Nothing is forever, neither flowers nor the long days of summer.

The Fortress Hill extended its shadows across the city earlier each evening, reaching up to our windows as a sign of early fall. The young nurse was at my side as we looked out into the idle darkness.

"Why don't you come with me to visit the Rose Lady?" I asked.

The question was unexpected. She gave me a frightened look: "I can't do that!"

"You can't or you wouldn't?"

"Oh *du lieber, dummer Kerl,*[9] I would love to."

"Then why not?"

"I am not allowed to go out by myself."

I must have looked disappointed. She seemed to want to comfort me: "Isn't there anything else I could do?"

"You could at least touch my face."

She appeared frightened. There were patients walking about.

"You mean now?"

"With your blanket."

"I can do that, if you like."

She had to break off our conversation. A young German nurse should not stand and have a long conversation with an orderly, specially if he happens to be a non-Aryan.

At night the lights were dimmed in the ward and turned off in the hallway. Our census was low and all was quiet at midnight as I lay on top of the pile of stretchers. My heart was pounding.

She came with a light blanket and pulled it up to my neck. While she was bending over me to tuck the loose ends under my shoulders, I lifted my head and kissed her neck: "You are beautiful, and I love you."

She got hold of my head and placed it gently down. There was softness in her voice when she said, *"Du bist ein verrückter[10] Kerl!"*

Then she quickly kissed me on the lips and left.

I could not fall asleep, wondering why happiness was always so short and was each time followed by the sorrow of absent love.

If head nurse Hildegard were to learn about the kiss, she would croak before she could dish out any punishments. This thought itself made me forget about the sorrow as I fell asleep, smiling to myself.

Fall was coming and I was eager to start my medical studies at the University of Tartu. I could not quit my job and face the draft board again. I came up with a plan. Even if it failed it wouldn't have any negative percussions.

Colonel Galt had been always helpful. I had to start my plan by making an appointment with him.

When the day and hour arrived I introduced myself, in case he did not remember me. He seemed to be in his jovial mood, "What can I do for you, young man?"

To help establish a good rapport, I started off by stressing the fact that the Germans had freed our country from the Russian occupation and how thankful we all were. In case *Herr Oberst* would find it convenient to take a ride to the countryside with a couple of his fellow officers to taste a home-cooked meal, my parents would be much honored.

I could see that the idea seemed to please him. He leaned back in his stool, fiddled with his thumbs on the top of his round abdomen and looked out the window.

A moment later he turned to me: "I do not see why not. I have to consult with my secretary and some of my fellow officers to find the proper time. I thank you for the invitation, and give my regards to your parents."

On my way out I gave a well-drawn map to his secretary, in case he decided to come.

My next step was to invite Leida Aunmann to my party with a special assignment. Leida was a lively girl from our neighborhood and a student of languages at the University. She was enthusiastic about the dinner party and promised to do her best to keep some lively conversation going. My sister Asta had only a basic knowledge of German, but with her blond locks and happy smile she would make a good decoy. My mother promised roasted pork with oven-browned potatoes and gravy and her "Floating Islands" dessert.

When Colonel Galt arrived with two officers, bringing along a bottle of cognac and another liqueur, the party promised to be a success. Within an hour the conversation was loud, with plenty of laughs. Leida was sitting next to Colonel Galt, conversing merrily about her studies at the University. Then a new thought just seemed to pop into her mind:

"Oh, by the way, Arved has been admitted to the university to study medicine," she said, touching the colonel by the sleeve and looking at him in a charming way. "Why don't you give Arved a leave of absence so he could start his studies?"

There was no hesitation in the colonel's voice. "By golly, why not. A splendid idea! I'll have my secretary do the paperwork so the young man can go and study to become a doctor." I stood up and bowed toward him with my thanks. Everyone applauded, including the other officers, while Colonel Galt seemed proud of his generosity.

Everybody drank to his health and to my success as a future physician.

Soon thereafter the party took off in a cloud of dust in their Opel convertible.

Three days later I went to see the colonel's secretary about my leave -of-absence certificate.

"Oh yes. They have had it ready since last Monday."

They were happy that I had finally come to pick it up. I was also told that head nurse Hildegard was informed of my departure.

Well, even though my work requirement had ended three days earlier, I decided to go in for one more evening shift.

First of all, I wanted to make a last visit to the old couple at the nursery, which had become my second home over the summer. I have always been fond of flowers. Even during the war I used to pick up wildflowers and keep them with me in my bunk, using an empty tin can as a vase.

This time I told the Rose Lady of my fondness for the young nurse in the hospital. I asked her for something special for the farewell.

"Well, red roses would fit the occasion, but I have something else in mind." She headed toward the greenhouse and returned with a handful of flowers. They were brilliantly showy, radiating several shades of red and yellow.

"Chrysanthemums blossom in our climate only in the fall. They are called "the Golden Flowers," going back over one thousand years, when they were featured on the Japanese emperor's coat of arms. I intended to show them to you when they were in full blossom. They are almost ready now, and will become more beautiful in your lady's room. I do not want them to wilt in a lonesome greenhouse, I'd rather see them bring happiness to the young lady or help lighten her sorrow."

At my last night in the hospital, I found Anne-Marie standing at the window. She sounded reproachful: "Why didn't you tell me you are leaving?"

"I did not know for sure until this morning."

"What shall we do without you?"

"I'll remember you."

"And I'll miss you!"

"I brought you flowers. They are for you only, hidden in the closet."

We stood silently at the window. She did not seem to be in her usual hurry. The city was semi-hidden in dusk. Only the cross from the church tower was still shining gold. She pulled out a white handkerchief from her uniform pocket, "Take it. It is for the flowers. *Mein Abschiedsgeschenk.*"[11]

Then my friends from the ward wanted to have an *Abschiedsgetränk* with me. I did not want to disappoint any of them. I drank more than I should have-the yearning and hoping and dreaming seemed to be entirely out of place in this crazy world. The only thing I could do was forget. I went to lie down on the pile of stretchers and fell asleep.

I did not wake until the next morning, when I found myself covered with the blanket. Light from the nurses' station shone into the hallway through the open door. I threw off my blanket and left the building through the back exit, avoiding the nurses' station and its open door. No encore, please!

The next summer the military hospital with its staff and wounded was being evacuated to Germany when The Red Cross transport ship was torpedoed in the Baltic Sea by a Russian U-boat. There were only a few survivors.

My leave of absence permit had excluded me from the fatal voyage.

Anybody who loves flowers has to also love poetry, as both require a sentimental inner core. From my high school days I still remember a poem by Henrik Visnapuu. I would like to quote it in memory of my friends and in memory of Anne-Marie and her perfumed white handkerchief. They all had to die when still young:

Ilus on surra, kui oled veel nor,
Nii päikesen magama minna.
Su umber on sõprade leinav koor,
sa nende südames igavest noor –
saad varakult Jumala Linna."

It is beautiful to die when still young,
To go to sleep with the rising sun.
Surrounded by a circle of mourning friends,
In their hearts you live - forever young,
Escaped early to Elysian lands

[8]you are romantic fellow
[9]Oh you dear, silly fellow
[10]crazy
[11]parting gift

Chapter 14

The Days in Autumn

It was hard to believe I was finally able to start the last stage of my education. I was a student in the 332-year-old University of Tartu, the only institution of higher learning in Estonia. My brains had been idle for two years. It felt good to hit the books and lecture halls again. Things seemed easy enough at the beginning: physics, chemistry, and botany, with their laboratory studies, the very basic stuff.

I met Endel Saar as a university student. I had dinner at his parents' home. Endel wore a tie and a double- breasted suit. He acted like a gentleman without any of his high school frolics. He was married to Helgi, the girl I had heard crying at Cat's Tail Road. Helgi, a lovely lady with a soft smile, was exquisitely dressed. The fine home, the good food, the wine-all contributed to a memorable evening.

I also met Velda again.

You remember the tear-moistened handkerchief of hers that I wore around my neck my last days in Väike-Maarja. I could not believe it. She was studying veterinary medicine.

She was slightly overweight, but in a way that stressed her femininity. She talked fast, was always excited about everything, and used her hands not far from my face to stress the points under discussion. She sometimes got one step ahead of me when we walked in the street, then tried to walk sideways so she could talk to me face-to-face. She had so much enthusiasm that I was afraid I might catch it.

On foggy afternoons, we took long walks along the paths at Cathedral Hill with its ancient ruins.

After a few months, the carefree days in Tartu came to an end. The German military was retreating. The Russians were not near the Baltic States yet, but the tables had turned in the Russians' favor. We had to face the reality of their reoccupation. A new decree was passed by the military government, requiring all men my age to register for the draft. University students had been exempt so far ,but that exemption was now lifted and my stay in Tartu was futile.

Enthusiasm for German occupation started to fade in the country. The Baltic States have always had a western orientation, and German aggression in western Europe became more and more apparent. True, the German military had freed us from the murderous Russian occupation, but they were not willing to allow the restoration of Estonian independence.

Their policy to eliminate Jewish and gypsy populations in Estonia was unknown to all of us. There were no Jewish farmers in Kullenga or merchants in Väike-Maarja, and no Jewish students in our high school. We had gypsies, but they were all migratory, and none lived in our area. The newspapers and radio, of course, did not carry any reports of their destiny.

I personally had met but few ugly Germans. The opposite was true. I met friendly and forthcoming soldiers who hated the war. Hitler, if ever mentioned, was described in negative terms. To lift the soldiers fighting spirit, the Nazi hierarchy had promised *Neue Waffen*[12]. It was turned into a joke by the rank and file, "Neue Waffen-alte Affen".[13]

It was late fall now.

I was heading home, planning to flee to Finland, to escape the draft. Trains ran on an irregular schedule. I had to wait for hours at the station.

Of course, Velda would not let me wait alone.

She laughed cheerfully proclaiming that things would turn out all right at the end. But every time she said "We shall meet again, my dear!" she burst into tears. That was Velda, Velda with the heart of gold. She tried to convince me, but could not even convince herself, no matter how hard she tried.

When the train rolled out of Tartu station at midnight, I was again the owner of Velda's tear-filled handkerchief. "For good luck and to bring us together again," she said after the last hug. Fate was to fulfill her first wish, but fail on the second. We never met again. My first try to become a doctor had also failed. I was forced to leave the university before the end of the first semester.

It would cost two thousand marks to be smuggled across the Finnish Sea. That was the amount an average worker earned in one year. My father had to sell sacks of wheat at black market prices to get the money for my crossing.

I left home for the last time just before Christmas. It was a foggy evening. As yet, there was no snow. I was on my way with my rucksack to Tamsalu railroad station to take the train to Tallinn. Across an open farm field, I saw light from the kitchen window until it disappeared in the thickening fog and darkness.

I wondered if I'd ever see that light again.

It was New Year's Eve, Friday, 31 December, 1943.

The temperature was a few degrees below freezing. Only a slight dusting of snow covered the ground. Here I stood with a beat-up suitcase at a poorly lit street corner in Tallinn, far from the center of the city, and waiting. An old pick-up truck came rumbling down the deserted street and stopped a few feet from the corner.

A short stocky man in a winter coat and floppy cap jumped out across from the driver's seat and asked: "What's your name, kid?"

Satisfied with my answer, he came around to the back end of what seemed to be an empty truck with a canvas cover, lifted up one loose corner, and told me to hop in. I had to crawl in as there was only a foot or two between the floorboards and the top cover. He handed me my suitcase. In less than a minute the truck was again bouncing along the cobblestone street. I tried to crawl toward the front but counted several pairs of legs and heard the warning, "watch it, you're sitting on my feet!" But, I found enough room to lie on my side. The occupants squeezed closer to each other. We were like sardines in a can in total darkness.

After awhile the bouncing decreased, and the truck picked up speed. We were heading north-east toward the sea somewhere, where a boat was supposed to be waiting to take us across the Finnish Sea. We unhooked the cab end of the canvas cover so we could sit in the open. The full moon stood high in the sky, shedding ghostly light on the woods and fields with an occasional prick of lantern light visible from some lonesome home. The air was dry and cool, making our faces burn. It was unlikely we'd get caught now, well outside the city, and all thirteen of us-twelve men and one woman-were almost in a festive mood.

A car with flashing lights was parked in the middle of the road about a hundred yards in front of us. Two men wearing helmets were standing next to it with powerful flashlights: the German military police!

The sharp beam of light seemed to blind our driver for a second, and it appeared that we were coming to a full stop just short of the policemen. But, then the accelerator was suddenly pushed to the floorboard, and the truck roared ahead. The light barricades flew through the air as the policemen jumped from our path. The right side of the truck's fender smashed through the open door of the police van as our driver took us into a roadside meadow. Luckily, there were no ditches on either side of the small road. We heard two pistol shots. Then, it was just us, in the full moonlight, driving without headlights. The ground was firm and a thin layer of frozen snow covered the meadow. There was enough light and only a few trees. The driver felt that the police car was sufficiently disabled to be unable to follow us. After a mile we were back on the road.

The right fender and light had been damaged in the collision, but the dimmed left headlight gave us enough light.

There were no other checkpoints. The truck approached the coastal village with its left headlight turned off-no need to attract the attention of the German Coast Guard. We came to a stop in front of a small house next to the sea. A 20-foot open boat with an outboard motor and two pairs of oars was tied to a short pier.

We entered the house with one room only, and ill-lit, with window shades drawn. A tall man, a Finn with a scarred face, seaman's cap, and superior grin collected the landlubbers' money. Everybody seemed to have the right amount and there was no hassle. The truck driver was paid off and left in a hurry.

After a short rest in the house to stretch our stiffened joints, we were led to the boat. There was room for everyone to sit. We held our suitcases between our knees. The boat was pushed off the pier and the captain, and his assistant attended the oars, rowing quietly off the coast. After an hour, there was nothing but the full moon, the sky full of stars, and the dark blue sea.

By then it was safe to start the engine. We picked up speed, heading out to open sea.

Conversation and small talk was again permitted, and someone shouted: "It is past midnight. Happy New Year 1944!"

"Happy New Year... Happy New Year...!"

The last day of 1943 had fallen on a Friday, and one could not wish for a luckier day. The military police did not catch us, and there was no snow to speak of. Even the sea was not frozen, truly exceptional for this time of year.

Someone added: "Besides being Friday, did you notice that the '31' backwards would give you '13'. Then take the year '1943' and the first and last numbers make another '13'. If you add the two middle numbers, what do you get but another '13'. How can you lose with a quadruple '13'?"

I was sitting next to the single female passenger, a woman about 30, who had been quiet throughout the conversation. She suddenly spoke up, "You better add the thirteen of us in the boat to your collection."

So much for the numbers game, the only subject we seemed to have in common and could talk about. But, the first of January found us still far out in the open sea in an open boat. Too many unknowns were waiting for us in the immediate and not-too-distant future. We remained withdrawn and total strangers to each other for the rest of the voyage.

At nine o'clock in the morning we reached the Finnish archipelago near Helsinki. The Coast Guard intercepted us and waved us to follow their boat to the harbor. The immigration officials were quite friendly when checking our ID's, and went casually through our belongings. It was routine for them. Thousands of young men had fled to Finland before us and many were likely to follow. "Welcome to the *veljen kansa* (brother country)," they said.

[12]New weapons
[13]New weapons – old monkeys

Chapter 15

Life in the Finnish Army

I volunteered to serve in the Finnish armed forces.

Here we go again, I thought.

After my stint as a volunteer in the *Wehrmacht,* I had promised myself not to volunteer for any state, group, or organization in my lifetime no matter how benevolent their statutes. Not even the public library. Why did I break my promise even before one year had passed?

It is hard for me to explain why I did certain things over fifty years ago.

Is it because at seventy one values each day of life more than at age twenty? How many young men have thrown their lives away for a cause which now appears hopeless folly? When there are so many days and years to spend, one is ready to spend them recklessly and without thinking that you might lose it all, even before you started shaving or had a woman.

I witnessed deaths of comrades many times over. I saw so many men shot that it seemed more normal to be shot than not. I'm sure I too had killed, but killing was like tossing a coin. It's either you or me, and the coin toss comes out in my favor. I have been asked how it feels to kill another human being. My answer has always been the same-I don't know.

I shot at moving dots in a distant landscape, but never face-to-face. I was never involved in hand-to-hand combat. In either instance, I probably would have been a loser, as I was born chicken-hearted. My battle experience has been confined to reconnaissance. Whenever there was shooting, we were shot at first, and when we shot we were just shooting back in an attempt to escape. We could never tell if we hit anyone specific in this blind firing with no visible target. We shot to help our buddies take cover for a moment or two, or so that we could get away.

There were occasions when Russian partisans were caught red-handed far behind the front line and were executed. Those cases were rare and I knew of only three instances over the span of a year and a half. Only front-line soldiers in uniform were taken as POWs. I am sorry to admit that there were a few faces in our company quite willing to try out their handguns on captured partisans. I clearly remember an incident one snowy evening on the eastern front, when two German soldiers brought us a prisoner, a partisan who had ambushed and killed one of the accompanying soldier's best friends well behind the front. Their commanding office had ordered the man shot, but they couldn't find anyone in their unit willing to carry out the order, and brought him to us in hope of finding volunteers. They did, and the man was executed.

Why do I say this when one should only speak honorably about the unit one serves in? I don't mean to show my disrespect. I'm certain there was no unit on either side, east or west, where this type of behavior did not take place during wartime-though it is not talked about. But, there was at least one company of Germans at one time who couldn't find a single man willing to shoot a partisan who had ambushed a soldier behind the front lines. Even the dead man's best friend wouldn't, so it was out of revenge. It is an event, one that I personally witnessed, that gives a human face to the German soldier. So, I don't think we should throw stones at every German who was forced to serve. Most of them served honorably.

I have let my mind wander to subjects I wanted to get off my chest. Another question I haven't really addressed, how could a person voluntarily join the Nazi military? The only way I can answer it today, if our foresight always had the benefit of hindsight, our sight would always be 20/20, as they say. I served my own besieged country honorably, solely against the Russians, and only a blind man could ask-why?

As far as calling the *Wehrmacht* a Nazi outfit, that would be like calling an entire city block a bunch of child-molesters if one happened to live there. The fact remains, the German *Wehrmacht* liberated us from hell, and their occupation of Estonia felt like salvation compared to that of the Russians. I had no contact with their *Sicherheitsdienst* or Special SS units. We learned about them only after the war. I did not know these organizations existed, but I sure did get to know the KGB.

I am writing my memoirs, describing my association with German soldiers and later on with civilians. I am not writing about Nazi cruelties that have already been well reported, and of which I have no knowledge. Joining the Finnish Army seemed the right thing to do. They were fighting the Russians only to regain part of their country that the Russians had occupied during the Winter War.

Perhaps I should explain the hostilities between Russia and Finland.

In early November, 1939, Russia demanded a "revision" of the existing peace treaty between Finland and Russia. Under the new treaty the Russians required the Finns to hand over part of their country-Karjala. Finland refused. Russia then canceled the existing peace treaty and attacked Finland on November 30, 1939. The League of Nations condemned the attack and kicked the Soviets out of the League.

General mobilization in Finland produced a military force of 300,000 men. Their military hardware included 100 airplanes and 50 antiquated tanks. The Russians attacked with a force of 460,000 men, 2000 tanks, and 1000 airplanes. The Russians lost ten times as many men as the Finns, but in the end Finland had to give up Karelja. (The new peace treaty was signed March 13, 1940 in Moscow).

So when the Germans attacked Russia in 1941, Finland used the opportunity to regain Karelja.

This will explain why I preferred fighting in the Finnish Army instead of the German, although both countries were fighting our common enemy, the Russians. What the communist occupation had done to me and my country left us Estonians with the moral obligation of retaliating by joining forces with any country fighting the Russians. The Germans gave us our first opportunity, but they were fighting the world. Any future association with their military seemed tainted.

In the Finnish army, my rank was still corporal-two steps higher than rookie and one step above private. There is a Finnish saying: *"Ei joku miesi ole sotamiesi, ei korporaali"* (every man is not a private, and a corporal ain't a general). That means I had to start two steps from the bottom.

I was sent to school to become a sergeant.

I want you to know that these schools were not in any city but were located in the wilderness surrounded by rocky hills, frozen lakes, and woods from horizon to horizon. There were no text books, but plenty of military maps covering the few miles of area around the campsite. Everybody had his own compass. The students had to learn how to sweat and freeze intermittently 24 hours a day, including Sundays. The instructor's vocabulary was rather limited, but did include many ways of swearing. The most common expression was "you are like a *tikku paskaan* (a match in a pile of shit). The days were all the same: drill practice without skis, with skis, without skis, etc. Our living quarters were a long barracks made of logs. There was a large brick oven at each end. We had to cut down trees to heat the ovens. Because the wood was freshly cut, it burned reluctantly and gave more smoke than heat. The average temperature was about 55° F, and ice-flowers inside the small windowpanes were the only decorations. The furniture consisted of two rows of double bunks. I don't recall having any table or benches, but I remember the strings wrapped around the lukewarm ovens where our wet uniforms were supposed to dry out overnight.

143

One spent the night in three ways, but you don't need to worry about choosing one over another. These decisions were made higher up, (remember, "a corporal ain't a general"). First, you slept in a straw-filled paper mattress without a blanket (the Finnish military did not distribute any). Added to the above arrangement was the so-called *kusen herätys* (urination reveille"). At an early morning hour the instructor, sometimes full of booze at this time, stood at one end of the long barracks, blowing a whistle and yelling *"Kusen herätys!"* You would line up in two neat rows next to the bunks, barefoot and in your underwear. "Right turn. Forward march to the latrine."

The latrine was just a right-angle extension at one end of the barracks. The urinal was a long tin gutter against one of the walls. We lined up shoulder-to-shoulder and faced it. The floor under our bare feet was covered with thick yellow ice, formed from spilled urine over the long winter month. One had to wait until permission was given to urinate. Soon, however, another signal came with the command *"pysähtyä!* (halt!), after which not a single drop of urine was allowed to fall. Then again "left turn…forward march!" and back to bed. If you were not quite finished by the second signal, you were free to return and finish your business.

As your third evening option, you might not go to bed after supper but would instead go though so-called "orientation skiing". In addition to your usual compasses, you and your partner were given a flashlight and a map with a few crosses penciled in. You had to find these spots in the wilderness, as designated with a red flag. All you had to do was find the designated spots, pick up the flags, and bring them with you when you returned, as confirmation that you really made the trip and could read a map and find your way with a compass. Orientation skiing was usually carried out at night when there was a full moon. You can't play Blindmans' Bluff when you're on skis. Even with a full moon, the downhill landscape might fool you and you might get hurt. That was the reason we were not sent out alone., in case one person broke his leg or neck, God forbid, your partner would ski back to report it. If alone, you would likely freeze to death because they would not come looking for you until noon the next day. Once my partner and I got lost on a frozen lake and wandered outside the boundaries of the map. If that happened, then you were *really* lost. The compass alone wasn't accurate enough to help you find your isolated campsite. Besides, you honestly did not know where you were. We were lucky enough to stumble on an isolated farmhouse. We slept the rest of the night there and the farmer was kind enough to give us a good breakfast and take us back to camp with his horse and sleigh. Nobody had been worried at the camp. Two men wouldn't break their legs at the same time, and to be on the safe side we were told to ski in single file, not side-by-side.

Our weekend leave to the city was canceled for the following Saturday, but we were not downgraded for our mischief since the instructors admitted that the cross was made almost at the edge of the map.. They hadn't given us enough room to get our bearings.

To tell the truth, there was no "city", only a village called Taaveti with one cafeteria where you could order a glass of artificially-sweetened cranberry juice called *mehu* and the only girl you might see was the waitress. When I said "a trip" to Taaveti, do not think for a moment that there was bus service to take you there and back. No sir. You had to ski the miles yourself. You and your skis were inseparable in winter. Wherever you went, they took you there. You could live without a girlfriend, but not without a pair of skis.

On those Fridays, when there was no full moon and it was cloudy and snowing, our platoon had a 15 km skiing exercise in the morning instead of orientation skiing at night. Friday expeditions started with a downhill trail we called "Suicide Hill". To one side was a barbed-wire fence, and about six feet to the other side, a pine forest. The slope was quite precipitous, making you speed downhill at least 20 miles per hour. One wrong move on your part, and you had to make a quick decision whether it would be the barbed wire or tree trunks you preferred to run into-a no-win situation indeed.

On one of those cloudy Fridays when there was a brisk wind singing in the trees and frozen snow-crystals stinging our faces, I decided to head into the trees to break at least one of my skis, hoping to escape the 15 kilometer ordeal. Then I would be sent back to the barracks to feed the ovens and wipe the floor.

I managed to break one of my skis in two places. You'd be mistaken if you thought this as simple as it sounds. First, your speed had to be just right-if you were too timid and planned your "big bang" too early without breaking one of your skis, you hadn't accomplished much. If you were too valiant, and the speed was sufficient not only to break the ski but also your neck, you had exceeded your intentions.

I was banged up, but didn't have any broken bones. What happened next wiped the smile from my face. Private Soomets followed me, with apparently the same idea. He hit just about the same time, and broke one of his skis too. The lieutenant arrived on the scene and made a quick decision; "Private Soomets, you give your remaining ski to Corporal Ojamaa and go back to the barrack, feed the ovens and wipe the floor. Corporal Ojamaa will use the leftover ski and come with us". I struggled the 15 kilometers with non-matching skis, one longer than the other, and could testify to the saying that "To win and lose at the same time is hard to bear." Was it Shakespeare or Byron?

When you join the Finnish Army, the first thing you do is buy yourself a sheath knife called a *puukko*. It was a "must" and everybody wore one. The sheath was of leather and made to hang from your belt, with a blade about six to eight inches long. It was manufactured from the very best steel and was sharp enough to shave your beard with. Brave men used it to settle an argument, and timid souls to clean their fingernails. It had many other uses, cutting bread, or fixing the bindings of your skis. When Finns got mad, you often heard someone threatened with a phrase that included the words *"puukko vatsaan* (knife in the belly)"*, but the threat wasn't usually carried out. I had a roommate (what I mean is, one of the 30 fellows I shared the barracks with) whose name was Vollard Koppel. He used his *puukko* all the time to clean his fingernails, even while he played chess. But, he was too refined to set up the chessboard, claiming that in private life he had a butler to do it. We believed such a luxury existed only in storybooks, never in real life, and we were willing to set up his chessboard since he preferred to play the game by himself.

Not even the Finnish winter lasts forever. First, the high-reaching rocks change their color from the gray-white of frost to different shades of brown. Then, small trickles of water become streams, rushing down the hills and gushing into surrounding lakes like fingers without end. Suicide Hill became a waterfall and our skis, just resting against the barrack walls or bleaching in the melting snowbanks, became useless memories of the past winter. We had learned all the military commands and could swear fluently in Finnish. We could orient the maps in a flash, and take apart the gun locks blindfolded. There was nothing left to instruct us in, and we were shipped back to our companies to teach squads of new recruits. We used the Finnish commands, but swore at them in Estonian, as they were just too "green" to understand the best curse words in Finnish.

Most of the company drill was not in squads but in platoons (one platoon had four squads). I marched along in a platoon as before, and the Finnish drill sergeants were in command. The old caterpillar march, where the sergeant is the only one with the brain, was endless and repetitious and dull. I started to feel worn out and feverish. Could one have battle fatigue without a battle?

When the regiment physician made his weekly call I reported myself sick with fever and weakness. The symptoms were so vague I thought he might laugh. The nurse checked my temperature, which was just a fraction above 99° F. The doctor had gray hair and a serious face. He listened to my lungs and looked at my throat, then took his seat behind the desk and looked out the window.

My back hunched, I stared at the floor boards, straight and slender, running with dark streaks between them toward the physician and his desk. I did not say anything, afraid to be labeled a malingerer. There was no sound, only the ticking of the clock at the table. The long slender hand, clicking away the seconds in short jerks, almost made a full circle before the doctor spoke up, "I know what you need... You need a few days of rest."

I stood up and smiled.

His face remained serious but displayed sympathy, an unusual trait in a military physician, "I will give you a certificate asking that you be freed of all duties for one week."

He handed me his hand-written note, and asked me to take it to the company office.

Spring had arrived and I had the whole week to do as I pleased. It seemed like an eternity. I needed to be alone and left alone, and this piece of paper in my hand promised to give me that chance to heal myself, to recharge my inner resources and make myself a new man.

The staff sergeant in the office seemed confused after reading the note. It was most unusual for the doctor to give a week off to someone who was not bedridden. He turned the note over to see if there was any additional explanation, but the other side was all blank. Then he looked at me with a puzzled face and asked: "How do you feel?"

"All right now."

"Do you intend to stay in bed?"

"No."

"What will you do?"

"I don't know."

He shook his head, and placed the certificate on the table in front of him: "I will keep your platoon sergeant informed".

When reveille sounded the next morning and the drill sergeant walked through the barracks yelling "ärätüs!(get up!), everybody shot out of their bunks, rushing to retrieve their garments from the oven strings. Mine were hanging neatly from the nail at the head of my bunk, all dry. I had missed the previous afternoon's rain shower.

The pillowcase of corrugated paper and the straw stuffing had a strong odor of mildew, bitter and sour. I rolled over onto my back to escape the smell and pulled my military overcoat up to my neck, exposing my bare feet. The rest of the platoon had departed by the time the sergeant walked through the barracks once more. He squinted in my direction, but did not speak. With both hands under my head, I wiggled my toes at him. Without my certificate I would have been eligible for 30 trips around the barracks for being late to the lineup, plus two weeks of latrine duty for the toe-wiggling.

The healing power of modern medicine was already working. This was only the first day of my "treatment", and I was strong enough to give "toe signs" to the sergeant.

I had to get up to claim my breakfast, since the mess hall would close at nine. I was handed a bowl of oatmeal porridge and four slabs of knacke-bread with a small sliver of butter. The coffee, called *"korvike"* was made from burned ground oats and acorns and served black with two lumps of sugar.

The officers shared the mess hall with enlisted men. But they had their own table, set closest to the kitchen and separated from us by empty floor space. Their food was not rationed and even their sugar bowls were still on the table when I arrived for my late breakfast.

Seeing the leftover sugar cubes reminded me of an incident at the beginning of our training. The officers had finished their breakfast when our platoon, leaving the dining area, passed the officers' table. Soon thereafter, a few sugar cubes were found missing from their sugar bowls. The entire platoon was lined up for investigation.

"Whoever has stolen the sugar cubes step forward!"

Nobody stepped forward.

But, the crime had been committed, and deserved punishment. If the criminal could not be found, the entire platoon was guilty and had to be punished. We had to stand at attention one minute and then crawl in the snow the next, then stand up again, then crawl again. New inquiries did not produce the confession, and the punishment had to be continued.

We were wet from the melting snow inside our coat sleeves and pants and even inside our collars. After hours of torment, we could barely stand from exhaustion. They couldn't extract a confession from us. I believe we were innocent of the "crime" we had been accused of.

Southeastern Finland, the area called Karelja that was now free from Russian occupation, is unsurpassed in its natural beauty. Now it was there for me to explore, alone. I wandered far out into the wild, climbed the highest rocky hill, and sat at the summit overlooking the horizon. The air was clear, without a trace of haze. There was no sign of human habitation, not even a trail of smoke as far as the eye could see, nothing but wooded hills intermingled with innumerable lakes. Weeping willows and birch trees on the shorelines, leaned over the still water, their branches drooping. The wind caused occasional ripples, which ran like shoals of minnows, breaking the silent surface in patches. Most of the periphery of the water, however, remained undisturbed in its blueness. Only the clouds with their running silhouettes were like changing shadows in one's mood.

When I felt tired from climbing, I leaned against a white tree trunk at the summit to rest. This tiredness is a sweet feeling one experiences while relaxing after physical labor, contrary to psychic weariness, which stays with you even in leisure.

When I was hungry, I made a small fire on a shallow of the rock, used my *puukko* to cut squares from my hardened bread, moistened it with the sugar cubes sweetened water from my canteen, and then toasted it over the open flames. This made them crisp on the surface and soft in the center, with a sweet flavor. After my meal I slept on the ground, which this high up was covered with dried moss.

The world was still at war, and men were dying in their youth, but here, all was tranquil-the birds nesting in the trees, the black winged buzzards circling motionless, carried up and down by the air currents.

I had traveled to the north-east, where the continuous rocky ledges had divided the lakes so that I could wander unhindered in the same direction, making return orientation easy with my compass. In case I missed the camp I would eventually reach the east-west highway and from there find the road to camp. The winter orientation ski trips had taught me to memorize land-marks without effort.

I could see from my observation post at the top of the cliff that the bright sun was still up in the sky, but shadows were creeping into the valleys below, darkening the narrow passages of the lakes between the rocky hills. It was time to return to camp where I was still a free man for a few more days. Close to home, but still halfway up the hill, I saw our platoon down below on a yellow road returning to the camp and singing:

> Dear maiden of my memories-
> How I remember your lovely charm.
> I shall never forsake you,
> Even in my dying days...

Then the days of marching near Taaveti were long past.

The "medicine" the doctor prescribed had worked wonders. It had cured me of my melancholy and replaced it with serenity and peace.

It was late summer now. We had been holding defensive positions in Vuokse and Luireniemel, and so far had suffered only light causalities from Russian artillery fire. Their aim left something to be desired, since most of the shells flew over our heads with a whining sound or exploded on the rocks in front of us. So far I had not seen a single Russian. The shooting I did was at the vultures that circled over the no-mansland. The real shooting was done by the first battalion, which had been at the front all winter and had suffered greater losses. I was in the second, held back for further training, and employed at the front when the war was already winding down. My arrival on the enchanted Friday with the quadruple "13" had worked wonders for me, I was hoping its charms would continue.

The Russians entertained us with propaganda broadcasts over their loud-speakers. They proclaimed the "unsurpassed freedom and prosperity" of their homeland. All this would be waiting for us if we would just walk across the strip of no-mans-land, waving a white handkerchief tied on a stick.

"Why fight and die for the fat-cats in Helsinki. Come and enjoy the easy life in the land of socialism!"

Of course the broadcast was in Finnish. If they had known that they were facing the Estonian JR200, they probably wouldn't have wasted their breath. Then they played Red Army marching songs for a while, followed by the announcement: "Five minutes smoking break, to be followed by two hours of artillery fire."

They kept their promise. Their shells exploded around us. I paid no attention as I was reading a book I found in an abandoned house. I remember crouching in my foxhole with the sun in my face as I read, Tämä haluta jotakin, ehka kotia mika, hänelle ei ole koskaan ollut." ("It made him yearn for something, perhaps for a home he had never known.")

I cannot remember how many times I've quoted this line to myself, memorized in Finnish. Neither can I tell you the title or the author of the book, since the front pages were missing.

Finland started peace negotiations with Russia in the summer of 1944, and the Estonian Regiment JR200 had become, in fact, a stumbling-block in the negotiations. The Russians requested extradition of our regiment, claiming us as citizens of the Soviet Union and thus under their jurisdiction. The Russian penal code classified us as traitors, calling for the punishment known as "25 + 5", meaning 25 years in a Siberian prison camp plus 5 years in exile. Finland could not very well go along with this request for obvious reasons. The only solution was to get our regiment off Finnish soil as soon as possible and then there would be no one to extradite. Or would there?

A rapid turn of events followed.

On August 12, 1944 we were pulled back from the front and given a train ride to Hanko, near Helsinki.

On August 16, Marshal Mannerheim signed a *Liquidation order* for the Estonian Regiment JR200.

On August 18, we held a parade in Hanko. Marshal Mannerheim praised us for meritorious service and gave out medals for bravery. I was promoted to sergeant.

On August 19, we were shipped out of Finland.

We were given a choice, go back to Estonia or emigrate to Sweden. Transportation was provided.

One thousand seven hundred fifty-two of us volunteered to return to Estonia and were aboard the transport ship *Vaterland*[14], hoping to prevent the Russian reoccupation. I was one of these.

Seven hundred fifty-nine volunteers were aboard another ship, headed to Sweden, where you could have your own bed.

To rest your head on a real pillow at night.

To sleep between white bed sheets, covered with a blanket.

To live in a city with colored lights.

To hold the hand of a girl instead of a cold rifle-butt.

And most of all, not to kill or be killed.

One hundred twenty-five of us did not have to choose, they had made the heroes' list and were buried in Finnish soil.

Today, over a half of a century later, I ask myself: why?

Why did I choose the fateful ship to take me back to the war?

Was it *Heimweh*[15]?

It was an emotional decision. When emotions become part of the equation, then reality is out, and only hope rules your thinking-hope wearing a fool's crown.

The odds of fulfilling our dream were less than a million to one. The

151

odds of losing our lives were real.

The only answer to the question I can come up with is: I knew I would not find inner peace in Sweden. It wasn't just my home I missed, it was my homeland, my country. We had suffered together and I could not desert her now. Hope was on my side.

But hope had never won a war.

Alas, some of the details of the peace agreement were not disclosed, thus jeopardizing the lives of the Estonians who had decided to stay in Finland. We learned later that after the peace agreement was signed, any Estonian remaining in Finland was in real danger of deportation to the Russian authorities. Only two ex-GIs had received Finnish citizenship and were safe. Three men had Finnish wives, and two of them were deported.

Some previous members of our regiment had enrolled in universities to continue their studies, and there were still wounded members of our regiment in Finnish hospitals. All of these were in danger of deportation.

Of course, the 125 men from our regiment who had fallen in battle on Finnish soil had nothing to worry about. The Russians were not interested in them. From the thirty men reported as "missing in action", twenty-three were already Russian POWs and serving their time in Siberia.

The exact number of Estonians deported to Russia is not known. The two-hundred Estonian soldiers who served in the Finnish military some time or other, and who did not return to Estonia or leave for Sweden, were listed as "unknown".

After the peace agreement a small article appeared in the back pages of the *Suomen Sanomalehti* the main newspaper in Finland) saying that Estonians in Finland were now *personae non grata.* At least a dozen Estonians who had taken up their residency in Finland saw the message and were able to flee to Sweden before they were arrested.

The saddest point in this whole affair was the fate of some two dozen Estonians that we know of. They had served in the Finnish military and were among the 1752 who returned to Estonia to fight the Red Army on their home ground.

After the Estonian front collapsed, they were the lucky ones who beat all odds by evading the KGB and the Russian Coast Guard and made their way back to Finland.

Alas, this time they did not meet the friendly Finnish Coast Guard, the ones who had said "Welcome to Finland from the *veljen kansa*". This time they were arrested by Finnish authorities and handed over to the Russian KGB, who "welcomed" them with the "25+5" year penal code.

There were also a number of other Estonian fighters, who made their way across the Finnish Sea after Estonia was reoccupied. They all met the same fate.

How many of boatloads of young men were sunk by the Russian Coast Guard or arrested by the KGB during their escape attempts, is not known.

[14]Fatherland
[15]Homesickness

Chapter 16

Home, Sweet Home

It was a strange sight indeed.

Along a curving footpath, one could see men walking in single file in endless column. They were all young, wearing strange uniforms not seen in these parts before. They were not flashy uniforms, but rather drab. They certainly did not look like the Russians who had their long shirts hanging outside their pants with folded tails.

They did not carry weapons. Each had a canvas bag the size of a pillow-case thrown over one shoulder, hardly half full and obviously light in weight, held leisurely in place with the right or left hand. They walked freely, looking all around them, taking in the sights, ignoring the fact that there was not much to see but empty farm fields, some already plowed under, showing their black underside and smelling of wet soil. The fields of clover had been cut earlier and since regrown, the only greenery in an otherwise drab landscape, not counting the weeds. There were thistles and catchflies. The tall cornflowers with their small blossoms were bent across the footpath of the passing men, who stuck the blue flowers in their buttonholes.

They all appeared excited for some reason, like kids at the county fair. They waved with their free hand to nobody in particular and talked loud in short sentences. They laughed in an easy-going way, like best men at a wedding party.

I think you've already guessed who these men were. They were the 1,752 of us back home after crossing the Finnish Sea. The Finns had collected all our weapons and ammunition. Our rucksacks were replaced with canvas bags to hold a few personal belongings.

"Finnish boys," that's what they called us at home. "The Finnish boys are back." It was the only news worth cheering about.

"They must know something we don't. The tide might turn. The eastern part of Estonia under the Russians might be liberated yet. We still have hope… We've heard that a new government was formed in Tallinn, and has declared Estonia an independent state. The Russians must honor our independence. Why would the Finnish boys return unless they knew something we don't? There is still hope!"

"What hope?" asked the realist. "Finland signed the peace treaty and no longer has any need for what you call the 'Finnish boys'. This also has freed the heavily-armed divisions from the Finnish sector, thereby

155

more than doubling their forces against us. The Russians' bellies are full of American corned beef, and they're driving around in American jeeps. Who is helping us? Nobody. A thousand or so "Finnish boys" with canvas bags across their shoulders-what can they do? Nothing, except get killed. They would be as effective against the armored divisions of Russians as a beaver trying to build a dam on Jägala Falls."

"How about the Germans? They freed us once and..."

"Don't be ridiculous. The Germans are fighting against the entire world and losing. Mark my words: they will be pulling out sooner rather than later."

"Do you mean we are quite alone, crushed between superpowers who have only their own interest in mind!?"

"Do you want me to answer that question?"

"No, I was just thinking loud..."

Early fall was in the air.

Under the thin clouds, the hazy sun did not leave any shadows as we continued our leisurely march toward the Hiiu railroad station.

All had been planned in advance by the Germans, who were still the rulers of the land.

They made the ship said some fifteen miles past Tallinn to a small harbor in Paldiski. An arrival at the capital city would cause too much attention and an outburst of national spirit they wished to suppress.

They kept us from the public roads, making us march out of sight, along a narrow path to the nearest half-stop railroad station.

They planned to hide us from our people in our own country. They only wanted our bodies to be added to the "heroes list."

But sometimes a fly can end up in the soup despite careful planning. Suddenly we faced a sight that puzzles me even today.

In the middle of the farm fields and next to our footpath we saw a small group of women, guarded by the German military. They were loading bricks from a pile to a waiting truck.

Close to me was a lady in her early forties with well coiffure hair, wearing a mid-length Persian lamb coat and fine textured leather gloves. She was busy wrapping up one of the bricks in a piece of wrinkled newspaper. When finished, she turned her back toward me to take the neatly wrapped brick to the waiting truck.

"Hey!" I shouted. "What's going on here?"

Before the guard could step between us, the woman turned around, still holding the brick. We were but three steps apart. When I looked at her I saw hopelessness and despair.

The guards rushed in, holding their rifles. They appeared frightened, seeing an endless column of soldiers in strange uniforms-but soldiers who were unarmed.

"Stand back. Stand back. We are guarding prisoners. Do not interfere!"

The confrontation was broken up grudgingly when our own officers separated us from the women and the German guards and ordered the march to continue. I am sure we would have freed the women if we had had our weapons. They did not look like criminals to us. Besides, civilian prisoners should be guarded by Estonian prison guards. They were, most likely, not communist spies.

I continued to walk without looking right or left. I could not get over the look in that woman's eyes.

Much later I wondered, were the women Jewish?

My resentment had been piling up unnoticed. I was just a naïve country boy ,and in my innocence I believed the German liberation of us was a compassionate act of kindness. The great western powers had done nothing to free us from Russian despotism. To the contrary, they were bosom buddies with Stalin the Terrible. Small nations, such as the Baltic States, did not matter to them. They could trade us or give us to the Russian Bear as presents and watch with indifference as he devoured our lives and liberty.

There was no justice. I had been fighting the Russians, believing the Big Brothers were with me all the way. The Finns got rid of us, and it would not be long before the Germans deserted us. They had been taking advantage of our feelings of revenge, which they had used for their own aims. I had done my share of fighting the "Red Tide" and suddenly I felt, no more. I was done with it. I did not want to be taken advantage of any more. Obviously, I could not expect a magic carpet to lift me out of the messy situation I was in. I did not plan to sit down in sorrow, holding my head between my knees but promised myself to make the best of every day whatever it might bring, and do whatever it took to stay off the "heroes list", to do only what was best for Arved Ojamaa.

I had been plain lucky for a long time already, I did not want to stretch it past the breaking point!

After a short railroad trip, we were stationed in Kehra, 30 miles east of Tallinn. Here, we were to register as an Estonian unit in the German military and receive identification papers, German uniforms, and supplies, including weapons.

While signing over to the German military, someone asked, "Do we have an alternative choice?"

"Most certainly," was the attending officer's answer.

"You will be given a spade instead of a rifle to dig ditches at the front."

The questioner must have been a lawyer in the old Estonian Republic, "Do we have to sign anything to choose that service?"

"No. That is not a voluntary organization. You will be under guard."

The questioner signed his name, volunteering for military service.

Outdoors in the sun there was a long line of people waiting to sign the document. I do not believe anyone refused. In fact, that was the reason we had returned, to fight the invaders and not to serve as ditch-diggers under enemy fire. I didn't hesitate to sign. Signing improved my chances for survival. When I reached the head of the line, I had only a moment to glance at the headline of the document, which contained the words "voluntary" and "Waffen-SS." The only thing I knew about the Waffen-SS was that those were elite fighting units with better weapons and supplies than I had known at the *Ostfront,* better than the regular *Wehrmacht.*

I tried to read the document after I finished signing, but was quickly pushed aside to speed up the proceedings for the rest.

Long lines were forming in the supply warehouse, where we were to give up our Finnish uniforms. Old German *Gefreiters* (corporals) glanced at you for a second or two, and then brought out a new uniform they decided would fit you. And then off you went.

When my turn came, I faced an old soldier with Hitler's whiskers. Most of the young men lined up behind me spoke only a few words of German.

"Greetings from Finland."

I started friendly conversation: "Do you care to try a package of Finnish cigarettes?"

I placed the package on the counter.

I guess he was tired of listening to the blabber in a foreign tongue all day, or to all that "pidgin German." Piling up foreign uniforms behind the counter and handing out brand-new German ones could become boring.

He gave me a half smile, "It might be good for a change," he said, putting the cigarettes in his pocket. "What can I do for you?"

I am attached to this old rag I wore fighting the Russians up north," I said, pointing to my Finnish uniform on the counter. "Maybe you can arrange…"

He did not toss my old outfit to the top of the pile, but left it on the counter.

What size do you take?"

"Oh, 40 short."

He laughed again, showing his gold tooth while the whiskers on his upper lip widened an inch. "Well, forget about the numbers. We have been recently promoted from 'haberdasher' to 'gentleman's wear'. You are about my size, and I know what you need." He placed the new uniform on the top of my Finnish one and shouted, "Next!"

I returned to my room with the bundle under my arm. The new uniform jacket was a good fit. It was superior to the Finnish shirt in material and in appearance. The jacket was a little too wide. There were a couple of Estonian tailors doing alterations for the commissioned officers, but a package of Finnish cigarettes came to the rescue. They not only took in my waistline but padded the shoulders and added the required silver band to signify my rank. They also cleaned and pressed my Finnish uniform, which I wore under the German one. Why not be dressed up if it makes you feel better, war or no war!

"How the hell were you able to keep your Finnish uniform?" I was asked. If I was in the right mood, I became philosophical, "Look. The soldier's life has many sharp bends and turns. If you have mastered the art of straightening them out, you would already know how, and would not be asking that simple question."

Next I had to register the Finnish rank and service I was in. When my turn came to face the officer's desk, I produced my Finnish military document, which gave my rank as sergeant. The officer was familiar with that term, "Ah, *Unteroffizier.*" What service were you in?"

I had my answer ready: "I was a medic in the second battalion JR200."

Of course I was a trained infantry sergeant, but it was not specified on my document, and the officer would not have understood Finnish anyway. Everybody knows that infantry chases the enemy or the other way around. The Germans were losing. That meant I would be doing a lot of running. My father had become an expert shoemaker on false pretenses and survived. It's easier to pretend you are a medic than try to convince people you are a shoemaker.

"Sehr gut," said the officer. "We mark you down as *Unteroffizier* and *Krankenwerter.*[16]"

I had to admit it was easier to maneuver in the German military establishment than it was in the Finnish.

When the supplying was completed, the first battalion departed for the front and was immediately engaged in fierce battle with the Russians, with heavy losses on both sides. My classmate William Märks fell in the very first battle. The second battalion, my battalion, was left behind in Kehra. There was no feeling of guilt on my part staying in Kehra and out of the action was fine with me. I had left Estonia with quadruple "13s" on New Year's Eve-how can one be in the First Battalion with lucky numbers like those!

I have already talked about how I lost any teenage-idealistic ideas of throwing away the German or Finnish uniform for the other. I did not feel myself a *"Romantischer Kerl"* any more, as I was when I was a flower-boy for the night nurses. Oh sure, I did not refuse the company of ladies-they could brighten any day in my life, but I did not fall in love with every female I spoke to. Oh yes, speaking of women, there was a 17-year-old girl in Kehra I was very fond of.

There is something mysterious about a woman at 17. She is at an unusual stage between being a mature woman and a child. One moment she can be one, in the next moment the other; and at times she can be both at the same time. She might start her sentence as a child and end it as a mature woman, or the other way around. The look in her eyes can switch back and forth in a fraction of a second, like a child watching fireworks and a woman admiring Apollo.

I've gotten lost again in my recollections. That statement about women goes back over 50 years. It does not apply any more. Not to 17-year-olds!

I started to wear my Finnish uniform openly, and nobody seemed to care. As I had to wear one, I preferred the Finnish over the German. It seemed to give me more of the identity I was looking for.

I had a distant aunt in Tallinn, just four train-stops west from Kehra. I heard that 48-hour leaves were given to men who had homes nearby. Again a German officer was in charge of distributing leaves. It made it so much easier for me to tell him a fictitious story. He would believe me outright, while the Estonian officers would find from my files that I was from the countryside.

To make my application more challenging, I decided to play it cool and appear in his office in Finnish uniform.

By now I knew my way around. I clicked my heels and gave a proper military salute, asking for permission to present my case. He just waved his hand.

"*Herr Major*, I have my parents living in Tallinn and have not seen them for more than a year because I was fighting the Russians in the Finnish armed forces. With your kind permission I would like to request a 48-hour leave of absence to Tallinn."

Then I saluted again and stood at attention. He pushed his chair back from the desk: "Haven't you received your proper uniform yet?"

"No, *Herr Major*." I continued to stand at attention.

I knew the proper code of conduct when one appears in front of an officer. The war was going badly, and enlisted men were less formal. He was an old reserve officer, had probably not seen a day in battle since the First World War. The younger men with their battle decorations did not give him much respect. Not like in the old days. As far as I was concerned, some of my Finnish counterparts were country hicks-they most likely presented themselves like "*tikku paskaan,*" but still managed to obtain their leaves.

I noticed that my presentation had made a favorable impression.

"Oh! At ease, at ease." He had noticed that I was still standing at attention, then wondered, "That's odd. I thought supplying of new uniforms had been completed."

That did not require any response on my part. I was now standing at ease and waiting for his decision.

"Well, young man, I believe you deserve to see your family again. I'll have my secretary type up the permit for you because of your Finnish uniform. You can pick it up this afternoon. It will be for 48 hours, starting at six this evening."

"Thank you, *Herr Major*."

I saluted again. (No *Heil Hitler* stuff.) He responded by lifting his right hand just a few inches above his desktop.

When picking up my permit later on, I read, "This is to certify that Sergeant Arved Ojamaa, wearing the Finnish Military uniform, is permitted..." A military seal with swastika and a signature were at the bottom of the right corner.

161

Well, with my uniform I would be "The toast of the Town." (The "Finnish boys" in their uniform will be a rare sight in any part of our country.)

Expectation and disappointment are twin sisters, and luck is their room-mate. That much I learned during my 48-hour pass to Tallinn.

Upon my arrival, the capital city was already in turmoil. According to rumors, Russian tanks had broken through the defending forces at Tartu. No true front existed any more, only occasional scrimmages. The Russians had practically an open road to Tallinn and might arrive in any day. The German forces were pulling out altogether.

My distant aunt, who lived alone, was excited about my unexpected visit. Her only daughter, Margot, had already fled to Finland and now lived in Sweden.

I slept in her study on the couch with bookcases and curtains and carpets. It appeared luxurious to one who had been sleeping on straw-covered bunk beds for ages. The pillowcase had the faint aroma of white clover, a summer sun in the country, and the perfume of a depart-ed young woman. Or perhaps it was just my imagination, my yearning for the serenity of the past, when there was peace.

I spent a restless night with haunting dreams of attempted escapes. When awake, I knew there was nowhere one could flee. North was the Finnish Sea and west the Baltic, while east and south was the Red Ar-my. People with money, influence, and connections might find a seat in a boat to take them where there was peace. I did not have any of these entitlements, and my ungodly dreams kept recurring.

The next morning was sunny and altogether peaceful.

The dreams and fears of the previous night seemed less threatening as we sat at the breakfast table in my aunt's small kitchen. She showed me a slip from the railroad station, where a sack of potatoes was wait-ing for pickup, my parents had sent her a supplement to wartime ra-tions.

Because the station was only a few blocks away, I volunteered to carry the sack on my back to her apartment. I left my rucksack on her kitchen floor as there seemed to be no reason to take it with me for the short errand.

The station was like a zoo.

People were milling about excitedly or rushing toward the waiting train. The engine was already bellowing smoke and puffing steam-getting ready to depart. Porters were hurrying with their carts, carrying trunks and suitcases that were still to be loaded on the already over-crowded wagons.

I got hold of a man in a railroad uniform. "What's all the big rush about, and where is the train heading to?"

He stopped for a moment since I was holding onto his sleeve, "It is heading south to Haapsalu. Whether the Russian tanks have already blocked the road is yet to be seen. This is the very last train leaving for anywhere for a while."

Forget the potatoes. Forget the rucksack and all my personal belongings. The wheels of the train were already in motion when I jumped onto the nearest railroad car. The very last thing I saw was a sweaty porter with his cart loaded with suitcases, standing at the platform while someone was shouting through the train window: "Forget about the suitcases!" followed by the final instruction, "You keep them!"

Someone next to me claimed they saw the tanks in the northern part of Tallinn that morning. This explained the chaos: the Russian tanks were coming at the same time as the last train was leaving the city.

God bless the potatoes my parents had sent to Maria. Without them I would have still been sitting at her breakfast table, sipping tea, missing the very last train out of Tallinn, which was headed south towards the Baltic Sea.

I was traveling light, that's for sure.

I had my Finnish uniform on, the *puukko,* my revolver in a leather holder hanging from my belt, and my *Urlaub* certificate in my breast pocket. This would come in handy for identification purposes if I came in contact with retreating German units. I tore apart my newly issued Waffen-SS document, ripped it into little pieces and fed them through the open window.

The train was full of people fleeing their homes: women with children, young men in German uniforms, older men in their 60's, some with their wives. The monotonous clicking of the wheels on the iron tracks gave everyone some degree of hope and security which might be shattered at the first tank-blocked rail-crossing.

The noon sky was almost colorless in the autumn sun.

Melancholy shadows fled through the train windows and across the faces of the passengers with their vacant expressions. After the woods came the meadows, where the sun caught up with us over the forlorn landscape.

I leaned out the hallway window, and looked at the small farms, old buildings with thatched-roofs, and few rolling hills with clumps of stunted birch trees, their leaves scattered on the nearby plowed field. Unpicked potatoes with their green tops ran in neat rows over the hillsides. Magpies were squatting on nearby fence posts. I could see no farm animals or human beings anywhere. It was as if a pestilence had devastated the land.

"What do you think of it?"

A soldier with scarred face was standing next to me. His uniform was dirty, he was unshaven, and he smelled of sweat. He was well armed with an automatic weapon and extra cassettes hanging from his belt. This man was not ready to give up, come what may.

"It looks like you have seen some action," I said.

"Action is my middle name, and I'm still around… One of the lucky ones. But the noose around our neck is getting tighter." He then added as an afterthought, "They're like locusts over our land and there's no chance to kill them all. My only comfort is knowing that they will not catch me alive. A few of them will kiss the dust before my number comes up."

Then he stuck his face with his stubby beard through the open window and after a moment of silence, wiped his eyes with the back of his hand. The draft from the rushing train must have made his eyes water.

He gave a short laugh into the wind and faced me again. "Sure, I would like to get out alive. It is more for my pride than anything else, knowing that the devils did not get me after all."

It was encouraging to meet a fellow who knew his worth. An idea flashed through my mind when I introduced myself.

"My name is Thomas," he replied. "But you can call me Tom."

We shook hands.

"You asked me first what I think. You want to hear my plan of action?"

"Shoot," was his response.

"Our common goal is to escape from the Russians. The way I see the lie of the land and the best way to keep our sap flowing is that we have to bunch up with a few of the best fighters on this train. We hike to the coast for search of a boat to take us to Sweden. If the Russians get in our way, we have to shoot our way out. We need men with guts who have light automatic weapons, good sense of humor with a fatalistic attitude. No complainers or maniacs. No kids who have just been drafted and might wet their pants when the going gets tough. We do not need a crowd, no more than six, counting us."

"That sounds like my way of thinking, alert," added Tom with enthusiasm in his voice. "I saw a man in Finnish uniform looking out the window and smiling to himself-worried about nothing. You must know that there's a greater than ten-to-one chance that the Russians will get you first before you find your boat."

"Well, that is the chance we have to take," I said. "We both have faced greater odds than that and made out all right. We'll make it again this time and will save your pride. There is another point I'd like to make. We are not fighting anybody unless challenged. We'll try to keep to ourselves and away from civilians. When it comes to shooting, my greatest fear is that innocent bystanders might get hurt. The sooner we get off this train the better. Let's go and find a few guys who feel and think the same. You take the front of the train and I'll take the tail end. We meet here in twenty minutes, no later. In half an hour we might reach the city, and we have to 'fly the coop' before that."

The hallways of the train were crowded: I had to step over suitcases and the old pops sitting on the floor. I had to push aside women and children, excusing myself repeatedly.

The very first candidate was a tall man in uniform, leaning against the wall. But, by the time I was closing in on him, he had pulled out a clean handkerchief to wipe his face.

Sorry! Wrong guy. A man with a white hanky in his pocket in times like this would be of no use to us. Perhaps he was saving it for surrendering.

In the next passenger car I immediately recognized two good prospects. One of them carried a light machine gun, and another had a German rifle. They appeared to be ruthless characters, talking loud, with their hands and elbows flying. There was even free standing room next to them, as civilians felt it safer not to rub shoulders with their kind. To me they seemed the right kind. I knew I could pick out a good fighter like some people could pick a winning horse.

I knew how to approach them.

It would be wrong to use the indirect method, working my way close and acting like I was minding my own business, leaning against the wall and cleaning my fingernails with the *puukko*. They would consider that an imposition, and any further attempt to communicate would be difficult.

How about a gentleman's approach, such as, "excuse me gentlemen for the intrusion, but I could not help but overhear..." They would take me for a clown.

I walked up to them and introduced myself:

"*Aliupseeri* Ojamaa, Estonian Regiment 200, Finnish Army. And an ex ski-trooper from the Ost-Front, Rebase Company."

My preliminary wiped off their perky smiles. One responded with, "We had the Finnish boys fighting with us in Pupastvere near Tartu. They made the Russians skip their beach-head on this side of the Erna River, and run. Hellish fighters. By the way, my name is Rik and he is Ants. What do you have in mind?"

I quickly explained my plan for forming a group of five or six men, all tough guys, well-armed and with battle experience. "We vacate the train after Ridala station to avoid the city. The train does not stop until Haapsalu, but we make it stop for us at the time and place we choose to bail out. It would be too dangerous to jump from the moving train with our weapons. Then we will hike to the Baltic Sea coast in search of a boat to take us to Sweden. If we find one, we have the weapons and we decide who will come with us and who won't. If the Russians get us first and there is no way to escape-none of us will surrender. We make them pay dearly before they finish us. You are welcome to join us. If the answer is no or if you want to think about it, I've wasted my time."

They looked at each other for a moment and I believe it was Ants who spoke up. "Our plans coincide with yours. We will join you, for better or worse." They both laughed: "It sounds like a wedding ceremony!"

We shook hands and that sealed the deal.

Then we met up with Tom. He had two men with him. One appeared rather young, less than twenty, but he had a light machine fun with two bands of bullets crisscrossing his shoulders, like a Mexican freedom fighter. He seemed to attract too much attention with his "armory".

Noticing my hesitation, Tom said, "This young man has been wounded twice. He has guts and is a virtuoso with the weapon he carries."

I shook his hand, saying, "Welcome to the party."

The other companion seemed an easy-going guy. His name was

Senka and he carried a Russian automatic weapon (the type we used to call a *kone*), its carrying-belt thrown over his right shoulder with the barrel pointing to the floor. He had both hands in his pocket, and he was leaning unassumingly against the wall with his feet crossed-like he was at the street corner on a Saturday night, watching the girls go by. The weapon he carried was used exclusively in ski-patrols, an excellent tool for close combat. It was light, short and stubby, hardly visible when held under the arm. Its cassette, the size and shape of a round humbug box, held 40 bullets each. The gun could be quickly positioned for firing by shooting from the hip with a spraying motion.

The four newcomers were all privates and Tom was a corporal. I was happy with their ranks, as another sergeant would have caused distractions. I certainly did not intend to be in charge of this group or give any orders. The war was over for us and rank was meaningless. Our common goal, not to be caught by the Russians, made us a cohesive unit with a fatalistic attitude.

I saw a man in a railroad uniform not far from us. I excused myself and went to consult with him.

"Are you familiar with this route?"

He looked at my odd uniform and noticed my side-arm. "I have been riding this Tallinn-Haapsalu route for many years," he said. "What do you want to know?"

"I was told the next station is Ridala. Am I correct?"

"Yes. We should be there in five minutes. The train does not stop before Haapsalu, however, which would be another fifteen minutes."

What is the land like, say three or five minutes past Ridala?"

"Mostly woods, small farms with poor soil, tends to be swampy."

"How far would you say the sea is from that point?"

"Perhaps 15 kilometers. You should go southwest, if you want to stay away from Haapsalu. The closest fishing village would be either Mäeküla or Rannaküla."

"Now listen carefully. We are a group of well armed soldiers." The tone of my voice might have sounded like an order. "Go to the locomotive engineer and tell him to stop the train exactly three minutes past Ridala station for us to get off. That is all I ask. We cannot take any chances with injury by jumping off from a moving train with our heavy weapons. To pull the emergency brake would cause too much commotion. Let's synchronize our watches. It is now exactly two o'clock. Remember, three minutes past Ridala. If five minutes pass, we will come to see the engineer."

The conductor was full of good will, whether true or pretended: "I understand. You boys have done all you could for the country, and I'm sure the engineer will be happy to do his part to help you get safely off the train."

I thanked him, returned to our group, and informed them of the plan. There were no objections. They all seemed satisfied that someone had made the arrangements.

"That's what we wanted to tell you," said Tom. "What the hell would we be doing in Haapsilu anyhow with a trainload of people. If the Russian tanks are that far west, the first thing they'll do is take Haapsalu, the city with the railroad station and the harbor. Fishing villages would be the last on their list."

The train came to a full stop at the designated time.

There were woods on both sides of the railroad tracks. We, the six sanguine soldiers, were the only ones to get off.

Somebody waved at us through the window and moments later we were left alone, standing on the deserted tracks in the middle of nowhere.

We started our afternoon march along a farm road toward the southwest, hoping to reach the coastline before dark. We had not traveled far when we came upon an old farm house, set in the back of old oak trees. The thatched roof was covered with deep-green moss. The door stood open to the dark interior. The weeds had grown tall next to the footpath, which led to an open well with its bucket on a chain and resting on the edge of the wooden enclosure. Ants rolled up his sleeves and lowered the bucket to the well. The water was refreshingly cool as we took turns drinking from the bucket. Tom and Senka sat on the porch steps, where the creeping buttercups grew high and their bitter-sweet smell hung in the windless air.

An old woman appeared from the dark interior. She had her babushka pulled down to her eyes and was holding her hands under an apron of undetermined color. She just stood there gazing into the afternoon sun, without saying a word or even paying any attention to us.

"Good afternoon, mother."

She pulled her babushka off from her eyes and gave us a toothless smile, "So you are not the Russians?"

"No, mother, we are not the Russians."

"You must be hungry then?"

Senka laughed: "How could you guess!"

She gave us an open-mouthed smile, showing her gums, pulled her hands from under the apron and crossed them below her breast, "Young men are always hungry. I do not have much to offer, just milk and freshly baked bread. No butter. It is bliss to feed you, young men, before them Russians come and take it all."

She disappeared into the dark interior bringing out tin mugs, their enamel crumbled in places.

It is better on the porch. The flies are fierce in the kitchen. They would not let you be."

Everybody dipped their mugs into the bucket of milk she had brought out, and ate fresh country bread from a huge loaf.

She continued to watch us with happiness in her furrowed face, handing out slices of bread she was cutting.

We questioned her, "How far is it to the nearest fishing village at the coast?"

"Maybe some twelve kilometers to Mäeküla as the crow flies." Then she added, "You better eat all you can, they ain't friendly toward strangers there!"

She brought out another loaf of bread and watched us devour it with obvious delight.

"Our young folks left a few days ago, afraid of the Russians. I decided to stay. What can they do to an old woman like me. They will let me die in my own home when the time comes." Then she added, "It sure tickles me pink to feed you, boys. Likely the last happy bit in my life."

––––––––––

We continued our march along the dirt road which was lined on both sides by mounds of field-stones cleared from fields over the generations. Occasional farmhouses were scattered near and far, but no tenants or farm animals were anywhere in sight. Even the barking dogs were missing.

The wind had disappeared and ribbon-like clouds were shrouding the low-lying sun. The stillness, with no living soul anywhere, gave us a premonition of plague:

The Red Plague shall occupy our land.

Country folks had gathered their livestock into their barns and hidden themselves in their homes-hoping to have the strength to endure the future.

The six of us would have no future in the "Red Dawn". The remote possibility of escape was our only option.

"Step up. Step up!" I tried to hurry them as early dusk was already in the air.

Rik was already sweating, carrying his light machine-gun, which was light only in name. "It's easy for you to say," he grumbled. "Look at my load!"

Sure, he had to carry a load, but then look at the youngest in our bunch. He was walking tall under a similar load. I learned later that his name was Leonard, but we called him Leo. So far I had not heard him say a word. Good fighters are not big talkers!

Next we came to a group of houses, where our trail ended. We faced a paved road with yellow sandy surface. A group of starlings were resting in long rows on the telephone wires. It must have been the road to the fishing village the old woman talked about. Well-grown alder and bird-cherry bushes lined the path, throwing deepening shadows on us as we walked briskly west towards the sea.

Stabbing twinges that I felt inside my boots with each step signaled new blisters, friends from the not-too-distant past. One doesn't speak of them as you do not speak of lice. If you don't have them, fine. If you do, so what? It's your private business and nothing to talk about. They were everyday events, like hunger and fatigue, little miseries you had to learn to overlook or they'd get the best of you. If they did, you'd lose the will to fight. Nobody would care if you started carrying a white hanky in your pocket and believed that 25 years in Siberia would consist of picking wildflowers. We chose our men with care. They might have blisters and lice, and they were hungry and tired, but they were willing to take it as a joke. When Rik said "It is easy for you to say, look at my load," it was a put-on and not a gripe. He was grinning when he said it, to lift his own spirit and the others'. We all looked at his red and sweaty face and laughed, "Hey, you do not need a shower tonight, you are already having one."

And he answered, "Shower? What the hell are you talking about? There isn't a cloud in the sky!"

We all laughed as we continued our march along the yellow road in the twilight hour, appearing carefree and young at heart.

After another hour, we reached a crossing in the road. The larger paved road, however, ran north to south. If we followed it south we would be traveling parallel to the coastline. We decided to continue west along the local road. After a while it made a sharp turn to the right, presumably leading to the fishing village. But, straight ahead was a clearing in the pine forest, and behind the scattered eelgrass was the sandy beach. Beyond that lay the open sea, restless in the late September evening.

[16]Medical orderly

Chapter 17

Adventure at Sea

The whitecaps were running high, falling on the wet sand with a rhythmic roar. Small boats, tied to the wooden pier, rose and fell with each in-rushing wave. With those, one would not be able to get past the breakers some 50 yards out, not to mention Sweden, well over 150 miles out at the other side of the dark and turbulent sea.

We took a path to the beach and were surprised to find people, single and in small groups, roaming about. They certainly were not fishermen from the village but fugitives like us, looking for an opportunity to escape. There were even a few trucks lined up next to us, parked where the sand was firm and dry. We sat down next to the pines.

The weapons were placed in a pyramid on the mound where the sea grass was tall enough to keep the shifting sand away from the barrels and locking mechanisms. I pulled off my boots and socks. My heel blisters had already broken and the raw flesh appeared inflamed, oozing bloody liquid. I had nothing to dress them with. The best I could do was place my boots under my ankles to keep the heels off the sand. Then I leaned back in the sand with both hands under my head and thought, "What else could happen!"

There was no reason even to speak and there was nothing to say. The crowded beach, with its aimlessly wandering people, like ants running away from fire, made our hearts sink. Maybe the word "hopeless" was in everyone's mind.

———

A tall, well-built man was approaching the truck parked next to me. It was too dark to see his face as he unlocked the cab door and swung it open. Looking over my right shoulder, I saw the decal:

KAINEL'S GENERAL STORE

ASSAMALLA

I forgot all about my bleeding heels as I jumped up and went over to the truck. The man's back was toward me because he was looking for something under the front seat.

"Mr. Kainel?"

He turned around and his friendly face was filled with surprise and delight: "Arved Ojaama! My God. The last man I thought I'd ever see again."

We shook hands warmly and his left hand got hold of my shoulder and he kept shaking it. My father and I had known him for years as a friend.

Then he noticed my bare feet and said: "Hey, haven't you got any boots?"

"I do, but I took them off to 'cool my heels'."

"What's wrong with them?... Let me see."

He got hold of my ankle and lifted up my right foot as he bent down.

That looks pretty bad to me. It needs to be dressed. I presume you have no such supplies, but I have my first aid kit."

He went looking for it, and I returned to my shoes and bloody socks, the only worldly possessions I had besides what I had on my back.

When he returned, I introduced him to my friends.

Mr. Kainel was full of enthusiasm, giving hearty handshakes all around. It sure lifted our spirits from their-to make an understatement-downward trend.

He cleaned my bruised heels with peroxide and alcohol, then applied some salve and wrapped them up with bandages.

"You cannot wear your boots for a while. I have a pair of soft leather *pastlad* for you." *Pastlad* were moccasin-like footwear, once worn by peasants.

Then he laughed. "In fact, I have practically my entire store in the back of my truck. What else do you need?"

I just shook my shoulders.

"Let me put it this way," he said. "What do you have?"

"I have my boots."

"Is that all?"

"The shirt on my back. That's about it!"

He slapped his thighs, still squatting next to my bandaged feet.

"The good Lord made me park my car in this spot so I could be of help to you and your friends. If my wife and I find a place in a boat, I could not take this stuff with me anyhow. If the Russians get hold of me, then good-by to the car and all that's in it, and that includes me and my wife. Need supplies? Blankets? I have blankets. Food? I could feed a company for a week."

Then he remembered the reason he had come to his car, "I forgot all about my wife. We have a small tent back there and I came to fetch another pillow for her."

He left with the pillow to pacify his wife, but promised to return.

Rik came out with a piece of wisdom, "Even your rooster will lay an egg if you are lucky enough, and I think he just did!"

"Do you folks realize we're going to be living next to a grocery store?" added Ants.

"And also a warehouse," said Senka.

"Wasn't it Jesus Christ who said, 'When the need is greatest, the help is nearest'?" inquired Tom.

At this point I cut in, "Let's leave Christ out of this. Besides, I don't believe he ever said any such thing. Mr. Kainel sure will lift our spirits and fill our bellies, but when I look at this crowd on the beach..." I shook my head. "The 'greater luck' hasn't materialized yet!"

"Well, who knows if this so-called 'greater luck' will ever come!" added Senka. It still feels better to die with a full belly than an empty one. They even give glorious meals before executions."

"Is that what they call the 'Last Supper'?" inquired Rik.

"Nay, the 'Last Supper' was in the Bible," said Tom. "It has nothing to do with executions."

I laughed to myself. My buddies had recovered from the blues even before we had a bite to eat.

By then Mr. Kainel had returned to his truck. He stopped there for a minute or two and when he approached us, he was carrying a basket in one hand and holding a bottle of the "Government brew" in another-the size we used to call "The President".

"The old Estonian custom is to 'wet one's whistle' on special occasions, and I do not know anything more special than this."

The bottle of booze made its rounds and returned nearly empty. Then we formed a close circle around the spread-out towel, and Mr. Kainel started to empty the basket.

Would wonders never end!

There was smoked ham, boiled eggs, sausages of different sizes and colors. Butter with hard rolls. Even chunks of smoked eel.

We were encouraged to dig in. "Eat all you can! When it is gone, I will go and get another load!"

And we did not "dine," we gulped it down, the biggest and tastiest meal of our lifetimes. We rediscovered the taste of things we had forgotten even existed.

After we had emptied two basketfuls of food, we unbuckled our belts and stretched out on the cool sand with our distended abdomens pointing toward the starry sky. Mr. Kainel brought everyone a blanket and wished us good night.

We built small mounds of sand for pillows and rolled into the new blankets with our weapons next to us. The roaring of the sea had ceased and only the rhythmic rumble of in-rushing waves remained as we slept through the dark autumn night.

The new day started with a cloudless sky and gently rolling sea. Mr. Kainel had brewed hot tea for breakfast. His wife, a good looking woman in her early forties, came to meet us. She shook hands with me and said just "hey" to the rest of the crew. She then retired to the cab because an early morning chill still hung in the air.

We ate our breakfast and drank more tea while we held a strategy session.

Mr. Kainel informed us that the people from the village would not bargain with anybody. They did not do so even when he offered his truck and all the supplies in exchange for a boat.

They had responded, "What would we do with the truck? The Russians will claim it as soon as they get here. We need the boats for making our living by catching fish." A reasonable argument indeed.

"Well," said Tom, "It is time for drastic action. It is our lives we are talking about, not about a few pounds of fish. We have to find a boat big enough to take us out to the open sea. If they have them-where could they be? Not in their houses: too small to hide a seagoing boat. So they must be outside. They would be too big to drag into the woods. What is left? Their backyards, hidden under haystacks or piles of straw."

"Correct," said Rik. "We have metal rods to clean our guns with. All we have to do is go through the village and poke the piles of hay and straw and see what we come up with."

I agreed, "We leave the machine guns behind and go out carrying the automatic weapons. We do not need to talk to anybody and we won't answer any questions about our intentions."

On Friday, September 22, 1944. the afternoon was sunny and mild with a light breeze from the south. There were no breakers over the shallows, where crying seagulls were diving and rising again, chasing minnows in the shallow water.

We had secured a 24-foot open boat and anchored it past the shallows in five feet of water about one hundred yards from the shore. It had an old-fashioned motor, one barrel of gasoline, and a pair of heavy oars on board. All six of us were guarding the boat from invaders. There were two other men aboard, whom we had specially selected for their skills. One was the carpenter, still tarring the reinforced sideboards he had installed ashore to prevent the choppy seas from flooding the boat. The other was the repairman, a specialist who could get the motor back to running condition after it had been neglected for months. He was confident he could get it into running order before nightfall.

So far we hadn't been able to find a seaman to captain our boat. Mr. Kainel was still ashore, looking for the right man. He had a way with people and we were still hopeful he would locate someone. It seemed to us that seamen who had decided to flee had left the country already, and the fishermen from the village had decided to stay put.

We had worked out a detailed plan for a Saturday morning departure. Before the crowd would be out at the beach, we would maneuver the boat as close to the shore as possible. I would stay in the boat with the two helpers to guard the weapons, while the rest of the crew would wade ashore to carry the supplies Mr. Kainel had laid out tools, drinking water, clothing, the canvas cover from his truck, plus a good supply of food, canned and smoked, to last for a good week or even up to ten days. He himself would carry his wife aboard to keep her from getting her feet wet.

Mr. Kainel had a good map of the Estonian east coast, showing two large islands: Saaremaa and Hiiu. We were only interested in Hiiu as it was located directly to the west, about 20 miles from the shore. It was a large island, shaped like a star and over 30 miles across. From the western tip of the island to the Swedish would still leave more than 150 miles of open sea-a formidable distance for a rickety wooden boat with a rusty engine.

We were only charting one step at a time. First, reaching the island of Hiiu would not be a very risky undertaking. We estimated the Russian occupation of the island would take at least two weeks and that would give us time to formulate our next step.

All plans, even perfect ones, have omissions, hidden flaws, and failed timing. It's best to take only one step at a time and then reassess the situation.

Our first minor omission was not taking any food with us for supper. We were anchored in five feet of water with one-foot waves. To wade to shore would soak us up to our necks, not an inviting option. We could have heaved the anchors and tried to maneuver the large boat with a pair of heavy oars closer to shore. This created the danger of making us drift and risk getting marooned on the shallows. The third option was to forget supper altogether. That one seemed to be the most reasonable. Of course, pushing the boat out to sea had made us all wet from the chest down.

Meanwhile the wind, still blowing from the south, had increased in velocity, forming whitecaps on top of the waves and making breakers reappear over the shallows. The cry of the seagulls had intensified. Their fishing must have improved when the shoals were exposed between the inrushing waves. The south wind brought in low-flying clouds and rolling fog, quickly shading the sun, which was now low on the horizon.

We were all anxiously watching the open sea and the fog closing in when Senka, who was keeping a lookout toward the beach, shouted" "What the hell is this!"

He was pointing toward the shore. What we saw frightened us all. About 50 people were wading in the water, rushing toward our boat.

"They'll drown us all!"

"Our boat might be able to handle 20. Anything beyond that will sink us," was my opinion.

"The Russians must have arrived, causing the panic!" said Rik.

We had to organize resistance, the strongest waders were only 20 yards from us, but now the deeper sea and one-foot waves were slowing them down. Some women among the early arrivers were short. The waves started to wash over their heads. They coughed after swallowing seawater. Some screamed for help. Some started to swim.

Our friend Kainel and his wife were not among the early arrivers. We yelled his name in unison, "Kainel! Kainel! If you are out there, wave!"

That did not work as many people began to wave. Some close to the shore started to wade back to the beach.

"Kainel! If you are out there, we will come get you!"

We couldn't hear anything like his deep voice over the high-pitched screams and rumbling sea.

"Senka," I yelled, "you keep count. The first 18 will be helped aboard, then everybody, including the newcomers, have to help hold back the rest and not only women and children! We need men to attend the oars and bail the water!"

After the short rescue mission, the scene became ugly. We were at full capacity, and couldn't let any more aboard. The railings on both sides of the boat were covered with grasping hands and it was difficult to pry them loose. They grabbed our wrists. There was the risk that they would pull us overboard. More drastic measures were needed as the boat was now starting to take water. Gun butts were used next to beat the hands away from the railing. This helped, and the boat rose well above the waterline. The crowd gave up one-by-one and turned back toward the shore, now occupied by Russian tanks firing blindly at the sea. The fog and rain obliterated the coast-line and only flashes from the cannon barrels barely outlined the front part of their tanks.

Bless the fog and the rain! They saved us from the tanks and their cannons. If the Russians had arrived half an hour earlier, they would have blasted us to kingdom come.

I was sitting at the bow and yelled loud, "Is there a captain aboard?"

A voice from the middle of the boat answered, "I am a captain."

"Captain of the navy?"

"Nay. Captain of the firefighters. Brigade # 6, from Tallinn," came the answer.

"Have you been on the water before?"

"The only water I am familiar with comes out of the end of fire hoses."

Well the captain at least had a sense of humor. But some women started to wail, "Oh my God... we will all drown...! Turn the boat around and let's go back to the shore! What will the Russians do to us anyway! These young kids will drown us all!"

Someone else got down on her knees and started to pray and wail with a high-pitched voice.

I recognized Tom's raspy voice, "That's enough! Madam, if you wish to go back, we'll heave you overboard." And then quite loud and firm, "You came here and we pulled you in. We are still anchored. Anybody, and I repeat anybody, who has changed his or her mind-leave now! We will help you get out. This is your last chance and the last complaint I want to hear." He walked through the crowded boat with

179

his "automatic" on his shoulder.

"Who wants to go back? Who wanted to go back? Speak up!"

There were no volunteers. Nobody spoke. The wailers and prayers had quit.

"Good. From now on I do not want to hear any complaints. We are all in this together. From now on we sink or swim together!"

"Understood? From now on everybody does what we tell you to do. If our sergeant asks you to jump overboard because of your whining, wailing or praying aloud, we will throw you overboard. You are our guests, remember! And uninvited guests besides. You have to behave accordingly!"

Somebody said "Amen", and that was it.

To get things going I yelled from the bow: "Anchors up. Man the oars. Two men on each!"

I took out my pocket compass. Its dial showed "N"-North. That was not where we wanted to go. The boat had no rudder. The men at the oars had to keep the boat on course, heading west.

"Right oar pull harder, ease up at the port side! Now we are on course."

And then loud enough for everyone to hear, "We are heading west to Hiiu Island. We have to row throughout the night. Men have to take turns. Everybody has to help bail the water, including the women. There is a bail at each end of the boat. When daylight comes, our mechanic will finish fixing the motor and then we just pop-pop to Hiiu."

The civilians were talking with hushed voices.

The panic was over. I heard a woman's voice, "This guy at the nose of the boat-he knows what he's doing!"

That was only marginally correct. I had my compass and could point the boat in the right direction. Without it we would be hopelessly lost in the fog and rain. There was one thing I didn't know anything about, but I would not announce my ignorance. It could only make things worse. It was the drift!

The wind was from the south, and it would make us drift northward with our low speed. Even if my compass showed west, our true course would really be northwest-making us miss Hiiu Island and end up on the open sea where there was hundreds of miles of nothing but water. To correct for the drift I decided to change course to the southwest. It was just a guess. My precious experience in orientation was not at sea but on skis where wind and waves had no impact. I even felt that experienced seamen could do no better than guess. The latter thought gave me confidence.

"Starboard, that means the right side, pull harder. Ease at port! That-a-boy. Stay on this course!"

The fog was still blanketing the sea. We were progressing slowly, possibly one or two miles an hour. The round-bottomed wooden boat was sitting deep in the water, the freeboard not over one foot, not counting the tarred boards the carpenter had added. That gave us another half a foot of grace. The boat had been on dry land for a while. That explained the slow leak that was making the water slosh against the floorboards. Continuous bailing was in order.

Meanwhile, we had taken a head count. There were 26 of us. I presumed Senka could not keep up the count when people were storming the boat and they were helping the first arrivers aboard. Only when the boat started taking on water did the boys have to become ruthless with their gun-butts. It was truly a wonder we were still afloat.

Twenty-six. Two times 13-my lucky number!

A single plane was circling overhead. Its circular searchlight illuminated the waves not far from us, probably in search of fleeing vessels to send them to the bottom of the sea. Thanks to the fog we escaped its light beam and the plane left, to continue its search further north.

I had been standing at the nose of the boat in my wet clothes, exposed to the wind, I found myself shaking from the elements, and decided to squat down against the rig-rails at the bow.

I was leaning against something warm when a woman's voice, sounding rather cheerful, invited me to join her. "Come closer. I am as wet as you are, but we can keep each other warm by being close."

Sure enough, I could read my compass down in the shade of the bow boards, close to a young woman, the two of us keeping each other warm.

"Right oar, pull harder. Ease at the left!"

We would keep our course southwest and see what happened in the morning, assuming we were still afloat.

The new day arrived with a bleak wind, high clouds, and a deserted sea. The rain and fog had vanished overnight. The rolling of the sea had subsided, replaced by ripples beating so close to the railing that one could just reach out and touch them.

The mechanic was not willing to start working on the engine yet. "My hands and fingers are too stiff to handle it. I might drop pieces overboard, and that would be the end of it! Let's wait for a couple of hours until it warms up."

We continued to row and bail water. We were cold, miserable and hungry but still afloat!

When the sun rose high over the horizon, we could see a faint blue line in the east where the sky met the sea. That was the mainland's coast, about eight miles out. How much we were north or south from our point of departure was anybody's guess.

I stood up from the bow-boards and looked directly into the wind. Our course was still southwest, which meant the wind must have shifted overnight. It had slowed our progress.

I could not help but ask myself "progress to where?"

The woman who had helped keep me comfortable through the night stood up. I was thankful to her for the warmth and the coat we could share. Of course, it was as wet as the rest of our clothes, but it had kept us from freezing. She had slept at intervals, resting her head on my shoulder. I had to be awake to keep the boat pointed in the right direction.

I looked at her for the first time, not that it mattered. She was taller than I, more slender than fat. She had a pleasant face with a few acne scars from her teenage years. She must have been about 30.

When I was 15 years old I tried to read a book with the title "Thirty Year Old Woman". I clearly remember my first thought, "What the hell is there to write about a woman who is already 30?" I did not know at 15 or even when I was standing at the nose of that crowded boat, that women in their 30s were at the most mature and desirable age.

She appeared uninhibited, with a pleasing smile, and asked whether I had found time to sleep. Suddenly she clutched my shoulder, pointed to the west and shouted, "The land! Can't you see the land!!"

People in the boat woke up from their somnambulistic state and started pointing to a piece of land just a few miles southwest.

But it was not Hiiu.

Hiiu would not look like a small island. It would stretch 30 miles across. But this tiny island was still an island in the open sea. It did not

182

take us long to reach a small bay, deep enough to run the boat to the beach. Nobody needed to wade deep in the water to get to dry land.

The island itself was only 300 yards in length and about 150 yards wide, with a few stunted trees and juniper bushes. The rest of it was covered with green grass waving in the breeze. The land itself was tilted toward us, leading to a rocky ledge with a hay shed at the other end. There were no other signs of human habitation.

We pulled the boat up and left it resting on the pebbled beach without any anchors or tow-lines.

By now the sun was high. The sea was filled with tiny ripples, and the wind from the south had the warmth of summer. The leaves of the stunted maples next to the hay shed had turned yellow and red, unique against the blue sea. Juniper bushes had branched out snake-like, close to the ground, hidden under the waving grass and now and then sending up a green bushy extension toward the sky.

The hay shed was half-filled with hay, scythe-cut and gathered by the young people from the village. They apparently came by boat, worked in the sun and in the wind from the sea. They ate a lunch of curdled milk and bread with fish and filled the hay shed with laughter. They went home in the evening, sunburned, and smelling of cut grass and the sea.

There was something enchanting about this small island, free from human misery; free of tears and sorrow, wars and dying. People had come and left, taking their ills and hurts, their joys and passions with them. They did not become acquainted with the loneliness they had left behind.

I could feel that left-behind loneliness when I was by myself. It was in the cobwebs, hanging heavy between the barn rafters. It was in the hay with its individual aroma, and it was spread over the faceless rocks behind the shed, which the sea washed. I wished I could be alone again.

But for me, it was a different world with little time for reverie. There were chores to be done. The first thing we needed was to dry our clothes.

The men took off their coats and jackets. The women went behind the barn and took off their wet underwear and spread it on the rocks in the sun. I had only my Finnish shirt and pants and I let them dry on my back. I took off my shoes, and spread out my wet socks and the heel bandages.

Senka had found a trickle of water running out from the stone-pile, and it tasted good. We collected the water in our bailing buckets and took turns drinking it.

In the northern part of the island sea sorrels were growing wild. We boiled them in the water to make sorrel soup and by the time the water was starting to boil, a lonely rabbit appeared on the beach. We poured all our fire-power on that rabbit and then wondered how we could have missed him as he ran in the open just 30 yards from us. He disappeared under the rocks at the end of the island.

We did not question our marksmanship, but wondered whether it was an enchanted rabbit, living alone on this Mysterious Island. We could only wonder also how our soup would have tasted with the rabbit in it.

The mechanic had taken the engine apart and reassembled it. We all cheered when we saw the cloud of smoke and heard the coughing of the engine. Meanwhile, after studying Mr. Kainel's map, I identified the island as Härjarahu, some six miles from the shore, and figured out the distance and direction to Hiiu. We had about 12 to 15 miles to go. By then the men's clothes were dry and the women had collected their underwear. We sat down to eat the sorrel soup-minus the rabbit, salt or pepper. The sun was still up when we settled in the fluffy hay in the barn for a restful sleep, to be ready for early departure the following day, which was Sunday, September 24, 1944.

The next morning our expectations of smooth "sailing" were shattered with an unexpected surprise. As soon as we had launched the boat it started to fill with water. With a unified effort we were able to pull its nose back to the pebbled beach.

Our carpenter went inside the boat to investigate.

He soon stood up, holding his hands like a man who was ready to surrender: "My God! There is a hole in the bottom of the boat!."

No wonder he was desperate. He had left all his carpentry tools ashore and thrown the tar-bucket with the brush overboard. We had not pulled the boat far enough out of the water. The wind at night had make the sea restless and the waves had tossed it against the rocks.

The state of affairs, so promising just a few moments ago, had become hopeless. We all stood on the beach as though possessed, and wondered whether anything else could go wrong.

We could not live on sorrel soup alone until the sea froze over. And what then? Return to the mainland and surrender to the Russians?

One thing was certain. We would not live long enough for that to happen.

The carpenter disappeared behind the boat railing once more. Was he reexamining the breakage?

After a short while he reemerged, holding up his hands like the pope, ready to bless the crowd, "You would not believe it, but it is true! I found a tool-box under the bench with lint and tar. Just the right things to fix the break."

Lightening had struck twice. We just stood there motionless, not knowing what to believe or what else to expect.

"It will take me but half an hour to fix it, and then we will be on our way!"

The carpenter kept his promise.

We lifted the women aboard before we launched the boat, pushing it further out until it was floating free. After boarding, we could see that the patch was holding and the boards at the bottom of the boat had swelled in the water, thereby sealing the previous leaks. There was no more need for bailing.

The motor coughed a few times, stopped and then started again. Soon its rhythmic beat became steady and the boat sprang to life, splitting the water in front of her. We were like tourists on a Sunday morning pleasure-ride.

I was standing at the bow to read the compass. The sea was calm. The sun was warming our backs as we headed west toward the island of Hiiu.

The woman who had kept me warm two nights before was standing next to me. It was she who had seen our "Mysterious Island" when we were lost at sea.

There was something hidden in her smile when she looked at me and said, "We deserve it!"

It took us about three hours to reach Hiiu Island near Orjaku. With better speed and a minimal southeast wind, I did not need to worry about drifting. We were heading straight west. One could hardly miss a 30-mile-wide island on a 15-mile boat trip.

———————

The village people ran out to meet us, all eager to get some news from the mainland. Our "passengers" melted quickly into the crowd, heading to the village with their adventure stories.

Senka could not hold back his bitterness, "Look at them! Not a single 'thank you'. Where are all the 'Hallelujah-women' now?...asking us to take them back so they could kiss the Russians' a-!"

We laughed. "You sure laid down the law in no uncertain terms… just throw them overboard and let them swim back!"

An old man with a seaman's cap and a crooked pipe stuck between his yellow teeth came up to see the boat. We watched him and he was looking at the boat. Senka broke the silence, "What's up, pop! Want to buy the boat?"

"Ain't for you to sell!"

He obviously knew that we did not buy it at the fish market.

To change the subject, I asked, "You have been boating and know the sea?"

"Near fifty years."

"What do you think about taking us to Sweden?"

"In this boat? If you want to drown yourself, there are easier ways to go about it!"

"The old man is yellow!" observed Senka. Obviously, he had plans and did not wish him to interfere.

"Now listen, you young punk. Because you made it from the coast to Hiiu does not make you a seaman. Wait until you get out ten miles in the open sea with this matchbox, you'll wish you weren't born. That's all I have to say to that."

"Cut it out, Senka," I said. "The old man knows what he is talking about. Now, we can't stay on this island forever. The Russians will be here in a week or two and there is no love lost between us. Any way we can get off this island?"

The old man puffed on his pipe. It smelled like rotten seaweed on fire. Too bad I didn't have any pipe tobacco to give him.

He took the pipe out of his mouth and said, "I hear lots of folks from Kärdla city have left with the real ships to Germany. That would be the safest way, if not the best. Whether you want to end up there or stay here, or drown yourself at sea, is for you to decide."

He was turning to leave, when I stopped him, "Listen, captain! If we decide against further sea adventures and leave the boat stranded here, would you take care of it? The boat belongs to some fisherman in Mäeküla. We just borrowed it for a short trip. It is in mint condition: all

186

fixed and patched up, no more leaks! Our mechanic even repaired the engine. See to it that the owner gets it back, will you?"

He turned to leave.

"Oh, one more thing. Tell them we're obliged!"

He touched his cap: "I'll take care of it!"

His humped back and swaggering gait spoke of his age and long hours at sea. When he was out of hearing distance, I could see that Senka couldn't suppress his disapproval any longer:

"What do you mean by leaving the boat?" he said. "Our plan was to head all the way to Sweden. Now as we are free of the civilian crowd, we have become seaworthy. Did you notice the carpenter and mechanic have stayed with us. We'll short-hop to the western tip of the island and then take off for the Swedish coast."

He realized that without me and the compass they would have difficulty orienting themselves on a cloudy day or night.

"You have made strong points. We all have to consider it," was my answer.

Then I added, "I've taken chances in the past, but I intend to take no more. I took a chance by coming back to Estonia, instead of going direct to Sweden. What have I accomplished? Nothing, except saving my own neck so far and becoming a buccaneer by taking someone else's boat, depriving them of their livelihood. No better than the damned Russians."

At that time it had been our only option ,and I would do it again under similar circumstances, but now we had other options and my intention was to return the boat to the rightful owner. I trusted the old man to do just that.

"How do the rest of you feel about it?"

Tom just didn't know for sure, and inquired, "How far is it from the western point of Hiiu to the Swedish coast anyhow?"

"More than 150 miles, but the current from the Gulf of Bothnia to the Danish Straits can change with the tides. The other point is, to reach the western point of the island we have to bunny-hop, according to my map, some 50 additional miles."

"How will our gas supply hold out?"

Everybody looked at the mechanic.

"I just don't know for sure. This old engine is eating it. I'm afraid we will come far short!"

"Rik and Ants, how do you feel?"

"We all have been more than lucky for too long," was Rik's comment. "We could not rely on it, or hope it will last forever. We have to consider the alternatives."

No one else spoke up and Tom had remained quiet. It wouldn't have been proper to question him further.

"I think we've agreed to leave the boat and hit the road again." Then I turned toward the carpenter and the mechanic, "Thanks for your help. Without you we would not have made it. You do not want to mix with us. You better join the others in the village and find your own way. It would be much safer for both of you."

They stayed there, leaning against the boat.

Chapter 18

The Farewell

It sure felt good to have firm ground under our feet again. We were heading west toward Käina. Our intention was not to hit the town, but to continue in that direction until we came to the main road that would take us south to an even larger island called Saaremaa.

There was no reason to stop in the local fishing village, which our boat crowd covered like a swarm of locusts, consuming anything edible over an area of a square mile.

Senka was first to bring up the subject of eating: "I am getting a bit hungry." It was the understatement of the year, but then he added, "Thinking about our last meal of sorrel soup makes my mouth water."

That was a joke. In fact that sour, boiled grass had given me heartburn and I said, "I hope I don't need to eat that stuff again as long as I live!"

"That might not be too long," predicted Senka, then added, "Let's walk a mile or two. Perhaps we will hit a farm or meet an old lady who happens to be baking bread. Let's hope our luck is still with us."

We were walking along a road with young pines on each side. This itself was surprising-I thought that Hiiu would have only juniper bushes and sand dunes.

But greater surprises might be just down the road.

The woods came to an abrupt end and suddenly we were looking at a good-sized field of potatoes, with some half-dozen persons on their knees picking them. They all looked up after Senka offered the greeting "more power to you!"

We saw smiling faces and stepped closer. Then we realized that the six smiling faces belonged to six young women. All of them were wearing men's old pants and hats, the customary garment for this kind of work.

An older man was guiding a horse and wagon in our direction.

"Halt!" he yelled to the horse. Then he looked at us, surprised. "By God. Six young men. I do not believe it! I just happen to have six daughters to marry off, but there are no men left in these parts." He then added with a grin, "At least till now!"

The girls leaned back, still down on their knees, and eyed us with amused faces. They all seemed pretty, with round eyes and lush brown hair that stuck out from underneath the hats.

A short pause followed. Everybody was thinking of something suitable to say. Only Leo, who had not spoken since we met, started to edge in the direction of the road. The rest of us just looked at him and at the empty road. We were not ready to leave. Our main interest was not socializing, although the conditions seemed favorable even for that. It would be nice to rest for a day and be attended by these red-cheeked girls, who looked like ripe cherries in the autumn sun.

When the farmer noticed Leo's movement towards the road, he seemed annoyed. "What's the big hurry?" he said. "Don't you know that patience is a virtue and the key to paradise?"

He might have been thinking about paradise on earth, like marrying off these seductive daughters of his. I noticed temptation in the eyes of my companions and I could not help but say, "Patience is also the key to *instant* paradise when the Russians get hold of us!"

"Ah, the Russians..." the farmer pushed his hat down to his eyes to scratch the back of his head, as if he was gathering his thoughts. "I do not believe they will come here at all, and if they come, it will not be for a while yet." He added, "We were ready to break for lunch when you arrived. I bet you could use a honest meal. Why don't you all join us!?"

It was an invitation we could not refuse.

When the farmer started to unharness the horses we were eager to help. In no time at all we were heading along the farm road, across the already-picked potato field and toward the not-too-distant house with its open door and smoking chimney. The girls were walking some distance from us, embarrassed to be wearing pants, which were old and patched besides. Pants belonged exclusively to the male wardrobe in this part of the country, though in some places the women might "wear the pants" figuratively speaking.

The landlady, seeing our hungry faces, brought out a large frying pan. She filled it with thick slices of pork and set it on her cooking range. When this was cooked, she broke a good dozen of eggs into the crackling grease. After a minute or two the pan was in the middle of the kitchen table in front of us. She brought out thick slices of rye bread, boiled potatoes, dill pickles, and a pitcher full of milk and placed it all on the table.

"Just go ahead and eat. The rest of us will have our meal after you are all finished. There is not enough room for all of us, and by the looks of it, you can hardly wait."

We ate and ate, our chins shining with grease and the perspiration running from our foreheads down to our cheeks. The last square meal was more than 48 hours ago, not counting the sorrel soup at Härjarahu. There was no time for conversation or even to wipe off the sweat. The older couple watched us, speechless but with obvious enjoyment.

The young girls were not in sight. They were most likely changing their clothes.

The next day we were back on the road afresh.

We had had three meals at the farm, including breakfast. We got cleaned up in the sauna bath the night before and spent the late evening hours sitting on the porch with the farmer's daughters, all six of them. They were dressed in female attire and looked like packages of pleasure. Their conversation was light, but they seemed to be extending the words they used beyond their original meaning, or used them in ways open to dual interpretation. It was a kind of guessing game, where they knew the answers and we only had to speculate as to their true meaning. Even before falling asleep in the hayloft, Rik and Ants were worked up, thinking of staying or postponing the departure.

The following morning, however, there wasn't a word spoken about staying. The night's sleep had melted away the evening's dreams of temptation and the new day brought nothing but harsh reality.

The sun was getting hot. What little wind there was, was blocked by the trees that lined the road.

Rik was already sweating. "Those damned Russians, he said, "I could have married any of those goodies and lived carefree on this island for the rest of my life. I'm getting tired of running."

"Now, now, Rik," warned Senka. "Look at it this way. If the Russians weren't chasing you, you wouldn't even be on this island, and wouldn't have met the girls. It is good for anyone to fall in love for one evening and leave the next day with a heartache. It breaks up the monotony of the daily grind. Gives you something else to worry about besides running and fighting."

That was Senka's viewpoint on life. He was quite a handsome chap, and must have left behind more than his share of aching hearts. He knew what he was talking about. It was true. The meals at the farm had supplied us with physical energy and freed us of our constant thoughts of food.

The road we were traveling was entirely deserted. We did not see any motorized vehicles. We seemed to have two choices: to be evacuated to Germany or to die in Russian labor camps. Just shooting it out with the KGB units when they arrived did not seem quite as appealing as before. The beauty of the young maidens had revitalized our desire to survive. We were all young, barely entering the third decade in our lives, and had not experienced but calamity and doom.

To escape from future tragedy, we had to make contact with the Germans. If they had abandoned the island, we were trapped like rats on a sinking ship.

We were all aware of that. There was no reason to discuss it. As before, you kept your hurts and ills to yourself. Your anguish and sorrows were not commodities for trading. Not talking about them made them easier to bear and kept the grief from spreading.

The road was firm under our feet, but covered with a thin layer of dust. It spattered over our boots and pants, even reaching up to our faces and caps. The trees threw their shadows upon us now and then, as the road curved and twisted along the wooded landscape. We left the road and stretched out for a moment of rest on a shady wayside, where the grass grew long and was free from the gray dust.

Stillness lay upon the road, the woods, and the long grass next to us. Even the broken clouds overhead were drifting unheeded. A purr of a distant engine broke the silence, getting louder with each moment.

"Senka!" I shouted. "You are the most gentlemanly figure among us. Why don't you get out and hold up your thumb?" He stood up with his "automatic".

"You better leave your shooting iron with us. The Russians ain't this far yet."

The rest of us sat up, leaving our weapons hidden in the long wayside grass so we wouldn't be taken for bandits. This was still a no-man's land, and one couldn't trust anybody holding a weapon in his hand.

The approaching car was an Opel convertible with three men wearing German military uniforms. The car came to a stop where Senka was standing. Two sergeants were in the front seat and a corporal was sitting in the back with an automatic weapon between his knees.

Senka was explaining something, tracing our coming-and-going directions with his hand. The men in the car were just looking at him, trying to make sense of his "half-baked" German.

I disregarded my strange uniform and stepped next to Senka, greeting them in the Finnish fashion with my hand touching the rim of my cap, "Sergeant Ojamaa here. We are hoping that you might be able to give us a lift to less hostile territory."

They looked at my strange uniform, with the two stripes on my shirt collar, while one of them asked in a less than friendly tone, "Who the hell are you?"

"This is the uniform of the Finnish Armed Forces," was my answer.

"Are you aware that Finland has declared war on Germany? In other words, you are wearing the uniform of our adversary."

"No. The last thing I knew, we were both fighting the Russians!"

I produced my German *Urlaub* certificate from my breast pocket, handed it over for their inspection, and added:

"I am an Estonian from the Finnish Armed Forces returned to my country to fight the Russians." Then pointing towards my friends at the roadside, I added, "We are the remains of the Estonian Division engaged at the Eastern Front."

After they had read my certificate, they started to laugh, "*Entschuldigung. Ein Missverständnis!*"[17]

They gave back my document.

Hang on to this! One of the Germans said. "It may have historic value. Might be the only one ever issued!"

The rest had joined us by now, leaving their weapons on the roadside grass. The German corporal remained in the car, expressionless, still holding his weapon between his knees.

A rather friendly question followed, "What are your plans for the future? You will have no safety net to fall into when the Russians land on the island."

Then the other added, "We are combing the roads on this part of the island, trying to rescue any stray soldiers who might have escaped from the mainland. Our last transport will leave the island of Hiiu sometime this afternoon for Kuressaare, the city with a deep harbor located on a larger island to the south, where transport ships are waiting to evacuate us to Germany. As you must know, Kuressaare is over 50 miles from here, across Soela Sound. If you decide to join us, we will supply the transportation. You may keep your weapons until then as our 'excursion' to Kuressaare might run into adversary bands and we have to keep our weapons ready."

This sounded like a friendly offer.

I looked at my countrymen, asking them if they all understood and agreed with what was discussed.

They nodded their heads.

Turning once more to the Germans, I said, "We are physically and emotionally drained and hungry besides. We accept your kind offer. Thank you."

"*Fabelhaft!*[18] It is still a few miles to Käina, and our small car cannot carry you all. Rest here, and we will send a truck to pick you up. It will not take more than 15 minutes. Just keep one man in the middle of the road so they won't miss you."

They jumped into their convertible and within a moment had disappeared in a cloud of dust.

When the dust settled and the road became empty again, Tom spoke, "Nice guys! Not pushing us one way or another. Entirely up to us. How can you turn down an offer like that! They even asked us to cool our heels until the limousine arrives to pick us up."

"I'll tell you what," Rik broke in, "If the circumstances were the same and we were in the Red Army and a Russian patrol found us here like this, they would execute us for desertion and only then send the truck to pick us up. See the difference?"

We had barely settled ourselves on the roadside grass when a new dust cloud rose from the direction the precious car had left. It was a canvas-covered military truck, having trouble making a U-turn on the narrow road with its soft shoulders. We gathered up our weapons from the roadside grass and lined up behind the truck.

A grinning face appeared from the window on the driver's side, "*Ach du liebe Zeit... ganz verloren, eh!*"[19]

And then his formal "*Einsteigen!*"

Senka was the first one aboard. We handed him our weapons first and then climbed in ourselves. The engine was thrown into gear, and the car picked up speed.

I could not forget Mr. Kainel, who had not only lifted our downcast spirits but filled our empty bellies with fancy food. He and his wife had disappeared from the face of the earth.

We all knew what that meant.

This was our first step toward forsaking the country of our birth. A new wave of red terror would rule our land with executions. An untold number of cattle cars filled with our people would soon be rolling again in forced repatriations to the labor camps far to the east.

Our new destination would not be the land of milk and honey, far from it. But it would at least give us a chance at survival. We would not end our journey as corpses in the back of a truck carrying a red star. Best we could hope for was to get a chance to push up dog-daisies in Siberia. Neither option deserved consideration.

The back of the canvas cover was open, and I could see the road behind us. It was almost white in the afternoon sun. And then came plowed fields on our left, black under the deep blue sky of autumn. It was almost like my first excursion to the Finnish Sea when the cut birches were waving in the wind and the women sang about never-returning youth.

Preoccupied with my memories, I saw a pattern of familiar colors, blue sky, black soil and the white road, colors once more forbidden in a reoccupied land.

But they will be there, in the Estonian landscape. Always.

[17]Excuse us, a misunderstanding!
[18]Great!
[19]Good heavens… quite lost!

Part Two - Capful of Wind

Chapter 1

In A Foreign Land

It was a sunny and breezy afternoon, September 29, 1944 when a German transport ship lifted anchor in Kuressaare and left for Danzig, about 350 miles southwest along the Baltic Sea.

The boat carried civilian refugees from Estonia, their suitcases and crates piled high on the deck. They all looked worried, recounting their belongings every so often and throwing suspicious glances at us, the only men in uniform among the refugees.

It is a fact of living through war that pessimism turns on itself and becomes optimism. Unlike our fellow passengers, we truly thought ourselves worry-free. Leaving Estonian soil behind made us feel liberated somehow. There was nothing else for us to lose. We had lost the country we had been fighting for and all we had now were our hands in our pockets and the shirts on our backs. But, even the shirts belonged to the Third Reich, a rather depressing after thought. We were naked enough to have joined Christ's Disciples. But then, on second thought, maybe we were too poor even for that.

Not that the proverbial shirts on our backs were unbecoming. Tom looked quite presentable in his new uniform, received from the warehouse in Kuressaare before we left. I, the one who was still in Finnish uniform, was provided with its German counterpart and a sergeant insignia. Nobody asked for my Finnish aliupseeril shirt in return, so I continued to wear it underneath the new one for good luck. With it I had obtained my leave to Tallinn and had made it to Hiiu Island on time. Now I was hoping its charms would continue.

I felt only emptiness when I saw the last green piece of land fade into the sea and the accompanying seagulls turn back toward home, a place I could no longer claim as my own. By the time we reached land again it was too dark to see any birds. We anchored overnight in a Latvian harbor called Liepaja, next to our sister ship, the *Nordstern,*[2] which also carried Estonian refugees, among them a group of teenage girls who waved at us frantically. A gangway was placed between the two vessels, and we made our courtesy call to the young ladies.

It was a lovely evening with a soft breeze, cloudless sky, and full moon. We promenaded on the *Nordstern* deck until the wee hours, talking, laughing, and holding hands. We were young and full of spirit and adventure. All the gloom was forgotten and miseries left behind, at least for those few moonlit hours. The girls invited us to continue our voyage on the *Nordstern,* but all the sleeping bunks were filled and we would be forced to spend the night next to the engine room, a hot and noisy place indeed. When we finally realized we were tired, we couldn't resist the urge to go back to our comfortable bunk beds. Senka, however, stayed overnight and didn't return until after sunrise the next morning. "Where in the world have you been?" asked Tom.

"Well, I was… delayed. They removed the gangway and I was forced to sleep on their boat."

"Ah, what a misfortune! May we inquire what caused the delay?" Eager minds wanted to know.

"I just happened to meet a very nice lady from Tallinn. An artist." He looked tired and cut the conversation short, "You guys don't know anything about art, and I'm not in the mood just now to teach you uneducated clods."

"Sure. But we clods think it must have been something from the Romantic period of art that you were reviewing…"

"I didn't get it straight what kind of artist she actually was," Senka went on, ignoring our good-natured digs. "She seemed more like a designer of fashionable clothes. Anyway, she told me our outfits needed some color. She knew from our visit last night that there were six of us and she felt, as a fashion guru, that blue silk scarves would be an improvement."

Then, with more clumsiness than showmanship, Senka pulled out a folded piece of silk cloth-enough for six scarves. I remember being surprised by the deep cobalt blueness, a color of such luxury that it seemed out of place, a refugee of its own kind. It was a color I couldn't remember ever seeing before. "This is her gift to you blockheads. We just didn't have enough time to cut it into six pieces."

Not enough time? He had spent the entire night with his artist lady. It would have taken only a few minutes to cut it up, as long as she had had some scissors. Senka's exasperated answer, that he was talking about time in relative terms, made me think of a populist definition I'd once read, "*When a man sits with a lovely lady for an hour, it seems like a minute. But let him sit on a hot stove for a minute, and it's longer than any hour. That's relativity.*" Senka's lady-love must have thought cutting cloth was like sitting on a hot stove, a waste of time. But spending the night with a young man must have seemed like a minute.

Bored with our hypothesizing, he leaned over the railing, spat once overboard and stole a glance at the *Nordstern.* Its deck remained empty. Our sweethearts were still dreaming of the night's adventures.

It was time to put the silk in its rightful place, where Senka's lady-fashion-artist had intended it to go. I used my *puukko* and found a wooden crate to serve as a cutting board: in no time at all everybody had a blue silk scarf wrapped around his neck, with an inch or two, showing above the collar. We tied it with a single knot in front, spread it out to its entire width, and then hid the loose ends inside, leaving the top button open to reveal the rich color and fabric. When I turned my head, it felt like a *Nordstern* sweetheart was caressing my neck.

We all had a good time joking about our newfound "wealth" and the generosity of the artist-lady. Too bad Senka had forgotten to ask her name.

It was still early when we were walking the deck, exhibiting the new adornments to our wardrobe. Sleeping late hadn't been an option in the past and rising early had become a habit. Our deck was still empty of civilians. Since the boat trip to Hiiu, we were keeping our distance.

The anchors were heaved and soon we were again free of seagulls on the open sea, accompanied by two gun boats, while *Nordstern* trailed us by a mile.

The day was uneventful and free of any temptations. Only one female, a preacher's daughter, followed us while her father stayed close behind. As far as charms were concerned, she wasn't blessed with much.

The next day was Sunday, October 1, 1944, our third day at sea. The wind had kicked up overnight. The water was in a high roll and we were leaning over the rail on the starboard side, watching the restless sea. At times the blue-green reached almost to the deck and the next moment there was only a gaping emptiness. When it retreated, the water left some twenty feet of the dark brown side of the boat exposed.

Suddenly an explosion at sea made us look up.

Nordstern was in high pitch.

The boat gave a mournful groan. Its bow went quickly under the waves and the stern rose up in the sky for a short moment. Then it too sank, and there wasn't a ship in sight, just floating debris and occasional black dots, the bobbing heads of a few survivors who were lucky enough to be on deck. Most of the passengers must still have been sleeping below and had no chance to escape. In front of our very eyes, a Russian U-boat had drowned over 500 civilians, most of them women and children. The young girls from the previous night were now at the bottom of the Baltic Sea. They would never return to laugh or dance again. Not even after 200 years, like Gertrude and her village of Kermelshousen in Mrs. Behrens's fairy tale.

I was frozen to the spot for a moment until our ship's sirens started to blare and the alarm bells rang. It brought me out of my lethargy and made me nearly panic-stricken, facing my own peril on the open sea.

"Alarm!... Alarm!"

These were the semi-garbled voices coming from the loudspeakers, urging everybody to leave the cabins and return to the desk-immediately! "Come the way you are!... Do not wait!... Do not take anything with you!..." This message was repeated over and over again: "Sofort[3]... schnell...!"

The women and children were then lined up along the ship's railing, hoping that the Russians would realize they were drowning women and children.

Our ship zigzagged in the heavy seas and pulling out a few of the survivors, all of them men. Our accompanying gunboats started to flop what looked like oil drums into the surrounding sea. These exploded under the surface, creating muffled rumbles and sending geyser-like columns of water high into the air.

I do not know how long it took before we quit zigzagging and started to move ahead with full speed. I only know we stayed afloat. The sun was low in the sky by the time we pulled into harbor in Danzig. There we were greeted by a huge banner, pulled across the landing, "*Räder müssen rollen für den Seig*"[4]

Not fully recovered from the perilous day at sea, we didn't have much enthusiasm for starting to roll the war-wheels just then.

To tell the truth, since the train ride from Tallinn our group had had nothing but luck with a capital "L". The devil had tempted us with the Orjaku sisters at Hiiu and lured us to switch boats in Liepaja. The Orjaku sisters were now picking potatoes for the Red Army, and the girls from *Nordstern* were resting at the bottom of the Baltic Sea. We had resisted temptation and were rewarded with firm ground under our feet in a thousand-year-old city.

The breeze from the sea caught us on an uphill road. The low-lying sun painted the medieval buildings yellow and red. We became elated walking the narrow cobblestone streets, realizing that there were no Russians breathing down our necks any more. At least not for a while, we hoped.

This all lifted our spirits and made us behave like kids at the county fair. We walked in the middle of the street, talked loudly in our native tongue, pointed fingers at the people and buildings and whistled at the ladies on the sidewalks.

The natives looked at us amazed, as though they hadn't expected to witness such things when they left their homes or apartments that morning. Dignified old gentlemen stopped on the sidewalks, leaned on their black umbrella walking-sticks and wondered what this world was coming to. Savages were loose in the land of Goethe and Schiller, Beethoven and Wagner!

We could not have been such boors in Estonia. It would have been like dancing on a casket at a funeral. Besides, there were bullets to dodge and hunger to endure. Here it was all different. We were in a country we weren't afraid of losing, because it was not ours.

Our loud blabber and odd behavior attracted not only the attention of civilians, but also two helmeted MPs who were now heading our way. In Estonia we called them the "Chained Dogs" because of the metal plaques they carried on their chests, held in place by an aluminum chain. As they advanced, there was still time to give my friends some quick advice, "None of you can speak German. I'll talk to them!"

We were facing two husky *Feldpolizei* officers.

"*Ausweis, bitte!*"[5]

"*Jawohl.*"[6] I handed over my document, now outdated by a month, which had given me leave of absence to Tallinn ("Reval" in German) for 48 hours.

One of the officers took it and spent quite a while reading the short note. Then he handed my *A usweis* to the other officer to read.

"*Meine Herren!* You are not in Reval any more, you are in a place called Danzig."

The only thing I said was my obedient "*Jawohl!*"

I decided the less German I spoke, the better.

"You come with us! *Verstehen?*"[7]

"*Jawohl.*"

We ended up in MP Headquarters, facing the officer in charge. If we wanted to establish some communication with them, it was not in our best interests to play total idiots. The best for me was to understand the spoken language, but my ability to speak it was extremely limited.

I explained our arrival by boat from Kuressaare and said something about the *Nordstern* being "Kaputt."

The officers interviewing us were aware of the fate of *Nordstern,* and now they had a connection between Reval and our presence in Danzig. The only thing he couldn't understand was, how we got through the checkpoint in the harbor. All I managed was, *"Räder müssen rollen für den Seig."*

It was a smart move. It made the officer laugh about the omnipresent slogan we had seen draped across the harbor. He had a sense of humor, an unusual trait in a police officer. In a friendlier vein, he continued":

"We will supply you with food stamps for tonight's meal and breakfast tomorrow. You will be staying overnight at *Urlaub und Unterkunft.*[8] One of our guards will take you there. Next morning you will be brought back here, furnished with *Marschbefehl*[9] to Neuhammer training camp. *Verstanden?"*

I clicked my heels, *Jawohl, Herr Offizier!"* and gave the usual military salute. His response was an agonized smile followed by a wave of his hand, signifying the end of our conversation.

After we had our supper at the military "Board and Refuge" place, we stretched out on whatever vacant mattress we could find on the floor, most of them already occupied by German soldiers sleeping, or talking and smoking. We covered ourselves with the supplied blankets, took off our boots, tied together, and hid them under our pillows so as not to lose them overnight. We even took the precaution of keeping our pants on. We'd hate to wake up in our new *Vaterland* without any pants.

The day had been full of tragedy and fear, but all had ended well for us. It was time to relax and be thankful for our good fortune, so far! That had been our most frequent phrase, "so far."

The next day we had our food rations and *Marschbefehl* to Neuhammer, valid for three days. The trip wasn't supposed to take more than 24 hours, but the officials considered us a bit retarded and gave us halfwits three days to find the place. They even exercised extra precautions by escorting us to the railroad station and helping us find the right train, service we were very thankful for. All we had to do was change trains in Posen.

"In Posen you have to come out of the train. *Verstehen?* You ask the MP or station master to help you. Just repeat the word 'Neuhammer, Neuhammer' and wave this document." They even showed us how to do the waving. *"Verstehen? Alles klar?"*

"Jawohl. Alles klar, mein Herr."

They didn't respond at all to our saluting, just smiled at us like mothers dropping their babies off at the nursery. I heard them say to each other as they left, "I only hope these nitwits don't show up in Danzig again!"

In the train we had an entire compartment to ourselves, though every other seat on the train seemed to be taken. Maybe our unconventional behavior, rowdy manners, horse-laughs and loud arguments in a foreign tongue might have kept the natives at bay.

We weren't embarrassed. If our wild behavior disgraced anybody, it must have been the Third Reich whose uniforms we were wearing. Besides, we were now "legit" with an official document in my breast pocket. Too bad the authorities had confiscated my historic *Urlaub* certificate from Tallinn.

We decided to leave the train in Posen and spend a couple of days in the city.

Only Rik objected, "What the hell would we do in Posen for two days without speaking the language!"

Then he had a second thought: "But how about visiting the art galleries! No knowledge of language is needed to dig art. Senka, remember, is familiar with it, mostly with the Romantic Art, which I favor myself. He will help us find the places. By the way, Senka, is it true that 'Art Houses' have red lights in front for easy identification? Maybe tonight is the night for me to become a 'patron of the arts'!"

Lucky for us, the language barrier kept Rik's daydreaming confidential. Or did it?

Two ladies had appeared at our compartment door during our conversation, and they queried in perfect Estonian, "What's going on here?"

We dropped Rik's line of conversation and becoming instant gentlemen, we all stood up and offered the newcomers our seats, which they took as an expected courtesy.

To us they both looked like they'd stepped out of a fashion magazine. Maybe not, but we were used to meeting quite different females. These ladies were distinguished looking, with coiffured hair. Their manicured hands showed determination as they adjusted their fur stoles. And their age, not more than mid-30s. If they were indeed refugees, they hadn't been refugees for long. They were too well dressed for that. But there they were, sitting with amused faces and offering no explanations for their sudden appearance.

The suave Senka spoke first. "Pardon me, ladies. May I ask how you happened to stop at our compartment? Are you our countrymen? I mean, women"

The red-haired lady, her freckled face giving her a slightly mysterious look, spoke first, "Well, your conversation was loud enough to be heard from the front of the train to the caboose."

Nobody seemed to know what to say next.

These two ladies had actually been hearing Rik's monologue about visiting the "art galleries" in Posen. To break the moment of embarrassment, I asked about their destination.

Posen, they lived in Posen.

You're from Posen? No kidding! We're planning a two-day vacation in Posen to visit all the art galleries there!'

Both women burst out laughing, tears in their eyes. We could only laugh along and feel awkward while doing it. But Rik's *faux pas* had broken the ice and the ladies opened up the conversation. They were Estonians who had been living in Germany since 1939. After the Molotov-Ribbentrop non-aggression treaty, the folks of German descent had left the Baltic States for their *Vaterland*.

Senka looked surprised, "You must be Germans then?"

"No, don't assume that. Anyone is welcome in Germany who could speak a few words of the language or claimed to have a few drops of Aryan blood in their veins. Our husbands felt we would be safer in Germany. Now they're in the military service and we have been living in Posen."

"Nice meeting you. My name is Senka." We all introduced ourselves to the ladies. The redhead's name was Silvia and the lady sitting next to me was Liidia Sommerfeld. Her husband was a lawyer, now a major in the *Felddienst*.[10]

I liked Liidia's style and her classy features. She had a canny smile and challenging glow in her eyes when she spoke to me. I wasn't sure if this meant anything in particular, or whether it was just the way ladies talked to strangers in this state. I was but a country kid, had never met or spoken to a lawyer's wife before and the privilege of conversing with a sophisticated lady now made me feel uncomfortable. Before this episode I had communicated with country girls who scratched their elbows when one spoke to them.

I found the encounter with this lady exciting and frustrating at the same time. Was this some kind of game? She seemed to enjoy playing whatever it was she was playing. I stopped wondering why they had joined a group of rowdy soldiers, not even officers, when the redheaded Silvia couldn't hold her excitement any longer:

"Oh, we haven't seen young men for ages!"

The Rose Lady in Rakvere had used the same expression in her flower garden two summers ago, but Silvia's statement had a different ring to it.

"Next stop Posen... Posen coming up!" The conductor walked through the coach and the train started to slow down. Dark landscapes flashed through the windows.

Liidia, Mrs. Sommerfeld, I mean- looked at me with a smile, "The 'Art Galleries' are closed at this hour. If it's agreeable with you and your friends, you are invited for supper in my apartment. We're not far from the military *Kaserne,* where you could spend the night, if that's what you want!"

We all accepted her invitation with a "thank you" while the redhead Silvia raised her hands over her head and applauded.

It was true. We hadn't been inside a private home since the kitchen in Hiiu, and an evening of tempting conversation on the Orjaku sisters' open porch. That all seemed another world now, something that had happened a generation ago.

Our stay in Posen was a memorable one.

The only thing apparently rationed in Posen was the food! Mrs. Sommerfeld's lady friends came over. Each brought a dish for the pot-luck supper, and after midnight were accompanied home with us as their "body-guards". The farthest thing from our minds was the local *Urlaub und Unterkunft.* That night we didn't need to sleep with our pants on or hide our boots under the pillow! I was the only overnight guest, sleeping in the *Herr Major's* study with it's oak paneling, varicolored tapestry and rows of leather-bound books. I took one, the nearest volume to my couch-bed, and glanced at its title: *Konversationslexikon des Sexualwissenschafts.*[11] It was the most unusual book with the longest title I ever had laid my eyes on. Even the illustrations were explicit and to the point. I decided to visit Mrs. Sommerfeld to inquire about the unusual encyclopedia.

I was gracefully received.

We were less gracefully received at our next encounter with the MPs. The few days in Posen had come and gone unnoticed. We hadn't even had time to visit the art galleries-our supposed reason for stopping in Posen in the first place. Now our *Marschbefehl* had expired and we ended up in custody, undergoing a pocket-search at Posen police headquarters. The only thing they found were colored photographs of Hitler and Goring, neatly wrapped in our outdated *Ausweis*. For some reason the officers seemed friendlier after viewing the postcards. Once more we had to "warm the benches" in the *Feldpolizei* headquarters while they prepared a brand new *Marschbefehl* for us, this time for two days only. Of course, we felt bad about the fact that we weren't able to communicate properly with them, hampered as we were by not knowing their language. It was regrettable that we had left a poor impression of ourselves. But the two words we knew in German, *"Jawohl"* and *"Neuhammer"*, came in handy. When the officers conversed among themselves, they tended to use the words *"Schwachsinnig"*[12] and *"Dummkopf"*[13] rather frequently.

Then the familiar routine followed. They took us to the railroad station and placed us on the right train. But this time they didn't leave us until the wagon wheels started to roll toward Neuhammer.

After the ordeal was over and we had a brand new *Ausweis* in our pocket, we were a relaxed bunch. If worse came to worse, we were making the best of it! There was nothing we could do to change the state of the world except save our own hide and so far we'd done a good job of it. We'd stopped being boisterous after meeting up with the Posen ladies, and were now steering our peaceful conversation toward the immediate future:

"Isn't it odd how easily we dupe the Military Police?"

"What else can they do but feel sorry for us? Look, we're lost in a foreign country, not speaking the language, and still carrying pictures of the Führer and his gang in our uniform breast pockets, next to our hearts. Did you see how they changed their tune after finding the pictures? They've given up hope themselves, but they have sympathy for some fools from Never-Never-Land who still seem to believe in the Third Reich."

"Are we to believe a compassion bug has become epidemic among the MPs, or is it confined only to Danzig and Posen?"

"I'm not talking about compassion. A cop is a cop, MPs particularly. I truly believe they are more tolerant toward foreigners in uniform than they would be toward their own citizens who might be AWOL. We have papers, outdated maybe, but still papers. Every time they give us a new *Marschbefehl*, there's no mention of our previous transgressions. They can't cross-examine us for the simple reason we don't speak their language. Along with a new *Ausweis,* they give us the benefit of the doubt."

"Then there's no reason we can't act like imbeciles just a few more times?"

"Yeah, we can repeat our act, but the closer we get to Neuhammer, the shorter the validity of the new *Marschbefehl*. If we get too close, we might get an escort instead of new papers. Once there, our own officers won't care less where we've been. We'll just be the latest escapees from our homeland. Might even receive congratulations. Most important in our cat-and-mouse game right now is never to cross old paths like Danzig or Posen where our faces are familiar."

"Selbstverständlich![14] How about jumping the train in the next station and switching to one heading in the opposite direction, away from Neuhammer. When they catch us further out, what else can they do but give us a new certificate and extend the expiration date."

It helped that the last MPs were nice enough to return our pictures of the Führer and his pals; no need to waste money buying new ones!

We had become the *Fliegende Holländer* of dry land.

Sadly, we never had a reception quite like the one in Posen, but there were still understanding Military Police to accommodate our "crusade".

It was another three weeks before we found the place called Neuhammer, the one we had been searching for so diligently and for so long.

[1]sergeant
[2]North Star
[3]At once
[4]The wheels must roll for the Victory.
[5]Credentials, please
[6]Yes (Sir)
[7]Understand
[8]Furlough, Board and Lodging
[9]Travel orders
[10]active service
[11]Encyclopedia of Sexual Science
[12]Feeble-minded
[13]Blockhead
[14]obviously

Chapter 2

Caged Freedom

Neuhammer in the late fall, 1944, was a weathered city of stone. Endless rows of two-story barracks, all alike, were occupied by thousands upon thousands of young men, separated according to nationalities, all made homeless by the expanding "Red Tide." Among them was a newly formed division of Estonians; men who had been able to escape from their now reoccupied country.

The camp was designed to fulfill all human needs with its row upon row of barracks for enlisted men, officers' quarters, warehouses, kitchens with dining halls, delousing stations and meeting halls, latrine barracks and sick bays. Further out and closer to the perimeter were the marching fields, rifle-ranges and a whorehouse.

The entire "city" was enclosed by a barbed-wire fence with guarded gates. Its inhabitants were called "soldiers" and "volunteers". Their living quarters were cold and damp. The food was poor. The autumn days were short, with frequent rain showers. Military drills lasted from dawn to dusk.

This was Camp Neuhammer, my new home for the rest of the coming year.

There were no hassles when we registered at division headquarters except that our "Sanguine Six" was broken up. I was assigned to one of the division's infirmaries and the rest were divided among different regiments. I never saw any of them, Tom, Rik, Senka, again. To this day I don't know what happened to them, or whether their luck continued to hold up. We had been successful in our common goal, which was escaping from the Russians, and we had done so against all odds. We were forced to go our separate ways and there were no corner bars in Neuhammer where old buddies could meet for a beer on Saturday night.

Back in Russia we had the saying: "A friend today, buried tomorrow." (Or a variation, "A friend today-poor devil tomorrow.") If the friend was just wounded, and recovering at a hospital in Vienna, he might send you a picture-postcard of the city with the penciled-in note "Wish you were here!" in that case he was called a "lucky bastard." So much for nomenclature.

Back in Finland I was once called a "poor devil" myself, obviously a mistake, or I would not be here to write my story. It all started with some similarity of names and a mix-up in counting the foxholes. We were holding defensive positions at the coast of Luireniemi near Viipuri and had come under fire from Russian battleships. In the dark of a nocturnal pullback to a protective pine forest, two men walking behind me mentioned my name. I turned in the direction of the voices and asked "What's up?" one of them gave me the sad news:

"We were talking about Corporal Ojamaa, the poor devil. His foxhole got a direct hit and they had to rake together what was left of him."

"That's news to me. I am Corporal Ojamaa, and I don't feel like I need any raking."

The word had spread however during the night, and it wasn't until the next day that I could set the record straight and prove that I was still very much alive. It turned out that the dead man was a young fellow with the name "Ojala". The names sound similar and the hit had left him unrecognizable. And Ojala had been in the first foxhole while I was in the very last one, the thirteenth. Of course, either end could be counted as first, depending on which end one started counting. But Fate had started his count from the Ojala's end, giving me the break. I even remember the date: 06/07. (Doesn't it give you another thirteen?) As you can see I had nothing to worry about with my double 13 protection.

I even remember carrying out a business deal on the very same day. I netted two packages of German cigarettes by going to a nearby German field kitchen and selling them a fish that had washed ashore after a Russian bombardment. It must have taken its time reaching the shore. Before I could complete the transaction I had to treat the foul odor by rubbing the fish with a lot of salt.

Anyway, my luck was still holding up in Neuhammer. Nobody questioned my qualifications when I reported to the designated sick bay. My rank as sergeant plus being an ex-medical student gave me status that many corpsmen did not possess.

Our pharmacopoeia was a limited one.

We had aspirin and codeine for cold, aches and pains, and fever. Then there was Prontozil, a sulfa drug, for sore throat and "walking pneumonia". It had the innocent side effect of turning one's urine the color of port wine. Of course this scared the daylights out of fellows, particularly those who were frequenting the previously mentioned establishment at the camp's perimeter. We had *tincture opii* to cure any diarrhea. Neosalvarsan was then the only known treatment for syphilis, and as far as I know there was only one man in our regiment getting the injections. We also had two kinds of salves. One was white-colored zinc oxide and the other, called Ichtiol, was black and looked like axle grease. The latter was for abscesses, infected wounds and blisters. The white stuff was for benign-looking lesions. If you happened to forget which cream was which, you just applied the stuff from the closest pot to the ailment you happened to be treating. According to my clinical observation, it didn't make one iota of difference which one was used.

Every soldier had to get an injection of tetanus toxoid. At first I observed the technique used by the experienced corpsmen. The subject stepped, drop his pants and lean forward, holding his head between his hands and resting it at the end of the examination table. Then the corpsman took a glass syringe with a needle from the sterilizer. First he injected some air into a one-ounce bottle containing the toxoid, creating positive pressure, making the clear liquid flow into the syringe by itself. During all this the recipient was waiting anxiously, his butt exposed and his pants resting on the floor.

Then came the experienced professional part. Using an arching motion, the corpsman threw the syringe like a dart with the needle pointing to the upper-outer quadrant of the patient's butt, pushed the plunger down to inject the stuff, and yelled, "Next!"

The patient from the "received" end pulled up his pants and left in a hurry while the first from the "receiving" line stepped forward and dropped his pants, and the entire procedure repeated itself.

Simple enough. Anybody could do it!

I have to confess, that the dictum "see one, do one" did not work, and the observed "dart technique" was a bust for me. Perhaps I was holding the syringe at a bum angle when I released it. Maybe it wasn't evenly balanced or it hadn't been launched with the right speed. I bent the needle badly with my first try and I had to catch the contraption in a hurry before it hit the floor.

There were too many variables involved and not enough time to sort it all out. I decided to switch to the technique my father used for making shoes. He did not throw his awl but used a screwing motion to pierce the leather. I tried the same method in giving injections and it worked splendidly, the first time and every time. The patients treated this way seemed to holler the loudest, but my explanation of "If it hurts the worst, it heals the best" left them satisfied enough and my waiting line moved along with the desired assembly-line speed.

At the end of the first day I felt like a pro, and nobody seemed to be any wiser. But I still had a lesson coming.

One morning Captain Tamm, the head doctor of the medical service, was sitting behind his desk and said to me, as the person standing closest to him, "I have a touch of a cold. Ojamaa, bring me some anise!"

I didn't have the slightest idea what he meant. Then I remembered a small glass-topped bottle in the medicine cabinet labeled *Oil of Anise*. I filled a glass half-up with water, added some 10-12 drops from the bottle, and placed the glass in front of him. The oil drops danced merrily on top of the water, and I realized than that this non-mixing mixture wasn't fit to cure anything, including the captain's cold.

His look placed me in the lower class of dimwits.

"What the hell is this?"

"The oil of anise, sir."

He ignored my answer and addressed his old corpsman, "Karl, bring me a half glass of anise!"

"Yes, sir!"

Karl opened a high cupboard and brought out a bottle with a fancy label, half-filled a glass, and placed it in front of the doctor. How the heck was I to know that he had anise-flavored liqueur somewhere for treating his fifty-year-old bones? The stuff he called "anise" was most certainly not listed in any pharmacopoeia. But then, in my stupidity I had served him oily water without asking the simple question: "What do you mean by *anise*, sir?"

Shortly after the anise incident, a new physician by the name of Leonard Kaupmees arrived in our medical unit. He was actually a senior medical student who had received a crash-course in treating battle casualties and had been declared fit for frontline duty. He was above average in height and rather skinny, with stooping shoulders and a stretched-out neck. He walked with a kind of staggering gait not seen in the military training camp before. He lectured each and every recruit who failed to give him a proper military salute. He talked too much and liked to tell "clean" jokes that weren't funny, and he was the only one to laugh after the punch line. He thought himself a swell guy without realizing that his behavior was not quite fitting for an officer and physician. He showed me special *Kameradschaft*, slapping my shoulder every time I was near enough and calling me "my colleague", knowing very well that I had only half a semester of medical school under my belt.

"Where is Sergeant Ojamaa. Get me Sergeant Ojamaa… on the double!"

Dr. Kaupmees was sitting behind the desk in his office, shouting orders at the corpsmen. He had just returned from an important officers' meeting and wanted to see me without delay.

I was found and brought to him and the others were asked to leave. When there were just two of us, he stood up, full of authority:

"I will be in charge of our regiment's first aid station at the front. I have requested that Sergeant Ojamaa be transferred to my medical outpost and I will appoint you as my staff sergeant. Besides treating the wounded you will be in charge of keeping a detailed list of casualties for the regiment's office and maintaining adequate inventory. Most important, you're not going out to the trenches, but will stay with me at all times as my number-one assistant. How does that suit you?"

I had been hoping that Dr. Toom would assign me to his crew at Battalion Headquarters, but this did not seem likely after the "Oil of Anise" incident. I did not think Dr. Kaupmees would be put in charge of anything, but it had come about and his arrangement would, *Got sei Dank*[15], keep me from treating the wounded on snowy battlefields that were under enemy fire. It was in the Rakvere military hospital, when I was about to enter Head-Nurse Hildegard's doghouse, that I coined the phrase "when the need is the greatest the help is nearest". Help had come from an unexpected source. I tried to suppress my delight, and managed to keep my answer to, "If that's what the doctor orders."

There was another hard slap on my right shoulder, "You bet your boots! And I have also asked for Sergeant Mägi (no relation to the Mägi from the Eastern Front) to be transferred to my outpost. To wrap up our team, a horseman with horse and sleigh will also be assigned to me. I'll pick out the right man myself and let him pick out the horse." Then he just stood there with his elbows out, rubbing his palms together with visible excitement.

"Oh-boy-oh-boy... I'll have my own outfit and in no time we will be ready for action...!"

Dr. Leonard Kaupmees came from an eminent family. They even had a butler! This fact made him well qualified to find the right man to complete his team.

He rushed out that same evening to the barracks to interview the "rank and file" for the job. I must admit, he found a needle in a haystack and came up with a dandy. The man exceeded all expectations, and his first name was, Napoleon.

The fact that Sergeant Mägi, a baby-faced young man with a soft voice and polite manners, was joining our outfit was good news for me. We had become friends at the camp and even spent a ten day vacation together in Germany.

Military leaves were being canceled that late in the war except for soldiers who were still in the training camp and extended only for those who had relatives living in Germany. Mägi and I did not know a soul, but we claimed to have aunts in Berlin. We filled out our application requests with fictitious names and addresses and were rewarded with a ten-day leave to Berlin.

Would you have liked to spend your vacation in Berlin in early December, 1944? Hardly. It is not much fun to inspect ruins in a cold and drizzly rain. Besides, if you've seen one street in ruins, you've seen them all. To be honest, we didn't have much time even for that as we spent most of our evenings and nights in air-raid shelters. Having lived through so many close calls in the past, I thought it might be a shame to get killed while on vacation.

My partner came up with an idea, "Let's assume our aunts have moved! But the question is, where they might have gone?"

Let's say Stockholm," was my wishful answer, remembering that I had once been offered the choice and turned it down.

My friend became annoyed. "I wish cows could fly! Let's be realistic. "Where else could we go?"

We stepped into a cafeteria, ordered *Kartoffelpuffern mit Sauerkraut*[16] for lunch, and studied the map. We picked out a small town called Hildesheim. Its name sounded friendly, ending as it did with "heim" (home). It was some 150 miles west and not a likely target for nightly air-raids by Allied bombers. There was no problem at headquarters after they found out we were not asking for extension of our *Urlaub*[17] rather a *Marschbefehl* to Hildesheim, to catch up with our elusive aunts.

The train trip itself was heartwarming.

Even sitting in the warm compartment and looking through the window at the fleeing landscape in the cold rain was itself rewarding. The passengers, mostly women, were friendly folks, eager to initiate conversations. Some of them were the motherly type. Seeing us in uniform made them worry about their own sons in the front. They even asked after our mothers, and wondered if they knew anything of our whereabouts.

There were always a number of lonely women on the train, women with husbands at the front or killed in action. They were eager to sit close to us with their legs crossed, their skirts short, showing a good part of their upper legs and their blouses open at the collar revealing flashes of their veiled bosoms. We could feel the warmth of their bodies and see passion in their eyes but did not know how to respond to their invitation. The evening darkness fell over us in the speeding train and over the besieged land. I did not feel lonely when sitting next to a young woman on a night train, without a flicker of light near or far.

---

[15] thank God
[16] potato pancakes with pickled cabbage
[17] vacation

Chapter 3

Blood in the Snow

On a snowy day in mid-January, 1945, our division left Neuhammer and took positions at the Eastern Front in the village of Berghof, near the Oder-Neisse River in the Province of Silesia.

———

As our advance scout, Napoleon had secured our first-aid station in the middle of the recently evacuated village by finding an appropriate building and nailing the sign *Verwundete Sammelstelle,*[18] with our division emblem, to the gatepost.

The building had been the village general store. Its spacious living room was reserved for the treatment of battle casualties. The furniture was removed from the room, a throw-rug covered the floorboards and pot-bellied stove was supplied the heat. Two tables were pushed against a wall without windows, and here our medical supplies were laid out in a hurry. Alcohol burners were lit under the sterilizers. The treatment table was piled high with bandages, tourniquets, and ampules of morphine, tetanus toxoid, and coramine. Below it were rolls of plaster of Paris, splinters, and a bucket of water. A few surgical instruments, such as forceps, curved clamps and needle holders, were laid out with catgut sutures to ligate bleeding vessels. Next to them were basins with boiled water and sterile sponges. Our supplies did not include blood, plasma, or intravenous fluids. Only whiskey and cigarettes could be offered as auxiliary "treatment," if requested.

With our preparations completed, we stood for a moment surveying our achievement and watching Napoleon break up furniture to feed the stove.

Soon the dry wood made it glow red, clearing the vapor from our breath and melting the ice-flowers off the windows. The cracking of the stove, dripping of the melting ice, and hissing of alcohol lamps under glass sterilizers were the only sounds in the eerie room. An ominous silence hung over our treatment room and the village, the snow-covered fields and the forest beyond.

———

The sudden thunder of guns broke the tranquility and soon melted into a continuous roar, at times breaking up into occasional firings, then was followed by bursts of machine gun rattle and the howling and hissing of mine-throwers. The deep roar of voices followed, as our regiment rose for the attack. The roar increased in volume, like something ready to burst open. I stood next to the window where the ice had melted. I could see a segment of the snowy field through a triangular space between two houses. Men were rising and falling, some rising again, then continuing their advance toward the opposing woods. I could not follow them further as the roof of a nearby house blocked my view. I kept staring at the triangle where men lay motionless, scattered at random.

Our first casualty was a young boy of 18 whose lower body had been run over by a tank. Dr. Kaupmees pulled down his pants to reveal testicles ballooned out to his knees, filled with guts. When the rapid quivering of his eyelids stopped and the few irregular heartbeats had come to an end, the corpsmen carried him out to the snowbank next to the entrance, his back resting against the treatment room wall.

Then they arrived, a few walking, others carried on a stretcher or pulled in on special sleighs. Late arrivals had to wait outside, as the floor in the treatment room was filled with moaning and bleeding bodies on stretchers, barely leaving room to step between them. If it weren't for the thick carpet soaking up spilled blood we all would have been slipping and falling.

If death came in the waiting line, corpsmen cleared their stretchers and sleighs and piled the bodies against the snow covered wall and rushed back to haul in another load. Wounded men had to be registered in our books, their condition recorded, treatment, if any, rendered. Their button-holes were then tagged with the information before they could be cleared for transport. Ambulances were standing by to take them to the nearest field hospital.

By late afternoon, the battle was won.

The enemy had been ousted from the nearby woods. Victory was ours. The ambulances had cleared the wounded and the corpsmen had collected the bodies from the field and added them to the pile at our doorstep. After the last corpsmen had faded into the early darkness with sledges that were now empty, I stood outside on the slippery steps to view the piled up corpses. All I could think was, "I don't have to identify them or break their dog-tags tonight. I could leave it for tomorrow!"

The main street remained empty containing nothing but drifting snow under the low-lying clouds. The only sound was the distant howl of a lonely dog. "The lucky one," I thought. The residents had their pets shot as a *coup de grace* before leaving. (There was no room for dogs in crowded trains.) This one had somehow escaped execution. Feelings of solitude overwhelmed me and I found myself standing there in the early darkness, howling along with the lonesome dog. No wonder we had so much in common.

The fire from the stove in the treatment room had burned out. The front door had been open throughout the day. It felt cold inside and smelled of disinfectant and discarded bandages.

After the newly-kindled fire had warmed the room, a thin cloud of vapor began to emerge from the blood-impregnated carpet. It rose toward the ceiling. I found a half-filled bottle of whiskey and took a good swig. It burned in my guts and helped me forget the bloodbath we all had witnessed.

Viva Victory! Was there anybody left to celebrate?

Attacking across an open field was murder! Whoever drew the battle plans should be demoted to corporal, I thought.

Oh, forget it. Take another swig from the bottle with a blood-stained label and remember the old dictum "A corporal ain't a general".

Our doctor was sitting on a lonely chair and resting his stretched-out feet on what was left of the treatment table. He seemed jovial. No wonder. He and his unit had stood up and handled a heavy load of casualties. The doctor had "held the fort" so to speak. I must admit, even after receiving the news of a Russian counterattack, he had responded, "Evacuate? Not in your life! I cannot desert my patients!" He went and got his gun belt, fastened it under his white coat and continued attending his patients and shouting orders as usual. Mägiand, I had no time to pay any attention to him. Get your own stuff! Well, he needed help applying a splint. His voice was like a foghorn, "Na-po-le-on!"

He had a habit of separating the name into syllabuses and stressing each one, but there was no Napoleon in sight, or even within hearing distance and he had to rest his vocal cords. Now that it was all over, he suddenly remembered his batman and yelled once more, "Na-po-le-on!"

A strongly built, rather short man with curly red hair appeared from somewhere. His eyes had a sly look. His freckled face was free of any expression. He stood at the doorway like a farmer who had finished his day of plowing and was at peace with the world and everything in it.

"Where have you been, Na-po-le-on!"

"I was prospecting, sir."

It was true. While we were attending the wounded, Napoleon had

219

chased down two stray chickens, and heated the stove with broken-up furniture. As the chickens were frying, he had crawled into the attic and made an important discovery, a whole sack of coffee beans and a case of champagne. Our doctor, however, was not yet aware of Napoleon's accomplishments, and he continued his mock investigation, trying to unnerve his valet.

"I am not sure what I will do with you, Na-po-le-on! Maybe I'll send you to the trenches instead of having you court martialed... Maybe I'll have you shot! How about it, Na-po-le-on!?"

Napoleon only had an innocent smile for an answer.

"Dammit, I'll have you shot for sure!"

As soon as the doctor heard what Napoleon had prepared for supper, his threats became praise.

We ate a candlelight dinner of fried chicken and oven-baked potatoes, all of it washed down with chilled champagne. The dinner was served in the dining room with a linen table cloth and fine cutlery. He even had found a gramophone in one of the bedrooms in the house, and entertained us with dinner music. The singer was somebody named Mimi Toma, and she sang in a low voice:

> Wer die Heimat liebt,
> So wie du und ich –
> Kann in fremden Ländern
> Nie glücklish sein...

> Who loves his homeland
> Like you and I -
> Could never be carefree
> In a foreign land...

It really is strange that after so many years I can still recall the name of the singer and the words she sang. Well, it was no ordinary day and not an ordinary meal.

Dr. Kaupmees drank two glasses of champagne and became quite talkative. He pardoned Napoleon, no execution, no court marshal. He promoted him from "Private First Class" to Na-po-le-on, the Miracle Man, praising his culinary skills and scouting ability.

He made a speech, more colorful than his usual monologue, "My friends, forget that I am the officer in charge. Forget that you are only sergeants and you, Na-po-le-on, that you are just the Miracle Man. We are eating chicken which is not ours and drinking someone else's champagne. I have never had alcoholic beverage before or eaten what is not legally mine. Tonight I have made an exception-because the true owner would never be able to return and enjoy his chickens or his beverages. The Russians will drink his champagne and belch, eat his chickens and pass gas. And that is the reason I, as the commanding office, give you, Na-po-le-on, my permission to use your God-given talent to catch as many stray chickens as you can and broil them to the best of your ability."

"Amen!" came the answer from Napoleon.

My God! Mägi and I did not believe it. He truly was a "lily of the valley", trying to keep us from feeling guilty for having a decent meal. By the same token, forgetting all his officer's crap, we had to admire his innocence, a mama's boy direct from medical school to the blood-bath. He should be preserved under glass in some museum. But just the same, he stood up under pressure and his speech made us feel good. Or perhaps it was the champagne!

Napoleon served us coffee. Not German *Ersatz,* not Finnish *korvike,* but real coffee made from freshly-ground coffee beans. His brew was too strong and hot. The steam from our coffee cups rose to the ceiling, blending with the vapors from the treatment room carpet, forming an arcane blend. We mixed the hot coffee with chilled champagne to cool it, an unusual drink indeed, pleasant in taste and easy to swallow. To save the candles, only one was left burning, barely outlining our faces.

The wind was up.

And the snow was falling heavy against the treatment room windows.

Our doctor had become one of us. He did not even mention his superior rank as he continued to reminisce. "We are having a feast tonight while our dead comrades are piled up next to our doorstep. Shouldn't we be feeling grief and keep wake throughout the night?"

"My friends, a doctor cannot share anyone's sorrow. Besides, there is not a hell of a lot of difference between us and the ones outside. Of course, we are still alive and they are not. Not any more. But the difference is only in time. Our candle is still burning tonight, but it might not be tomorrow. The way I look at it is, our friends outside are actually a step ahead of us and we all have some catching up to do. Until we do, I say, *Freut euch des Lebens,weil noch das Lämpchen glüht...*"[19]

The lonely candle had burned close to its end. The melted wax looked like frozen tears on the tablecloth. Our doctor's spirited speech called for another sip of our acrid punch.

With an odd felling of nostalgia, I started reminiscing about a funeral procession in the deep Russian winter of 1942. I was again there, sitting on the straw-covered sleigh and holding the casket made of weather-beaten boards. The Russian women gathered in silence and wiped their eyes with babushka corners. The rest of our squad stood motionless at the doorstep with hands crossed or in their pockets, eager to return to their card game. They made their bids and frowned if they drew the queen of spades. Then the driver pulled the reins and the horse started its slow walk through the snowbound village to the edge of the forest -our burial ground. The horse did not need any guidance to find his way back to the village. We had plenty of room on the straw-covered sleigh. The space previously occupied by the casket was all ours. We stretched out, lying on our backs and watching the low-lying clouds drift in the early nightfall and our arms and backs were still aching after shoveling the semi-frozen earth. To alleviate our discomfort, physical or otherwise, the quartermaster had supplied us, the undertakers, with a bottle of whiskey. We took turns tilting its bottom toward the darkening sky while a few snowflakes started to fall. Then my buddy, the driver of the sleigh, announced that he was drinking to Külmoja's health. That was the name of my friend whom we had just buried. His statement, as funny as it was, lifted my spirit, "Why not!...Here is to you, my friend...!"

The liquor burned in my stomach and made my head spin. We were still laughing as we pulled next to the horse barn in the village. The lesson learned, if you feel gloomy because you've lost a friend, drink to his health! It will lift your spirits and mend your misery, heal your pain and wash off your sorrow.

A moment of silence followed at our dinner table. We could hear the wind in the chimney and ice crystals beating against the window.

The candle flickered.

A horse-like laugh broke the silence as our doctor lifted his glass, "Let's drink to the health of our dead comrades out in the cold!"

The new day came with pale sun and freezing temperatures. The wind had died down at dawn but the night's storm had left snowdrifts high in our back yard. The pot-bellied stove in the treatment room was fed once more with broken-up furniture. The ice-flowers on the windowpane-regrown overnight-started to melt, dripping water on the still-soaked carpet.

The bravado of the previous night was forgotten.

We ate our breakfast in silence until Dr. Kaupmees reminded me of the casualty report I had to finish and take to battalion headquarters.

Napoleon went out to clear the back yard of snowdrifts. I was to identify the dead while Mägi, holding the pencil and a number of large envelopes, became the recorder. To my dismay I found the bodies frozen together by their blood-soaked garments. I had to cut their clothing with my all-purpose *puukko*. It had served me faithfully for over a year now and I had never realized the variety of tasks it would be called upon to perform.

I now had them all separated and lined up in a single row on the ground where Napoleon had cleared away the snowdrifts. I reached for their dog-tags, broke them with a snapping sound and read out the numbers. Mägi had a hard time recording them, his fingers stiff from the cold. I had to repeat the numbers to avoid mistakes. Identification badges and personal belongings were placed in the designated envelopes and sealed. This sequence of events repeated itself until all were registered and the yellow tags were tied to their shoe laces. When the final body count matched the number of sealed envelopes, we hurried back to the warmth of the pot-bellied stove. By then the ice had melted from the windows and I could see a canvas-covered truck pulling up. The driver and his assistant hoisted the frozen bodies like logs into its dark interior, raised up the back and bolted it shut. Then they rushed to the shelter of the cab and took off in a hurry. I stood for a moment at the window which was still dripping from the melting ice, as though it was shedding the tears nobody had for the men in the truck now on their way to a common grave. I remembered with nostalgia the tender funerals of my dead comrades a few winters ago.

In the same afternoon, riding horseback, I took the casualty reports to the regimental headquarters and brought back a gallon of milk from the nearby village, donated by friendly women. Napoleon could now make hot chocolate from the cocoa powder he had found in the pantry.

Days and weeks followed in the deserted and snowbound village. The front remained quiet except for an occasional barrage from the Russian cannons, their random firepower exploding harmlessly in the distant fields. Life in our field station became routine. We treated an occasional wounded soldier, smeared zinc oxide on frozen toes, and handed out aspirin and sulfa drugs for the winter colds. The only excitement was a fire in a nearby military warehouse, netting us two dozen cases of champagne. The initial excitement over our cache soon dwindled as Mägi and I realized we could not drink it all by ourselves. The doctor had switched to hot chocolate and Napoleon did not count as a drinking partner. We did not associate with low-ranking privates.

Do not assume that the rest of the winter consisted of leisurely living, drinking champagne and dining by candlelight. Quite the opposite was true. The front was moving and mostly in a western direction. Once we were entirely surrounded by Russian forces, and when our division had broken through we could escape only by foot. The battalion aid station was already closed, and we were ready to pull out, our rucksacks on our backs, when the corpsmen brought in a wounded soldier. He was unconscious with a bullet in his brain, but very much alive. Dr. Kaupmees made a quick decision, "We cannot leave him for the Russians to brutalize him. Sergeant Ojamaa, how much *morphium* do we have?"

"Fifteen ampoules 10 milligrams each, 150 milligrams, total. All packed away in my rucksack."

"Dammit. Get it out and give him 100 milligrams at once and intravenously," then mumbling to himself: "That should depress his respiration and he can die in peace."

Well, it was ten times the normal dose, but I followed the doctor's orders, and gave the stuff by IV. Then we just stood around him with our packs on our backs, waiting for him to die in a hurry.

He started to snore instead.

"Sergeant. Give him the rest of our *morphium* IV."

"Yes sir. 50 milligrams coming up IV!"

Our patient continued to snore even louder.

The battalion's last patrol was going through. Seeing us, they were alarmed, "What the hell... The order to pull out was given order an hour ago and you are still here!"

That annoyed our good doctor immensely. He was the God and Jesus Christ all in one in his station and nobody would push him around-Russians or no Russians, "Can't you see we are busy. I make the decision here when we should pull out and when to stay!"

The guys in the patrol shrugged their shoulders. They were just sergeants and our doctor was an officer's candidate. Who is ordering whom around anyway?

"Suit yourself!" they said and left in a hurry.

With every passing moment Mägi and I got more restless. The boys at the front might not be able to keep the Russians at bay much longer.

Napoleon was standing at the window.

224

"See any Russians yet?"

"Not yet."

The good doctor's frustration grew. "Dammit. I am not going to leave my patient for the Russians to kick around. He has a bullet in his brain and he will never recover… Sergeant Ojamaa, you better shoot him."

"Not me, sir. This would be a major operation and only doctors are qualified to perform those."

"Now, you give it to me straight," he said, "If you were in his position, what would you prefer? To be shot by me or left to the Russians?"

"Not the Russians. You shoot me!" was my quick answer.

"The same here," was Mägi's response.

"How about you, Na-po-le-on?"

"You shoot!" Napoleon replies.

"Dammit!" our doctor swore, I'll have to do it. I'm not looking forward to it but I have to do my duty. Help me drag him out to the horse barn."

We helped do this, and then our good doctor shot him.

I am not saying it was wrong, but I don't know for sure. It still bothers me because he was not all there to give us permission. I could never have shot him, but on the other hand I gave him all the *morphium* IV, and this does not leave me scot-free. I am quite sure that I'd rather have my friend shoot me than leave me to the Russians. On the other hand, I am not sure, whether I would have been able to give *coup de grace* to anybody. I could not even shoot dogs brought to us by their crying owners before evacuation.

Until now, I have kept this incident to myself, but I feel better now that I have spoken about it.

We all made out all right, but barely. The Russian artillery fire was quite fierce over no-man's land as we crossed the muddy fields half-running and half-walking, each boot feeling like it weighed a ton.

[18]casualty clearing station
[19]Enjoy life, while the lamp is still burning…

Chapter 4

The Yellow Road

I was alone.

Walking, at times running with a typical military jog, along the yellow road. It was spring day in early May with a soft breeze blowing in my face and the green rolling fields on both sides trying to keep me in a cheerful mood. I had nothing to carry, no rucksack, no bag. I was still wearing my military uniform with a shield of Estonian colors on my left sleeve and a pair of soft-leather officer's boots which Napoleon had found in our cellar and which fit my feet exclusively. I had no hat, belt, or weapon of any kind. I swung my hands freely, making good progress along the road without knowing where I was going or even what to expect. But these unknowns didn't upset me, since I had lived with the unexpected since my late teens.

The dust from the road made my throat and mouth dry, but there were no wells or houses close by, and I was reluctant to leave the main road which became crowded at times with soldiers, all without weapons and belts. I did not like to look into their sweaty and anxious faces, and let them pass so I could be alone, at least until another flock caught up with me.

I happened to be alone when a couple of locals, a young man and woman, caught up with me. I stepped aside to let them pass but the young man grabbed me by my shoulder and held on, pointing to my boots. He was tall and muscular, and there seemed no way I could win an argument over ownership of my footwear. I displayed passive resistance, just standing there with desperation in my face. Compared even to bullets, this was probably the most hopeless predicament to have faced. I could not see how I could continue barefooted. It was too late for me to realize the hazards of traveling alone.

His lady-love looked into my panic-stricken face, then gave her companion a powerful and unexpected push, making him stagger backwards and lose his grip on my shoulder. Whether she took pity on me or just didn't approve of "highway robbery" remains a mystery to me. She accompanied her physical interference with a forceful accusation in a language I did not understand. I turned my back towards the struggling couple and continued with a leisurely walk, trying to give the impression that the episode had come to a peaceful conclusion and I had no reason to make haste. This event made me feel less a transient guest in this country, as promised at the border, and more like a *persona non grata.* But perhaps I've lost you here, and need to go back to May 8, 1945.

That was the day Germany surrendered.

My encounter on the yellow road took place three days later. Our Estonian division, along with countless German units who had been fighting the Russians, were fleeing west to surrender to Allied forces. No one wished to be captured by advancing Russians, already breathing down our necks. Alas, disaster struck us at the first road-crossing where processions of men, heavy weapons and supply columns from three directions had to merge into one-going west. It was pandemonium of indescribable proportions. When the Russian planes showed up, we hit the road on foot, leaving everything behind. To get to West Germany we had to cross through part of Czechoslovakia, which had declared itself as an independent state just a few days ago. The temporary Czech border guards did not allow anyone with arms to enter their territory. By then we were like a flock of loose sheep without any bargaining chips. We gave up our handguns and rifles at the border and in return we were promised safe passage through their country. A spoken word in a hostile country, evaporating further down the road, is like a morning fog.

The guards were riding bicycles and encouraging us, "...Hurry ... Hurry!! The Americans will leave Jaromer at noon. If you make it there in time, you will be in their hands. If not, you will have to face the Russians."

Run, rabbit, run...

Hours passed. The crowd of fleeing men in messy uniforms, with neither caps nor belts, was scattered along the graveled road as far as the eye could see. They kicked up dust, which hung in the windless air, curving and bending along with the road like a hangmen's rope.

It's only 10 kilometers, and only eleven o'clock. Forget the sweat burning in your eyes and the thirst choking your throat. Above the cloud of dust one could see the shining city on the hill, Jaromer, our new Jerusalem! Our salvation!

I threw a glance over my shoulder.

A Volkswagon was off the side of the road, its doors open; suitcase still tied to the roof, lid ripped open and garments still scattered in the dust. An elderly couple was sitting in the front seat, motionless. The dashboard was covered with blood and swarming with flies.

"Hurry, hurry! You've only got 10 minutes...!"

We were already in the city.

The sidewalks were crowded with people. When they looked into our sweat-streaked, dusty faces, women laughed, "Look at the monkeys!"

The men swore and spat into the roadside dust not far from our running feet.

We were led into a fenced-in, grassy soccer field. The gates were closed and rifle-carrying guards began circling the perimeter. To run the last 10 kilometers and end up in a trap! No Americans in sight.

The Russian troops arrived two days later. They took over the camp and we officially became their POWs. They searched us thoroughly, man by man. They claimed the wristwatch my father had given me for my 15th birthday. Many of them had their sleeves turned up. Their forearms were lined with watches from wrist to elbow.

After the search they took us back the same road we had come running in on, but this time forcibly directed back to the east. Well, it had finally happened. The cat-and-mouse game had come to its final chapter. My transgressions against the Soviet regime were too numerous to be forgotten or forgiven. I had evaded their draft and fought against them with the Germans and Finns. The KGB was not exactly known as a humanitarian fellowship.

All this did not bother me. The only regret I had was getting caught. Besides, I still had some options open. First, I was among a multitude of German prisoners, and I blended well into the crowd. I had already removed the Estonian coat of arms from my left sleeve and the Estonian Division's insignia from my uniform collar. I did not have any identification papers, but then neither did most of the German POWs.

My name was now Alfred Schulz, and I was from Baden Baden. That was the information I gave to the Russians and if you would have asked me about Estonia, I would have shook my head and answered, "Did you say Estonia?! No, never heard of the place!"

I had never heard of Baden Baden either, in fact until I struck up a conversation with a fellow POW who was from that city. He was about 30, an intelligent-looking chap. His eyes had a dreamy look when he started to reminisce about Baden Baden, his small home town. It was in the beautiful Schwarzwald Mountains, with all its mineral springs and health spas. What's more, it was quite far to the west, close to the French border. I became interested in his home town for obvious reasons. The Russians had premised to send everybody home and Baden-Baden seemed an ideal destination. The friendly fellow prisoner had even supplied me a street address, scribbled on a piece of paper in my pocket. There were also few Estonians in that prison transport. I do not know how many or where they were from, but most certainly not from Estonia. Someone in front of me in the line stumbled, and then swore:, *Oh sa kurat!*[20]

"What was that?" I inquired.

"Mind your own business," was the answer.

The Russians claimed to be having "difficulties" completing the paperwork, the only thing preventing them from sending up home the next day. That was the reason we were made to march east for a few days, so they could get us to the place where they were keeping all our discharge papers. Meanwhile, we were marching five abreast in an endless column, in sun and rain. Drinking water and occasional slice of bread was supplied now and then, but when it came to eating we were left to our own devices. The predicament was, we were not allowed to break rank. Fellows who had eaten grass were having trouble with their bowels. A sudden urge made one jump across the ditch and drop his pants in a hurry. The nearest guard had his frolic by firing a volley from his automatic weapon, hitting the ground just a step or two in front of the diarrhea Charley. This of course, scared the daylights out of him and he ran back in a hurry, trying to pull up his pants with one hand while the liquid excrement was still running down his legs, inside his pants. The guards loved playing "Russian Roulette" with us and getting a bellyful of laughs in return.

"Yoptvoiu mat!... That'll teach him a lesson!"

I abstained from eating grass, knowing well that diarrhea takes more out of your system than you can ever put in by eating grass! During our march I kept my eyes glued to the nearby ditch, looking for empty food cans. Spotting one, I had to time my jump to retrieve it before the guards had time to play "Russian Roulette" on me. Sometimes there was a little meat left inside the can. If not, you could still wipe the inner surface with your finger and pick up a small amount of grease.

We reached a Czechoslovakian village on Sunday.

I know it was Sunday, because the church bells were ringing. Our guards ordered us to lie down in the roadside ditch, and then most of them went into the village, where they were greeted with flowers and treats of all kinds.

Church goers went by, dressed in their Sunday best. They were talking and laughing and gave no sign of noticing us down by their feet.

There was a house close to the ditch with an open window.

Its lace curtains were fluttering in the breeze, the sunlight falling on a white bed cover and pillows. I was dreaming of being at home again, and felt myself ready to lie in that sunlit bed. All the misery had only been a bad dream and now all was well again. I could hear them talking with hushed voices so as not to distract me in my tranquil sleep. Their prodigal son was home again.

The ditch I was lying in was damp. The chill cut through my thin garments, dulling the gnawing pain in my empty belly. The balance between real and unreal had become cloudy, with only a nebulous line between imagination and delusion.

Still in a state of semi-awareness, I stood up and walked into the house with the sunlit curtains.

Nobody stopped me.

The room was unfamiliar, the people at the breakfast table, strangers. They stopped their forks and spoons and gawked at me in hostile silence. I realized this was not my home or my folks.

I asked for a slice of bread.

A man at the end of the table pointed with zest behind me, saying, "There is your bread."

I turned to look and saw a slice of bread floating-fluffy and swollen-in a half-filled bucket of urine.

I left the house and returned to my ditch.

The visionary dream had turned into a nightmare, and my first attempt at begging had ended in humiliation. I remembered Nietzsche's line, *Whoever gives bread to the hungry, invigorates his own soul.*

I do not intend to recount the miseries of my imprisonment. The subject is superfluous, hurtful, and dull. Still, I cannot forget that Sunday morning episode in a Czechoslovakian village out of my mind.

The next day we left Czechoslovakia behind and entered East German territory. We saw only women with solemn faces, some of them crying. The guards were reinforced and they nervously manipulated their automatic weapons. The prisoners were back in their *Heimatland*, and there was danger of desertion.

There weather was mostly sunny, with heavy dew at night.

Occasional rain showers streaked our filthy hands and faces, making us look like painted clowns. Another night spent in the plowed fields would then cover the streaks uniformly with dirt. Only eyeballs, teeth, and smooth fingernails would flash out from the universal color which was gray.

Evening came with early fog and scattered rain showers. The guards herded us into a tight circle on a recently-plowed field, surrounding us with camp fires and sentries. We were to lay down in the mud and were not allowed to stand up without permission. If anybody felt the need to "obey nature's call", he had to give a hand signal to the nearest sentry, who would walk him outside the perimeter to relieve himself.

A fellow next to me kept mumbling and tossing around, as if he were fighting the devil himself. The circumstances were less than favorable for sleep, and his behavior did not make it any easier. Before I had the chance to kick him, I understood two of his words, *"Kuradi venelased!"*[21]

"Ah-hah! A fellow country-man. Not happy with your sleeping arrangement," was my inquiry in our native tongue.

If he was surprised, he did not show it.

"So what! Mind your own business."

I could well understand his being sore. I had blown his cover of impersonating a German prisoner. Of course, one had to be careful about the informers, the ones looking for a companion to desert with. For an extra slice of bread he might pass the information along, and the guard would keep an extra-steady eye on you. In case you had an "urgent call of nature" and jumped across the ditch, you'd never make it back alive.

Since I responded to him in Estonian, I had blown my own cover of "Alfred Schulz from Baden-Baden". He did not need to address me in German. I was no snoop. I offered to share a piece of sod which I was using as a pillow. The rain had departed. The wind was up, blowing away the last patches of fog but bringing in smoke from the smoldering camp fires. We were wet in the mud and too miserable for sleep.

I started a hushed conversation in our native tongue, "What do you make of the situation?"

"Scheisser![22] The worst mess."

"Well, same here! '25+5' is the best I can hope for, thank you."

"You're welcome. I consider myself lucky to claim Siberia as my permanent residence." Then he added, "It's odd, the Germans started the war and German POWs are better off than us. The war is over and they will be going home sooner or later. We, who fought only for the freedom of our own country, we have to hide ourselves behind the true villains. Heads, you lose and tails, you lose. Is that fair?"

He became agitated again, "When the time is right, I'll clear out. All or nothing! Taking the chance to be a free man is better than hiding behind German prisoners. I'd rather be under the roadside turf here than buried in Siberia."

His firm stand gave my own downcast spirits a lift. Saying it aloud had helped him make up his mind and reinforced my own decision. So far we had been marching along an open road with farm fields on both sides. An escape attempt under these circumstances would be suicide. It would have been easier to desert in Czechoslovakia, but one would not get very far trying to sneak away in a hostile country. Here we would at least have the sympathy of the natives. They would be afraid to hide you, but would not report you to the Russians.

"Well, I go along with the decamping idea," I said, "but when the time and place is right. I haven't counted all my chickens. Not yet!"

"Good. We'll stick together and see what might happen. By the way, my name is Kask, Vello Kask."

He turned on his other side, a reckless move. Before this, he was muddy and wet on one side, and just wet on the other. Now he was muddy and wet all over.

My own hip was sinking into the morass and this spread the chill throughout my body. I still owned my canvas wallet which the Russians did not feel worth taking. Way back they had claimed my officer's boots, but had left me a worn-out pair of regulars. My officer's boots were too small to fit the Russian who took them, but he took them just the same.

This all went through my mind as I pulled the canvas wallet out from my inside pocket, which was still all dry and warm, and pushed it under my right hip. This relieved my chill and I couldn't help but think how nice it was to own something, something handy in a time of need. I was not as careless as my countryman. I did not change my sides, just tried to get some sleep and disregard the smoke from the campfires.

The next day was sunny from the start.

By noon my clothes were almost dry and the caked mud on the side I had slept on started to crumble and lose its stiffness. We had a short break at noon, and continued our shuffled walk into the night. According to the rumors, a freight train was waiting for us at the Polish border to take us to the East. The trains had been busy hauling war booty to

Mother Russia during the last stages of the war, and they could not sit idle for long. That was the likely reason the guards marched us at this late hour along an unpaved road through a pine forest. The circumstances made the guards nervous. They tried to speed us up by shouting, and shooting their weapons at random.

Flashes from the guard's automatic weapons illuminated the tree trunks behind us as Kask and I implemented our "leap for freedom" with good timing. The pine forest and low bushes were only a few steps from the road and gave us instant cover. All the guards could do was shoot blindly into the forest. They could not chase us and leave the prisoners unguarded.

It was a foolish move anyway to take the transport through the woods at night, but who was complaining? They had made us free men in the pitch-black forest. After the first wild dash, we stopped to catch our breath. Because of darkness and a heavy canopy of trees overhead, we could not see enough stars to orient ourselves. The worst scenario would be to head in the wrong direction and run into Polish border guards. The best would be to spend our night here and try to find our way in daylight.

The stillness was both overwhelming and pacifying. It was such a welcome change from the guards and their random firing. Here, one could almost hear pine needles dropping on the dry ground and restless birds adjusting their wings in their nests. We piled up dry pine needles for a bed. It was a far cry from the muddy fields of previous nights.

I could not help but think that once again I had beaten the odds and escaped. Each new danger had led to a new escape. Round and round, like a dog chasing his own tail. Had I opened Pandora's box, leaving nothing but hope and no final escape? I was getting tired of hoping. Would I ever find my own "rock-pile" to hide in, like the enchanted rabbit at Härjarahu who so fortunately escaped a boiling pot of sorrel soup?

At the moment there were some 300 kilometers separating me from my protective "rock-pile", and the escape route was infested with the Russian military and the red-armband-carrying German militia. Besides -there was no bed of roses waiting for us at the other end of the road.

Run, rabbit… run.

[20]Oh, you devil (swearing in Estonian)
[21]Damned Russians
[22]shit

Chapter 5

Run, Rabbit, Run

The yellow road was fading into the green landscape.

There was a long line of refugees from Ober-Silesia Prussia, from Danzig and Frankfurt-am-Oder, and many other places in between.

Poland had claimed the eastern provinces of Germany and millions upon millions of people were evicted from their homes, towns and villages. The term of "ethnic cleansing" was not invented yet. There were women with children, a few men on crutches, and one with an arm and shoulder missing and his empty sleeve stuck under a military belt with *Gott nit uns*[23] on the buckle. There were people pulling play wagons and pushing baby carriages, all packed with a few of their belongings, meager food supplies, and dangling kitchen utensils. Their clothes and their wagons were covered with dust and they walked in a dreamlike state.

I was one of the sleepwalkers myself, helping to push Mrs. Meyer's baby carriage full of her bundles and dragging my right foot like a man with a wooden leg.

At Red Army checkpoints they waved us through, *"Horosho*[24]... keep going..."

Mother Russia needed only full-bodied men... no use for the one-legged and the armless, the old women and children. There were so many of us, filling the road for miles. There was no way to check them all. Nobody came to lift trouser-leg to check my wooden leg. The way I reasoned, even if they did, they were no orthopedic surgeons or neurologists to diagnose my affliction. A man with a horrible limp, twisting his butt to take a few steps, it makes no sense to drag him to Siberia just to croak there. If any of the guards at checkpoints gave me a second look, I limped up to him and asked for a smoke," *"Yest li u vas tabak? (*do you have tobacco?*)"*

I received a sympathetic look. Rank and file soldiers had a soft spot in their hearts for cripples. They handed me a handful of "makhorka"[25] from a pants pocket, a piece of *Pravda* from the other, and waved me on.

A funny thing happened the very first time I tried this trick. I must have been nervous. My hands were shaking and I was unable to roll my own cigarette. The guard noticed this and volunteered to do it for me.

He even sealed it with his own spit, lit it in his own mouth, and handed it over. All I had to do was smoke it. I could not thank him enough, repeating my, "Spasibo... spasibo... (thank you... thank you)"

"Pozhaluista! (you're welcome)"

One could not limp only when there seemed to be immediate danger. No sir, that would be dangerous. I limped even at midnight when going alone to the nearby bushes. Al this had, in fact, rearranged my brain centers and I forgot how to walk in a normal way.

In the evening we stopped at a roadside farmhouse to sleep in the barn. The farmer did not need to worry, lame or armless men could not run down any of his lively chickens! I washed my face under the pump and filled my cup with cool water. Then, I sat on the steps and watched the farmer's wife feed the pigs. The stuff she was handing out smelled so good it made my mouth water.

You might wonder what became of my buddy Vello Kask, since I haven't mentioned anything more about him.

I have to go back to the first fateful morning after our escape. He was a brave fellow, but too reckless. It is a lousy combination of traits and can get you into a mess in no time. That was what happened because of his anger and impatience.

He was rushing in front of me at the first village we came to, plowing ahead in the middle of the road like a drum major in an Easter parade. If he wanted to be the decoy, that was his business. I had misgivings about the place from the start, no soul in sight and an ominous tranquility hanging over the road, the orchard and nearby houses, I stayed on the right side of the road, walking on the soft grass next to the fence with cranberry and lilac bushes. When I reached a sharp turn in the road, I stole a quick look ahead. What I saw made me jump over the five-foot fence, and I landed under some wild currant bushes. I could see him through the fence, flanked by two Russian soldiers, their bayonets attached to their rifles, coming this way. I buried my head in the long grass and held my breath until their footsteps faded down the road. It was obvious that he hadn't snitched on me. The soldiers would have had an easy time spotting me under the nearby bushes. I sure was thankful to him for not telling them about me.

Before I could make my next move I heard a high-pitched squeal from the next house. I remained where I was and kept close to the ground. Haste under certain circumstances can be fatal!

All remained quiet, however, and I attributed the squeal to the pigs in the adjacent barn. Then, the front door slammed, and I could hear heavy footsteps in the gravel. Two Russian officers walked past me on the other side of the fence, only a few steps from me. They were holding their heavy caps in their hands and wiping their foreheads with the sleeves of their uniforms. "*Yoptvolu mat*" was all they had to say as they laughed and continued drying their sweaty-red faces.

All remained quiet after that incident and I was convinced the Russian patrol had left the village.

The anxious moments under the bushes had made my throat and mouth even drier, and I was in dire need of drinking water, even more than food. I felt safe approaching the house.

"Go away... go away!" said a woman in her early 40s as she hurried to the back porch: "The Russians will burn my house down if they find you here!"

"Now you listen... I am thirsty and hungry. Give me a mug of water and a slice of bread and I'll be gone," ...adding "please" at the end.

She stood on the porch and appeared confused for a moment. Her face was covered with perspiration, her hair in disarray with the ends stuck to her sweaty neck. Her blouse was torn in front and her dress was crumpled.

That explained the Russians' laughing spell.

She brought what I had asked for and then watched me with an empty stare until I disappeared behind her trees and bushes. She was not all there.

I kept her mug.

She wouldn't miss it!

I stayed with the *Flüchtlinge*[26] one more day, until we reached a small town with a railroad station. A passenger train was there to take the refugees further west.

The platform was packed with people and their belongings. The train had standing-room only. I did not go into a compartment after helping Mrs. Meyer's baby wagon aboard, but stayed in the hallway next to the window, keeping my eyes open. Sure enough, there were two pairs of Russian MPs with red arm bands, their rifles thrown across their backs, checking passports. They had started their control from both ends of the train, closing up in the middle. Every time the train stopped, they emerged from the previous wagon and stepped into the next. That made it easy for me. As they were closing in on the center, I mingled with the crowd on the platform and stepped leisurely into one of the already controlled wagons. I forgot to mention my military coat. I did not have it any more. The lady whose back yard I had been hiding in gave me a civilian jacket, not too large or too new to attract attention. My military pants looked like any ordinary pair, caked with mud a few times and then dried, now the color of roadside dust.

I blended in with the folks in the train. My German was fluent enough and if I took care, I could imitate a Berlin accent. You know, *"Ich bin ein Ber-r-liner"*[27].

I have to chuckle now when I think of a train incident that happened well before the end of the war. I was taking two Estonian soldiers with hepatitis from Neuhammer to Cottbus Hospital. I did not feel like sitting too close to them, and took my seat in the next compartment. There were always young women in trains during the war. The wagons were not lit, and I had found a seat next to a real nice girl, Soon we were holding hands and gazing together at the moonlit landscape through the train window and saying nice words to each other.

My buddies in the next compartment started to laugh and talk loud in our native tongue. I could not help but smile. They sure were happy with their disease! Actually, they even let me in on their secret. All one had to do was save up the butter rations for about two weeks and when it turned real rancid, eat it all at once. Just the butter and nothing else for a couple of days and presto. After a week or ten days your skin would turn yellow-green and your pee the color of dark beer.

Anyway, those guys started to celebrate their good fortune. That did not please my lady-love's romantic mood and she made a fleeing remark, *"Verrückte Ausländer!*[28]*"*

How could this slur come from my sweet lady's mouth, the one I had been cozying up to? Her remark started to bother me. I stood up, and said, "So am I, my lady-love, so am I."

And I left to join my yellow comrades-in-arms in the next compartment. Too bad. It broke up a beautiful relationship, but I was rewarded for holding onto my national pride. In Cottbus Hospital I met a bunch of vivacious Estonian nurses, and I spent a most memorable evening in their company.

I woke up from my daydreams to face post-war reality.

I didn't know a living soul and didn't own anything but a muddy wallet and a beat-up mug. Besides all that, I didn't even know where I was going. Mid-day had passed. The train with its bellowing engine threw long shadows on the green and yellow landscape where the dandelions were in full bloom. And then my old battle-fatigue fell over me. The same kind I had experienced near Taaveti, but more pronounced. I had felt quite cheerful a few moments earlier. Now, feelings of hopelessness sneaked over me at the least-expected moment. I realized my physical and mental reserve had been depleted for some time, and I had lost much weight as a prisoner. I even wondered how I had been able to manage the stress that far.

I felt faint and nauseous. I had to get out of the train, because it was the last place I wanted to be if I passed out!

When the train came to a screeching halt in the next station, I pushed my way out. The sign at the station spelled out "Zahna", the name of the town.

A few women in summer dresses were promenading on the platform. Were they just to meet the train or were they hoping for arrival of a lost son or husband? They were quietly staring at me. A few walked by, giving me a quick look and then continued their peaceful stroll. I had to disappoint them. I was the only newcomer in town and, of course, no one came to claim me.

After the train had taken off I continued to stand there, unable to decide which way to go. I should have known better: A fugitive must never stand alone on an empty platform. It was too late. A man in a black uniform with a red arm band was heading in my direction. I would not get too far by running. I turned and started to walk towards him, acting like he was the one I wanted to see, a member of the new East German Militia. His first statement was far from friendly, "Who are you and what is your business in Zahna?"

In situations like this, one could not win with a smile and apology. Hostility calls for self-assured response. I challenged his authority to detain a Soviet citizen. Of course, it was a bluff, and it did not work. He took me to the police station to be interviewed by the chief himself. My story was a simple one, I claimed to be a Soviet citizen, surviving forced labor in Nazi Germany and now on my way back to Mother Russia.

"Well, the Soviet Union is to the east. How come you are traveling west?"

"Very simple. As you know, the trains are jam-packed and people are standing even in the bathrooms. I was forced to use the station-house a few stops back, and by mistake boarded the wrong train."

The chief did not seem to know whether to believe me or not. But at the same time, he did not want to detain a Soviet citizen.

"It is out of my hands," he claimed. "If you are a citizen of the Soviet Union, I have to call the Red Army post in the city. They will know what to do with you."

Now I had really cooked my goose. It was distasteful for me to claim Soviet citizenship in the first place. It was a put-on, and it had backfired.

He rang up the military post but seemed to have trouble getting his message across. Nobody there seemed to understand German.

The chief hung up. "Well. The officer in charge is out, and I did not get a satisfactory response."

That meant the tide had turned again in my favor. Once more I stressed the importance of Soviet citizenship. Who won the war anyhow! and so on. We were not arguing over peanuts-my freedom was at stake.

It worked. The old chief let me go with a warning, "The next train to Frankfurt and further east is due here tomorrow morning, and you better be on it! If my men find you loitering there after the deadline, you will be arrested. And I do not want to see your face here again!"

I could have pressed him for a "freebie", but thought better of it. What would I do with a ticket to Frankfurt anyway?

I left the police station with both hands in my pockets. I had made out all right.

I could stroll around in Zahna tonight without any worry, a rare commodity. To spend the time, I started to wonder about its name-Zahna. It did not sound German. More like some Greek goddess. Zeus' wife could be called Zahna. Close enough; besides, it had the right *Klang* to it - Zeus and Zahna. Zeus was a womanizer and one of his wives or concubines could very well have been caked Zahna. She must have been something to look at, Zeus would not go for the ugly ones. Somehow I felt I had Zahna's blessing, and that I'd make out all right in a town named after her.

The sun had set, and a pleasant stillness hung in the air. The hours of dusk added to the feeling of serenity as I walked in the middle of the cobblestone street. The sudden anxiety I had felt in the train had left me and besides, I liked this place! Who knows, maybe somewhere in this town supper was waiting for me. There were no refugees here to make the folks stingy and cold-hearted. Besides, a young man about town was a scarcity, might even be a conversation piece. My encounter with the police could testify to that.

There were still a few people out taking their evening walk. They turned their heads or even stopped as I walked by. It did not take long until two women left their sidewalk and were heading in my direction.

One was tall and slender, rather good looking with short dark wind-blown hair and large brown eyes in a small suntanned face. The other lady was shorter, maybe 50. She had the pleasant look of a kind-hearted housewife.

We all stopped, facing each other. I know I was nothing to look at-unshaven and all dirty, with my clothes full of dust. For some reason they did not seem to mind. The older woman spoke up, "Can we be of some help to you?"

I knew how to behave. Getting overly emotional and chummy would frighten the women. It was best to act cool, and make them feel you were making out all right and not out looking for handouts.

"Well, I arrived by train and have met your Chief of Police or Militia Chief, whatever you might call him. He asked me to clear out of town by tomorrow morning. Until then," I shook my shoulders... "Until then, I guess I'm just taking in some sights!"

The older lady was the sentimental type. Must have seen the hopeless look in my face that I was eager to hide.

"You come with us and we'll take good care of you!"

She took my arm and pulled me along down the middle of the street, the younger lady on my right, the other on my left.

I felt as if I was going home. Up to that point in my long journey nobody had addressed me with kind words. I had been told *"you come with us"* only by the Russian KGB and the German military police. The phrase never had such a tender ring to it as it did with this German *Hausfrau.*

What else is there to add? They drew a hot bath for me. The young woman, her name was Hannah, let me use her husband's razor. I was given a new shirt and underwear. The husband's pants fitted me, almost. When trying them on I noticed many trophies decorating the bedroom. Hannah's husband was a boxer, the middle-lightweight champion of Germany.

"Oh," I thought to myself, "you better not get too chummy with the lady with windblown hair. The boxer might not approve of my using his razor or wearing his pants." She must have read my thoughts, and tried to pacify me, "He is or was in the service, and I have not heard from him for over a year."

Then she gestured toward the kitchen with her head. "She is my mother."

I tried to believe a "thank you" was all she wanted, but, with the way she looked at me when I was trying on her husband's pants, I had my doubts.

Things would work out all right. They always had, so far!

I was ever so careful to add these words "so far". So far, so good. What tomorrow would bring was a different matter. Don't get cocky. Luck is fragile. Treat it tenderly or it will forsake you. Luck is temperamental, like young love. The moment you believe it is forever, it will leave you. They speak about "bad luck", but is there such a thing as "cruel luck"? Yes indeed: if luck would have left me then, it would be cruel, cruel from the very beginning.

That same evening after Hannah and her mother had fed me and made me look human again, they took me to a farmer who needed help.

Life was not too complicated on the farm.

The hours were long and at the end of the day I was very tired and sometimes fell asleep at the supper table. I gained back all the weight I had lost. Even my wardrobe improved through the generosity of young Mrs. Konrad. She presented me with her husband's new sport coat. It made me feel and look like a million bucks. I wondered if she's given up hopes of seeing him again. How else could she be so generous with his wardrobe?

The farmer contributed food and shelter toward my physical well-being, but man cannot live by bread alone. Loneliness mixed with isolation and anxiety were my bedfellows. I didn't even sleep in bed most of the time. The Russians made occasional raids at night and young men on the premises made them suspicious. It can become stressful working hard in the daytime and hiding in the barn at night.

One day when I was pitch-forking hay to the farmer as he loaded the cart, a bunch of field mice realized they'd lost their shelter and started fleeing in all directions.

The old man hollered, "Kill them... kill them... hit them with your pitchfork!"

I could not do it. They reminded me of my own fate, running for their lives!

The farmer swore, "What kind of a man are you, who can't even kill a mouse?"

Regardless of his curse, I just could not do it!

But help was coming again from an unexpected source, from a lady I call Mrs. Grace. After so many years I have forgotten her name. But I remember you, Mrs. Grace, wherever you are. I did not want to use a fictitious name, it would be dishonest. I remember she used to call herself *altes Schlachtross*,[29] but it would not be proper for me to call her by that name.

I met her a few weeks after I started working for Mr. Konrad. During their evening walks many of the townspeople, mostly older women, walked past Mr. Konrad's farm. At that point they turned around and walked back to town again. I used to sit on the porch steps and watch their comings and goings. For several evenings I had noticed a woman who walked alone at the other side of the road. I could not guess her age from where I was, but she walked with a bounce like a young woman. Every day she looked towards me. One evening she crossed the road, stopped a few steps from me, and said, "You are lonely, young man, aren't you?"

Her hair was all gray, but she did not seem to be over 40. She was neither slender nor fat, and her face and eyes had an inner beauty visible only to the few who had eyes to see it.

"Come and visit us, my husband and our two daughters. We would be happy to listen to your worries and tell you ours. Sharing thoughts and longings will make us all feel better."

I visited their home that Sunday afternoon. It was small house in a green landscape. White curtains, full of the wind that entered through the open windows, looked like sails on a ship.

The husband was a slender man in his 40's with a sad face and happy smile. He had lost his right leg above the knee through an accident years before. He had not served in the military because of his disability.

"Leg or no leg! I could not have killed anybody."

When I told him I was unable to kill the farmer's mice as demanded, he proclaimed with conviction.

"I wouldn't either, my friend... When a fly sits on my nose, I only encourage him to move on. I do not intend to harm him."

"But I have killed men during the war!" I said.

"Well, this is different, in my opinion. You and your adversary had

243

two identical goals, to kill the other, and you both had the means to accomplish it. The fly sitting on my nose had no such intention or means. You and the field mice had no opposing duel in mind. All they were trying to do was save their own lives, not endanger yours in any way or form. So there is a difference between killing a mouse and killing a man. And I should add, not killing a mouse would redeem you from the sin of killing an enemy soldier if the fates happened to be in your favor. If you had killed the mouse, I could not vindicate you."

His two daughters were in their early teens. They were flying in and out of the house. I do not remember their names or faces.

We sat at the tea table in a room that was fragrant with the jasmine blossoms. Mrs. Grace told me how she had been a teacher of high-school literature, and that she liked to read poems. Those twilight hours were like ichtiol or zinc oxide salve for my ailing spirit. She recited the poem of Rainer Maria Rilke:

> *Reiten...reiten...reiten...*
> *Durch den Tag and durch die Nacht.*
> *Reiten...reiten...reiten.*[30]

Or Heinrich Heine's:

> *Wir sassen am Tee-Tisch*
> *Und sprachen von Liebe viel...*[31]

Those are the lines I still remember from those poetry hours. I used to remember the entire poems she read, but I've done no reinforcing and the passing years have eroded most of the lines. It would be easy for me to write down the additional verses from some library books, but that would not be part of my memories and would be deceiving.

After my first two weeks at the Konrad farm, police distributed registration forms to be filled out by each member of the household and to be personally delivered to police headquarters for verification.

The farmer handed me my application forms and asked me to register. He would not let anybody live in his house without registration. There was even a warning on the form:, "Anybody having unregistered persons living in their household will be penalized for code violations, and the person without papers will be arrested for further investigation."

This, of course, put me in a predicament. I was a transient and my registration would not be routine. Besides, my face would still be familiar at police headquarters.

I took my worries and application forms to Mrs. Grace. She promised to find out how the registration would be conducted and whether each applicant had to be seen by a police officer. After a few days she had all the information and had even arranged my registration with a female clerk she knew who would not ask me any questions, just stamp my papers and hand out my ID and food stamps. There would be no police involved in a routine registration.

Just don't worry. You go to the police headquarters on Tuesday between 9 and 12. There is a policeman at his desk downstairs. You ignore him and take the stairs to the second floor. There will be five female clerks, each behind her own window, registering people. You go to the third window from your left. There is a lady with gold-rimmed glasses, slender with graying hair. All you have to do is hand over your application papers and say, "My name is Schulz. Greetings from Mrs. Grace."

Come Tuesday, I put on my new coat and smeared my hair with brilliantine cream to straighten out the curls. The house philosopher lent me his glasses for disguise, and off I went. There were people coming and going on the first floor. I passed the police officer's desk. He did not give me a second look. When upstairs, I took off the glasses. With them, I wouldn't be able to see the registration windows, let alone identify any female clerks behind them. True enough, there was the third window and the lady with gold-rimmed glasses. I stood in her line and when my turn came, I did just as I was told, handed over my registration form all filled out neatly with my true birth date and name, as Alfred Schulz, born in Danzig, Germany, presently employed by Mr. Konrad as a farm laborer.

The lady gave me a surprised look, excused herself and left her window. Oh, my... perhaps she was an informer and went to call the cops. Before I had the chance to let my imagination run amuck, she was back with my food ration cards and ID, all stamped and signed, and she pushed it all over with a knowing smile, "Here you are, Mr. Schulz. *Alles ist in Ordnung.*"[32]

That was all there was to it.

I had become a lawful citizen of Zahna, complete with food stamps and as Id. From now on I could sleep peacefully in my own bed next to the old farmer and not worry about nightly raids.

The following Sunday I went to visit my philosopher friend and his wife for evening tea as usual. I thanked my benefactress when I was standing face-to-face with her. "There are no words to express my gratitude and all you have done for mc. You have saved my sanity and made me feel at home. You might have even saved my life by getting me registered." I said.

She looked at me with her gray-blue eyes, "We love you dearly and would hate to lose you, but you must know that there is no future for you in Zahna. We all hate the thought of the day you feel strong enough to leave us."

That evening we took our tea in their small garden, the three of us sitting at the triangular table with three legs. The sun had set and only the western sky was lit with the faint outline of an old moon near the horizon. The stars came out. There was Cassiopeia and the Seven Sisters, and the Northern Star. She quoted poetry by heart and her husband talked about the book he was writing, *"Die Melodie und Rhythmus der Welt."*[33] I cannot faithfully repeat his thesis-I am surprised I can even recall the book's title. Long forgotten, it has now suddenly come to me like a bolt from the blue. It makes me feel as if I was still at the same tea table under a starry sky, in a city named after the goddess of illegitimate love. In essence, given the way the planets circle the sun, he thought even time had circular motion, saying, "Just as we are sitting at this tea table tonight and do not remember that we have done so before and will do so again in the future history of the universe. All is circling like a carousel, and we are like puppets on a string, not knowing when our circular motion in time will bring us back to this tea table again."

I was gazing at the stars during his animated presentation. When a moment of silence fell over us, I asked if I could quote a short poem in Estonian, written by a fellow soldier before we were forced to leave our native country.

Oh yes. They would love to hear it.

> Suur Vanker, sõiduta koju,
> Põhjanael, juhata manatee.
> Olen kui pisike poju –
> Eksinud võõrasse laande..."

"They seemed genuinely moved by the emotion in my voice and somehow realized the poetry in it, but then they wanted to know the meaning. All poetry loses some charm when translated. I hesitated for a moment, before continuing,"

> Big Dipper, take me home.
> North Star, show me the highway!
> I am like a little lad –
> Lost in an alien forest...

Then, we just sat there in the starry summer night, feeling happiness in each other's presence, believing we had done it before and would enjoy it again in the circular history of time.

---

[23] God be with us

[24] O.K.

[25] homegrown tobacco

[26] refugees

[27] I am from Berlin

[28] crazy foreigners

[29] old bettle-horse

[30] To ride…ride…ride.. Through the day and throughout the night/ …to… ride…ride…ride"

[31] We sat at the tea-table and spoke about love…

[32] All in order

[33] The Melody and Rhythm of the World

Chapter 6

The Deliverance

"The brakes!... apply the brakes!"

I was in the Thüringer Mountains, sitting atop an ox-driven cart loaded with manure, and presently in danger of crashing into the ravine below. Karl was driving the oxen and I was the brake-man.

I have never done any of these things, namely being in the mountains, sitting on top an ox-driven cart, and braking a manure wagon. No wonder I was slow finding the handle. I pulled as hard as I could, locking the huge wooden wheels, and the wagon came to a full stop. Karl, a well-grown 17-year-old boy, grinned over his shoulder, "That was close. Just hold onto the brake handle and pull as soon as the wagon starts pushing the oxen!"

He took off his cap, dried his forehead, and pointed to the west, "See that valley down there, between the hills? That's the best place to get to the American Zone. I would not try the hills. As soon as you kick loose some stones, the racket will alert the Russian border guards and their dogs and then you'll have no place to hide."

"OK... thanks for the hint."

"That's OK. Always ready to help a friend in need. Kindly loosen the brakes gra-du-al-ly, or we might end up in the American Zone, oxen and all, buried under a load of manure. Ha-hah-haa!"

I laughed along, not a very dignified was to reach Paradise. Either on earth or in heaven.

The sun was bright, the mountain air was fresh. If I turned my nose into the wind, it would neutralize the bittersweet odor rising from the wagon. I had come a long way from Zahna, the little town some 150 kilometers to the East. I was now next to the American Occupation Zone. From where I was, my spit would land there if the wind happened to catch it.

The border village was filled with all kinds of folks trying to get over to the *Amerikaner*. The village people were tired of the foreigners and were not handing out any food packages. Somehow I had struck up a conversation with Karl, and he had hired me as a brake-man to haul manure to the fields between the mountains. Pay was good according to the going rate; free meals, a place to sleep and when we were done with the manure, he promised to take me to the spot where border-crossing would be easiest. At least in his opinion… he stressed these last four words and asked me to forget the rest, "It ain't easy anywhere, or the people would not be hanging out in the village like lost souls. If you are not sure about going, then forget it. My old man had a stroke and we could use your help even after the manure hauling."

I had made up my mind already in Zahna, and I would not change it. This would be the last step in my predicament, and all I needed was luck. If you wonder how I had managed to get so far west without a hitch, then I'll tell you.

I used to go to Saturday night dances in Zahna. There were many teenage girls without partners. It would have been inconsiderate of me to pick out one girl and hang around with her all the time. I was on friendly terms with everybody, and so it happened that one evening I was visiting two sisters and just shooting the breeze. They were good talkers and full of vim-and-vinegar. We were talking when their older sister walked in in a Railroad uniform. Well, we got talking about railroading and I learned that she was a conductor on the train going all the way to Dessau and Aschersleben.

She was off the next day, but the morning after that she was going as close as five kilometers to the *Amerikaner.* The train would not go any further. "How about the Russians. The Russians MPs, I mean?" "Only spot-checking from one station to the next." she said.

This all sounded too good to be true. There was only one problem.

The ticket.

To buy a ticket, one needed a note from the police department. I might as well ask for a ticket to the moon. According to her, passengers without tickets would be put off the train or handed over to station police. To travel 150 kilometers without a ticket was, in her view, quite impossible.

I sat down again.

All the hot air had escaped from my hope-balloon, but the sisters' sister was not finished with me:

"If you are really as nice a guy as my sisters are telling me, I might be able to help you."

"How?"

"I can buy a ticket without any note from the police, but I do not need the ticket. I am the conductor, remember?"

That was the answer to my problem.

If I had been keeping company with the boxer's wife, I would have missed the sisters and their sister conductor. Amazing! I had made all the right moves, so far!

I took her ticket, which of course had no name on it. The Russian MPs might ask for some kind of certificate, but I had my ID to show them.

For me Zahna had been a place of rejuvenation and a new beginning. I still have many fond memories of the amiable people. I had even accumulated assets. The friendly philosopher gave me his rucksack, saying,

"This thing is older than you. As a young man I used to wander in the mountains-that was back then when I still had my two legs. I can't go anywhere now and I am happy that you, my friend, will take my old rucksack out of the closet and onto the open road."

Hannah gave me her husband's razor, "I do not think I'll ever see him again, and if he returns he would not miss it."

There was veiled accusation in her eyes as we faced each other the last time. She and her mother had rescued me when I was down and out, but I could not make her happy. She was just too eager, sophisticated, and mature and I was too young to know the true value of a 30-year-old woman's friendship, full of passion and longings.

Young Mrs. Konrad made me sandwiches for the road, and said, "We will miss you!"

She tried to hide the yearning that all young married women must have when their husbands have been gone for months, perhaps years on end.

Mrs. Grace had given me her motherly love and cured me of my afflictions. Like a good trainer. She had made me strong for the road and was herself happy and sad to see me leave. *"Lebewohl, mein Freund!"*[34] was all she said after we embraced. "...There is more lasting beauty in heartache than in fleeing moments of happiness."

That's the story of Zahna and the ease with which I arranged my trip westward.

After we had cleared the cow shed of all the manure and spread it on the fields this side of the mountains, my friend Karl said, "It is time for you to go."

We had passed the border guards with our oxen team every day for a week, using the dirt road that led to the fields further back in the mountains. Their small sheds, painted in stripes like candy sticks, were about 100 yards apart across the already-harvested potato field, flanked on both sides by sharply rising hills with low bushes and uncut grass. There, the guards marched back and forth between their sheds, rifles thrown across their backs. They seemed bored and time seemed to hang heavy in their hands. They sat inside their cubicles to escape the heat of the midday sun and had no guard dogs to keep them company.

The sun had already sunk behind the Thüringer Wald and mountain range when I, with the rucksack on my back and Karl as my guide, walked the winding footpath toward the border.

Take your bearings now and wait until it is too dark for you to see the guards, then just walk past them-and good luck!"

He slapped my shoulder and the next moment I was alone, staring toward the narrow strip of land where only one hundred yards separated me from my freedom. Darkness without shadows closed in after an hour of waiting and then I started my slow walk towards the guards, hoping to miss them. At times I stopped to listen and look. I could see nothing but plowed and harrowed fields in all direction. I continued my slow advancement and thought I was past the demarcation line when I heard a sharp shout, *Kto eta?*"[35]

Over my right shoulder I could see a faint shadow of a man yards behind me. That meant I had already passed the guard posts and was now on the American side of no-man's-land. I tossed off my rucksack and ran. I was a ways out before I could see flashes from their guns and bullets hitting the soft ground a few steps from me, kicking up small puffs of dirt and trailing with the sound of gunfire. I kept on running. After a short while there was no sound except for my muffled footsteps and heavy breathing. I had disappeared into the darkness. The border guards did not see any point of shooting aimlessly into the night.

Then the plowed field ended and I continued to walk now on grassland with scattered bushes that were tall enough to come to my shoulders. In some spots they had grown into each other and I had to keep my hands and elbows in front of my face to struggle through the thickets. I came to an elongated mound: railroad tracks. I felt my way up and saw a river, perhaps twenty feet below me. It was not side, since I could make out trees from the opposite side against the lighter sky.

I heard voices coming from the road on the other side of the river. I could not see anything, but I was sure the language they spoke was not Russian, but English.

I was elated.

All I had to do was slide down this embankment, swim across the river, and then I would be a free man. I started to descend along the graveled embankment and must have kicked some stones loose. I could hear them running ahead of me and splashing into the river below.

"Kto eta!..." came a low-pitched voice from the river below, and I froze. I did not move or breathe and could not see anything below because of darkness.

There must have been another line of guards next to the river. All remained quiet below. Certainly no one was trying to climb up to the embankment. Then a thought came to me. Maybe they thought it was just a rabbit.

That helped to settle my nerves, but obviously I was marooned between two rows of Russian border guards. Did I have to try to "re-escape" back to the Russian zone, before the guards and their dogs would find me?

I got down from the embankment, away from the side of the river and started to follow the railroad bank, taking cover between the bushes. Soon the bushes opened to a meadow and there was a village with people milling around.

That's odd, it must have been well past the Russians' curfew hour, or perhaps… perhaps…

I walked next to two women, still staying close to the bushes, and asked if I was still in the Russian-occupied zone.

"Das glaub' ich nicht ..." they laughed, *"Hier sind die Amerikaner!"*[36]

I grabbed the shoulders of the nearest woman and laughed in her face with tears in my eyes. She did not seem to mind, but added, "Don't celebrate too soon!"

"What do you mean?" was my anxious query.

"Do you see that bridge there, across the river? And can you see the flickering light in the middle of it?"

"Sure, I can see it."

"Well, there is an American MP guarding the bridge. If you are trying to cross it without a certificate with an American stamp; that proves to them that you do not belong here. You will be locked up overnight until the Russian truck comes in the morning to take you back where you came from."

That scared me beyond belief.

What a night! I had been through this win-and-lose event so many times and had no "fuel" left to go through it again anytime soon. I must have looked like the Statue of Gloom.

"Now, now... don't give up as easy as that. Just look some 50 yards beyond it and you can see a railroad bridge."

"Well. Nobody is guarding that one. You could walk across it in broad daylight and the *Amerikaner* from his bridge would not give a hoot where you are coming from or going to. He is sitting in his chair and guarding only his bridge. What is happening in the rest of Germany, or the world for that matter, seems no concern of his."

To set my mind at rest, the other lady spoke, "Once you are on the other side of the river, nobody will ask you any questions or want to see your certificate."

I walked to the railroad bridge. The full moon was out now and only shreds of clouds were rushing towards the west. I waited until the clouds had covered the moon and then I walked across the bridge, carrying my boots in hand so as to not make any noise walking on the steel bridge.

After crossing, I walked back to the regular road and found a barn full of hay to spend the night in. I pulled my coat over my head, and laughed myself to sleep.

I had nothing-no money, no provisions, and nowhere to go, and I did not know anybody. But I had gained something more valuable than all this put together. I had gained my freedom and the right to live as a free man.

[34]Farewell my friend
[35]Who's there
[36]I believe not,... here are the Americans

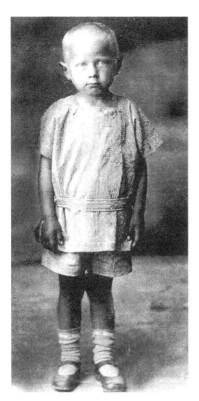

Sunday, June 23, 1925

That Sunday was Memorial Day and our family with the rest of Kullenga farmers were attending the church service in Vaikee-Maarja about 3/4 of an hour ride. It was six weeks before my third birthday and I remember the day well, as I was photographed for the very first time in the old Laurus' General Merchandise store and his so-called photo studio. Old Laurus was a tall skinny man with goatee and pince-nez glasses. His studio held a black wooden-box camera with a small lens in front. I was line up ready for the photograph, when old Laurus stooped under his black shroud quickly appeared shouting, "Shut your mouth, boy." His rude remark worked better that any "Look at the birdie." I stood there tough and determined, mouth tightly closed, eyes defiant.

Väike-Maarja High School, 1939

255

Above: August 1952, Ashby receives a live rooster from his friends in Fresno to act as an alarm clock.

Below: Christmas 1952– the loneliest for Dr. Ashby. Spent in San Francisco. For months there had been nothing but text books, lectures and exams. He spent hours watching the restless waves.

 Left: Dr. Arved Ashby in his home.

Below: July 5, 1956, Hazel and Arved arrive in Kansas City for Arved's training in the field of Obstetrics and Gynecology at the University of Kansas. Their 1953 Chevrolet, held all their earthly belongings, including a TV with rabbit ears.

Above: Dr. A.O. Ashby shoveling out his car stuck just a short distance from his home. He had been called on to deliver a baby girl to the Voss family of Sheboygan.

Below: 1963- Dr. Ashby was a speaker at the Sheboygan Rotary Club, where they were honoring recent citizens of the United States.

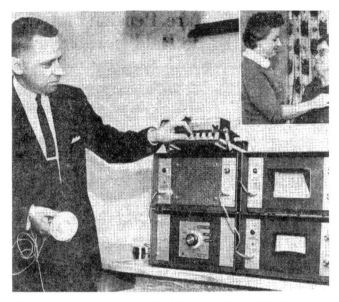

Above: Ashby examines a new machine for recording babies' heart beats. Donations came from the Memorial Hospital Auxiliary.

Below: Christmas 1960, the Ashby's first in Sheboygan. Dr. Ashby is seen drink and cigar in hand celebrating his new home on South 27th Street.

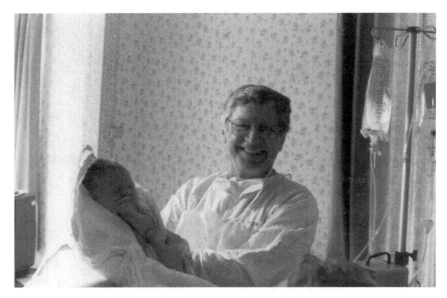

Above: Dr. Ashby just after a new delivery in 1985.

Below: Retirement day for Dr. Ashby in 1989.

RETIREMENT OF DR. ASHBY

THE WIND AT MY BACK

Arved Ojamaa Ashby, M.D.

Chapter 1

The First Day

The year was 1945.

The Great War had ended six months ago.

I was walking down the open road with my hands in my pockets and the wind at my back. The sun was shining bright in the morning sky, and dewdrops glittered in the autumn grass. Shreds of clouds drifted towards the Harzgebirge, the mountain range I had crossed the previous night. It was a narrow escape from East Germany, the bullets whistling around me as I ran for my life. The Russian border guards did not have the dogs to chase me, and I reached the American Occupation Zone in West Germany in one piece. I could not run with my rucksack bouncing on my back and had dropped it during the pursuit.

Once more I was free of any worldly possessions.

I saw a few military trucks approaching, and the sudden fear, an old reflex, flashed through my head – the Russians!

But, in an instant I was laughing over the silly notion, knowing very well that these could not be Russians. Not in the American Zone. These trucks were big, canvas-covered vehicles with powerful engines, a far cry from the Russians' old boxes rattling down the roads of East Germany.

Nobody would take pot shots at me any more.

Having lived with hidden anxiety for years, it was hard for me to imagine a day without it.

I practiced my old limp, just for fun, and peeked over my shoulder knowing there could be no Russians in sight. No red banners either. No black-clad militia anywhere in sight. What a relief. But, could it all be true and not a dream? Really?

Another over-the-shoulder look at the empty road and another feeling of joy. It must be true, no Russians as far as the eye could see.

What a beautiful morning to walk down the road on this side of the mountains, carefree and light of heart!

I came to a road crossing that had many signs pointing in all directions. They carried numbers and insignias I had never seen before. Those must have been for American military use, and meant nothing to me. Almost hidden behind these signs was another road sign with names of villages and towns and how many kilometers one had to travel to get there.

I was not familiar with any of the places listed, until I read, Hildesheim 78 km. A year had passed since I took the train from Berlin to Hildesheim.

It was late fall then. A cold rain had been falling all day. It was getting dark, and because of the war there was no light in the compartment. Next to me, sitting at the window in shadowy twilight, was a young woman. In the meager light I could see only the outline of her forehead, her rounded cheeks, and the curves of her lips. Everything below was hidden in darkness. The sight thrilled me, made me feel like I had entered a hidden and mysterious world. I was like a five-year-old boy again, getting secret pleasure by watching prepubescent girls in short skirts skating on the blue ice behind our barn.

One does not need speech to communicate with a young woman next to you on a night train. Words can be insensitive, tactless, or even rude.

I could feel the heat from her shoulders and hips as we sat there at close quarters.

Perhaps she had a fever?

She turned her face towards me and said just one word, "Oh." All she said was, "Oh."

Her name was Cora and I was to spend the rest of my vacation in Hildesheim with her.

Hildesheim must have been hundreds of miles away, I thought, but I had not seen any maps and my sense of geography must have been deceiving me. After all the running and shooting since then, I had not had time even to think about Cora and her sleepy medieval town.

Just think of it, thousands and thousands of road signs in the world and the first one I ran across said HILDESHEIM, the town of Cora, the only person and place I knew on this side of the mountain. Anything on the other side would be no more accessible to me than the Nordstern on the bottom of the Baltic Sea. Poland had her Posen and all Ober-Silesia to boot. The Russians' red flag with its hammer and sickle was now flying over Danzig. The girls from these places who had treated our "Sanguine Six" with way-out hospitality must have been evicted from their homes. They very well could be on the road that very moment, pulling their play-wagons and pushing their baby carriages, all loaded high with roped-up bundles and hanging kitchen utensils. I remember it all like yesterday: the manicured hands, the fur stoles, oak-paneled studies with their leather-bound volumes of lascivious books. Where were they all now?

I sat on the roadside, next to my sign and continued to reminisce.

I could feel her eyes looking at me once more.

Cora was a nice girl, a few years older than I. That in itself was a plus. The teenage girls seemed immature now, after all I had been through. The dreamy-eyed seventeen-year-olds were good for holding hands and looking at nightscapes together through the train window. That was about it. But, Cora was different. Mature.

I was thinking about her eyes, and then and there an old poem from high school English class popped into my mind. I continued to sit there, pulled my knees against my chest and pronounced with a loud and clear voice, reciting to the road signs and to the empty road beyond:

> How many have loved
> your moments of glad grace
> And your beauty with love false or true.
> But one man loved the pilgrim soul in you.
> And the sorrows in your changing face…
> *By Irish poet W.B. Yeats (1865 – 1939)*

Then I just put my head on my knees and cried.

I really do not know why. I had not cried for a long time. I could not even remember when. It was not customary to cry in our family back in Kullenga, not even at funerals or weddings.

Way back, when I had left home for good, we just shook hands. No hugging or kissing, no backslapping. I know my mother cried in secret. She just went to the pantry to get something for me for the road. It took her a long time to find whatever it was she was looking for. She came out all cheerful and in smiles, but I could tell from her eyes and the way she blew her nose that she had cried a spell all by herself in the cold pantry, which smelled of moldy bread and salt pork

So I just sat there and cried next to the road sign, somewhere in the American Zone, mostly because of being free at last.

I don't remember for how long.

The tooting of an old fashioned car-horn made me look up.

A beat-up truck was parked on the roadside with a crudely painted sign, spelling out, G E M U S E[1]

An old man was leaning through the open window: "Was ist los, Junge?"[2]

I stood up and wiped my face with the back of my hand, "Not much. I was just resting on the roadside."

He offered me a free ride to the next town. I found an open space in the back of his truck between the crates of cabbages, celery and cucumbers. I ate one of his carrots for breakfast.

I was sure he wouldn't miss it.

I arrived in Hildesheim in late afternoon. I do not remember much about the railroad station, but I knew where she lived. Cora's room was almost in the center of town, next to the river and its ancient bridge.

I sat with her in her room upstairs watching the evening fog roll into the city along the river bed, filling first the valley below, then creeping up to the bridge, hiding its columns and shielding its distant end and all the buildings beyond.

The bridge seemed to hover, as if suspended in the clouds.

Her hair spread over her shoulders when she poured us wine, "Look at the bridge...up in the air...going nowhere!"

We laughed and drank the wine. It tasted sour and bitter. That was the wine they had, what with the war and everything.

I found the street and the bridge.

Or what was left of them. There were no houses as far as I could see. The bridge was gone. Its support columns were still standing and pointing like fingers towards the sky from where the destruction must have come down like rain.

No house, no window, nor the girl I knew – all had evaporated like the fog from that river. I washed my face and sat in the tall grass in the middle of the town. It seemed there was no one to cut it. I did not see a soul.

I felt tired and slept dreamlessly. It gave me refuge from the present and helped me to forget the past.

When I awoke, the sun was low at the horizon. The shadows of the bombed out city were creeping across the river.

———

I walked back to the railroad station and bought a ticket to Hamburg, a harbor town at the river Elbe. Hamburg was up north in the British Occupation Zone. When I was still a prisoner I heard rumors that Churchill had suggested that the Russians should get out of the Baltic States, and thought the British might welcome an Estonian refugee. As for the U.S., Roosevelt was dead by then, and I wasn't sure how the Americans would treat a person whose home was on the other side of the mountains and who did not possess the right stamped certificate.

That was the reason I took the night train to Hamburg.

I said earlier that I had no money. That wasn't quite true. I had overlooked the Deutsche Reichsmarks in my back pocket that the farmer I had worked for gave me. It was not a sign of his generosity; the money was worthless unless you had a wheelbarrow full of it.

I had also saved my food stamps from Zahna, but the old lady selling hotdogs next to the Hildesheim railroad station would not take them. She said they were worthless. The paper money was still technically legal tender all across Germany, but she wouldn't take that either. She gave me the hotdog just the same.

God bless her. She did not know how hungry I was.

———

What is there to say about the train ride from Hildesheim-over-Hanover to Hamburg just after the war? It was well over 200 kilometers. If you had been in that train, or any train for that matter, back then there would be no need for me to describe it.

It was no fun compared to today's standard of travel, but it seemed a great luxury to me at the time. A fellow from a prison transport who was traveling by foot knew a good thing when he saw one.

The wagons, of course, were packed to capacity with warm bodies, bodies from every country imaginable. The multitude of personal odors was mixed with the scents of perfume and stale cigarette smoke. Perhaps one could count out the number of Finns and Swedes, maybe the Austrians and Swiss, but anything more than that would be difficult. There were Poles, Yugoslavians, Ukrainians, Hungarians, and Jews.

And of course there were Germans.

Most of them were so-called Flüchtlinge, refugees evicted from their homes when their land and property was taken over by the Russians and

Poles. They had all their belongings with them in packs and bundles. To get from one end of the wagon to another, one needed all the skills of a mountain goat.

And there I was, part of the crowd, not smelling any better or worse than the rest of them. I had been successful in obtaining more than a half-seat in the crowded train, and this says something about my survival skills. It required patience and know-how to get one, as you can imagine. At first you had to find a bench with a few inches of vacancy at its free end. The next step was to lean towards it. You couldn't try to sit yet. After waiting in this semi-sitting position until the seat owner had dozed off, you could start leaning more inward, half an inch at a time, until you could claim the entire seat.

No sudden movement or the present occupant might notice your intrusion and push you off altogether.

This invisible intrusion worked in many ways, and under different circumstances, it became part of your survival instinct. I had been an apprentice of a fellow prisoner who had cultivated it to perfection.

I did not even want to think about imprisonment, but being cooped up in that night train there was not much else to think about. When it came to Cora and Hildesheim, things were just too personal for comfort, and if personal things didn't work out, then the best thing is to say "forget it" and let it go at that.

I leaned back in my seat and tried to catch some sleep.

Hamburg, here I come!

[1] vegetables
[2] What happened, young (fellow)?

Chapter 2

My First Day In Hamburg

A garbled sound from the loudspeakers announced the arrival of our night train in Hamburg station.

The main terminal was something to see, with its steel stairways crisscrossing and connecting various platforms, climbing and descending above and below us, crowded with people. And of course, there were trains, bellowing smoke and blowing steam, entering and leaving the huge steel-framed building.

There was no time to admire the scenery, as the rushing crowd was pushing me towards the exit. It turned out not to be an exit at all, rather one of those steel stairways to take us up to another platform. A sleek train with large windows was waiting.

I made use of my insidious intrusion technique and was the first one aboard. I rewarded myself with a seat at the window, so that I could have a birds-eye view of the city. What I saw first was a reflection of my own face, covered with a stubby beard and a red rash. No wonder my beard had been itching lately! It would not have taken a brain surgeon to diagnose the condition as a Staph infection.

Well, my unhygienic living habits had finally caught up with me. The very last time my face had met soap and water was about two weeks earlier in Zahna. That was when I had had my last shave with the razor the boxer's wife had given me as an *Abschiedsgeschenk*.[1]

Oh yes! I had washed my face in that river in Hildesheim, and I recalled the water as having an unpleasant odor. Which made sense. Many houses had fallen into that river during the bombardments and had most likely taken their occupants with them.

Well, at least I hadn't drunk the stuff!

As far as treatment was concerned, I had few options except keeping my face glued to the window.

The train soon departed, and the new scenery made me forget my own miseries. There was nothing but ruins and more ruins.

A few walls were still standing here and there, alone and in groups, some of them bleached white by the sun, like skeletons in the desert. When the train slowed down for an upcoming station, they appeared menacing, closing in and looking at me through their windowless eyes.

Someone sat next to me.

There was the rustle of a dress and a faint smell of perfume. It had to be a woman. This in itself lifted my spirits a notch or two and raised my curiosity. Besides, looking only at the scenery outside had given me a stiff neck.

Then something unexpected happened.

The lady next to me grabbed my arm with nervous fingers, then let it go with an apology, "I am so sorry. I took you for someone else."

After her emotional outburst she kept looking down at her lap, then pulled a handkerchief from her fur-lined sleeve to dry the tears from her eyelashes.

I looked at her more closely.

She was in her forties, dressed in a fur-lined coat and hat. She had round cheeks and a smooth face. Her eyes appeared unusually large and had fine wrinkles at the corners.

Somehow she reminded me of Tanya's mother from the deep Russian winter of two years earlier, when the three of us were drinking tea from a copper samovar and listening to the wind as it piled snow up against the wood-carved window frames.

Then the lady next to me started to speak haltingly about her son. She had not had word from him, and the war had ended six months earlier.

"You remind me of him. At first I was dumbfounded in belief that I was sitting next to my son!"

She gave me another long look, saying: "Forgive me for staring at you. But you look very much like him!"

That sounded like some kind of confession. I had not dealt with anyone's grief but my own, and here was a strange lady who was entrusting me with hers. I had been only a face in the crowd and suddenly I was somebody, even if that somebody was someone other than me.

She wanted to know more about me, and like a fool I opened up some and then felt embarrassed. I should have known better, should have kept my mouth shut and kept my inner feelings to myself. Such feelings made me curl up inwards like a porcupine, and I became hostile. She busied herself with her handkerchief for awhile, then looked up and asked me to come and rest in Blankenese for a few days. That was the suburb where she lived with her husband, untouched by air raids, "I want my husband to meet you and see the resemblance between you and our son!"

This turned me off.

I did not want to be a stand-in any longer. Perhaps I was even supposed to feel sorry that I, a homeless man, had survived and their son, who had so much to live for, had probably perished.

I declined her invitation outright, "No thanks. I can manage on my own. She did not insist.

Then she fiddled with her shopping bag, opened it, and took out a package of pastries, which she then placed on my lap.

I once more tried to refuse her, but she insisted, "Now listen, young man! I know when someone is hungry and I want you to have it." She then added, like an apology, "It is really a selfish move in my part: hoping that someone would help my son, if he still happens to be alive."

I left the small white pastry box tied with blue and red ribbon on my lap, "Thank you very much!"

She had won that round and her motherly instinct told her that she could help me more, "Two stations out is a physician's office. I am sure the doctor there would be able to give you something for your face. He has his sign just outside the station. You cannot miss it!"

The train was slowing, and people got up from their seats.

"This is where I get off. I'll give you my address in case you change your mind. You know you are always welcome!" That said, she shoved something in my side pocket, gave me a quick smile, and disappeared into the crowd.

I found her calling card and a bundle of German *Reichsmarks* in my pocket. I opened the white box and found four mince pies, still warn from the oven. I ate them all then and there, and left the *S-Bahn* at the designated stop to look for the doctor's office. I found a good-sized sign outside on the station wall just where the lady said it would be. It read:

Doktor R. Schneider,
Fachartz für
Haut- und Geschlechtskrankhieten[2]

"Well," I thought, "I think I'll stick to his first specialty."

It did not take me long to find a cluster of stone houses still standing, and in one of those our good doctor had his office.

I sat down on a waiting room chair with a curved bottom, and looked around. There was no receptionist in sight, only two females sitting in a far corner, talking a mile a minute and smoking up a storm. Both were blond, but I did not think it was their natural hair color.

Cued by all the powder and paint, I placed their age in the "has-been" category.

They did not have any skin rashes, as far as I could see.

Soon they were called to the doctor's office, and about half an hour later the three emerged and continued their conversation in the waiting room for a spell. They spoke with hushed voices and I could not make out what the conversation was all about. But the painted ladies soon took their leave, and the doctor turned to me with a broad gesture:

"Next!"

His office was semi-dark and sparsely furnished.

There was just one tall and narrow window, and the treatment chair faced it. It reminded me of a barber's chair with one exception: it had odd contraptions on both sides of the seat to support the customer's feet. Next to the chair was a long wooden table with rows of white pots, containing all kind of potions and ointments in different colors. A wood-tongued blade was sticking out of each for handy application.

I sat down on the barber's chair, but kept my feet off the contraptions.

The doctor was a young man with a crew cut and suntanned face.

He was wearing an informal white shirt with rolled up sleeves. He had black framed glasses, and appeared to be in his thirties with friendly features and easy-going manner. I spoke first, "Well, doctor. What I have speaks for itself. It might not be leprosy, but is close to it in my 'street doctor's' opinion"

He appeared amused, "I would take your predicament any day, my friend. You should have been in my office half an hour earlier and seen what a real disease looks like."

Having detected my accent, he inquired, "You are not from this part of the country. May I ask what brings you to our fair city, or whatever's left of it?'

I gave a short summary of recent events and tried to make a favorable impression by mentioning my medical background in the service.

"I know," he said. "It was hell out there, but I was lucky to get out when the going was still good."

After he had finished inspecting my face, he concluded, "First of all you need a good shave."

"Well, no barber would touch my face with a ten-foot pole, and I don't own the tools to do it myself."

"That's no problem, my friend. I'll fix you up!"

He gave me the needed shave, and I would call it the most painful episode in my young life. Off came my beard – and part of the skin on my face.

He seemed pleased with his barbering skills, and added, "That's more like it!"

Then he sprayed my face with some kind of solution. This made everything burn like hellfire. I brought up the subject of pain, but he brushed it off as a necessary part of the healing process.

Next my chin and cheeks received a heavy coat of yellow salve from one of his potion-pots. When he was finished with his multi-stage treatment, he handed me a mirror so that I could admire his handed-work. There was a noticeable improvement, but the distress I was still in made me omit my praise.

Before taking my leave, the good doctor gave me the razor he had shaved me with. Perhaps he didn't want to bother with all the work involved in disinfecting it! He gave me a jarful of that yellow sulfur cream too.

When I inquired about his charge, he patted my shoulder, "Professional courtesy, my friend!" After the departing handshake, he gave me his final instruction, "Keep away from those blondes with painted hair. They are nothing but trouble with a capital T."

On my way back to the station I was taking stock of the day's events. First of all, I did not consider myself poor any more.

I had started my first day in Hamburg like a beggar, and now I felt like the king of the castle. A few kind words and mince pies from the strange lady in the train had given me emotional as well as physical support. The food had quenched the fire in my belly.

The free treatment and supplies from the friendly doctor made me feel like a million bucks.

And money. Oh boy, did I have money!

I could easily afford a ticket to Baden-Baden, the place with the health spas and mineral baths I had dreamed about in the prison camp. On the other hand, maybe it would be best to stick around and have a short vacation at Blankenese as a stand-in for a couple's lost son.

But above all -- I had my freedom!

Without it, nothing would have counted for a wooden nickel.

Before I knew it, I was sitting again in the high train, heading back to the main railroad station. The way I figured, it would not make any sense to head further out and end-up who-knows-where. The one good thing about all this traveling was, I could not get lost. It is impossible to get lost if you have no destination in mind. There was no need even to ask for directions, because I didn't know where I was going.

This time I had secured an aisle seat. I was in no mood for the ruins. I had become indifferent, and they all looked the same to me.

The clicking of wheels and slight swaying of the train made me feel untroubled and content.

More people were entering the compartment.

Someone, a woman, was standing in front of me and holding onto a metal post. I looked up half-leisurely and met a pair of eyes I recognized in an instant.

As strange as it sounds, I knew this girl. Her name was Eevi Eenpalu, and she had been my classmate at Lasila Elementary School back in the early 30s.

She took me with her to Schwarzenbeck, a few stations from Hamburg. I registered there as a Displaced Person (called DP) in an UNRRA[3] camp for refugees.

----

[1] parting gift
[2] Specialist in Skin and Venereal Diseases
[3] United Nations Relief and Rehabilitation Administration

Chapter 3

New Beginning

Days became weeks, weeks became months and then years.

Time is like shifting sand, running down the hourglass. Its steady flow has no beginning and no end. There is no today, only yesterday. Like a long dream, it is only a flash in your somnambulistic brain. It is over before it begins.

Those were my five years in post-war Germany. And what enchanting and wicked years they were.

I lived in a Displaced Persons camp, a few miles from Hamburg. I had a roof over my head, a bunk to sleep in, and a shelf in a beat-up cupboard to store my bread rations. The cupboard was an unneeded convenience. Bread always managed to get eaten before it could make its way into storage.

Just the same, this was all prodigious luxury for a fellow who had learned to get by with very little. There were times when I had less than that.

After a long time, there was no need to pretend.

Nobody was chasing me. Not any more.

I could forget all about my alter ego Alfred Schulz from Baden-Baden, the fictitious name I had given to the Russians in the prison camp to hide my identity. Siberia with its labor camps appeared close to me then, but now it was but a distant memory to menace me only in my nightly dreams.

I could take pleasure from blissful leisure when stretched out in my bunk bed with both hands under my head, occupying myself with nothing more pressing than counting the cracks in the ceiling boards.

In the evenings all was still and the early dusk fell on the table under the solitary window, where sleepy flies chased a few breadcrumbs and gave out a high pitched whine that sounded like a faraway song in my reveries.

There at the road crossing was my uncle's liquor store with its rusty weather vane on the roof and a tin sign next to the sun-bleached window, exhorting passersby to drink only Saku

Beer. The ancient drying house for rye and wheat stood be-
hind the store, on the knoll where the firemen's horses would
graze and the men would pass around a bottle of government
brew.

And when the bell rang in the tower, a flock of frightened
crows flew across the surrounding fields of rye, which were
waving in the wind and blossoming. Their pollens filled the
air, softening the shadows of the summer clouds as they float-
ed across to the store, the blacksmith's place, and the knoll
with its horses grazing.

I saw her there, her hair in the wind and her breasts daringly
full under a summer dress as she drove her father's cows
along the winding road towards the settlement called Kul-
lenga. I could rest the tip of my tongue against my hard pal-
ate and make the word sing with its double "l" ---

"Kul-l-enga".

After one week had passed, I ventured out from my tar-roofed barracks to get acquainted with my surroundings. The so-called camp consisted of a group of neatly arranged buildings, previously occupied by
the *Luftwaffe*. There were living quarters, offices, classrooms, and the
Community Hall with its own stage.

I learned that the total number of refugees in the camp was well over
one thousand, and they all were compatriots who had fled Estonia before the Russian re-occupation in the fall of 1944. There were people of
any profession imaginable. They had even started a high school in the
camp, one with more teachers than students. There were writers, news-
papermen, politicians, actors, opera singers, doctors, nurses, and dance
instructors to name a few. And there were young people, men and
women in their teens and twenties, who had been students or were in
the work force. Men of my age, all possessors of resilient luck, were
fairly few.

Upon my arrival I had no problem in the registration office, where
the secretaries were all Estonian. A single "foreigner" among us was
the camp commander, an Englishman with the rank of captain.

During my get-acquainted walk I did some thinking.

First of all, what was I supposed to do? How was I to occupy my
time?

The only thing I came up with was attending the high-school-level
classes. I obtained permission to sit in on the senior class as an observ-

276

er. I was not permitted to participate in any discussions or take part in any of the student activities. I observed for a couple of weeks, and then just quit. I wasn't learning much, and it seemed degrading for an old soldier and ex-university student to sit in the same class with greenhorns.

A few days passed where I did nothing but claim my bread ration and stand in line at the soup kitchen.

Then a new idea hit me: why not become a ballet dancer?

I had read the bulletin board about the starting class.

The way I figured it, ballet dancers did a lot of running.

I myself had done some recently, and I was anxious to learn whether there was any similarity between these two pastimes. Would my previous experience give me a head start in the ballet class?

As you might well imagine, there were no common features between the activities. I did my running and jumping for a couple of lessons, but when the first assignment came, I did the only sensible thing possible --- I quit!

Perhaps you would like to know what the stint was that broke the camel's back, so to speak.

To start off with, I had to imagine a beautiful flower.

Well, I could do that. But it was harder to manage the suggestion that the flower was supposed to be growing from the middle of the dance floor.

Then came the assignment. One had to dance to the imaginary flower and stretch out both arms for a caress... when a hissing head of a snake was to appear, scaring you out of your wits.

Kindly dance out the entire sequence of events.

I believe you would have done the same thing I did, walk out and give up your future career in ballet altogether.

I was back in my bunk bed again, counting the cracks in the wallboards and ceiling. Out of boredom I started to shoot the breeze with a young fellow sleeping in the bunk below. He was a joker with a good sense of humor, and we had a great time together making up wisecracks about life in the camp. It did not take long for a few carbon copies of our "creations" to make their way into circulation.

I wouldn't bring up this minor episode if it hadn't had consequences.

The Entertainment Committee must have read our jokes, one thing led to another, and I became one of the four newsreaders at the Thursday evening gatherings.

Everybody was eager to know what was happening in the home country or in the world in general, but hardly anyone had a radio or could get hold of a newspaper. A newsgathering committee was formed that did nothing but gather the news. They listened to the radio broadcasts from the BC and *Deutscher Rundfunk,* and collected clippings from the Estonian weeklies from New York and Stockholm. The announcers had to have strong voices and clear diction as there were no microphones or loudspeakers, and the main hall was usually filled to capacity.

Entertainment followed the news. Perhaps the folkdance group performed, or a former opera singer from the "Estonia" Theatre sang an aria from *the Marriage of Figaro,* or a pianist played Bach. This all was followed by a dance that lasted well past midnight. A German band supplied the music, and they were the only ones who were compensated. The entire band received two packages of Lucky Strike cigarettes for their all-night effort.

Soon, I was well integrated into the new lifestyle, and kept busy with rehearsals and newscasts. The only thing I missed was female companionship. In this dominion I was definitely an underdog. I had arrived late to the camp and with my "laid-back" attitude I would not have had much of a chance anyway. Besides, the boys outnumbered the girls in the camp by three-to-one.

At times, when in my bunk bed at twilight, I recalled the days in East Germany when I did not feel neglected. The women-folk were there to initiate the conversation, and their companionship lifted my spirits and relieved my loneliness.

Or during the war when we were stationed in an isolated village in Ober-Silesia, just a mile from the Russian front, and Mägi --- my fellow medic --- and I missed the companionship only a woman can provide. After having attended wounded comrades all day who wouldn't become physically and mentally drained? The only tranquilizer was a good swig of firewater, but that did not put out all the fire inside of us.

In the late afternoons, when all the shooting had died down and the setting sun colored the snowy fields virginal pink, Mägi and I would call on the girls in the next village. I carried a few bottles of the champagne that handyman Napoleon had "rescued" from the warehouse while sergeant Mägi lugged the gramophone on his shoulders. For the next few hours young women surrounded us with romance in their eyes

278

and affection in their smiles.

Their attention cured all our ills.

We used to call them "the miracle workers", as they could heal us without laying a hand on us. Their magic spell, thank God, did not last forever and required perpetual replenishment.

I seem to keep getting lost with my reminiscences….

What I really wanted to talk about was the odds against me for finding a suitable female companion in the camp.

"Forget it," that's what they said, but to tell the truth I ended up with a very nice girl, in a fashion.

Whether it was just a coincidence or a stroke of luck is anybody's guess.

We all had seen her walking by with her blond hair flying in the wind and her steps light, as though she were dancing. Hungry eyes followed her comings-and-goings wherever she went. I was a realist. To me she was like a picture in a storybook, just nice to look at!

But, the look alone did not cure my loneliness.

A new sign on the bulletin board did not improve my disposition:

Lessons in Modern Dancing
Tango, Fox-trot, English Waltz

Starting soon:
Register in the office with your partner.

Of course there was no charge for those classes or any other activity to be participated in. We were all refugees and had plenty of time on our hands. To overcome their boredom, the professionals were happy to teach their trade to the younger generation.

My very first and last dance lessons had been back in 1938, when I was 16 and still in high school. I sure could have used a "refresher" course, but I had no partner. There might have been a few girls still available, but taking a chance with an unknown cohort would be like buying a horse from a gypsy trader. She might turn out to be defective merchandise, and then I would be stuck with her. I'd rather have had a tooth pulled than a lame duck for my dance partner.

Anyway, when the lessons started I could not stay away. I stood like a wallflower next to the dancehall exit and watched the performance.

And then it happened. The door opened and a gust of wind behind me brought in cool autumn air and a faint smell of perfume.

I turned to look and there she was, our "picture-book-blond".

With a sly smile, she asked me why I wasn't dancing.

The answer must have been obvious, and all I could muster was, "It takes two to tango!"

Her answer was music to my ears, "Would I do?"

––––––––––

I remember practicing the basic steps, each of us holding our hands behind our backs, and I had to lead her with my shoulders. She tried to press her shoulders against mine, but her curvaceous build made it hard to accomplish.

To dance the Tango properly you have to feel your partner's entire body against you, from the tops of her shoulders down to the knee-caps. It has a tantalizing rhythm, slow steps alternating with fast ones, and at times you and your partner are standing still. This motionless unison episode might be the most ardent part of the entire dance. The memory of it could stay with you even after the dancehall lights had been turned off and the band had departed.

––––––––––

For me she was *"Die Madonna der sieben Monde"*.[1]

She was my Aphrodite, my unfulfilled adventure, and the dream of my twilight hours. She was a disease without a cure. A blossoming red poppy, addictive with her opium seeds.

––––––––––

Long after the lessons, I went looking for her in the crowded dance hall. She rushed to me in eager anticipation and we danced again in intimate togetherness.

To reveal one's feelings through dance can be more meaningful than any verbal confession. Physical intimacy beyond the dance would spoil the mystery of romance.

With the passing of time, such a relationship had become badly outdated.

But so have I, so have I.

[1] "Madonna of Seven Moons"

Chapter 4

BACK TO HAMBURG

It was mid-winter of 1946 when I signed up to start my medical studies in Hamburg.

What else was I to do with myself?

How does a person make decisions in life? Usually by "falling into" them, and I must have "fallen into" this decision at the age of three when the country doctor visited my ill sister and my admiration for him knew no bounds.

Until now all I could think was how to survive from one day to the next. Making plans for the future back then would have been hopeless folly. Before, it had been staying alive; now staying alive meant getting into and finishing medical school. When the British Authorities offered free tuition and board I was quick to grab the opportunity.

I could not produce my original high school diploma for obvious reasons, but I saved the day by tracking down two of my old high school teachers. With their help I secured the needed certificate through the Public Notary Office, and that solved my matriculation problem.

But there were other issues, such as having no overcoat or hat, and only one pair of "air conditioned" shoes which offered little protection against snowdrifts. I changed my mind, the life of leisure in the DP Camp had weakened my willpower, and I couldn't muster enough energy to face the challenges ahead.

The question became moot the following day. The British commander in the camp simply refused to take my name off his completed list of "goes", and would not restore my privilege of staying. Bless his heart, I was forced to become a student!

With a few belongings in my beat-up suitcase, I walked a mile through the snowdrifts to Schwarzenbeck railroad station and took the afternoon train to Hamburg.

I registered at the newly established campus, called the *Zoo-Lager*.

It was formerly a graveyard, but during the war they had leveled the ground and built rows and rows of wooden barracks with tarpaper roofs and weather-beaten siding. This collection of buildings became the dormitory for some 600 students from Estonia, Latvia, and Lithuania. It was called the Baltic University Campus.

The living conditions during the first winter after the war were marginal at best. Our barracks were cold, the food was poor (1550 calories per day), and the entire city looked dismal in fog and snow. The electric power was turned off at 10 p.m. Candles were sold only on the black market, with prices hardly anybody could afford.

There was nothing one could buy. The food items and few consumer goods available were all rationed. You couldn't even buy razor blades, but you could trade in your old blade for a re-sharpened one.

The only thing that saved us was an allowance of six packs of American cigarettes per month, with a black-market value of 1200 German marks per pack. With that money we could buy plenty of salt herrings to add badly-needed protein to our daily diet.

The only two things not rationed in this drab city in ruins were prostitution and dying.

We didn't witness the dying firsthand, but it did keep our Anatomy Department pretty well provided-for, since a few of the corpses ended up in *Formalin* instead of a grave. As far as prostitution was concerned, we confronted the proceedings every afternoon on our way home from the *S-Bahn* station.

After the snow had melted from the hillside in the nearby park, the young British draftees added color to the landscape with their open-air lovemaking. The services of young women could be had for only a few cigarettes or a Hershey bar. The Hamburg paper *Die Welt* reported on the concerns of English ladies back home. They were worried about the virtue of their offspring in the morally corrupt city, but it had to be said that "the young and the restless" were taking advantage of deflated prices on an open market where supply had exceeded the demand. Later on at the nearest subway station one could recognize recent patrons by the wet elbows on their uniforms.

Well, I had witnessed similar goings-on in the Russian Occupation Zone, but with a notable difference. The idea that the other person *offered* their services was entirely abandoned. Every woman was considered a potential customer, her approval was not sought, and no compensation was offered.

The Red Army considered it part of the reparations the women had to pay for a war they had lost.

Perhaps, I've deviated a bit from my subject, but instant gratification and dying were part of daily life back then, and both are to some degree related to the field of medicine.

In our dormitory, I shared a large corner room with three other students. We hung up old military blankets to divide the room into four separate sections. Everyone had his private corner with a window, a small table with a chair, and the bed to sleep in. There was no central heating of course, but we had a pot-bellied stove, its pipe going out through one of the windows. In the depths of winter we had a small allotment of coal to keep the frost out of our room and the inkpots from freezing.

Everyone attended the lecture in the morning, and so there was no need to heat the room until the afternoon or evening. On our way back we always tried to snitch a piece of wood to supplement the heating allotment, but it was not an easy task. One had to have Houdini's talents to find anything combustible that wasn't nailed or chained down.

Courses in freshman year of medical school were in the basic sciences such as chemistry, biochemistry, physics, and botany, with additional laboratory work. I had a rudimentary knowledge of these subjects from my high school days, and it didn't take too much effort to keep up in those classes.

What made me feel like a medical student was the course in anatomy. It took four semesters of hard work to complete, and it started off with Osteology, the study of human bone structures.

It wasn't easy. Every hole and groove had its Latin name. I was later to learn that in America the terminology was modified to English. Not so in the old country. For instance, what was referred to as the *optic chiasm* in American schools was, in our textbooks, the *sciasma faciculorum opticorum.*

Our mimeographed compendia in anatomy had poor reproductions. They were legible enough when it came to the long bones, but the skull was a different ballgame. The skull holds innumerable protrusions, grooves, hollows, shafts, and holes, and you had to remember not only the nomenclature, but also match the name to the proper site. Here our drawings were far too smudgy for orientation and none of us had the *Gray's Anatomy* book. Skeletons were only available for study in the university classrooms.

Luckily, help arrived from an unexpected source. The Sanitation Department started to dig for a water main, and the workers had piled up a mound of soil with parts of human skeletons. Remember, we had supplanted an old cemetery.

This dirt pile became a goldmine for the medical students, and skull bones were like pearls in the rough. We scrubbed them clean, and placed them on the barracks roof to be bleached and dried by the sun.

When we returned from lectures in the afternoons, we brought down only the bones we happened to be studying that day. Another benefit not recognized at first, the skulls on the roof helped us find the living quarters of our classmates.

If all this sounds gruesome, think nothing of it.

I would be honored if future physicians were to use my skull to help them along in their learning process.

––––––––––

My recollections about the course in anatomy in coming years get grislier as we start to remove the muscles, blood vessels, and nerves from the bones.

It is called dissection of cadavers.

I was referring to the abundance of corpses and to the fact that the skull is the most difficult part of Osteology. Once you got into the advanced anatomy class, you'd get to dissect someone's cranium with all its "attachments" still in place.

Let's assume your assignment was to dissect the facial nerve, but the whole caboodle had the unfortunate tendency to roll off the table. Thanks to the foresight of someone in the department, flowerpots were made available to stabilize our specimens.

Our instructor, Dr. Zauna, was particular about handling dissected tissues, they were to be placed in a container and buried. The same principle was not followed in the university Pathology Department. There, after someone obtained tissue samples, the rest of the surgical specimen was fed into a disposal.

––––––––––

When you had finished your two-year course in anatomy and you knew every bone, muscle, nerve, and blood vessel in the human body and had already passed innumerable *practices* and *colloquiums* and mini-exams, you were qualified to take the final exam. The professor who was the head of the department would throw questions at you for two hours and you had to defend yourself by using the Latin terms in their proper place and sequence.

You'd pass, most likely, because the meek had been weeded out long before.

When the professor was satisfied with your answers, he would ask for your "study book" and write your grade in the proper place. You were rewarded with a grade of *sufficit, bene sufficit,* or *maxime sufficit*[1]. Then he would sign and stamp the page with the department seal, hand back your book, shake your hand, and you were able to go out and celebrate. You had accomplished a major milestone in your goal of becoming a doctor.

Well, there was always the possibility that you might fail.

In that case he was not interested in your "study book," and he did not shake your hand but might add something like "go over it one more time", or "better luck next time".

I'm not sure what happened if you failed on your second try. Later on I became acquainted with a student in Sweden who had failed her Anatomy twice. She was working in the Pharmacology lab and waiting for the anatomy professor to retire so she could give it another go.

I am getting ahead of myself. All told, I was still studying the bones and there was no variety in this kind of diet, only cold and impersonal Latin terms to torture your brain with. When I finally registered for the Osteology exam I could shoot out those Latin terms like bullets, hitting the right hole and groove in the skeleton without a miss.

Of course, I passed, but for all the effort they didn't even give you a grade, only a note in your study book "Osteology --- accepted" and Dr. Zauna's signature.

Meanwhile, spring had come to the *Zoo-Lager.*

A young chestnut tree that grew under my window had new leaves. Some black starlings were walking in the morning grass, still wet with dew. Slender-leafed yellow crocuses were flowering at the gate and the hillside park had become an open-air market for lovers.

I decided to go out and have good time and flush out the skeletons from my brains.

It had been a long time since the last dance with my tango partner. She had immigrated to England. I was in the crowd of well wishers when she said, "Remember our last dance!"

Oh, I do remember it all, her smile, the look in her eyes when she spoke the words.

Well, she was gone now, gone for good, and one couldn't live on memories alone. There had to be more to life than recollections, especially and wonderfully, when you are only 25 years old.

There had been much talk about St. Pauli.

It was the most famous entertainment district in Hamburg, if not in all of Germany, and I intended to go and check it out. I had asked Rick to accompany me, because he was the most conservative fellow I knew. He had shown no interest in females in the camp, and was thus a safe mate to take along for seeing with one's own eyes what this supposedly "wicked" city was all about. I had sold two packs of Camels to have what I thought would be enough spending money to cover the expenses of our conservative exploration.

I'd better say a few words about Rick.

He was studying pharmacology and lived next door to us. He came over almost every evening when we all sat around the open-coil cooking plate and toasted the slice or two of bread we had saved for supper. I liked to watch him when he did his toasting. His hand movements were composed, even precise as if he was still handling the test tubes and beakers in his lab.

He was above average height and slender (weren't we all), with short-cropped sandy colored hair and a sober look on his face. He liked to listen to our light-hearted conversation, and only occasionally added a word or two which were usually witty and to the point.

"It's my treat!" I told Rick.

We took the S-Bahn to *Millerntor* and there we were walking down along the *Reeperbahn,* the main thoroughfare in St. Pauli.

To our left was the harbor with bulky ships, semi-hidden in the evening dusk, and huge cranes with their steel cables like hangman's ropes still visible against the darkened sky. To our right were restaurants, bars, and dancehalls, their loud music filling the cool evening air. While the rest of the city was buried in darkness, everything here was lit up in colorful lights. As for people, the street was full of them: mostly men and couples, and the occasional single woman. The place was out-of-bounds for members of the British military, only the MP's were making their rounds.

Rick and I continued our slow walk along the crowded street and saw nothing unusual except for a place where bikini-clad women were happily wrestling in a mud bath. At the end of the match one of the girls pulled down the opponent's panties and slugged a handful of mud onto her bare butt.

We turned into a side street called *Grosse Freiheit* and by the time we had reached a disco place, called *Jungmühle,* Rick thought the time had come to rest our feet and have a glass of beer. "This place looks as good as any," he said.

It was a struggle to get in through the crowd, but once we were inside, we realized how big the joint really was.

All the tables seemed full. The customers were talking, laughing, singing, and drinking. The dance floor was filled with couples hanging onto each other and swaying while the orchestra played the popular song:

Unter der roten Laterne von St. Pauli
Sang mir der Wind heut' zum Abschied ein Lied[2]

In one corner there was a bunch of women in evening dress standing in a row and facing the dance floor. Now and then a male customer would approach them and hand something to one of the girls, then together they would head towards the dance floor.

Over and above that pandemonium was a huge mirror-covered globe hanging from the ceiling, spinning slowly and flashing rainbow-colored light all over the place.

We found an empty table on the balcony and when a waiter showed up I ordered two glasses of wine. It tasted for lime.

Not the lime from a citrus tree, rather the lime they used to disinfect outhouses. We drank it but when the dude showed up again we asked for something better than the previous Alka Seltzer mixed with bird-droppings.

Well, the waiter just stood there in his black outfit with a bow tie and all, shook his shoulders, and gave us a laconic answer, Well, gentlemen, it will cost you!"

I placed a full pack of Camels on the table in front of him. A package of American cigarettes was worth more than a pocket full of German *Reichsmarks.*

"This will be good for two glasses of *Liebfraumilch* for each of you," he said, and prepared to collect the cigarettes.

"Not so fast!" Rick said as he placed his hand on the package. "Bring us two glasses of your *Liebfraumilch* and you'll get ten Camels. OK?"

Well the new wine arrived, and it turned out to be unpolluted.

In fact it was quite drinkable.

The whole package of cigarettes was gone in no time at all, and the third round of *Liebfraumilch* took all the cigarette-money I had.

By then, for some reason the smoke-filled dancehall had become a cozy hide-out filled with glowing lights and sweet romance.

We started to look around, and glanced down over the railing.

The flashing lights from the spinning globe produced only colored spots in my eyes, but Rick had shielded his eyes and surveyed the action below, "Hey, those ladies down there in the evening dresses are dancing-girls for hire. I'll go and get some tickets! I feel like dancing tonight!"

Well, that's what he did.

I danced with a decent-looking girl in her early twenties. I felt like starting a conversation, "Hey... how's the business?"

She looked put out and told me that she was in no "business", but was a medical student earning extra money by dancing at night.

"Oh yes! Have you passed your Osteology exam yet?"

She gave me a nasty look and changed the subject!

Rick really surprised me.

He was such a bookworm at the camp, but here he was full of enthusiasm and action. The *Liebfraumilch* must have cleared his empty stomach in a hurry, and the liver had no previous experience in detoxification. How else could he have got up the courage to ask our dance partners to join us at our table?

Will miracles never end. The waiter was already waiting for us, saying, "Gentlemen, what can I bring you for refreshment?"

Rick took the word "gentlemen" as an obligation, and ordered champagne.

"Take it easy!" I warned him in Estonian: "I don't have that kind of money!"

"Well, I thought you said it was the night to celebrate! You've been living and sleeping with your graveyard bones too long! Look what we got tonight, young beauties of flesh and blood. Mine is an accountant, and I hear yours is practically a doctor. Isn't that reason enough to celebrate with these fine ladies?"

The girls appeared offended, "Speak German, please!"

"Sorry, a *lapsus linguae*. With your academic education you will recognize that Old Latin expression as meaning: a slip of the tongue!"

He then added quickly in our native language, "Don't worry. I'll take care of it!"

Well, that took a load off *my* mind.

Why not! Let a thousand flowers bloom!

I knew he had an uncle in Australia who owned a chicken farm, but according to Rick, he had not contributed any material support for his nephew. All the old man wanted was for Rick to go the Outback country and run the chicken farm for him.

Our ladies became friendly again when the champagne arrived, but after the first drink they asked for a new set of dance tickets, "You see," they explained, "we are losing out by not dancing!"

Rick did not want the girls to come up short.

He went downstairs and came up with a handful of tickets.

He placed the pile on the table:

"Help yourself, and don't be shy!"

Rick was so smooth with the ladies, but these so-called "accountant-doctors" did not show lady-like manners:

They continued to drink our champagne and every five minutes collected their tickets. They seemed to be happy enough with the arrangement, but Rick and I felt that we were at the short end of the bargain.

"Let's have another dance," was my suggestion.

We might at least get something in return for Rick's money!

This time I danced with Rick's girl, and it turned out to be a near disaster. She was taller than I and tried to dance too fast to the beat, and I was not able to slow her down. We returned to our table in the middle of the dance, and she collected her full ticket.

Soon the champagne was gone.

The girls swooped up the rest of the tickets and left.

Rick had no money left after he had paid for the dance tickets and champagne, and I was broke long before that.

The waiter came to collect the empty bottle and glasses, cleaned the table, and wanted to know whether "the gentlemen would like to have more refreshment."

We had come only to observe the action, but somehow things did not turn out as planned.

We had to give up partying and go back home.

Back in the S-Bahn and speeding through the ruins of the dark city towards the Zoo-Lager, Rick was still in a joyful mood.

He slapped my shoulder: "Didn't we have fun, dancing with two fine ladies?"

"They were some ladies alright," was my less enthusiastic response.

The next day was Sunday. I went to see Rick. He was still in bed and did not have much to say.

"You sure dished out a lot of dough!" I started the conversation in cheerful fashion. Where did you get it all?"

"Saved it up for about a year. Was planning to buy a new suit."

"Anything left?"

"Not a dime."

Obviously he wasn't interested in discussing "how wonderful a time we had" the previous night, or "the good-looking dames we danced with." I could well imagine why!

There wasn't much else to say or do, and so I went back to my own place and stretched out in bed.

I felt sorry for Rick and all the money he had lost. Besides, it was at least partially my fault. I had asked him out for an evening walk along the *Reeperbahn,* and the way things looked now, Rick would not have a new suit for another year.

The more I thought about that night, the more it bothered me. I did not know the money we had spent so foolishly had been saved up for a new suit he obviously was in dire need of.

Then an idea hit me like a thunderbolt:

There was a way we could make money, plenty of money, and Rick could get his needed suit.

I got so excited that I sat up in my bed.

I might as well tell you what I had in mind.

It had happened a few weeks before the *Reeperbahn* incident.

I had taken a wrong streetcar, and ended up in the industrial section of the old town where most of the old buildings were leveled to the ground but some were still standing with burned-out interiors. I could hear a humming sound coming from one of the buildings that was still standing, marked with a weather-beaten sign. I could barely make out the words, *"Hahnemanns Kofferfabrik"*.[3]

I stopped to listen. True enough, I could hear machine noises coming from inside the building.

"I sure could use a new suitcase," I thought. "Perhaps a pack of cigarettes will do the trick?"

I found my way upstairs to a narrow office. An old man came through the swinging doors, placed both his hands on the dusty counter, and with a probing look inquired, "Y-e-s-s?"

I had a habit of carrying an extra pack of Camels in my pocket – just in case, like people carry extra cash. I placed the cigarettes on the counter in front of him and said, "I would like to purchase a suitcase."

He did not say a word. He turned around, and was heading towards those swinging doors again, when I shouted my final instruction, "A good-sized one too, please!"

I waited for a while in that dusty and noisy place.

It was obvious that no customers or salesmen had called here for decades. Suitcases were not sold on the open market during the war, and the owner was not interested in selling them now for worthless German marks. On account of my accent, the old man did not need to worry that I might be a revenue agent snooping around.

By then the swinging doors opened, and the old man was struggling with a new suitcase that he finally managed to place upon the counter.

I had not seen anything that new and shiny for years, and then only in shop windows. It measured about three-feet-by-two and had a pair of neatly molded wooden braces all around it for extra strength. Of course, what I had would fill only half of it, but who knew – perhaps one day I would become prosperous enough to fill it up to the brim! Then the wooden braces would be handy to hold my wealth together under lock and key.

At the time I didn't give a second thought to any possible future dealings with the old man, but after Rick had lost all his money, I started to wonder:

Why not become a suitcase salesman with Rick as my partner!

The displaced persons were starting to emigrate, and most of them had nothing but plain cardboard boxes and wooden crates for holding their meager belongings. I knew for a fact that families and older women had saved up cigarettes by the cartons and on top of that had cans of Maple Leaf butter stowed away from their CARE packages. That meant purchasing power!

The market could be unlimited and the way I figured it, the profit margin could be as high as 500%.

––––––––––––

Well, that's what we did, and our *Koffergeschäft* passed all our expectations in volume and earnings.

At the factory we paid one pack of American cigarettes (plus a nominal amount of German marks) for one large suitcase.

We sold the same suitcase for four packs of cigarettes.

Let's do some calculating: 1 package of American cigarettes could be sold for 1200 marks. The profit from one suitcase would be 3x1200 = 3600 marks. By selling just two suitcases you would make 7200 marks. If you compared it to a university professor's monthly salary of 6000 marks, the disparity became obvious.

Rick and I had no guilt feelings about the business.

Our prices were reasonable, and there certainly were lots of folks in need of a nice suitcase. For four packs of cigarettes, one could become the proud owner of a new and shiny suitcase with two keys to boot. Most of our customers could put all their earthly belongings in one, lock it up, pocket the keys and voilà, they would be ready to emigrate to Australia, New Zealand, Canada, or any other country that was willing to accept them.

––––––––––––

There were a few limitations and precautions we had to consider. Rick and I could not carry more than two large suitcases each at one time. To overcome that handicap, the old man in the factory was able to fit a smaller suitcase into the large one, and then a third, still smaller one into the second. This arrangement increased our combined carrying capacity from four suitcases to twelve. The smaller ones did not have a profit margin as high as three packages of cigarettes each but still doubled our take.

There was not much of a market in Hamburg, and we had to make trips to the nearby DP Camps. The police at the railroad stations kept their eyes open for black marketers, who would be carrying large suitcases with contraband, but there was no law against carrying empty ones.

Let's assume you arrive at Hamburg *Hauptbahnhof* with your large suitcase. The police would became suspicious and ask you to open it for inspection. You open the large one, but there's nothing in it except a smaller one. The officer orders you to open that one too. Well, you do as you are told, and in the process expose a third one.

At this point, the policeman was getting irked, "Open this one too!"

You open the smallest one, and the only thing in *it* is a pair of worn-out suspenders. (You are trying to convince the police that you're transporting personal property and not involved in any shady back-alley dealings.)

At this point the policeman turns his back on you and walks away slowly, trying to retain his dignity and keep his temper under control.

The other detail you had to follow to the letter was, never let anyone follow you!

There were enough enterprising young men who would love to invade your turf and take away part of your business, if not all of it. You had to use evasive moves to shake anyone from your tail. First, take the subway, preferably one going in the opposite direction. Then switch to the S-Bahn and make your exit just a fraction of a second before the doors close. Did anyone jump out of the train after you? If you're not sure, take a streetcar to anywhere. If you got lost, well, that would be even better. By the time you found your way to the *Kofferfabrik*, you would have lost all "tails".

The next rule, You do not over-saturate any camp. If you have no more orders to fill, switch to a different camp!

That reminds me of the trip we took to Oldenburg, a place about a hundred miles from Hamburg. The railroad tickets, fixed to the old German mark, were ridiculously cheap. The round-trip to Oldenburg and back would cost us perhaps the value of three American cigarettes.

We were ready to leave with our suitcases when Ed, the waiter at the Riviera Club, gave us an address near Oldenburg where we could purchase good home-brewed whiskey at a very reasonable price. That meant increasing our profit margin further.

It was obvious that we couldn't take the booze back to Hamburg in bottles. The only way to get past the cops in the Hamburg railroad station and deliver the liquor safely to Ed was in rubber enema bags. One bag in front and another one in back, balanced and secured in place with a pair of suspenders and buttoned up inside our waistcoat.

It would be as easy as skinning a cat.

Unfortunately, all did not go as smoothly as planned.

The suitcases sold like hotcakes all right, and we picked up the booze without any hassle. All we had to do was to tuck it next to our undershirts, and nobody would be the wiser.

But bouncing around in that milk-train made Rick mighty thirsty.

He wanted to have *"nur ein Schluck"*[4] from the enema bag hanging inside his buttoned-up waistcoat. He got a straw from somewhere, opened his overcoat, let all his breath out, then held it in, unscrewed the rubber cork from the bag, and inserted his straw. It all took time and his face started to turn blue from lack of oxygen.

He looked so funny that I burst out laughing.

Well, it tickled his funny bone too, and he laughed along.

A person cannot laugh when he's exhaled!

Try it. It won't work.

To laugh you have to inhale first. And what happens if you inhale when there's an uncorked rubber bat inside your buttoned-up waistcoat and it's filled up to the brim with booze? You don't have to be an engineer of hydraulics to figure that one out.

Most of the three quarts of booze will burst like a fountain into your face and hair, and part of it will run inside your collar down to your underpants while part of it will soak your outer clothes. Only a fraction will sink back into the bag.

And that's exactly what happened to Rick.

I left Rick to himself in the Hamburg station. The aroma he carried made him a living commercial for illicit booze. The cops could smell him a mile away.

Lucky for Rick: it was one of those rare evenings when there were no policemen in sight, or even in smelling distance.

He missed his chemistry classes the next day because his suit hadn't dried out yet and he didn't own a spare one.

By now you must think we were Mafiosos, alchoholics, and woman-izers.

Not true.

Wheeling and dealing was the way of life back then. Survival of the fittest, and it didn't interrupt my study. Delayed things a little perhaps, but we remained students in body and soul. You have to admit that the little jests in your early twenties are more vividly remembered than the hours and days of hard work. Besides, remember that Rick had lost all his savings through an "unfortunate incident". Perhaps that's what we truly deserved as simpletons in the *Reeperbahn* at St. Pauli, but with my old survival skills we were able to pull ourselves up by our bootstraps. To tell the truth, our wheeling-and-dealing put us ahead economically by a mile. Rick was now wearing a tailor-made suit of the best English wool, and I had become the proud owner of a full-length leather coat and wore a sea captain's hat.

Soon these frolics became repetitious and dull.

This temporary fad of merry-making, walking down the *Reeperbahn* in my leather coat and sea captain's hat, seemed foolish.

I don't want to go into deep analysis on how I had managed to elude that highlife web on the wrong side of the tracks. Deep down I must have had enough common sense to pull myself out of that trap without any soul-searching or looking for excuses.

My brakes had not been defective.

I was like the volunteer-firemen in Kullenga decades ago.

One Sunday each summer they had their parade, drank their booze, and raised hell. The next day they returned to their backbreaking job in the farm all refreshed, and hit the plow-handle with renewed vigor. Did they feel sorry for their excessive indulgence? Heck no!

They loved every moment of it, and had their fond memories of the foolish behavior their wives wouldn't let them forget. They had a good laugh when the missing events were filled in for them. They didn't quite remember drinking too much booze. The celebration was like a booster shot for them, and it made the endless working days and hours easier to bear.

I must have inherited some of that "peasant-fireman" mentality. Live it up for a while, and then call it quits. Wake up one day and say to yourself: enough of this foolishness. So you had a good time, but re-member: no party lasts forever, and there is more work to be done. The studies that I had temporarily left at the wayside, I was picking up with renewed vigor. I hit the books harder than ever before and found happiness in the progress I made.

I was still lagging behind the rest of the bunch, but the finish-line was light years away and I had plenty of time to catch up with the rest. Who knew, perhaps I could become one of the first ones to retake the exams.

At first it took some self-discipline to convert myself from a businessman-student to full-fledged student. It wasn't all just a cakewalk, that's for sure. Who cared to attend lectures all day and then be cooped up in the barracks to study the rest of the daylight hours and into the night? (Electric power had been fully restored by then.)

On Sunday afternoons I used to give my brain a "breather". Rick and I had a "Social Hour" at the small Riviera Club, a classier joint than the rest at the *Reeperbahn*. Ed had reserved us a table in the corner next to the band. Through the high and narrow windows the afternoon sun threw streaks of yellow light on our table and to the dance floor. At times we took along a couple of fellow-students who had signs and symptoms of mental "meltdown" due to excessive brain strain.

We never did go back to *"Jungmühle"*, never hired any dancing girls, and never again asked anyone we didn't know to join us at our table.

Only on rare occasions did we get up to dance. It would have clashed with our melancholy mood and the serenity of the quiet afternoon, which was reserved for doing nothing.

It was a good way to unwind, drink wine, listen to the band, and grade the girls on the dance-floor. On occasion we did dance with the female guests, a common practice in the old country. Even then we would ask Ed's advice before dashing out to pick a girl and take her for a short swirl. He was our waiter, and we trusted him implicitly. He could tell the difference between the innocent ones and the semi-professionals. If he said "better not", we skipped it, even when the girls looked as appealing as yellow butterflies on the dance floor.

Sometimes we tried to fool old Ed and asked his opinion when it was clear as day that we wouldn't drag that particular one out for all the tea in China. He knew when we were just kidding. He would give us a short smile and announce neither his approval nor disapproval.

The pages in my study book started to fill up with signatures of passed *compendia*, lab work, and exams.

To be completely honest I did flunk the zoology final at my first try.

It was due to oversight, and not stupidity.

The mimeographed book in zoology I used was missing the last chapter, called *avia* --- the birds. I knew everything I had in *my* book from cover to cover: I had memorized the entire classification of bugs and all the individual names in Latin, from fleas to frogs to the mammals. I had already made an appointment for my oral examination when I became aware of the missing chapter. A few fellows who had already taken the exam reassured me. No questions would be asked about birds, The subject was thought to be too easy. Bugs were what the professor had been bugging everyone with so far.

Well, I don't need to tell you what happened at my first exam attempt! You were right if you guessed that his very first question was about the birds. I flunked, naturally.

Well, I hit the book again and after two weeks of study I knew every bird, living or extinct.

I took the exam again, and wouldn't you know it. On my second try the professor's interest was confined exclusively to bugs. But bugs had been my "bread and butter" all along, and I was practically on a first-name basis with any insect he wanted to attack me with. However, my previous blooper about the birds was neither forgiven nor forgotten: I was awarded the grade of *bene sufficit.*

During my biochemistry examination the professor and I had to struggle, not because of my inadequate knowledge of the subject, but because of the failing lights. The electric circuit in the building must have become overloaded, and every five minutes or so the lights went out. What was so odd about it, was that the old prof did not utter a word during the blackouts. As soon as the lights were on again, he resumed shooting me with his bio-chemical "bullets". We had played this Russian Roulette in reverse for less than an hour when he asked for my study book and awarded me with the glorified grade of *maxime sufficit.*

I wasn't quite sure whether I deserved the honor, but I was complaining about neither my grade nor the power interruptions. The prof obviously didn't want to play this "night-and-day" game any longer, and the blackouts had made him generous with his grade.

The only other topic I have vivid recollections of was histology, the microscopic study of human tissues.

I had become acquainted with two Latvian female co-students. The first one was called *Goldchen* on account of her blond locks and lively disposition. The second girl's name was Michelson (I can't remember her first name). She had a square face and wide shoulders, but after ahe had shed her broad overcoat her slender waistline and well-developed upper anatomy gave her a striking figure. It made me feel good just to look at her! She helped me to overcome the eyestrain suffered because of stooping over the microscope for hours on end. It invigorated me more than any glass of *Liebfraumilch* at that joint in the *Reeperbahn.*

After we had all passed our "Practical Works in Histology I and II" at the *Microscopische Versammlung.*[5] we were allowed to sign out the microscopes and boxes of slides so we could prepare for the final exam in our dormitories.

Histology with microscopic anatomy was like detective-work. At times one had to pick out the semi-hidden segment or cell and ignore the obvious to reach the proper conclusion. Histology was a subject where my visual memory came in handy, and my ease with the slides did not go unnoticed by the two Latvian co-eds. Before the final examination they became frequent evening visitors to my room, where the only attraction was the microscope and the slides with their kaleidoscopic colors and structures. One needed only to move the slide a fraction and a new world of fabrics, looking like colored cobwebs would fill your visual field.

Of course, we didn't have the advanced microscopes where two persons were able to look at the same slide simultaneously. To speed up study we had to keep our heads close to the binocular eyepiece and take turns to view the myriad of tissues under the same microscope. As an instructor I sat in the middle, shoulder-to-shoulder with the girls. Their hair got into my face and when they turned their heads for a comment, our faces almost met while the indirect light from the concave mirrors gave their eyes a soft glow. It would be superfluous to mention my eagerness to be the co-eds' instructor.

Goldilocks was the cheerful and easygoing girl. She laughed frequently and without any obvious reason. Perhaps a *monocyte* under the microscope reminded her of a witch's head or an occasional red blood cell (called the target cell) might remind her of a doughnut. When she laughed, I had to smile without even knowing what she was so amused about.

The three of us had signed up to take our final exam together.

The examiner, an associate professor with a gleam in his eye, took Goldilocks first. Things went without a hitch. If there was a small difference of opinion between her and the professor, a quick smile and shake of her head (curls flying) usually pacified the examiner and brought the point of discussion to a satisfactory conclusion. Michelson, the taller and more serious girl passed her exam with a few minor

298

"bumps".

Each of them received a *maxime sufficit* for their efforts.

Then came my turn.

The slide part of my exam went too smoothly. I had the answers without taking much time to study the slide. If I came across as a "show off", it was not intentional, but it rubbed the professor the wrong way. Besides, he had already distributed two *maxime sufficit* and he did not want to give the impression that histology was as easy as all that. In the question and answer period he went into methods of staining the tissues, something described in the histology books but not discussed during our lecture series. I still remember the questions about the stain called *Evans' Blue*. Well, I did not have all the answers to his liking, and when he took my study book he had a feigned smile on his face when he announced that he could not give me a higher grade than "*bene.*"

You should have been there to see the prompt response from my co-students. Michelson places her study book back on the professor's table, and Goldilocks did the same. Both of them requested to have their grades changed to *bene sufficit,* explaining:

"Herr Ojamaa has been our instructor. Whenever we had to struggle with a certain slide, he was there to help us. If he gets a *bene,* it is unfair to him, and unfair for us girls to get *maxime sufficit!*"

A long moment of silence followed.

The associate professor kept his eyes on the three study books in front of him.

He could not very well downgrade the girls with their grades already written in the books. The only way out of his predicament was to add the word *maxime* in front of my scholastic rating in histology.

The change in my grade didn't really mean much then or for the future, but I can't forget the determination those two Latvian co-eds showed on my behalf. After this episode a beautiful friendship was established between us. I found Goldchen's vivacious demeanor good for my disposition, and Michelson's physical make-up was restful for my eyes.

Our symbiotic relationship was short-lived. Both migrated to Australia. I know nothing about their later careers in the outback country, but with their determination and looks, I am confident they reached their goal and became doctors.

Meanwhile, our Study Center was relocated to Pinneberg, a few stations from Hamburg, forcing us to commute. Rick stayed back in Hamburg, and a year passed that I didn't see him. Our common days of business and carefree hours had passed.

But, I felt overwhelmed when the sad news arrived that Richard Siidam's life had come to a fateful end.

A few days before Christmas 1947, his body was found floating in the Hamburg harbor. He had met his end during a final visit to the *Reeperbahn,* a day before he was to leave for Australia to run his uncle's chicken farm. Nothing else was known about the episode. Foul play was suspected.

I had lost a sometime friend. I had lost many in the past, but this was different. I had invited him to accompany me to the *Reeperbahn.* I should have realized his unconstrained nature when he blew his entire savings for a few worthless moments, but I was his accomplice and let it happen. I had helped replace his monetary loss, but the devil's finger had touched him before he could escape to the outback country away from the evils of St. Pauli.

[1] satisfactory
[2] "Under the red light of St. Pauli…The wind sang me a farewell song"
[3] suitcase factory
[4] just one swallow
[5] microscope classes

Chapter 5

CHANGING TIMES

The summer of "49 had been beautiful.

Our dormitory, surrounded by rolling meadows and clumps of red rosebushes, was a few train stops from Hamburg. The weather was unusually sunny, with high billowy clouds and nightly showers.

I had finished the first half of my medical studies and could call myself *cand med* or medical candidate. But after the spring semester, the IRO[1] announced closure of the university campus. We had to choose between immigration or being integrated into German society.

A number of students had obtained scholarships to American universities. Canada had been accepting young men as lumberjacks for over a year, and England was in need of farm laborers and hospital workers. In both countries one had to sign a contract to remain employed in the designated pursuit for at least one year.

Only America gave us a free choice. The immigration officials told us, "It is against the American way of life to force you to work in a place you do not like." I had found a Reverend and Mrs. Carlson as my sponsors, and filed my immigration application to the USA like most of my fellow students.

––––––––––––

For the first time after three years of study, I had time I could spend to my own liking. I took long walks along the footpaths to a café in the forest. The waitress had an easy smile, brought me a glass of lemonade, and left me alone to admire the locale with its flowers and yellow butterflies. The long grass beyond the tree line was bending in the summer wind, as if praying.

In the Liberal Arts department there was a girl with dreamy eyes and a tranquil disposition who had become my companion. Together we walked the lonely paths between the recently-cut hayfields smelling of last summer, we visited the art galleries in Hamburg, and took cruises on the river Elbe. Or I would rent a boat and row in a small lake in the park where the willow branches dipped into the placid water.

We held hands during the train ride back home as dusk fell over the distant fields.

I like the mental make-up of the female sex.

It is more refined and introspective, perhaps even more imaginative and creative than that of the male. My temper is closer to that of the female gender than to the harsher male counterpart. I have had very few male friends over the years, but needless to say I never held hands with any of them.

***

Then came fall. A foggy mist covered the fields.

The girl with dreamy eyes had left for America, as had most of my roommates and fellow students.

I was still waiting.

Nobody told me the reasons for the delay.

I could guess. I had been fighting *against* the Russians and not *with* the Russians during the war, and had broken the old rule of "don't ask --- don't tell".

There were only three of us left in the attic room with high and narrow windows. The windows showed only clouds, and were washed by frequent rain showers. One of my companions was Endel Peep, a youngster from the back woods of Estonia who hadn't taken any steps to find a country to go to. The other, we called him *der dritte Mann,* was Sven Wichman, who was trying to finish his engineering studies in Hamburg before immigration.

***

The whole scenario had become depressing.

I had nothing to do, and didn't know what to do next. I walked alone along the summer trails, now wet from autumn rains.

It seemed that luck, my old and faithful companion, had deserted me.

***

There was only one female student left behind. She was a quiet girl with a dark complexion, slim and full of individual charm. Kai lived in Hamburg in a semi-cylindrical metal structure they call a quonset. I re-arranged her electrical wiring and in return she prepared and served supper. It was just wonderful to sit at a cloth-covered table with plates and cutlery. I couldn't even remember the last time anybody had served me a meal. It didn't matter that the dinner table was just a reinforced crate. We were both lonely, and our friendship meant more to me than the one I'd had with a dreamy-eyed liberal arts student the previous summer.

Another spring arrived, and I hadn't heard anything about my immigration to America. I had a distant cousin in Sweden named Margot Üksi, Kaarel Lehiste's mother, and wrote her about my plight. Margot quickly took up a crusade to get me to Sweden.

The immigration office in Stockholm, however, refused to issue me the visa. According to the existing rules, only first-generation relatives of Swedish citizens would be eligible for such a document. Margot had always been a "doer", and she wasn't giving up her quest that easy.

Gustav V, *Bernadotte af Wisborg*,[2] was the king of Sweden. It was one of his close female relatives in the royal household whom Margot had written a tear-filled letter claiming to have only one living relative outside the Iron Curtain, a young man in a Displaced Persons' camp in post-war Germany. Would the honored lady help to find a way so that the young man could join Margot in the free and prosperous country of Sweden?

Margot's letter must have been a moving one.

She was invited for an interview, and her timely tears helped the old lady reach a quick answer:

She would call her cousin, Count Carl Bernadotte of Wisborg, in Frötuna and ask him to write a note that Margot could take to the immigration office. In that note the Count would ask the officers to issue a visa to *Estniska medborgaren* Arved Ojamaa, as he was needed as a farm laborer on his Estate in Frötuna.

When Margot returned to the immigration office with that note, her visa request was given immediate attention. If a member of the Royal Family was in need for a farmhand, there most certainly was no regulation for denying such a request.

I had put all my hopes in one country --- America.

I was tired of waiting, and willing to go to any country to escape my predicament. If it was Sweden, so be it. But still, I was very much hurt that America had rejected me.

I would be a farm worker again, but it would be only a temporary arrangement.

Perhaps I could finish my studies in Sweden instead and become a doctor there, the goal I had worked towards in Germany. I couldn't even fantasize about staying in Germany, with its high unemployment and dislike of foreigners.

The royal note did wonders. It took only two weeks to get a notice from the Swedish Consulate in Hamburg to come and pick up my visa. I was asked to bring my passport, a recent photograph showing both ears, and 20 DM of newly issued German currency.

All this might sound simple enough, but for a DP, a displaces person without a country, like me, it was a different matter. The International Refugee Organization (IRO) had made it clear in its constitution that no authority had the power to issue me a passport because I did not enjoy the protection of any government, and thus was not in a position even to apply for one. Plain and simple.

The military government of Germany came to the rescue by issuing me a red cloth-covered document that looked like a passport, though it stated on its cover in three languages (English, French, and German) that it was a "Temporary Travel Document *in Lieu of* a Passport".

That solved one of the requirements. Next I went to a professional photographer to have my picture taken with both ears showing. It cost me 7 DM, depleting my monetary resources.

I overcame the currency shortage the next day, when I ran into Oskar Puusepp. He was a generation older, and had been a professional soldier in the old Estonian Defensive Forces, where he had attained the rank of captain. At present, he was a student at the Lutheran Seminary in Hamburg. Once, we shared a room in the student dormitory, and I remember him "burning the midnight oil" studying Latin and ancient Greek. That was part of his curriculum for being ordained as a Lutheran minister.

He was living now in a rented room on the outskirts of Pinneberg.

There was something mysterious about that square room of his. The stunted and twisted birch trees crowded his outside window like emaciated ballet dancers. On the opposite wall was a grandfather clock with woodcarvings of cherubs holding up the timepiece. The odd thing about it was that the landlady had removed the clock to save the delicate mechanism from wear and tear. This left the angels reaching for an empty hole. It gave me the willies seeing the faceless clock and ghost-like birch trees staring each other down through the window.

I felt kind of sorry for old Puusepp.

You try to live in such a crummy room all by yourself when you're already past fifty. No female companion even to bring you a cup of coffee or make your bed in the morning. Nothing but an old landlady shuffling around in worn-out slippers with her fat dachshund at her heels.

When Oskar heard of my predicament, he gave me 20 DM, saying, "Pay it back when you can. If you can't, well..." he made a sweeping move with his left hand, put his wallet back in his pocket, and took off to one of his Greek seminars.

Later on, when I was able to pay it back, he was rather reluctant to take it. "Young man," he said, "you have expenses!" But his wallet was empty when my 20 DM disappeared into it.

It was one of the sunny afternoon in August 14th, 1950 when I took a seat in the *Nord-Express* and entrusted it with taking me to a new unknown. The few roots I had grown in Hamburg were being torn up. I had to start yet again from the beginning, from the bottom of the ladder.

It was time to leave all the books behind and "take up a plow".

[1] International Refugee Organization
[2] name of the Swedish royal family

Chapter 6

MY YEAR IN SWEDEN

The *Nord-Express* arrived in Stockholm about noon the next day.

I am not going to describe the city or how I felt in the new country. What I saw seemed somewhat strange. There were no ruins anywhere! I had become used to crumbled-down buildings as part of any cityscape, but here everything appeared neat and orderly, almost unreal.

Besides, I did not see much of Stockholm anyway. By Monday morning I was back at the railroad station for a 40-mile ride to Uppsala, about seven miles from my final destination.

In Uppsala station a black car with chauffeur was waiting to take me to Frötuna. It sure was an unconventional way for a farm laborer to travel, but I was not going to work for some sharecropper. No sir! The Count Carl Bernadotte himself had hired me to work at his estate which extended far and wide. His land holdings included two or three villages, and endless woods.

My friend, Sven Wichman, who had finished his engineering studies in Hamburg and was now making a buck an hour pushing a wheelbarrow at some construction site in New York, pointed out my situational differences in a letter: "You won't be hauling the s--- of just ordinary cows, no way! You'll be servicing Royal Cows, and that puts you in a higher social bracket than you realize!"

The Count was a man in his early sixties, with a serious face and reserved manners. The Countess, on the other hand, acted like a commoner. She was in her late forties, a slender woman with a sensitive face and lively eyes. She walked among the farmhands and servants wearing slacks and had a kerchief tied around her head. She personally came down to arrange the delivery of my groceries, told me how to get milk from the creamery, and asked the farmer's wife next door to do my laundry and clean my small apartment.

I could not speak a word of Swedish.

I could communicate with the Count and Countess, since they spoke fluent German. But, I was only a farmhand on their large estate, and not a weekend guest at the mansion.

To speak with my fellow farm workers I used one-word sentences and plenty of hand signals. In their eyes I was a novelty. I had arrived in a car driven by the Count's personal chauffeur, a truly unconventional way to transport a farmhand who couldn't even speak their language.

They had never met such a creature before.

The farm work itself was physically demanding, with long hours.

I was under the weather one Saturday afternoon.

Since eight in the morning we had been pulling turnips in a drizzly rain and loading them into a wagon. They were big, and their roots hard to remove from the clay ground. I had a stiff back and aching arms well before quitting time at 12:15 p.m.

When the hours were finally up, I went to my room and plopped myself in an armchair, wet clothes and all.

The rain seemed to get heavier. It beat on the roof and rattled against my window. This kind of weather always put me in a melancholy mood, and this Saturday was no exception.

Minutes and hours are long in solitude. I had nowhere to go or anyone to speak to. I should have been studying Swedish, but didn't feel like it. All I could do was sit there and keep looking out the window at the pouring rain.

Someone knocked at the door. This itself was most unusual. Nobody had visited me so far!

They waited until I was working in the fields before they cleaned my apartment. When I went to the creamery to get my milk allowance, I didn't say a word. It was all pre-arranged. The container was waiting for me at the designated corner. The last time two teenaged girls sat on a nearby bench, giving me an open-faced smile. I didn't know how to respond, and kept on walking back to my deserted house with downcast eyes.

After hearing the knock, I opened the door and stood face-to-face with a young man, a farmworker. We had baled hay together.

He pulled out a beautiful radio from under his raincoat, and said a single word, "The Countess...!"

Back then radios were not a dime-a-dozen, and this one was special. It was in a beautiful mahogany case with a lit screen, and had all three wavelengths.

Bless her heart!

I plugged the radio into the wall socket and was instantly connected with the outside world. I found the West-Berlin station and listened to the *"Bunte Stunde"*, a variety broadcast with music and laughter. What a wonderful feeling to listen to a language one could understand.

My spirits were buoyed up by the unexpected gift. I shed my wet clothes and fixed myself a sandwich.

Then I started wondering why I was getting all this unsolicited attention from the ladies, from East Germany to the West, and now their intuition was extending even as far as Sweden. Was there something about me that made all motherly types rush to pull me out of the particular tar pit that I happened to be in at the moment?

I had to laugh. Whatever it was, I hoped I wouldn't lose it!

In their quiet way, the Bernadottes were wonderful people, and I owe them a lot. But let's face it, I was a stranger in their world and to their way of life. They treated me with respect, or with rather stiff kindness, maybe I should say. I could never imagine any back-slapping or belly laughs from their social class, but underneath all this formality was a hidden warmth and even affection. When dining in their mansion I couldn't exactly start praising their place or asking questions about their family or how many kids they had. But, I could talk about how much I admired the birch trees lining the rocky roadside, or even ask questions about that centuries-old fieldstone barn I had admired. Then they would visibly brighten up and tell stories about the road and the barn.

After five weeks of farm work I was discharged at my own request.

Meanwhile I had become the proud owner of a used bicycle and had made several trips to Uppsala, where I intended to settle.

I want you to know that Uppsala is not a hick town in the middle of nowhere. Far from it. Uppsala is a medieval town with cobblestone streets and historic buildings, located six miles from Frötuna and 40 miles from Stockholm. Its population was then about 60,000.

It has the largest Gothic cathedral in the country, which took over 150 years to build and was finally finished in 1435. There are other famous landmarks, such as the 16th century royal castle of Gustav Vasa.

Most important, Uppsala claimed the oldest university in all Sweden and its library, called *Carolina Rediviva,* contains the famous 6th century illuminated *Codex Argenteus* manuscript. Carl von Linné, the world-famous botanist who was the first to classify plants and animals into genera and species, died here in 1778 while he was a professor at the University, and Anders Celsius founded an observatory here in 1730.

I had rented a room at Runstensgata in a one-family home for 20 crowns, and the Count had sent me on my way in a chauffeur-driven car.

It sure impressed my new landlady, but reality presented quite a different picture. All I had was a bicycle, a fancy radio, two large volumes of *Internal Medicine* in German, and a suitcase from Hahnemann's *Koffernfabrik* now filled with my earthly belongings and 100 Swedish crowns.

The night before my departure, I was invited to an informal dinner at the mansion. I found the number of forks and knives confusing, and most of the dishes served by the butler in black attire were unknown to me in both taste and appearance. The only thing I remember from that room was a large painting of Karl XII on the wall just behind the Countess's chair. I knew enough of my table manners not to gaze around at the dining room during the meal, or to place my elbows on the table.

At the end of the meal, they both shook my hand and wished me luck. The Count gave me his recommendation for application to the University and asked me to keep him posted about my future endeavors in Sweden.

Well. This fancy dining and chauffeuring had been yesterday, and today I had to face reality.

I could hardly dream of starting my university application process right then. My currency reserves of 100 crowns were enough to buy groceries for a week or two, and I was far from being proficient in Swedish.

First and foremost, I had to find work.

I scrutinized the "Help Wanted" columns in the evening newspaper and made inquiries during the day. The first stop I made was at the bicycle factory. They were in need of help, according to a newspaper ad. Things looked promising as first, but they quickly lost interest when they noticed how I was struggling with the language.

The Hotel *"Tre Liljor"*[1] needed someone to wash dishes.

I made a silly mistake, and went to the delicatessen of the same name.

I was embarrassed to no end. I kept asking when I should come to work while the manager recounted patiently the fact that I was in a bakery and they had no dishes to wash. The salesgirls had inane smiles on their faces when I picked up my rain-soaked hat and left.

I was feeling tired and depressed.

By now I didn't even feel like going to the Hotel *"Tre Liljor"* to inquire about the dishwashing job. On my way home I remembered having only milk and bread in the corner of the basement steps, the coolest spot in the house. (The landlady had a small refrigerator, with no room to share.) I needed something more substantial for my next meal, so I went on a spending-spree and bought a can of anchovies for 1 *krona* and 25 *öre*. I needed a can-opener, but I didn't know how to ask for one. It took me awhile to find it in the dictionary. I still remember the Swedish word for can-opener as *knoservöppnare*. By God, it sure can be frustrating not knowing the local language!

After a few days of useless searching, I got a job at *Ekeby Bruk* --- loading wet clay into wagons on the graveyard shift.

I had no choice! It was this or go hungry. The day I applied was Thursday, and I was supposed to start at *Ekeby Bruk* on Monday.

That meant I had just one working day left to find less strenuous work, and hopefully to find something that would divert me less from my medical studies.

The following day was 13 October, Friday --- the day I wouldn't forget. I got up that morning, flipped the day-leaf on my calendar, and saw the date, Friday, 13 October.

Well, the day and date startled me at first. But, then it came to me that "Friday" and "thirteen" used to be my lucky day and number. Perhaps they still were... To hell with the newspaper ads!

The only way to get anywhere was to get on my bike and see if there was a pot of gold at the other end of the rainbow. I decided just to drop in on one of the University laboratories and ask for a job.

I got dressed and ate some leftover sprats with bread, washed them down with some milk, and I was on my way. My confidence-scale was going up and down like the blood pressure readings of a person ready to go into irreversible shock, but instead I pressed harder on my bicycle pedals.

It didn't take long to get to the outskirts of the city. There was no use fooling around in the old downtown. All they needed were janitors and maintenance men, and I would not qualify for those.

The first building on the right side was a three-story brick structure, some 50 yards from the main street. A gravel road led to the entrance. The letters on the glass paneled door spelled out, Institute of Pharmacology.

Unable to get up the courage to enter, I stood there on the doorstep for a minute or two and pondered my next move: should I go in or not?

"Well," I thought, "it's supposed to be my lucky day Friday the thirteenth! All they can say is 'No'; they won't shoot me!"

I opened the door and stepped in.

A middle-aged lady wearing a white lab coat asked me something I did not understand.

"Could I see *Herr professor?*"

Her answer was apparently "yes".

She went and knocked on the door behind the desk, and a moment later I was facing a tall man with a pale and expressionless face. He was wearing an open-collar shirt and suspenders.

I asked for permission to speak German.

"Yes, you may."

At that moment, for some reason my confidence dropped to an all-time low. Instead of asking for a job, I started to stammer something about my pharmacology studies in Hamburg and whether I might get credit for my previous work.

The professor seemed annoyed, "Well, put in your application and then we'll see!"

He turned away, but before he could retreat to his office I added in desperation, "There was something else I wanted to ask you, *"Herr Professor...*"

"Yes?"

"I... I have very little money, and no job!"

"Well. Why didn't you say so in the first place? Come in and we'll talk about it."

In his office we were facing each other.

"How much money do you have?"

"98 kronor and 75 öre."

"That won't get you too far!"

Then he started to think out loud, "Hmm. We don't have any openings at present, but something always comes up here. But you can't wait. You need income now!"

"Let me see. For a start I could let you take care of our rabbits and white mice and the frogs. I'll pay you two crowns per hour. It wouldn't take more than three hours every day, with a monthly salary of 220 crowns."

I couldn't hide my delight --- it was all over my face.

I had been working eight hours a day plus four hours on Saturdays for 200 crowns a month and it had been all hard physical labor. Here I'd make 220 crowns a month, working only 3 hours a day --- feeding rabbits! Now I'd have time to do some reading!

Glory be, on this rain-soaked "Friday the 13th" I had finally found a job beyond what I could even imagine.

The professor noticed my happy face, which had turned red by now, and added for reassurance, "This will get you started. We'll come up with something more substantial later on!"

He asked for the *vaktmästare*[2] Mr. Eglund and instructed him to show me my duties as the new *Versuchsperson und Versuchskaninchen Fütterer.*[3] Mr. Eglund, the maintenance man, seemed pleased. It was a duty he was happy to lose.

Goodbye *Ekeby Bruk* with your graveyard shift in the clay pits! Life was worth living again.

It didn't take more than two hours each day to feed the rabbits and clean their cages. I felt sorry for them, I really did. They didn't have much to look forward to anyway. It's not easy to be a *Versuchskaninchen,* so I talked to them. They stopped chewing hay and listened with their big white ears all perked up.

On a shelf on the opposite wall were white mice in glass jars, each with a perforated top holding a glass bulb full of water with pipette-like extension so they could have a drink any time they felt like it. Their other urges remained unfulfilled, as they were carefully separated by sex. One could well imagine the outcome if their living quarters would become co-educational!

Down in the dungeon were the frogs, about a hundred of them. They had to be fed only twice a month, one-by-one. You had to catch them and shove a piece of raw liver in their mouths. The piece had to be entirely inside the mouth, or they'd spit it out and be dead by the time the next feeding came around.

I had barely gotten acquainted with my mammals and basement reptiles when I was called back to the Professor's office to meet Miss Hermanson. She was a senior medical student who had received a research grant, and Professor Barany had appointed me her assistant with added salary of two crowns an hour.

I don't remember how many evenings I worked with Miss Hermanson, but I can tell you, those were the shortest two hours I have ever lived through, work or leisure.

She was a good-looking young woman with a Mona Lisa smile and lively eyes.

She asked me to call her Gun (pronounced *gu: n*).

We worked evenings from 5 to 7 giving shock treatments to rabbits before and after DOCA injections. She kept looking at me with her brown eyes, even when she should have been looking at the rabbit's hind legs I was holding for her. No wonder she stuck herself with the myelogram needle! We both had a good laugh, but she did learn quickly to use the needle without sticking herself --- looking or not looking.

Her short hair had fallen across her face, and there were her eyes and smile again. I couldn't even look up --- she had me under her constant surveillance.

We used an odd language to communicate in. It was a mixture of German and Swedish. She wanted to improve her German, and I my Swedish.

I gave her one rule about the German language, though on looking back I think I might have made it up: "Any noun ending with a *–chen* means small, like *Kanin-chen:* small rabbit."

She was making fun of my rule.

"How about a *Mäd-chen.* Does she have to be small?"

"Well, the German language has many exceptions!"

"If instead of Gun you called me *Mädchen,* then would I fall under your rule or would I be the exception?"

The rabbit's sudden move made both of us grab one of his legs --- her reflex must have been fast, how else would it happen that my hand had landed on top of hers.

As a precautionary measure we both continued to hold that foot without even noticing that the rabbit soon gave up his struggle.

We had supper together in the cafeteria.

We didn't speak.

She didn't challenge me with her wit anymore, and for some reason seemed to have changed since I had held her hand accidentally.

She paid the bill and when I protested, she simply said, "You are just a poor boy!"

That was a fact, and the way she said it --- well, it didn't bother me a bit.

Then she went up north on a deer hunt, and I was out twelve *crooners*. Well, I had to admit I missed her more than I missed the money.

There was another experiment I participated in. Marie-Lou Scholten was in charge of it. She was a tall, small-boned woman with red hair, and a face and hands full of freckles. She was the medical student I spoke about earlier who had flunked her anatomy exam twice. She was working in the lab and waiting for the professor to retire so she could give it another go.

To pass the time she was doing an experiment with different cough drops. Like all the other participants, I had to put on a mask and inhale some kind of gas mixture (I don't remember what it was exactly), in a concentration that was increased until it made me cough. Then I had to chew certain cough drops, and after five minutes or so be tested again to see if she had to increase the concentration to activate my cough-reflex. She was trying to find out whether the brand-X cough drops really worked.

One of the students in our cough experiment told me he was going to buy his wife a vacuum cleaner with the "cough-money" he was making!

As for the results of the experiment, if I remember correctly, there was no difference, cough-drops or no cough-drops!

When we had completed the "cough drops experiment, Professor Barany had a new and rather more exciting job for me.

Dr. Linner, a 35-year-old ophthalmologist had received a grant and needed an assistant. Professor Barany was in charge of all the experiments in his Pharmacology Institute, and he appointed me as Linner's assistant with a salary of five crowns per hour. This was "top of the

315

top" pay.

Dr. Linner was a rather short but well built man, with thick eyeglasses and a serious face. According to the department grapevine, he was "all work and no play". All his energy was directed to his patients in the hospital and to his research in the lab. He was very frugal with his grant, and acted like all the money was coming out of his own pocket. His German was excellent and it was the language we used for communicating. Perhaps that was one of the reasons I was slow in picking up the native tongue everybody I worked with liked to speak German with me!

As far as our experiment was concerned, it consisted of ligating the left side of the interior branch of the rabbit's carotid artery and then injecting vitamin C intravenously. After a certain length of time I had to aspirate a few drops of *humor aqueus* from the anterior chamber of each eye and then use microanalysis to determine the concentration of vitamin C in the fluid. I was, in other words, trying to see if there was any difference in concentration between the ligated and non-ligated sides.

This work was interesting and as I mentioned, well paid. My monthly salary surpassed that of some of the lab technicians.

Was there a touch of jealousy, a bit of "look at this guy who can't even speak proper Swedish and is making more than I do"?

Everyone's salary was common knowledge. Mrs. Bundesson in the front office paid it out in cash. She was a good-looking woman about 30 and shaped like a model.

She had beautiful black hair and black eyes, and if you happened to hear a hearty laugh all the way down the hallway, it was Mrs. Bundesson for sure.

She was supposed to withhold income tax, but if you were short of cash on a payday, you could ask her nicely to give you all of it. She would look at you for a minute, then declare, "I shouldn't be doing this but --- alright! This time only! You'll be facing the double-whammy next time around, you know!" And she would count out your entire salary, all in cash.

Mrs. Bundesson was just too kindhearted to say no, even if she was putting herself in hot water with the tax collector.

Who could criticize my income?

Most certainly it was not Mrs. Gertz.

She was the head technician, about 40, short and pleasantly plump, with fifteen years experience.

She liked to hum. She hummed tunes while doing lab work, and she hummed when high up on the ladder... almost touching the ceiling, and she hummed!

Her assistant Miss Ingalill was a 24-year-old tech. She was a bird of a different feather, moody and cocky, and definitely a suspect.

I had been told that she was beautiful. But I do not know where or how she, with her shortness and wide hips, hid that beauty. And smoke, my God, could she smoke, always a cigarette in her mouth.

According to our old doctor Goldstein, Ingalill smoked to suppress her overheated sexuality. Dr. Goldstein knew everybody and everybody knew Dr. Fritz Goldstein, *Kinderarzt aus Berlin.* He visited me every day to speak his native tongue.

He always started with, *"Wie geht's"*

Every time my answer was the same, *"Ganz gut! Wie geht's Ihnen?"*

Now I had asked how he was doing, and that would always take some time to answer. Before replying he would sit in the chair next to me, stretch out his legs, and unbutton his jacket. His tie had sunk down halfway to his waistcoat, showing the rusty collar button in the front. He was what the Swedes called an "archive-worker".

The older refugees with an academic education, the artist, the writers and composers, received a fixed salary from the state averaging perhaps 300 crowns each month. They, like Dr. Goldstein, had their own small offices in different university departments, in libraries, civic offices, in art galleries, museums, and the like. They kept the filing cabinets up-to-date, arranged the department periodicals and wrote little mementos to themselves, which they also catalogued.

Dr. Goldstein's answer to my question of how he was doing was always the same"

"Schlecht."

And if I inquired why things were bad, he went into detail, Sweden, the robbers. The government robs its own people!

Doctors, rabbit-doctors, all dimwits! Don't have the slightest idea about disease or how to treat it! The medical literature, rubbish! Waste of the good paper it's printed on!

He would continue along the same vein for awhile, but I always noticed a gleam in his eyes, as if he were telling a joke.

I took a break and offered him a cigarette.

We smoked together and talked. He had a wide knowledge of drugs and their effect. He was an expert in opiates, and told me that the Peru Indians were able to survive in the harsh environment only because they chewed coca leaves. That gave them endurance, satisfied their hunger, and strengthened them.

I liked Dr. Goldstein. He was kindhearted. He became happy if someone came to his tiny office to borrow something, like a sheet of paper or a magazine.

If you happened to go past his office you could hear a hammering sound, it would be old Dr. Goldstein typing a reminder to himself on his old upright typewriter, with one finger.

If you happened to be out of cigarettes he was ready to put on his coat and go downtown to fetch a pack for you. Not as a messenger boy! God forbid! Only as Dr. Fritz Goldstein, *Kinderarzt aus Berlin.*

And there came Dr. Edlund.

He was a tall man with a crew-cut, with a serious face and a nononsense attitude. He ran a tight ship while Dr. Barany was in England on a lecture tour. I do not believe we ever exchanged a word between us. Once I heard him speak English, with the visiting delegation from a Brazilian University.

These doctors and candidates, they all spoke English.

When they published their research papers it would be in English. To receive their doctor's degree after graduation, they had to do research and write their doctoral thesis. During that time the Swedish government would pay their salary and cover all expenses, including the technicians' and secretaries' salaries and the lab supplies.

Friday the 13th had come through for me with flying colors.

If I had ended up in *Ekeby Bruk,* I would have soon been dead, I am convinced...

I have fond memories of the people I worked with at the Pharmacology Institute, located at Stockholmsvägen 19, in old Uppsala.

I had meanwhile enrolled at the University of Uppsala, and received credit for my previous work in Hamburg. I could have started spring semester but decided to wait until fall 1951. It just did not make sense to rush into things in the middle of winter. I had to become more fluent in Swedish and build up my bank account.

I only had a visitor's visa to Sweden, good for six months, but it was extendable, if you behaved yourself and turned out to be a useful citizen for the country and community. This arrangement allowed me to remain on the IRO waiting list for immigrating to the USA --- I had not immigrated to Sweden, I was simply visiting the country. This way I could have my cake and eat it too!

I received a letter from the Hamburg D. P. Regional Resettlement Center, dated June 6th 1951, with the warning, *"We have to call your attention to the fact that the IRO and DP Commission will close your case unless you return to Wentorf Processing Center immediately."*

The tone softened a little toward the end, *"Please let us know at once of your intentions."*

Well, this sure was a surprise; it looked like my emigration application to America was at last going through!

For the moment, I was confused at the same time I was happy. I was constantly in hope of getting this message my first few months in Sweden, but now I was kind of settled. I had put down a few roots in Uppsala.

I had a good job, and was admitted to the University as a continuing medical student. Had my own bicycle and radio, too. And as far as the language was concerned, well, I was getting "over the hump," so to speak.

But the old question was still there, go to America, or not? If I left for America, I would have to start again from the very beginning. After each "new beginning" it was becoming harder to keep going and easier to sink into an "I don't care" morass.

Did I have what it took to make a go of it on a new continent, in a new country..?

America had been the land of mystery to me since I received my first Christmas present from that faraway country at the age of three. Lady Luck had kept me afloat all those turbulent years and together we'd manage to overcome any adversity that might cross our path. Perhaps in America more than anywhere else!

What had happened in the meantime so that my application to the USA was finally approved? Was it the Korean War?

The war was in full swing by now, and the Americans were taking heavy losses.

The Russians' jet fighters had been shooting down American bombers. Did this war finally convince U. S. legislators that Stalin and his Red Army were not friends for keeps?

I believe the Americans must have finally switched their categorization of Stalin from friend to foe, and rightly so. Surely it was the Korean War that had erased my "sin" of having fought the true enemy, the Socialist Republic of the Soviet Union, all along.

I decided to go, of course.

My last day in Stockholm was Sunday, 11 June, 1951. It was a bright summer day, and I still remember the fresh and promising breeze that was blowing in from the sea.

Margot and I had breakfast in her Klubbcken apartment and then we attended the Estonian Songfest-in-exile in the nearby woods. The choir stood on the side of a forest hill, and conductor Olav Roots perched himself on a tree stump.

It was a memorable day in many ways.

I also met Miss Eller, my beloved literature teacher from years before.

We spent the rest of the afternoon together. She not only remembered me, she could even recite the poem we had studied together in Väike-Maarja some 12 years ago.

My train finally pulled out of the Stockholm railroad station at 9:40 p.m., and I left behind the white city on the hills with its blue waters. In my memory, I can still see Margot's white handkerchief, waving in the early dusk while Miss Eller covered her face to hide her emotions.

It was goodbye to beautiful Sweden.

[1] "Three Lilies"
[2] maintenance man
[3] researcher and feeder of research-rabbits

Chapter 7

On My Way

It was Tuesday, 14 August, 1951 when the old military transport ship *General Blatchford* lifted anchor from Bremerhaven on its way to New York. It was a good-size ship, 1700 reg. tons and some 500 feet long. It made 14 to 20 miles per hour depending on weather conditions. Its "cargo" consisted of some 600 immigrants, and it took ten days to cross the Atlantic. Every other night we had to turn our clocks back one hour.

The weather was warm and sunny when we crossed the English Channel. The White Cliffs of Dover, yellow in the afternoon sun, were the last sights of land, soon to fade into the blueness of the North Atlantic.

The ocean can be stormy in the fall, and so it came about that on the evening of August 17 the wind blew with a gale force and waves became mountains. In order to overcome the dangerous roll and yaw, the ship changed its course to face the wind and the waves.

There were no luxury cabins, I can tell you.

We all slept in cargo rooms, in hammocks arrayed from floor to ceiling, perhaps 200 bodies in one compartment. In the upper hammocks the air was hot and mixed with the smell of engine oil. It was cooler for the lower sleepers, but they had to deal with the stink of urine and vomit, overpowering because of clogged toilets and seasickness.

It sounded like the repetitious and mournful roar of a hundred lions when the ship hit a big swell, pitching and rolling, and between the giant waves one could hear deep moans coming from the ship.

Nights are strange in a room filled with hammocks, and you see the entire enclosure swaying all in one direction but in a disorderly manner. The red lights scattered through the huge cabin made it all look ghostly and unreal.

Towards morning the gale had blown itself out, but the sea remained restless under low clouds. A few people started to show up in the dining rooms, but the sight of food made them cradle their stomachs with their hands. When another deep water-swell buried the bow, the few dining-room stragglers quickly left.

321

The sea was running high. All the in-rushing waves were white-capped, and when one of the swells broke over the bow the wind ripped it into white foam. Fine, mist-like droplets filled the air. They made my clothes damp and covered my face and hands with a layer of powdery salt. My shoes, originally brown, were now white.

The breath of fresh air and opportunity to look at the horizon seemed to clear my head and relieve the squeeze in my stomach.

From the very beginning I was assigned to the ship's clubroom to lend out books and chessboards, domino sets and picture puzzles.

It freed me from tedious manual labor, unless one counts as labor holding onto one's inkpot when the ship made its dives.

So you want to know how I became a librarian..?

The same way I kept my Finnish uniform way back when everybody else had to give up his. I used to call it "Insidious Intrusion", modified to fit the time and the circumstances. This wasn't the same thing as being "pushy", which was sure to get you nowhere in those circumstances.

In this case I was doing voluntary work even before the work assignments were handed out. At least it turned out that way, by a coincidence:

I had found the ship's clubroom, and I started to pull out some books and read the covers. Someone with authority stepped by, "The clubroom is still closed. What are you doing here?"

My old rule-of-thumb: if you don't know what the best answer is, be evasive at first and try to find out which way the wind is blowing. Like this, "Nice library, nice clubroom, but look at this mess! Whoever is in charge should be fired!"

"What am I doing here? Just trying to straighten out a few things!"

He asked for my name. I gave it to him.

"Good. You just stay where you are and keep things under control!"

See, that's how it works!

And I didn't touch a single broom-handle or work a single day in the kitchen all the way to New York.

As the Librarian and Clubroom Manager of the *General Blatchford,* I had the unusual opportunity to meet all kinds of people. I did not pay much attention to anyone, except for one girl. Her name was Marta.

She was from Lithuania and I thought her something special. I had noticed her individual poise, charm and beauty already in the transit camp, but there was no way I could approach her --- being of different nationality and all.

It was my opinion from my university days that the Lithuanian co-eds had a special charm. They were free-spirited and easy to talk to. There were more beautiful girls among them than any other group I knew.

One day Marta came to the ship's clubroom to borrow a book.

I became most attentive of course, inquiring about her tastes and what kind of a book she had in mind. We did not have much of a choice in our so-called library, just paperbacks and books the previous passengers had left behind.

She liked the works of Thomas Mann.

Mann is pretty heavy stuff, but when I was still a student in Hamburg I had read his novel *Der Zauberberg,* in the original German.

Well --- she had read it too.

Any two people who have read *Magic Mountain* from cover to cover must have much in common!

I brought this fact to her attention, and proposed, "Perhaps we should get together in the evening and discuss the subject in more detail. We could even try to define the 'Magic Mountain disease' named after the title of this book."

She pulled in her upper lip and gave me a cunning smile.

Perhaps she had intuited that the book was not the only thing I was interested in.

I do not know if anyone has ever catalogued smiles, but I would classify hers as "promising".

"How about tonight at eight? Could you meet me on the deck after supper?"

And there was that smile again

"Why not!"

When the sun was low in the sky, making the waves transparent, we were leaning side-by-side at the rail, mesmerized by the seascape and feeling the odd happiness of each other's presence. There is mystery and charm when two people are strangers and full of affection for each other.

I became convinced that we both had the affliction called "Magic Mountain disease". It is a disease of the mind. Its victims gradually lose their perception of time and reality. For them the present becomes an eternity.

The stars came out early at sea.

They came out even before sunset, and when there was nothing but stars the mist rose from the sea and covered our lips with salt.

As my old friend Senka had said on Hiiu Island, way back when we were running for our lives, "It is good to fall in love one evening and have only heartache the day after. It helps break up the monotony of life."

Marta and I had the whole week to ourselves.

She became my unofficial assistant in the library. When young men came to take out a book or a deck of cards,, they seemed to congregate at her table. I don't blame them --- it was worth waiting just to have a short conversation with her and hear her say "good-bye".

The weather for the last seven days had been sunny and warm, with a soft wind and calm seas.

The tempo of life was leisurely on the boat.

The minutes and hours passed by like the waves from the sea, rolling along without beginning or end.

Friday, 24 August was our eleventh day at sea.

At 8 a.m. that day faint outlines of New York skyscrapers appeared in the morning haze, and at 11 a.m. the ship dropped anchor at the city pier. Exactly at 1:20 p.m. I stepped onto American soil.

It was an unforgettable moment!

After years of intermittent hope and disappointment, it had become reality. I was full of high hope and exhilaration.

My years in the old country had been lessons in survival.

I had been like a floating buoy in the windblown sea, overrun by waves but always managing to surface. It didn't matter that I was 29 years old and had only a few worldly belongings in my suitcase. When I opened it for the customs officer, he took just one look and waved me off.

The waiting bus took up from the harbor to New York Penn Station where smiling ladies from the Traveler's Aid Society tied labels on our buttonholes --- mine read "CHICAGO". (My sponsors Rev. and Mrs. Carlson lived in Fresno, California, and that was where I was headed.)

The next thing I knew I was on a train speeding west. Everything was different, new, and strange. There was so much… It all tired me and made my eyes ache.

A few station lights flashed by the window, and then there was nothing but darkness and the wagon wheels beating on the iron tracks in a restless hurry.

Our train arrived in Chicago at 9:30 a.m., but my watch showed 11:30. I must have lost two hours somewhere. Our large group was broken up and a new tag hanging from my buttonhole spelled out "Fresno. Cal." - my destination.

Another Traveler's Aid lady took our small group grocery shopping. She was patient and friendly, advising us to buy only ready-to-eat food items to last for three days. She laughed, running from one basket to another with her "no-no's" and taking out items that needed baking or cooking. We just didn't know any better!

When crossing the wide Missouri, I remembered the Weser, a small river near Wentorf, where we used to sit on the sand next to the willow bushes and watch small steamers sail by.

The people were on their Sunday outings, all waving to us merrily. And Gerda, a Jewish lady from Berlin sat on the sand next to me and sang:

"Leise rauschen die Wellen von Missouri…"

A sudden spell of homesickness fell over me --- and then I had to wonder how a homeless person could feel homesick!

But I could not help remembering the Sunday afternoon at the Weser. It smelled of dead fish and cut grass, and all those friendly people on that one-horse steamer were waving at us.

Nobody had waved at me since!

For supper I ate my dried-out bread and some sausage. The lady from Traveler's Aid had asked me to take along bottles of a strange drink called Coca-Cola. It was warm and had an unusual taste, bitter and sweet at the same time.

Then I folded my jacket, placed it against the window sill as a head-rest, and slept.

On the third day, I saw palm trees for the first time in my life. In the Finnish army we used to march and sing, "I'm sitting under a palm tree on the Island of Capri…"

But that was nothing but a song since none of us had seen a palm tree, something one could only sing about. These palm trees were real, growing next to the red brick platform. The train had stopped to take on water for the locomotive before entering the desert.

A single woman on the red platform was waving. And far out be-yond the desert there were snowcapped mountains, their summits hid-den in white clouds.

I was bound west, beyond even the mountain range, all the way to Fresno, California.

Chapter 8

Another New Beginning

At first I lived in a room on the top of a pump-house and commuted to work with my '36 Ford. I have to confess that I didn't have a driver's license, but the place of work, the Kingsburg Cotton Oil Co., was just a few miles from my residence and the road I drove ran between vineyards with only one stop sign to negotiate.

Kingsburg was a peaceful town of a few thousand residents.

It had a couple of churches, a high school, a pharmacy, and a private hospital with ten beds. Older people went there for a few days of rest and had their blood pressure monitored. The hospital also gave first aid, delivered a few babies, and removed hemorrhoids and tonsils.

One day I was walking past this one-horse hospital and had the fancy hat on I had bought in Sweden, when an older lady grabbed my sleeve and inquired, "Are you the doctor?"

"No ma'am, I ain't no doctor," and added to myself "not yet!"

It kinda cheered me up. If I looked like a doctor to that old lady, perhaps it was a good omen and one day I wouldn't only look like a doctor but be one. And I promised myself: next time I got back to Fresno, Mrs. Carlson would help me put together and mail out a few applications to some universities.

As far as my work at the Kingsburg Cotton Oil Co. was concerned, it was a no-brainer.

I had to collect and analyze samples of cotton meal they used to feed the cows. The law required it to contain 3.5% oil.

If the feed contained less than that, the company could be penalized for cheating the cows, and if it contained more, the company would be losing money.

I worked alone from four to midnight, five days a week, and earned $250 a month. My office was on the second floor over the mill and nearby, behind the willow bushes, were the South Pacific railroad tracks.

The hoboes gathered there every evening.

327

This was the place where the freight trains slowed down, making boarding and disembarking convenient for the vagabonds. They sure seemed to be a happy bunch, stretched out in the grass in a circle. They passed around a gallon-size wine bottle and cooked their supper over a small fire.

It was only a month since my arrival from New York, and I had my life in order. To tell the truth, I owed it all to the generosity of Reverend and Mrs. Carson from Fresno.

They were religious people and had been missionaries to South America, and the reverend liked to tell stories about the life among the Indians in the jungle they had been converting to Christianity.

One of his favorites was about the devil and the pig.

One day the natives had rushed to his trailer with an urgent request: the Devil had got inside one of their piglets and made it sick. If the good reverend would not come over and drive out the evil spirit, the little pig would die for sure.

Reverend Carlson had rushed over that very minute, knelt down next to the pigpen, and said a powerful prayer. It sure did the trick — the devil had fled in a hurry and the piglet got well and grew up to be a prize hog.

When the time was right, they slaughtered the hog and the reverend was an honored guest at the feast of the blessed pork.

They all had been very much impressed with the power of the white man's God.

The Carlson's were my American sponsors, and shortly after I had arrived in Fresno, Mrs. Aliide Carlson threw a potluck supper party in my honor. She had already collected the donations, and I was presented with a check for $200.

The first $50 went toward the down payment on my '36 Ford. They both co-signed the contract to guarantee the balance of $150 to the used-car dealer.

That was not all they did for me. Not by a long shot!

Mrs. Carlson helped me scrutinize the *Fresno Bee* want-ad pages, and that was the way I found a job at the Kingsbury Cotton Oil Co.

It so happened that the Carson's older daughter Lydia was married to a winegrower, Mr. Waldon Johnson, and they lived close to the place I worked. They had an empty room on top of their pump-house. They let me live there, rent-free.

It was a nice square room with a bed, desk, and chair.

Through the multi-panel window I could see the endless vineyards, and far out at the horizon was a snow-covered mountain range, the Sierra Nevada.

Then Reverend Carson drove me in my old Ford from Fresno to the Johnson's place, and before leaving he gave me a fifteen-minute driving lesson. After I had driven a few miles on the roads between the vineyards, he declared me a good driver, good enough to drive myself to work and back.

I tell you, it wasn't an easy task to synchronize all your movements to please a temperamental car made in the mid-30s — especially the one I had. It acted like an old mule by stopping unexpectedly in the most inconvenient places.

If I would forget the clutch and start to shift gears, the gadget under the floor would sound like it was losing all its marbles and teeth. Then the car would jump in horror, and before I knew I would be sitting in the middle of the road with a dead engine.

Together, the gears and clutch and stick-shift handle were like the contents of Pandora's Box.

Trust me when I tell you it is impossible to shift gears with the right hand, signal turns with the left, and steer the car at the same time! The car would take advantage of my moments of indecision and head toward the ditch. In desperation I would drop everything I was doing, grab the steering wheel with both hands, and jump on the brakes. This action would throw me almost through the windshield, and the car would end up halfway in the ditch and with a dead engine again.

My first trip to work went without a hitch, but driving back to my "Water-tower apartment" at midnight was a voyage of horrors. If I alone had to do all those things at the same time — like watch the road in the dark, use the clutch to switch gears, apply the brake, and steer the car —I would say it's almost impossible!

It was simple enough to get gas in those days, but my car had decided it didn't like gas stations. It either stopped before the pump or rushed past it. After a few such struggles I got the hang of it. The attendant pumped the gas, cleaned the windshield, and all I had to do was dish out $2.60 for the tankful of gas.

There was no end to my old clunker's surprises. At times it acted like a stupid mule refusing to respond to my commands, and at times it was like a wild stallion that ignored all my attempts to pacify it.

It took a month and many miles of driving along the quiet roads between the vineyards in that beautiful San Joachim Valley, before we were able to make a tentative peace between us. A short time later I passed my driver's test, and became a legal motorist on the open road.

In these accounts I have always described the events of New Year's Eve, whether it was spent on a *gulanye* in a Russian village or crossing the Finnish Sea in an open boat. Nothing dramatic happened in Kingsburg when the New Year of 1952 rolled in, quiet as a lamb. I worked my usual shift at the Cotton Oil Company lab, but snuck out fifteen minutes before midnight to witness the New Year celebration in the small town. I found Main Street entirely deserted. The single bar in town was closed and all its chairs were neatly lined upside-down on the tables, giving the recently scrubbed floor a chance to dry. All windows in town were dark. The only thing brightly lit was the sign in the front of a church announcing the hours of service.

When past the outskirts of town, the only light in the entire universe was my old Ford illuminating small stretch of the road where I was the only traveler.

Winter comes and goes almost unnoticed in the San Joachim Valley.

The warm days become gradually hot. The dead gray fields become green again. The lilac bushes next to the pump house become heavy with blossoms, and their aroma filled my small room.

At the end of April my company closed for the summer, and I was without a job. There was not much that Kingsburg could offer and I returned to Fresno. I was told it would be hard to find a job, given the high rate of unemployment.

You might not believe it, but they hired me at the very first place I inquired.

Of course I had to do some pretending, but if you don't have confidence in yourself, nobody will!

Douglas Aircraft had recently purchased the Ventilator Company, and they were busy making parts for a variety of airplanes. It was Monday morning, and one of their inspectors hadn't shown up.

The girls in the front office wondered if I could qualify for the job and asked, "Can you read blueprints?"

I did not know what the word "blueprint" meant, but I also knew if I were to ask "what is a blueprint?", that would be the end of it.

"...Of course I can read blueprints!"

Then the secretaries called for Ron, the foreman in the machine shop. He was a friendly-looking chap in cowboy boots and a hat.

He gave me a friendly wink.

"So you can read blueprints, but do you know how to use a hightcase?"

Well, this word didn't ring a bell either.

"Sure thing! I can use... whatever..." I didn't quite catch the term, and I was afraid of pronouncing it wrong.

Ron turned toward the girls. "What the heck! He looks like a nice guy! We'll give him a try." Then he explained, "My parts inspector didn't show up this morning and I need someone right away. Can you start now?"

"Sure thing."

"That's the spirit! After the girls have registered you, come right back here and if you don't see me, ask for Ron."

The so called machine-shop was a huge and noisy room filled with heavy punch presses, milling machines, and cutters, men and women working behind them. Almost in the center of the room was a table with measuring instruments and an upright gadget looking like a miniature gallows without a rope. It must have been the hightcase Ron was talking about. Next to it and spread out was a light blue-colored sheet of paper with some drawing and numbers.

Ron came over and gave me a few hints how to check the first article against the blueprint.

"If it meets the specifications, then sign the order-slip and they will make hundreds of it. If however the first article does not match the blueprint and you sign the production order —— you'll be in hot water, my friend!"

Well, it turned out to be as easy as falling off a log.

The machinists made the first article according to the blueprint, and then they came over to have it approved. The articles were rather unsophisticated and easy to check out. Ron came by in the evening.

"Good show. I think things will work out okay!"

Then I remembered to ask about my salary.

"$1.68 an hour. If things work out, there'll be overtime."

I made a quick calculation: 40 x 4 x $1.98 = $316.80 a month. Not bad for a start.

The first month went by without a hitch. I was happy to be working days instead of nights, and with people around me. There were middle-aged women working some of the presses. Their work was repetitious and boring, their faces were expressionless and dull. I don't believe I exchanged a single word with any of them. All the machinists I had contact with were men.

Right around the time I showed up, the company started to make wing components for a new military plane.

The first thing needed were the "tools", the so called iron blocks over which heavy presses would mold the wing components. When you press a metal sheet against a block it does not stay exactly the same shape as the mold, but straightens out somewhat called "spring-back." Depending on the type and thickness of the material used, different sheets of metal had their own "spring-back allowances." There were thick manuals listing these allowances. The engineering department drew the blueprints according to specifications.

The machine shop needed an inspector to check out the so-called "tools" so they would match the engineering department's drawings.

Ron thought I could do it and so it happened that after one month at the Ventilator Co. I was promoted from "parts inspector" to "tools inspector".

The machinists were slow making the forms, as the new work was unfamiliar.

I had time and the manuals at my disposal, and I tried to do mu own calculations with my high-school trigonometry. After a few days I had things figured out and my numbers matched the ones on the blueprint.

One day, however, I came across a blueprint where my calculations did not match the Engineering Department ones. I went over my calculations a couple of times — still no match!

I called Ron and told him my problem.

"By God!", he exclaimed. "The 'Whiteshirts' must have goofed!"

We called the engineers "Whiteshirts". Well, that's what they wore –– their sleeves turned up and their hands in their pockets –– when they walked through our machine shop, bitched about this and that, and gave Ron a hard time.

Well, Ron went to the Engineering Department with the blueprint:

"What the hell's up with you Whiteshirts! It takes one of my men in the production line to figure out your mistakes!"

He threw the blueprint on their table –– let them figure out what's wrong with it.

Before quitting time, Ron came to see me:

"Have time for a beer? By the way, I can't pronounce your first and last names. If you don't mind I'll just call you 'Duke'…?"

There was a place across the street called "The Happy Hour Club", and when we got seated at the bar Ron said, "My treat, Duke! What'll you have?"

I hadn't tasted American beer yet, and I didn't know one brand from the other.

"I'll have the same thing you'll have!"

"Two 'Buds' coming up!"

I liked the taste of American beer. Not as bitter as those made in the old country. It had been a hot day at the shop, and it sure was nice to sip cold beer in a cool bar.

Ron ordered another round.

"How do you like your new job?"

"You know, Ron, the work is interesting and the pay is good. And having you for a boss, well, the best thing that ever happened to me."

Ron didn't say anything for awhile. We just drank our beer, but I could see that my statement had hit the right spot, just like the cool Bud we'd been drinking.

Then he wanted to know whether I had anything planned for the coming weekend.

"Not a thing. Not a friend or girlfriend in town."

"Care to work this Saturday? Pays time-and-half. Now you are making $1.98 an hour, that will come to three bucks!"

"At your service"

I started to work ten hours a day plus Saturdays. There was so much work piling up because of the new contracts, while up until then they'd been making vending machines.

My take-home pay became more than $400 a month, which at that time was a darned good income.

I no longer lived in the pump-house, needless to say. It was a one-room apartment with all kinds of characters as my neighbors, no better than a hole-in-the-wall. With my new income I could have a decent place to live. And so it happened that I rented a small house in a nice neighborhood, with trimmed lawns and shady trees. I even had my own telephone. My landlady was a young and good-looking woman. She lived next door and brought some of her baking over almost every day.

It was the most splendid summer of '52.

The sun shone all day in Fresno. It never rained.

As far as my new social life was concerned, there was always something cooking. I belonged to a small and loose-knit group of newcomers and locals. On weekends we might drive out to Bass Lake for an overnight camping trip, and sit around the fire until past midnight.

Or we might spend a long weekend at Yosemite Park. It was so inspiring to listen to the sounds of the late-evening bugle and watch the rangers pour glowing bits of charcoal from the top of *Glacier Point* into the valley below. It looked like millions of fireflies lighting up this side of the cliff, rising some 4000 feet toward the sky.

On weekdays we went to the city park, ate watermelon, and did square dancing. The city supplied the band and the caller. There I became casually acquainted with two Canadian nurses from Alberta.

One Sunday afternoon there was a grand entertainment in Washington Park. Xavier Cugat and his Latin orchestra performed while Abby Lane wiggled her hips and whispered into a microphone.

The two Alberta nurses had their new roommate with them. She was from Ontario, and like the Alberta girls had come down from Canada to work at Fresno County Hospital for higher pay.

Her name was Hazel.

She had dark hair, a beautiful face and slender body, and wore glasses. She did not say much, and did not laugh at all.

By then the sun had settled behind the palm trees and the heat of the day was replaced by a pleasant coolness. The Cugat Orchestra started to play "Love Me with All Your Heart".

I asked Hazel for a dance.

She liked to dance close.

Not intimately close. She was too conservative for that, but still close. While dancing she would hum the melody the orchestra was playing.

After the second dance, she even smiled and said she liked a Latin beat.

Then the Alberta nurses wanted to leave, and Hazel had to go.

We shook hands and she wrote her phone number in my notebook by using her lipstick.

Neither of us had a pen!

I had accomplished everything I could dream of in my first year in America.

Nobody I met minded my accent. Perhaps even the opposite was true: they all seemed to be forthcoming and ready to go the extra mile to give me a chance, and then were genuinely happy to see me succeed.

Oh, I almost forgot to mention that besides meeting Hazel, I was finally admitted to medical school for the fall semester of that year.

Getting in was actually a good deal more complicated than all that...

Chapter 9

Visiting Academia

It was just after New Year's 1952, when I was still working at the Kingsburg Cotton Oil Company, that I started to send out my applications to different medical schools. Mrs. Carson not only helped me draft them, as my English was still rather "bumpy". She typed them up for me. I mailed the official-looking applications first to the University of California in San Francisco, and then to several universities in neighboring states as well.

All the places I wrote to sent me a "we are sorry" note. There was one exception though.

The University of California Medical School in San Francisco did mail me an application form to fill out. They also asked me to include copies of my previous academic work, to have a physical examination including a chest x-ray, and mail the information promptly to the dean's office. At the same time they asked me to "cool my heels"; there were seven applicants for one vacancy, which was reserved for a foreign student.

With the Carsons' help I filled out the forms, had my physical exam, and made copies of all the pages from my study book. Reverend Carson wrote his recommendation and I mailed the whole thing back to San Francisco.

Two weeks later I was asked to come for the interviews but I was reminded once more that there was only one chance out of seven. According to my calculations, my probability of becoming a medical student was 14.29%.

These figures didn't worry me — I had beaten lower odds than that in the past, and my enterprising spirit was still intact.

The interviews were set for 27 February, 1952.

The three doctors I had to see were Dr. Bostick, Professor of Pathology; Dr. Crede, Professor of Pediatrics; and Dr. Guttentag, Associate Professor of Homeopathy.

That was not all they asked me to go through before I could face the "Big Three" at the admission board. I had to call on a whole bunch of professors at the Berkeley campus to seek their approval of my previous academic work. The list of subjects included anatomy, histology, zoology, physics, chemistry, and a few others.

On 26 February 1952 I took the Greyhound bus from Fresno to Berkeley and that afternoon went out to collect the needed signatures.

There were a few nervous moments at first when I faced the high and mighty professors, but their friendly and at times humorous disposition eased my fears. They just took my sheet and signed it, no questions asked. Some even complained about the bureaucracy that required these "useless" visits — wasting my time and theirs.

"Well, I am practically over the hump!" I said to myself in the late afternoon, viewing my signature collection. The subjects had been listed alphabetically and there was only one signature missing — in *zoology*.

That shouldn't be a problem, I thought. Although I flunked my first try taking this exam back in Hamburg, this was not mentioned in my credentials, which specified only an above-average *bene sufficit.* After all — I was not applying to veterinary school!

Never count your chickens before they're hatched!

The zoology professor was a young man, perhaps a few years older than I. He viewed my mimeographed copy of *"The Textbook of Zoology"* and couldn't find a chapter on Zoological Embryology.

Well, he couldn't find it because there was no such chapter.

German zoologists apparently didn't feel important to teach the embryology of caterpillars and chameleons to the medical students. I had even taken a special course in "General Embryology" as recorded in my study book.

But that didn't satisfy our good professor, "I am sorry, but you don't seem to have had enough of *animal* embryology."

He then added, "I'll sign your sheet with an asterisk, and add a note of your short-comings on a separate sheet."

His words cut my optimism down below the freezing point.

I do remember that episode even today, standing there in a semi-dark room, next to his desk. The only sound was the scratching of the professor's pen running across the white sheet of paper, writing the obituary note for my medical school application.

My old survival instinct of "fight or flight" took over as I spoke slowly, "Your note would make me ineligible to compete for my spot in the sophomore class. I've already secured all the other needed signatures. But if you feel that my shortcoming in animal embryology would be reason enough to disqualify me, then I'll accept it and must bear the consequences."

He hesitated for a moment while his pen had stopped in the middle of the sentence. Then he picked up his sheet, crumpled it into a ball and threw it into the wastebasket. He then took my sheet, added his signature to complete my list, shook my hand and said: "Good luck."

Next thing I knew, I was out in the open air.

––––––––

The cool fog I had seen through the Zoology professor's window was now wrapping itself around the campus buildings. The streetlights gave off a soft glow. I felt peaceful and tired.

It had been a successful day, and I hoped my success would hold through the next day, when I was to interview in San Francisco.

The medical school with its hospitals is located on Parnassus Street, high on a hill overlooking the city and the Golden Gate Bridge.

Dr. Bostick, the Professor of Pathology, was a young man, perhaps less than 40. He asked only a few general questions and took notes. The second interviewer was Dr. Crede from the Pediatrics Department.

He was about 60, somewhat rotund with gray hair. He did not take notes or ask any questions. He just listened to my presentation, nodded his head now and then, seemingly agreeing with all I had said.

The interview took perhaps fifteen minutes. At the end of these two interviews, I felt I had made progress.

––––––––

The third and final interviewer was Dr. Guttentag.

His small office was not in the main hospital building, but hidden in back in one of the late 19th-century structures. His official title was Associate Professor of Homeopathic Medicine.

To my knowledge, this subject hasn't been taught in any medical school for years. Homeopathy was a teaching of minimalism. Somewhere I had read an anecdotal recipe for homeopathic chicken soup, "Fill a kettle with water, and bring it to a boil. Hold a slaughtered chicken over the pot so that its shadow falls into the boiling water. Boil the shadow for ten minutes. You have made homeopathic chicken broth.

One or two teaspoons three times a day will cure the most persistent cold or cough, and perhaps many other ailments for that matter."

Dr. Guttentag, in his late sixties and full of vim and vinegar, was a small man with a thin face.

"So you have studied in Uppsala! Very famous university. Very famous. Probably the best in all of Europe! ...very good, very good.

"I have heard that they have an illustrious manuscript in their library, but at this moment I can't remember what it is called?"

"Do you mean the *Codex Argenteus,* called also "Silver Bible", which dates back to the 5th century?"

"That's it, that's it. Thank you for reminding me!"

"It is kept in the main library, called *Carolina Rediviva.*"

"As I recall, there were also world-famous professors who have belonged to the faculty in the past?"

I started to wonder whether he had been cramming up for my interview — either to be a show-off or to bungle me.

"Do you mean Carl von Linné, the professor of botany who cataloged plants into genera, classes and orders? Of course, Professor Celsius's name is in use even today in temperature recordings. They both belonged to the faculty in the mid seventeenth century."

"Very good, very good!"

His hand was already stretched across the table.

"Could I see your study book from Uppsala?"

I opened my voluminous briefcase and started to look for it.

I got more nervous with each second of going through my papers and notes. The only thing I could *not* come up with was the study book our good professor wanted to examine.

I knew I had had it with me, because I had looked at it on the Greyhound bus on my way to the interview. I must have left it on the bus!

Dr. Guttentag pulled back his hand.

All his "very goods" had changed to suspicion, and he looked at me like I had robbed a bank or something. He was not interested in the photocopy in my files, did not want to see my study book from Hamburg or my membership certificate from the Östgöta Medical Fraternity in Uppsala.

I was asked to leave his office so he could make a phone call.

After I had paced the corridor for ten minutes, his ancient secretary asked me to come back in.

Professor Guttentag appeared less hostile, but not as suave as he had been earlier. He continued with his cross-examination.

I do not recall all the avenues he investigated, but at the end the dialogue went something like this, "Young man, what did you do during your free time in the big city of Hamburg?"

"Well, there wasn't much of what one could call 'free time'. I went to the theatre, and to the *Kunstausstellungen.*[1] I was also the editor of an Estonian-language periodical called *"Scientia et Artibus"*[2] that took up time."

"That's nice. When in Hamburg *Kunsthalle,* were you impressed by any particular paintings?"

"I was more or less a casual observer, but I was really frightened by Munch's "The Scream". I also remember Kokoschka's landscapes. I'm afraid that's about it."

"You were Lutheran, right? Went to a Lutheran church in Hamburg?"

"Yes, sir."

"Now, if you went to church, can you recite the Lord's Prayer for me?"

"You know I am Estonian, and could recite it in Estonian."

"A young man with a good memory should, in my opinion, be able to recite it in German, if you really attended church as you said you did?"

I hesitated for a moment.

"… or wasn't that what you just told me?"

I inhaled deeply and shot the words out with determination, *"Vater unser der Du bist im Himmel, Geheiligt werde deine Name. Deine Wille geschehe, Im Himmel wie auf der Erde…"*

"Good. Good. *Das ist genug!*[3] You may go now."

———————

When I got outside, I looked at my watch. The entire interview had lasted 90 minutes. I must admit, that I felt exhausted after that grilling.

It had upset me to a degree that I couldn't even find my way out.

I sought help from a young woman in a white lab coat with heavy black-framed glasses. She gave me a friendly smile and the directions.

I still remember her smile as she stood there with both her hands deep in her lab coat pockets. Amazing, how just one smile at the moment of distress could be remembered half a century later.

I stayed at Sibul's place while I was in the Bay area.

He was a countryman of mine, and another of Mrs. Carson's sponsored Estonian students from Germany. He was doing post-graduate work in hydraulic engineering.

We had lunch together.

He had just returned from a 35¢ matinee about cowboys and Indians.

"Whenever my brain gets flooded with 'water-works' and I can't keep focused, that's where I go to unwind."

Good idea. Perhaps I should try it too to wash out the painful memory of my recent interview.

"Naah," I rejected the idea. I was just too jumpy to watch any cowboy-Indian flick on a screen!

After lunch I started to think.

The Greyhound bus wouldn't leave until the evening, and I had the whole afternoon to spend somehow. Perhaps there was something else I could do to promote my application.

I went to the University Library and started to leaf through "Who's Who" at the Berkley Campus.

My eyes stopped at one name, Professor Emeritus Herbert M. Evans.

Wasn't it *Evans' Blue* I was tormented with during my histology exam in Hamburg, when the Latvian co-eds came to my rescue? Might it be the same Evans? I read further that he had studied in Heidelberg. That meant I could speak German with him and express myself more fluently than I could in English. Perhaps he could give me some advice with my application?

"Well, that's the least I can do to promote myself!"

I left the library to look for his office.

Lucky for me, I didn't know just how famous this man really was or I would have dropped the idea then and there.

The more I've learned about him since my encounter, the more I've become amazed at all the things this man accomplished.

First, already as a medical student at John Hopkins he had written a section on "The development of the human vascular system" for the two volumes of the *Manual of Human Embryology*.

Back then, when surgeons removed the thyroid gland, they frequently destroyed the blood supply to the parathyroid gland, which caused tetany. Dr. Evans, still in medical school, did detailed neck dissections on cadavers, injecting dyes into the arterial and venous system of the thyroid gland and thus identifying and showing the variation in the blood supply to parathyroid gland. He had done research with analine dyes and their ability to stain tissues and measure blood volume (thus "Evans' Blue"), and had done extensive work in human embryology.

In 1915 he returned to California as Professor of Anatomy and the Chairman of the Department. He was the first to identify and use ACTH and propose that the anterior pituitary had endocrine functions essential for normal bodily growth, normal ovarian function, and normal thyroid and adrenal cortical function. By the time he retired, his laboratory had identified FSH, ICSH, and prolactin. And there was much more.

It has been suggested that he should have been nominated for the Nobel prize four times over. But problems might have been caused by his personality, which one source describes as "dominating, being both captivating and exasperating".[4]

Lucky for me, I had no knowledge of his supposed personality difficulties. Knowing that, I wouldn't have given a second thought to seeking him out.

After my visit with the distinguished professor, I coined a new utterance:

"What you don't know, will help you."

It isn't easy to see such high and mighty professors without an appointment, but I created enough of a commotion with his secretaries that Professor Evans himself stepped out of his study to see what the row was all about. He was a tall and slender man in his early 70s with a serious face and friendly manners. First he pacified his office girls and then he came to open the swinging gate to accept me into the back of his office with, "Come in, young man!"

Well. He was the nicest man one could ever hope to find among scholarly professors. After Dr. Guttentag had put me through the meat grinder, it was little short of salvation to see a friendly face in high academia.

First, I explained the purpose of my visit which was to get into the Medical School. Because I knew he had been a professor of anatomy, I opened my old anatomy notebooks with colorful drawings, some were perhaps even better than those in anatomy books. I could remember the muscles and nerves better after I had drawn them out on paper.

Professor Evans was visibly impressed, "I know academic standards are high in the old country, and I like your drawings. When I was still a medical student, I also liked to draw out subjects. Well, I'm retired now, and no longer a member of those admission boards.

Then he started to rub his chin, and seemed lost in his thoughts.

"You are an ambitious young man, and I believe we have an obligation to let you finish your studies."

Then he seemed to come to some kind of conclusion, "I tell you what, Professor Althausen is an old friend of mine, and he is the Chairman of the Admission Committee. Perhaps I can arrange a meeting between you two."

Lucky for me, Professor Althausen happened to be in his office, and the connection was quickly established.

Their conversation started with the usual niceties, but Professor Evans came to the point quickly, "I have a very nice young man in my office, who has applied for admission in the sophomore class. His file must be on your desk this very minute. Do me a favor and meet this young man sometime today. He is from Fresno, and has to leave in the morning."

Then Professor Evans just listened for a minute or two without uttering a word. It was obvious that Dr. Althausen was not interested in meeting an applicant, but my "mentor" emerged as the winner at the end of the conversation, "Tonight at eight be on Main Street in downtown San Francisco, next to the Fox Theatre. Professor Althausen will be coming out of a conference and will meet you there."

He shook my hand. "Good luck, young man, and I hope our efforts will be rewarded!"

I found the street and the theatre.

It was getting dark. There were lights flashing red and blue from the movie theatre entrance. The wind was up, blowing paper wrappings along the gutters, and I was chilled to the bones and shivering. Was it the cold humid air blowing in from the bay, or the anxiety about the upcoming meeting?

A tall man stopped in front of me with drooping shoulders and a tired face. He was holding a briefcase under his right arm and didn't wear a coat or a hat.

"Are you the young man from Professor Evans' office?"

I started with my prepared speech, but Dr. Althausen raised his hand.

"As a rule I do not meet the applicants. I listen only to the Admission Committee reports and then we'll decide which candidate will be admitted."

I started to say something, but stopped.

There was nothing to add to his statement. I must have looked like a sad sack, bareheaded with my hair blown all over my face.

"What country are you from?"

He asked the question without any particular interest. Perhaps he wanted to ease my misery, which was written all over my face. I said, "Estonia."

His drawn face brightened, and there was some softness in his voice when he confessed, "I was born in Estonia."

He paused, then continued, "My father was a German, but my mother was Estonian. I left the country as a young boy, moving to St. Petersburg in Russia. When the Bolshevik Revolution started, our family fled to America. I had part of my medical studies in St. Petersburg, but ended them here."

His voice had become even more muffled when he asked, "Whatever happened to that country...?"

He probably was recalling his childhood days in that small nation. I was ready to use his short episode of reminiscence to my advantage, "Communist Russia re-occupied the land, and I have lost everything to the Bolsheviks: my country, my home, and my relatives and friends. All I have left is the wish to complete my medical studies."

"I am in the same position you were a generation ago!" I added.

For a moment we just stood there.

The cold wind blew a torn newspaper page around us, and blew his dark hair over his face, "Well, we'll have to see what the Admission Committee comes up with. At this time I can't promise you anything. It was nice meeting you."

He shook my hand, waved for a taxi, and a moment later disappeared into the evening traffic.

A coincidence perhaps?

A million-to-one coincidence that the Chairman of the Admission Committee happened to be born in Estonia. Obviously my previous work had to be at the level of the other applicants, but if all else were equal, this encounter might have given me an edge.

After having met Dr. Evans and Althausen, all the tension and anxiety I had piled inside of me had suddenly vanished. I felt only peace and serenity deep inside. I had gone the extra mile to promote my application, and it was not up to me any more.

On 8 August 1952, my 30th birthday, I received the notification from the UC Medical School Dean's office that I had been accepted into the Medical School, to start on Monday, 22 September as a sophomore.

The notification contained also a sobering thought; it called my attention to the fact that it was customary to admit such students "on probation". One "D" grade or lower at the end of the semester, and I wouldn't be allowed to enroll the following term. In other words, I would be expelled.

This warning placed a psychological millstone around my neck.

I had never questioned my ability to keep up with my fellow classmates in the past, but at UC I was among a very select group of students. (Some 500 had taken the entry exams at Berkeley, and only 85 had been admitted to the Medical School for the freshman year.) Besides I had been away from the school for a spell and all my previous studies had been in German. One had to be a moron not to recognize that the road ahead was filled with bumps and potholes.

Well and good. I recalled the proverb I had coined years ago, "If worst comes to worst, I'll make the best of it."

When I told Ron at work that I was leaving to attend medical school in San Francisco, he thought it the dumbest thing he'd ever heard.

Look here, my friend, you are making a major mistake! You're earning top dollar helping build airplanes. It's a rapidly growing industry, and your future would be secure here at Douglas!"

Then he sounded even annoyed, "What is this? Going to chase a bird in the bush when you already have one in your hand!"

It was all true to some degree, but the bird in the bush was a bluebird, and the one in my hand was a common sparrow. Besides, I didn't want to mortgage my future for present success.

It was a Sunday morning, 21 September, when I got ready to say my good-byes to Fresno. All my belongings were in the back seat of my '36 Ford, with plenty of room to spare. I filled the tank with gas and the radiator with water. I couldn't do anything about the windshield wiper.

It entirely had a mind of its own.

It worked splendidly when the sun was shining, but quit as soon as a few raindrops started to fall. That wasn't much of a problem in Fresno: it never rained there, but San Francisco was a different ballgame. It was Hazel's suggestion to leave the wiper on all the time: perhaps it would continue to work when it started to rain. She told me about an old doctor in Oshawa who never turned his windshield wipers off, rain or shine. He had left them on because he couldn't remember how to turn the darned thing on once it started to rain. Well, my problem was not the shortcomings of my memory, rather the capricious mindset of my windshield wiper. It seemed kind of foolish to depart from Fresno on a sunny day with the wiper jerking across my windshield, and I ignored her advice.

My financial status was as follows, I had closed my checking account, and had $1,200 in cash in my pocket. My expenses were as follows: The tuition fee was $165 per semester. Two semesters in a year would come to $330. I had rented a room within walking distance of the university for $25 a month. A school year was roughly 10 months, that makes $250. After subtracting $330 and $250 from $1200, it left me 625 dollars to live on, not counting car insurance and gas, and school supplies and books. I had to manage with $12 a week.

From Fresno to San Francisco was 180 miles.

This was the longest and the most important, and perhaps most perilous, trip for me and my '36 Ford.

---

[1] art exhibitions
[2] "Science and Art"
[3] That's enough!
[4] L. Bennet, "Herbert McLane Evans," *Alumn. Fac. Bulletin,* vol. 27 (special edition)

Chapter 10

MY THREE YEARS IN SAN FRANCISCO

The word was survival.

My first year at the University of California Medical School was no bed of roses, as you can well imagine.

I was not familiar with medical terminology in English. To read the day's assignment of 40 pages of Anderson's *Pathology* by using an English-German dictionary and trying to memorize the text as well, it was almost beyond my capabilities.

At the end of the week our Pathology teacher Dr. Bostick wrote "Quiz Monday" on the blackboard. Poor soul, I didn't know what the first word meant, and so I had no idea what the short sentence meant.

Well, Monday came and I found out.

My first face-to-face encounter with Dr. Bostick was also a painful one. It was a session in microscopic Pathology.

Everyone had his own microscope, and we were viewing the epithelium of the human bladder with some kind of tumor. Dr. Bostick stopped at my table and asked me to name the epithelium.

I said I was not familiar with the English term.

"Well, what is it called in German then?"

I just froze. I couldn't come up with the answer.

He stood there for a moment and then continued his slow walk between the tables. The instant he had turned to leave, it came to me:

It was called *geschichtetes* Epithelium (and *stratified* epithelium in English).

Almost 50 years have passed since that episode, and I have forgotten most of my histology, but I will never forget the name of the epithelium lining the bladder, as long as I live, in English or in German.

But for me it was too late. I couldn't very well run after him and shout, "Sir, sir... it is called *geschichtetes* Epithelium!"

———————

To overcome my anxiety form these negative experiences, well, the only tranquilizer I had was to hit the books even harder. It isn't easy to study a pathology text with an English-German dictionary when there are only 24 hours in a day.

Somehow I managed, and after one month I could discard the dictionary altogether and read the English text with minimal effort.

Even today, leafing through the pages of my old Anderson's *Pathology* and seeing my penciled-in translations, I feel a bittersweet nostalgia for bygone years. Today, however, the situation has reversed itself; I know the English terminology, but to understand the penciled-in German I need a different dictionary.

———————

The Professor of Microbiology was Max Marshall. He had a round face and wore black-framed glasses. He was pleasantly overweight, which went with his easy-going manners. He held long sessions with the auditorium lights turned off while he projected all kinds of microbes on the wall sized screen, whether blue or red with *Gram* stain. Some of us used the time for a short nap, but Dr. Marshall had an antidote for that: he threw in an occasional slide of a bikini-clad dame. The howl that followed from the auditorium woke up even a premium snooze. We had only two female students in our class of 85, and they just laughed along. The term "Sexual Harassment" wasn't invented yet.

———————

This was also the time when the first polio vaccine was introduced.

Dr. Marshall was a strong supporter of the orally administered vaccine over the injectable one introduced by Dr. Salk. According to Marshall, Dr. Salk had more political pull and friends in high places to give him all the credit and glory. But in a year or two the oral form had quietly replaced Dr. Salk's injectable one.

Nobody knows today that the wrong guy got all the credit because he knew the right people.

Who was the other guy? I don't know. Perhaps it was A. B. Sabin, but I'm not sure.

———————

During my sophomore year, Dr. Goldman was the lecturer in Surgery.

Like most surgeons back then, he was sure that anything that ailed you had a surgical solution (remember lobotomies!). You guessed it, our relationship was less than cordial. In one of the surgery written quizzes he gave me a "D". Perhaps rightly so, but it sure scared me out of my wits. In a hurry I had named the gallbladder ducts in reverse: in my drawing I had the cystic duct originating from the liver and the common duct leading to the gallbladder. I knew that a "D" at the end of the semester would mean curtains for me.

The other blooper I pulled in my first month was in Public Health. I had mixed up the words rural" and "metropolitan", but Dr. Lucia forgave me. The following summer I was pumping gas at McKale's gas station, and Dr. Lucia drove up in his pink Cadillac. I filled his tank, and while paying he asked me who I was. I must have looked familiar to him.

"I'm the student who didn't know the difference between *rural* and *metropolitan*!" He had a good laugh, added *"errare humanum est!"*, and drove away.

Well, I got ahead of myself. I was still worried about my silly mistakes and as I said before, to improve my chances for the next semester I had cut down on my sleeping hours even more.

I prepared my own meals on a hot plate in one corner of my room. My menu consisted of Spam and potatoes and milk with bread, day-in and day-out. There was no more enjoyment in eating than filling a gastank with gas. I even ate my meals standing up, the same way I fed my car. The only difference was, my car ate gas and I ate Spam.

The fall semester ended in February, and I didn't hear from the Dean's office, meaning I was off probation. That sure took a load off my shoulders.

The spring semester started with Dr. Paul Gliebe, a psychiatrist in charge of the mental ward in the County Hospital.

He was short rather than tall, more fat than thin, and when he laughed, it was more sinister than kind. Dr. Gliebe was an intriguing man with a colorful background of talents. Among other things, before medical school he had been a Catholic priest and then an alcoholic. Now he was the head of the psychiatric unit at County Hospital, and practiced a take-no-prisoners brand of psychiatry. Everybody, including the students, was fair game to be a teaching example for psychopathology.[1]

Before the advent of mind-altering drugs, psychiatry occupied a fascinating middle ground between Freud's psychoanalysis and voodoo medicine, between shock treatment and group therapy.

Dr. Gliebe was good at them all, and this morning he was about to give a shock treatment to us, the small group waiting in front of the locked psychiatry unit.

He arrived in a jubilant mood, and full of friendly spirits, "I have the most interesting case for you today!"

He made his announcement while unlocking and locking doors as we advanced toward the darkest part of the psychiatric wing. Finally he came to one of the cell doors and unlocked it.

A dim light was shining through a high window guarded by steel bars. There was no furniture in the entire room except for a bare mattress on the floor. A man was lying there motionless with his hands at his side, paying no attention to us.

Dr. Gliebe gave the short history, "This gentleman is Mr. V., one of your ex-classmates.

"At the end of last semester he was expelled from the medical school because of his academic shortcomings, and he ended up here, in a catatonic stupor."

I could very well imagine myself there on that soiled mattress, and I felt deep sorrow. I knew him better than any other of my classmates. He had been friendlier than the rest and we had even done some studying together. I wondered if it was only the expulsion that had pushed him over the edge, or if there was some underlying disease beforehand. The way Dr. Gliebe exhibited his prize specimen, the two events seemed interrelated.

I felt the experiment that Dr. Gliebe performed to observe our reaction was rude and even traumatic, like witnessing an execution.

There was another experiment of his, where *I* became the prey.

During a roundtable session, he flashed an 8 x 10-inch cardboard picture of a young boy sitting in a chair and looking down at a violin in his lap. After a quick glance we all had to give a title to that picture, the very first thought coming to our mind. I was sitting next to him at the round table and after he had flashed his picture I said, "It is hard to learn."

Even before I had finished my sentence he had turned to the rest of the group with quick "Did you notice that?"

I still believe mine was the best title. My classmates were afraid to be classified as half-brainers, and gave descriptions like I'd rather play outside," or "I have a headache."

I thought their answers were phony, especially the second one given above. Dr. Gliebe should have analyzed *that* one, a kid sitting with a violin in his lap has a headache. How stupid can you get!

I would say the student who offered that phrase should have been analyzed. Perhaps he was repeating what his wife had told him that morning to turn away his amorous overtures.

So much for Gliebe and his shock treatments…

The next service was Obstetrics.

As sophomores we were not allowed in the delivery room during partition, but stood in the next narrow room with a wall-sized one-way mirror where we could observe the happenings at close quarters.

These episodes were not peaceful ones.

At times there were parturient bone-chilling screams, but without exception it all ended with happiness and laughter. It was the only service where the house-staff had a "let's go and get it" attitude.

After deliveries, residents of the house-staff used to sit on the tables in the utility room, shoot the breeze, and answer our inquiries. It was a common courtesy that medical students and interns were to stand rather than sit, and it was unheard of that any of us from the "lower class" would try to sit next to the resident physician.

After a flurry of deliveries, all the parties involved had a feeling of accomplishment. Even we, separated from the "action" by the deceptive mirror.

I wonder about the legality by today's standards, could we be called peeping toms?

One course I have unusual memories of was Nutrition.

Nina Simmonds, who had a Ph.D. in Nutrition, gave it. She was God's Gift to her field, and no deviations from her teaching were permitted:

I ran into some trouble with her and ended up in the Student Health Service. It all started innocently enough. We all had to write down what we had eaten the previous week.

Well, my list did not vary much; *Breakfast – bread and milk with a slice of cold Spam; Lunch – the same; Supper – as above, except fried potatoes replaced the bread and the Spam ration was increased to two slices. Multiply the above by seven.*

The next thing I knew I was called to see Dr. Olson in the Health Service.

It did scare me for a minute, but I calmed down quick, thank God it wasn't the Dean's office. When I entered and sat down next to Dr. Olson, I noticed she had my week's meal-list in front of her. She was a nice lady in her 40's, pleasantly overweight and the motherly type, "Dr. Simmonds referred you to me after reading about your diet.

"There is no variety, but most significantly it lacks vegetables and fruits. We are very much concerned about your future health.

"What seems to be the problem?" she asked.

Their worry about my diet surprised me. It really did.

There were some 60,000 students in the university, and they were concerned about what I ate.

I remembered one afternoon at the Czechoslovakian prison camp, eight years earlier, *We had been herded into a fenced-in soccer field without any food for a day and a half. I was stretched out close to the barbed-wire fence when I noticed a piece of moldy cheese in a tin wrapping barely three feet from me, but outside the fence. It took some time to find a small twig and fish it in, slowly and carefully, afraid of either being seen by the guards or breaking the tiny twig. I ate the whole thing, including the mold and dust!*

Look at me now in San Francisco, living like a king, eating Spam three times a day and washing it down with milk. And they were worried about a lack of variety!

All this went through my mind as I sat next to that lady doctor with misgivings in her eyes.

"Well, doctor," I said. "There are more than three months left until the end of the semester, and I have only $200 left."

She asked me to go and see Dr. Johnstone, the Chairman of Tropical Diseases, who also handled Student Affairs.

When I went to see him in his office, Dr. Olson had already called and he was familiar with my predicament. He came at once to the point, "There are no scholarships available this late in the school year. How much do you need to see you through?"

"$200 would be enough."

"Are you sure about the amount? Good! We can give you a loan of two hundred. We'll charge you 2% interest and you don't have to pay it back until you open your practice, regardless of how many years it takes. You can pick up the check at the business office by tomorrow."

"If any time you are in need of help, you just come and see me. Good luck."

It was as simple as that.

That $200 was the first loan I ever had.

I could hardly spend it on my culinary needs because there were more pressing priorities, such as rent, car insurance, and even clothing.

I went all out and bought a natty double-breasted suit. It was on sale for twenty-eight bucks, and the kind of ribbon ties then in fashion set me back fifty cents. The unwritten rule for students was to wear either a suit or tie or a lab coat and tie. Any sloppiness in your appearance might be interpreted as a sign of being a sloppy doctor in the future. With my insecure status, it was best for me not to challenge traditional dress codes. Nobody would see the Spam and potatoes in my alimentary tract, but what I was wearing was visible to everyone.

By the end of my sophomore year I had lost most of my anxiety about getting expelled. When two weeks had passed following final exams and I received no notices from the Dean's office, it meant that I was off probation and could look forward to the junior year.

All the winter and spring fog had lifted, and the sun was shining all day long as I crisscrossed the city to find work during summer recess. As a junior medical student, I was qualified to take the State of California Laboratory Technician's exam.

What the heck, I thought, I'll take the exam. If I pass, good. If I don't, so what?

Well, to my surprise I passed.

As a certified technician, I could work alone in the lab over the hours nobody wanted. I got a job at Children's Hospital working the night shift every Friday, Saturday, and Sunday.

That took care of three nights, but that wasn't enough to see me through the coming junior year at the school. It's a fact of life: if one puts all his efforts into finding a job, he'll find it!

I started working at a San Francisco shipyard as a carpenter's helper for five days a week. The foreman was an old German fellow with a raspy voice and stubbly beard. When he heard me speak German, his favorite language, he hired me on the spot. They were building a mine-sweeper made entirely of wood. We even used only copper nails. You know shipyard workers were paid well and besides, it was a government job. Nobody worried about an expense overrun. My only job qualification was to know how to hold onto my hammer. So I carried the hammer around from eight in the morning until four in the afternoon and was well reimbursed for my effort.

Working at the harbor offered a certain splendor.

The sun over the water. The smell of the sea. The white wooden boards reeking of the forest, the unique, clean sound they made when loaded onto our deck. And there was always the deep, wailing sound of the merchants' ships as they pulled out of the harbor.

That still left me four open evenings a week, and for those I became an attendant at McKale's gas station, where I worked from 6 p.m. until midnight closing time. We got to wear a uniform and fancy cap, sort of like a policeman's, with a shiny company emblem on the front. In those days we were called service station attendants and we were proud of the title.

When a car pulled up at the station, two attendants would rush out, one at each side of the car. The senior attendant opened the door at the driver's side and I, as a junior, the passenger side. With synchronized motions we pulled brushes from our back pockets and wiped the floor mats in the front. Both of us had to finish the job at the same time and close the front doors with a harmonized bang. The next step was to wash the front windshield. Again, all of our movements had to be like mirror images, the wiping hands had to meet each other in the middle of the windshield. My duty was to pump the gas while the senior attendant gave the sales pitch. He had to memorize the slogans pointing out the advantages of McKale stations, and he also tried to sell tires and batteries. I also learned how to do a lube job and change the oil.

There were evenings when I was alone until close-up time at midnight.

Those were tranquil hours with an occasional customer. I still remember one summer night when a lady drove up in her Cadillac requesting a "fill-up". It took only two gallons to fill the tank, making me wonder why she had driven in.

Her bill came to 58¢. She handed me a dollar and a bouquet of red roses.

By the time I had recovered from the unexpected gratuity, the tail-lights of her car had already disappeared into the evening darkness.

It made me wonder about the true source and meaning of the flowers.

Was it something she'd gained participating an illegitimate love affair? She most certainly didn't wish to take them home, neither could she toss them out the car window.

This would also explain the small gas purchase. Maybe she was topping off the tank so the car wouldn't look like it had been driven somewhere.

I ended up with three jobs that summer: 40 hours a week as a carpenter's assistant, 4 x 6 hours as a gas station attendant, and 3 x 8 hours as a lab tech. The latter job was mentally demanding, especially on Sunday nights, when I had to cross match blood for patients going to surgery Monday morning. At that time there was a gray zone between compatible and non-compatible blood, with the final call left to the technician's interpretation: when a patient's plasma was mixed with the donor's red blood cells and examined under the microscope, the RBC's had to float freely. If they formed clumps, it was incompatible. But if three or four cells were stuck together back to back, that was called rouleau formation and the types were still considered compatible. How about five cells or even six RBC's riding on each other's back, did that indicate compatibility or not? Remember, it's past midnight and you are the only one in the lab. It's your call!

Let's assume the patient was group B, Rh negative and you had only three units of B-negative blood in your icebox. You are a conscientious man and so you check out all three. One is definitely a "no match", and the other two have the same amount of rouleau formation. What do you do? Call the night supervisor and tell her you don't have compatible blood for the patient? She would have to notify the surgeon, who would be mad as hell to be awakened at this hour. He then asks his case to be switched to the afternoon. In the morning he will call his appointment desk and ask the receptionist to cancel his afternoon appointments. He comes to the lab when the day's shift is in and you have left for the shipyard. When he finds out that the blood is indeed "compatible", he would raise hell. First in the lab and then in the pathologist's office. I would lose my job if my reading was cautious, and the patient might suffer a severe reaction if it was too "loose".

I think you could see that I was under some stress some mornings when driving to work in the shipyard in my old buggy. I said a little prayer that some of the cross matches with heavy rouleau formation I had called "compatible" would not give too bad a reaction if transfused.

The other problem was that I had to be at the shipyard at 8:00 a.m., and was also supposed to work in the lab until eight in the morning. I took off half an hour before quitting time and left the lab unattended. If any urgent requests were to come in and there was no one present, it would mean curtains for me for sure.

Anyway, I quit worrying since there had not been any bad reactions from the blood I had released when even six or seven erythrocytes were stacked like a pile of coins. Later on, when I saw them riding piggy-back like headless caterpillars under my microscope, swimming merrily among the free-floating RBC's, I just said "howdy" to them and OK'd the match. At first, as you can imagine, it was a nail-biter all right!

I took the attitude of the baseball umpire, "I calls them as I sees them", and let it go at that.

As I said earlier, I was working in Children's Hospital and children were admitted here most frequently at night.

Polio was one of the diseases common back then, and so was meningitis. If it was viral then the doctor had to sit it out, so to speak. If however it was meningococcal, prompt treatment with an antibiotic was a must.

One summer night a child was admitted to Children's Hospital with a stiff neck and high fever. Her symptoms were not my concern, but it was my job to analyze the spinal fluid brought to the lab by the attending pediatrician. He sat down then and there, waiting for the report and watching my every move. Under such hurried circumstances I would have preferred to work without supervision, but I couldn't easily tell the doctor to scram.

The spinal fluid, normally clear, was only slightly cloudy and only a few leucocytes were visible under the microscope. One of the white blood cells had a biscuit-shaped object inside it, and looked as if it had swallowed a hula-hoop. I had never seen anything like it before. Was it an artifact or a bug hiding there? I marked the spot and searched for more of the same kind, but couldn't find any. I returned back to the spot, and the "hula-hoop" was still there. I tried to remember from my microbiology class whether the meningiococcus was oval-shaped, and if it could be inside the cell.

Things were getting exciting now.

My hands were even shaking a bit when I prepared it for the final test by adding a specific antiserum (called the "capsular swelling test") and putting it in a slide. Believe it or not, the bugger was now wrapped in a thick coat, meningiococcus, no doubt about it!

The pediatrician rushed out to start the treatment with antibiotics while I set up the cultures. The cultures would have only confirmatory value. The child would be dead if the doctor waited for a culture report.

When I returned to the lab next weekend, everyone in the lab cheered. The culture had confirmed my preliminary diagnosis and the child was now afebrile and well into complete recovery. I moved from "one of them" to "one of us" overnight.

They gave me a German beer mug as a wedding present.

Oh, did I forget to tell you that I got married that fall?

It was true. ...To the serious Canadian nurse whom I had met a year earlier in Washington Park in Fresno. We had danced to the music of Xavier Cugat then, and now she was my wife.

We got married in a Lutheran church in San Jose on a Saturday afternoon, 29 August, 1953. We had a one-day honeymoon drive along the so-called "Seventeen-Mile Drive" on the West Coast and then returned to our furnished apartment at 4248 California Street, close to the Children's Hospital, where I continued to work weekends through the year for added income. (I quit at the shipyard, and no longer worked at McKale's service station either.) Hazel started to work at Henry Kaiser Foundation Hospital on Gary Street. Life fell into a peaceful pattern.

We were a happy young couple.

Hazel was a wonderful wife, and I could appreciate married life at the age of 31, after having lived as a loner and surviving on my famous diet of Spam and potatoes.

Soon we had enough money to make a down payment on a 1953 Chevrolet from "Horsetrader Ed's" used car lot. I'm sure you've seen that huge neon sign at the corner of Gary and Market Streets, showing Ed standing on his head with a cowboy hat and all, and declaring, "Horsetrader Ed Would Stand on His Head to Complete the Deal!"

In my free time I used to shine the car up and drive down California Street, convinced that everybody was looking at the fancy car I was driving. We even bought a television set with rabbit ears so we could watch the Ed Sullivan Show. Well, to get the facts straight, back then it was called "The Toast of the Town". Saturday nights, Sid Caesar and

Imogene Coca and their "Show of Shows" could make your stomach hurt from laughter.

To be honest, I didn't see those shows until the end of my senior year because before then I was still working at the lab on Saturday and Sunday nights.

Not to worry, every lab had its radio, and ours was no exception.

The songs they sang in those days were full of mystery and romance. It made my heart ache to listen to Robert Merrill sing "They Called the Wind Maria," Vaughn Monroe doing "Ghostriders in the Sky," or good old Gene Austin singing "Ramona". I couldn't name them all.

I personally didn't go for the real chummy things like Eddie Fisher's "Wish You Were Here", and stuff like that.

Hazel was also an excellent cook.

For our first Thanksgiving she had stuffed turkey and I had the responsibility of putting the turkey in the oven at two o'clock in the afternoon. We didn't have anything like plastic bags in those days, and the turkey came wrapped in wax paper. Well, come two o'clock, I set the temperature to 350° and I put the turkey in the oven, wax paper and all.

Alas, by the time Hazel got home from work and opened the oven door, the turkey had suffered irreversible harm, the wax paper had melted and soaked into the turkey.

We ended up eating hot dogs instead.

Hazel didn't say much, but that was the very last time she asked me to do any kind of cooking or grilling. For me it turned out to be a blessing-in-disguise that I had spoiled our first holiday dinner.

———

The only thing I could make in the kitchen was Estonian pancakes, but by now I've forgotten even how to do those.

———

I spent the year 1953-54 at San Francisco County Hospital.

About two weeks into my junior year, I received an ominous looking letter from the Dean's office.

At first I was too scared to open it. I went to the bedroom to be alone, ripped open the envelope, and read the short note.

Then I rushed to the living room to tell Hazel, "It's a congratulatory note from the Dean with a check for $500, a Scholarship from the Henry Kaiser Foundation."

If you can imagine being in Hell, and then a minute or two later being in Heaven, then you can picture how I felt.

I hadn't even applied for a scholarship, but the University of California with its sixty thousand students remembered my inadequate diet and with this scholarship they wished to supplement my culinary needs and thereby help me withstand the rigors of junior year.

Five hundred dollars! Just to think that before the wedding I wanted to borrow $100 from "Household Finance". They had been advertising "Household Finance, Money When You Need It" all over the place.

Well, they turned me down. They told me I had no collateral, and my '36 Ford was worth nothing.

A couple of months later, I had five hundred bucks in my pocket and I said to hell with Household Finance. Who needed their money anyway!

The following two years in medical school were full of fun and hard work. The SF County Hospital emergency room was like a museum of diseases and suffering, and at times it was even fun.

At the end of Market Street, next to the bay, was the winos' territory. They were city folk and different from the hoboes.

No one had yet invented a new social class by calling them "homeless" and making everybody feel guilty for their lifestyle.

America back then was a free country, and as they used to say: "You can be what you want to be." If they wanted to be hoboes or winos, that was their free choice.

At times a few of them were found sleeping in the street and brought to the emergency room. The junior medical students had to take their medical histories. The trouble was that none of them seemed to know their age.

A good way to find out was to ask: "Do you remember the great earthquake?"

They usually remembered that.

Then you asked: "How old were you then?"

If the man said "about ten", then a quick calculation would give you his age.

The big earthquake in SF was in 1906. So, $1954 - 1906 = 48$; $48 + 10 = 58$.

That made him 58, give or take a few years.

The senior year was spent again at Parnassus Avenue, and my last assignment before graduation was at the Pediatric Clinic.

Before any of us could start that service, throat cultures were taken to rule out any streptococcal carriers. It so happened that my throat culture was positive. I was given penicillin shots for the better part of the following week. I ended up with a sore bottom while the throat cultures remained positive, and I was told to have my tonsils out before I could start my service at the pediatric clinic.

I went to see Professor Morrison, the Chairman of Otorhinolaryngology. He was a gentleman of 60 years, always meticulously dressed with a white carnation in his buttonhole. When I told him that I had never had a sore throat in my life, I still remember his short and to-the-point answer, "If your car has brakes, do they always squeak?"

Saturday morning came, and the professor himself took out my tonsils. Hazel was working and could not get off, but she sent two French-Canadian nurses to help me recover from anesthesia.

I must admit they were young and good-looking, and they gave all their love and know-how to assist a poor patient after such a life-threatening tonsillectomy. They were sure well coordinated: one held my hand and supported my back while the other held my head and the emesis basin.

I told Hazel how thankful I was for all the French nurses' help, and added: "I wouldn't mind having my tonsils re-operated on if given such tender aftercare."

She didn't think I was being funny at all, and the only reply was "watch it!"

I must admit I recovered quickly and that same Saturday night Hazel and I went to see the movie *Bad Day at Black Rock* with Spencer Tracy and a French movie called *Mr. Hulot's Holiday.* I laughed so hard that my tonsils (or what was left of them) started to bleed again.

My last month as a medical student was spent in the Pediatric Clinic on the sixth floor of the hospital building.

---

[1] as per D.W. Furnas, M.D. Class '55

Chapter 11

NEW YORK, NEW YORK

I received my MD degree on June 17, 1955. It took me twelve years and four universities, each in a different country, to get there. I had been interrupted by the war and other circumstances beyond my control. Not only did I survive all ordeals, I had fulfilled my life-long dream of becoming a doctor. It would be hard for anyone to understand or appreciate the happiness I felt back then at the Golden City by the Bay.

The graduation ceremony itself was no big deal. There were thousands of graduates lined up at the Berkeley Football Stadium, each standing in his or her own line, from MDs to DDSs to PhDs. Also included were BSs, Bas, MSs and DCs, and many more.

All the graduates wore black broadcloth, but only the doctorates had the bell-shaped sleeves barred with a stripe of velvet, and their hoods were a foot longer than any other. Our caps were also made of velvet and carried a gold tassel. I had to spend five bucks to rent the outfit for the occasion and stand in one of those lines with my classmates. Each of us received a roll of paper with a handshake from the Dean while the real certificate could be picked up from the Dean's office.

Five days after the graduation ceremony, I took and passed the California Board of Medicine's examinations. The written tests lasted for three days, six hours each day with breaks in-between.

All I needed now was one year of internship and then I could open my own medical practice anywhere in the State of California. Goodbye to McKale's gas station, the shipyards in the harbor, and nights at the Children's Hospital lab. All in all, I had had a good time wherever I worked, whether it was in Bay area or back in Kingsburg and Fresno.

During the senior year we had applied for internships in different hospitals across the United States and after the State Boards were over, the members of my class scattered in all directions across the country.

Nothing was keeping Hazel and me on the West Coast.

I had accepted an internship in Queens General Hospital in New York. It was a city hospital without any private patients and the interns and resident physicians "ran the show", so to speak. I had accumulated enough book-knowledge and it was time to put it to practical use.

Queens General was happy to have me.

Why should they turn down a young doctor who would be willing to work day and night for $62 a month, the amount they paid interns back then? The city could hire five interns for the money they paid for one maintenance man, and the maintenance man would work only eight hours a day, five days a week. It was no wonder that the floor scrubbers tended to splash murky water all over our white shoes with a grin, saying "sorry, doc..." In recognition of their superior standing, all we could do was respond with, "Well, don't rub it in!"

It was June 25, 1955 when Hazel and I packed our few belongings in a not-yet-paid-for gray Chevrolet from "Horsetrader Ed's", and took off toward Donner Pass, across the salt flats of Utah all the away to New York. The car had a gallon-size water bag that hung off the hood, in case the radiator overheated.

Back then there were no turnpikes to speak of and motels were few and far between.

The best ones even had a TV in the room.

If the place had TV, that was advertised with a neon "Pay TV in Room" just below the vacancy sign. You had to drop a quarter every half an hour and fiddle with the rabbit ears before you could see *Death Valley Days* or *The Jimmy Durante Show*.

We drove until late, and by then there were big "NO"s stuck in front of the "VACANCY" signs. But then, we were traveling on a tight budget, and had no use for the $10-a-night motels anyway. Who would be fool enough to waste a quarter to watch their snowy TV when you could buy a whole gallon of gas for that money!

Instead we chose to live off the land, so to speak.

There were plenty roadside homes, their folks sitting on the front porch ready to wave in late travelers. You could rent a spare bedroom from them for five bucks a night, and they'd be nice enough to share the family bathroom with you.

It took us five days with long hours of driving through cornfields and small towns until we reached New York. We arrived during rush hour, got immediately lost, and ended up in the Bronx. We did find our way to Queens, eventually.

It just so happened that Arnold Pärnama, a buddy from my Hamburg days, lived in his own house in Queens, perhaps two or three miles from Queens General. He was a bachelor and the nicest guy you could hope to run across in that town, or anywhere, for that matter. He had polite manners, spoke slowly, and never raised his voice. He was so reserved that even his smile appeared apologetic.

The neighbors' wives helped him out in many ways.

They even brought rosebushes for his small garden and all Arno had to do was show the ladies where to plant them.

He worked as a civil engineer at the City of New York Transportation Department in Manhattan, ate his meals at the Estonian House at East 34th Street, and came home late.

I trust you've put two and two together and figured out that Hazel and I would be living like a king and queen in Queens. The whole house was practically ours for $60 a month.

Arno's icebox didn't hold much besides *Burgermeister Beer*. It came in two-pint jugs and, being a good tenant, I refused to let any of the stuff go to waste. I polished off all the half-filled bottles so Arno wouldn't have to put up with any stale brew.

––––––

Queens General Hospital was a huge pale-brick building at 164th Street. It had over six hundred beds and its grounds covered two city blocks with full-grown elm and maple trees and was separated from the city by a high wrought-iron fence.

Next to the main hospital buildings were two one-story brick structures: one for the house staff and another for the young ladies attending the School of Nursing. Tennis courts were next to it where the student nurses in their blue-striped uniforms used to play with interns dressed all in white. A paved walkway led to the dining rooms, where the interns and residents took their meals, free of charge.

Nurses and the rest of the hospital staff had to pay a minimal fee.

––––––

The house staff was a mixed breed.

There was a sizable group of interns who had graduated from a medical school in Switzerland. What amazed me at first was their perfect English, while two of them had apparently picked up Brooklyn accents in Zurich. Later on I learned the truth: they were all Americans, who for one reason or another had attended medical school in Switzerland. It remained a mystery to me whether they preferred the continental flavor of medicine or simply did not pass the entry exams in the old USA.

There was one female intern among us, a true Swiss with limited English. To work with her in the ER was most confusing. She would start a case, fail to understand the patient's complaints, and then walk away in the middle of her exam to take up another case. She usually didn't finish the second one either, leaving a lot of confusion in her wake.

Dr. Phipps, an intern from England, was a nice chap to work with. After two weeks I came under his influence and started to say "now, now" instead of a simple "no". He came to my rescue once when I had an English seaman as a patient: the trouble was I couldn't understand a single word he said.

He soon returned with the remark, "He's a jolly good fellow, but I can't understand his cockney either." I believe Dr. Phipps said it just to make me feel better because he was a gentleman with his classy English.

Two of the interns were straight from Japan.

They were both hard workers. Doctor Yamauchi was so duty bound that he even *ran* from one bed to another when he drew blood in the morning. With my name of Ojamaa I was thought to be a Japanese. In fact, when pronounced "O'yama" (stress on the second syllable), in Japanese it meant "small mountain"; if you said "Oo'yama" instead, it became "big mountain".

The trouble was that my face and blond hair did not match up with Japanese mountains. Well, "Ojamaa" meant "Brookland" in Estonian and Riverland" in Finnish, but then there were no Estonian or Finnish telephone operators and I was paged with everything from "Omaha" to "Pajamas".

We also had three African-American residents on house staff. Two were in Internal Medicine and one, Dr. Dickerson, was the chief resident in Obstetrics & Gynecology.

There was no Affirmative Action back then, and they had made it without any preferential treatment.

Dr. Dorsey and his physician-wife were indeed the tops. They were both residents in Internal Medicine without Dr. Dickerson's show-off qualities.

I remember one episode with Dr. Dorsey, which puzzled me at first.

There was one patient who was admitted in a semi-stupor state with a high fever, and no one had figured out what was wrong with her. Without going into the diagnostic rigmarole, I'll cut to the quick and divulge that she soon died.

Because the case had puzzled everybody, the visiting staff almost made an ultimatum to the house staff to get the autopsy permit signed. Dr. Dorsey had to drive out to Long Island to meet the next of kin. When we finally got there and found the small house in a residential district, and I had parked my car at the curbside, Dr. Dorsey announced in his quiet voice, "YOU go in there and get the permit signed."

It was a most unusual, and to tell the truth, unexpected request. A poor and unsophisticated intern was sent to do a man's job. He knew very well if I came back empty-handed, he would get all the blame.

It was his responsibility and he knew it.

After I had returned with the signed permit Dr. Dorsey, who had been so incommunicative on our way down, became elated and full of good spirits:

Good show, man. Good show! How in the world did you manage to get her sister to sign it? You know the phone call I made, she was dead set against it!"

"Well, I was truly unprepared for that task. It made me shy and apologetic, even embarrassed, asking for her signature. She must have felt sorry for me."

I hadn't been around long enough to know the shadowy side of American society called discrimination. Dr. Dorsey knew what I didn't know then, that a woman in a blue-collar neighborhood wouldn't have opened her door to a colored man in the 50's, let alone sign an autopsy permit he was delivering.

Dr. Dickerson, chief resident in the OB department, was quite the opposite of Dr. Dorsey.

He was cocky, sure of himself, and reckless by today's standards. Back then the word "malpractice" was just a word in the dictionary, and some doctors took chances with patients in order to sharpen their medical skills. He was competent all right and knew it, and he made sure that everybody in the department knew it, including the patients. He called himself "painless Dickerson", and he was that, too.

His "routine" was as follows: when a patient was ready for delivery, he became an anesthetist first by using open-drop ether. There was no anesthesia machine or suction equipment in sight.

After he had put the patient asleep, he scrubbed and then went to the rear end of the table and delivered the baby with forceps. If during the episiotomy repair the patient started to move and the attending nurse happened to be busy resuscitating the baby, anyone in harking distance was asked to become an anesthetist and drop more ether on the patient's mask.

Any invasive procedure had to be okayed first by the attending board-certified physician. One day he had put his patient to sleep and was ready to use forceps to deliver the baby, when one of the attending physicians stuck his head through the delivery room door with a "What's up?"

"I would like to do inversion and breech extraction."

"What's the indication?"

"Practice."

"Go ahead!"

And Dr. Dickerson pushed the baby's head up and out of the pelvis, inserted his hand deep into the uterus to grab the baby's feet, turned the baby all the way around, and delivered the child as a breech. It was skillfully done without rupturing the uterus, and the baby and mother weathered the procedure well. The mother was under anesthesia and would never know that the attending physician had performed a danger-ous procedure for the sake of practice, and had done it without her per-mission!

Well, one could conceivably say "what you don't know won't hurt you," and let it go at that.

Dr. Pescatore was the senior resident in Internal Medicine.

She was a female physician all the way from France, perhaps thirty years old. She had red hair, wide hips, and a bulging bosom. She loved to play table tennis in the late evening hours with young interns. The way she "played the game," she probably enjoyed double victories.

Whether the opponent considered himself the winner or loser de-pended on his point of view.

Because of her senior status, she was also the doctor in charge of the interns' health care, beyond helping them exercise at "table tennis for two", that is.

One day I had a sore throat and went to see Dr. Pescatore. She exam-ined my upper anatomy and prescribed Chloromycetin.

It is a powerful antibiotic, not suitable for minor ailments. It might cure your sore throat all right but the side effect, such as aplastic anemia, might kill you later on. I had her prescription filled in the hospital pharmacy but decided to let nature take its course without the help of Dr. Pescatore's miracle drug.

Twenty years later, when I was practicing in Sheboygan, my German shorthaired pointer became gravely ill from infected wounds he had received in fighting a neighbor's dog.

I still had the old vial of Chloromycetin and put it to good use; my dog's life was saved, thanks to Dr. Pescatore's prescription!

My first service at Queens General was in the Department of Internal Medicine. I worked under a second-year resident who became my only friend among the house staff.

His name was Dr. Tofig.

He was an Iranian, with a pale face and two dimples on his cheeks when he smiled, which was most of the time.

Everything Dr. Tofig did was done in a hurry, the activities that I witnessed, at any rate.

He talked fast, had the wonderful habit of throwing his arms above his head as if he were chasing devils, and could change the subject of discussion from medicine to girls in the middle of a sentence.

I asked him to call me Duke, the name Ron had given me back in Fresno. I just did not want him to call me "Pajamas".

My first assignment was to draw blood for the lab. Queens General was a teaching hospital and patients' blood was drawn to run tests for everything under the sun. Who knows, one might accidentally hit the jackpot and make a rare diagnosis, such as "Tsutsugamushi fever" or "Fisheye disease", and then you could proudly announce that you had had that disease in mind from the start.

To run the gamut of tests, the lab needed blood and lots of it! It wasn't unusual to see a blood transfusion in one arm while the intern was taking it all out from the other. The patient would be perfectly justified in suggesting that the stuff be taken straight from the bottle and his arms be left alone.

We did not wear gloves when drawing blood.

AIDS was unknown then and the etiology of many types of viral diseases had yet to be discovered.

Medicine in the 1950s was a simple and straightforward thing.

For instance, take the case of jaundice (hepatitis). Back then doctors only concerned themselves with two kinds of it: the obstructive kind and non-obstructive kind.

If you turned yellow, the doctors wanted to know if you had rocks in your gallbladder.

If you did, you had obstructive hepatitis and had to have your gallbladder out. If you did not, you had non-obstructive hepatitis and the surgeons lost all interest in you. In the second instance, you had most likely been a lifelong boozer and you liver was shot to hell, and that was the price you had to pay for having had too many "happy hours".

There was also a third, more nebulous kind called "viral hepatitis".

Doctors in the Old Country loved their Latin and during the bedside rounds called this third type *prognosis infausta – terapia nulla.* They couldn't just come out and announce in the presence of their patients that the case was hopeless and there was no way of treating them.

In this country some doctors called it "just one of those things", and the prescribed treatment was to "let nature take its course".

Well, no doctor would come out and say: "Forget it, you're a gon-er!"

Who would need a doctor for such a diagnosis, anyway!

We had pages of printed instruction for cases of non-obstructive jaundice, telling patients what not to do or eat. Whether it made any difference in the final outcome, nobody knew, but the instruction sheets sure made the doctor and their patients feel a load better.

That reminds me of a story one of the pediatric residents had told us back in San Francisco. He had been seeing a child with epilepsy, and at the end of the visit the mother had wondered, "How about the window in his room at night? Some say it is good for his condition to keep it open, the others tell me quite the opposite. Which way is the right way, doctor?"

The doctor's answer was very instructive and to the point, "Leave the window open four inches. No more and no less!"

Of course it wouldn't make any difference whether the window was closed or left open, but if the doctor had said, "it doesn't matter", then the mother would have thought the doc didn't really know his stuff.

And the "four-inch only" story made her feel so much better by knowing what was best for her child. She followed the doctor's "four inches" order with a measuring tape.

Coming back to our hepatitis story: researchers started to confuse the simple issues and divide the straight viral condition into three groups: "A", "B", and "neither A nor B".

It took them a lot of further research until they discovered that the third kind was not really "neither A nor B", but rather a separate class, called "C".

Was there a different treatment for each group?

No, sir.

In fact, there was no treatment for any of these conditions. The only difference was that the one might kill you quicker than the other.

Surely it would take a load off *your* mind to know whether it was A, B, or C that had wrecked *your* liver?

Diabetes could be a tricky condition at times for the interns to treat because it involved a lot of guessing. The basic guidelines were simple enough.

When the blood sugar was high you treated it with insulin, if it was low you had the patient drink orange juice. It was just like driving your car: accelerator or brake, accelerator or brake.

The trick was: when to use which one and how much.

The intern had taken a sample to test the blood sugar in the morning, and the patient happened to complain of being sweaty after he had had his breakfast. (What did he expect? The temperature in the ward was 90°F.)

The nurse got the lab report. Aha! Low sugar, the patient is having an attack of hypoglycemia!

"Nurse, give him a glass of sweetened orange juice!"

Two hours later the same nurse would call you:

"Your patient is snoring and cannot be roused."

A quick urine test would reveal 4+ sugar and 4+ acetone.

"Jesus!" you'd say, "the patient is in a diabetic coma!"

And so you load him up with rapid-acting insulin.

The patient wakes up, feels great for a while, and then conks out again.

This time your guess is "hypoglycemia again". Perhaps you shop in too much of that rapid-acting insulin stuff?

The intravenous line is in place, and you order the nurse to run sugar solution in rapidly. Then you add, "When he comes to, give him a glass of orange juice!"

If the perpetual swing between diabetic acidosis and insulin shock continues you'll write "brittle diabetic" in the patient's chart.

The attending internist will explain, "You have to learn to handle the patient like you handle your car: accelerator or brake, accelerator or brake, and not both at the same time!"

Dr. Tofig was all smiles.

He was trying to establish a cozy relationship with the head nurse, who was giving him the cold shoulder. That did not seem to bother Tofig for a moment, though. She was all iceberg when they stood next to each other to discuss patient care, yet he remained so suave.

I felt so embarrassed. "It is hopeless!" I said. "She just plain hates your guts!"

Tofig raised his eyes from the chart he was looking at and smiled, "You do not know women. If they reject you outright, then you have a good chance. If they ignore you, then there is no hope. This is the basic rule of the game. The sooner you learn the facts of life, Duke, the better off you'll be!"

"What do you mean? I'm married."

He became visibly annoyed:

"What the hell has marriage got to do with it!"

We took a break.

Across the street was a drugstore where we sat down in a small cubicle and ordered glasses of cold coke. He deposited his nickels in the jukebox and played "Come Down, Come Down from Your Ivory Tower..." over and over.

She ain't gonna come down," was my prediction, which he countered with, "Man, you do not know Iranians!"

Then he started to worry about one of the patients he had sent home from the ER the night before. The patient's symptoms had been so vague that he hadn't even bothered to look at his EKG until this morning.

"This guy had a heart attack, that's for sure."

Then he laughed his short laugh and threw his hands over his head, as if ready to surrender, "I can't get hold of him. He has no phone. All this drives me crazy."

He liked the word "crazy".

Everything drove him crazy: his patients, the head nurse, and cardiograms.

But he was not worried about any of it. Everything was just fun and games and yes, perhaps, crazy!

We worked all afternoon.

I took histories, did the physicals, and started IVs. He was studying his cardiograms and went over the morning's lab work.

The p.a. speakers were almost constantly busy with telephone operators paging the new interns. Sometimes my own summons sounded like "Dr. Pajamas", and other times like "Omaha". But Dr. Tofig told me to relax, I was under his jurisdiction, and no one had any claim on me.

After a short while the operators quit chasing the doctors and had an important announcement to make, "Attention all doctors, the Liver Conference starts at 3 p.m. in Ward X. House staff to attend!"

"That's odd," I thought. In California, the rounds in Ward X had been autopsy rounds. Besides, I was eager to finish my work and get home to see how Hazel was making out by herself at Arno's place. If I went to that damned liver conference I wouldn't get home much before midnight.

But Dr. Tofig was very persistent and wouldn't take "no" for an answer. "This is 'must' conference," he told me. "I am going, and you'll come along if you know what's good for you!"

We had to cross the ambulance entrance.

There were wheelchairs and stretchers with patients, some wrapped in bloody bandages. One of the ambulances was unloading a pregnant woman who was calling for Jesus in a high-pitched voice. The way things looked, the baby might drop out then and there!

"Let's get out of here," was Tofig's suggestion, "or they might ask us to help!"

As we approached the alleged conference room, he continued:

"That's the way it is on Friday nights. People get their paychecks and then have a good time stabbing and shooting each other."

"They sure seemed to be having fun whatever they were doing, and when you ask 'who shot or stabbed you?' the only answer you'll get is, 'It was my friend, he didn't mean it.'"

After a short pause, he added, "And we, poor souls, have to take care of them for a flat fee of two bits an hour!"

By then we had arrived at the room that had been reserved for the liver conference.

It was no conference room at all.

There weren't even any chairs to sit on.

It was just the table-tennis room in the interns' quarters.

The tables had been pushed against the walls. The water cooler was filled with what looked like orange juice with paper cups all lined out next to it. A record player was blasting some Dixieland music while the young interns and residents were doing some kind of Mambo with the nurses, who had just finished their shift at the hospital.

Tofig was all smiles. "See," he said, "you would have missed an important conference!" And then he laughed, his two dimples showing.

He got a cupful of that "pre-treated" orange juice for both of us, in some quarters it would have been called a "screwdriver", and we were ready to settle down for the Friday afternoon "Happy Hour".

Suddenly his body seemed to stiffen and his face turned serious.

He had noticed his favorite nurse across the room, standing all by herself at the open window.

He mumbled something about wanting "to catch a whiff of fresh air," and was soon heading towards her at the window.

I had to admire Dr. Tofig's taste. She was something to look at, with her nurse's cap off and her brown hair fallen down to her shoulders. Because of the mid-afternoon heat she had opened a few buttons of her uniform, exposing her swan-like neck.

"Well," I thought, "they sure know how to hold 'liver conferences' at Queens General. My compliments to the hospital administration for supplying all the right ingredients."

I had to admit the atmosphere was much friendlier and more relaxed here than at the no-nonsense place high up on Parnassus Street. Life over there was all books and study, and so it needed to be. Here we worked long hours for pennies, but Friday's social hour made us all feel better about ourselves and the world we lived in.

Well, to borrow a phrase from Dr. Tofig's favorite tune, my internship at Queens General truly felt like "coming down from the ivory tower".

Only a few weeks later, Hazel and I went to a movie.

I do not recall any of the action on the screen, but I remember seeing a couple ahead of us that were in a cozy relationship.

I knew them both.

I guess Dr. Tofig was right when he said I didn't know Iranians.

After the happy hour, I went back to the medical ward and worked until dark. Before leaving, I was called upon to pronounce a 104-year-old man dead and sign his death certificate.

I remember that late evening well.

The ward was all dark with sleeping patients. Only the low-hanging light threw a circular beam on a single chart, left open at the nurses' desk. At the ward folding screens had been placed on both sides of one bed, shielding it from the rest. Behind it were the nurse with her flashlight and two orderlies with a stretcher.

The old man was on the stretcher, covered with a white sheet, and one of the orderlies rolled him toward the service elevator at the end of the hallway. Then the screens were folded up and carried to storage.

The nurse returned to her desk, wrote a short note for the open chart, removed it from its metal folder, and threw it into the "out" basket.

I sat with a piece of paper in front of me.

By signing it, I would become a part of American history, I pronounced dead a man who had been a youngster when Lincoln was president and the Civil War started.

Through the window on my right, I could see the lights of the city below. They were alive in different colors: flickering, flashing, and blinking, while some threw circular beams of light onto the sky, making it glow in gold.

I signed the death certificate before me, placed it on the open chart in the outgoing basket, and left the floor.

The attendant opened the high wrought-iron gate with a "Good night, doc!"

The road was downhill.

The sky was still ablaze with washed-out stars over Manhattan and the Bronx. I drove my old Chevy towards Arno's place on 183rd Street.

My first day as an intern at Queens General had come to an end.

Chapter 12

After the First Day...

After the six weeks in internal medicine I started my three months in the obstetrical service. That added up to twice the time required, but I wanted to have a good start in my future specialty and had skipped the ENT service entirely. I had witnessed numerous deliveries and assisted in a few, but now I had become number one on the "firing line".

To tell you about the Labor Department at Queens General, first I have to admit that it was the most boisterous place imaginable.

No cuss words could be heard, but Jesus's name was frequently invoked. At times it was the only word used to make up long sentences. The volume and strength of the vocal cords compared favorably to opera singers'.

The other aspect of obstetrical practice back then was routine administration of Scopolamine with Demerol to the labor patients. Scopolamine had an unusual effect, it robbed the patients of all recollection of time and events. When they woke up the next morning, the first thing they asked was if they had already had their baby. And when the baby was brought to them, they wondered aloud, "Are you sure it's mine?"

The drug rendered women less vocal all right, but they became physically violent and hard to manage. It sometimes helped to raise the side-rails on their beds, but this didn't prevent them from doing all kinds of acrobatics like crawling over them or "riding shotgun" by sticking their legs through the upright divider and beating their pubic area against the steel bar. At times I had to help the nurses wrestle them back into bed and retrieve their legs from the steely traps.

During the day the resident staff was around to help the interns through the "tight spots", so to speak, but at night you were on your own. No wonder there were anxious "what to do next" moments.

I'll tell you about my first delivery. If it becomes graphic in parts, so be it. If my story appears flippant, I assure you it would only be so in the eyes of the reader.

It was nighttime.

The baby was large and the woman violent. Her hands had been restrained, but before the right leg could be fastened to the stirrup, she hit me on the head with it and knocked me off my stool. That itself shook my confidence, and I felt like a boxer who had been knocked down on the very first round.

The nurse helped me up, and I had to re-scrub and re-drape myself. By then the nurse-anesthetist had arrived and pacified the patient with ether.

When the baby's head came to a good bulge I made my mid-line episiotomy, but after two contractions I realized my cut wasn't sufficient and the patient would suffer a tear into her rectum. This itself would not have been something to worry about, if one knew how to repair it. So far I had only heard about such repairs, but had never seen it done. I decided to make a second cut in the same part of the of the lady's anatomy, lateral to the first incision.

I ended up with two episiotomies. I had never heard of a two-episiotomy delivery before! Perhaps it would have qualified me for the Guinness Book of World Records?

Well, the birth itself went ok. I did not drop the baby, but placed it on the mother's abdominal drapes, and cut the umbilical cord while the nurse took it to the crib.

Then I sat down again and looked at my patient's lower anatomy. I had to confess: it looked like an earthquake had struck.

After the birth of the baby the lady's stretched-out perineum had shrunk to its natural state and the two episiotomies, so far apart a few moments ago, had become close neighbors.

How to repair it became the $64,000 Question. You could well imagine the stress I was under looking at the piece of vagina and perineum hanging out between my two cuts. It sure looked like a tongue sticking out at the wrong end!

Should I cut the hanging piece of tissue out altogether or try to sew all of it back together again? If I cut it out, would it make the vagina too narrow for future use? Would the tension created by pulling the two sides together break the catgut sutures and make my repair-work fall apart?

On the other hand, if I included the hanging part of the vagina and perineum in my repair, would it have an adequate blood supply? If not, it would become necrotic, unable to hold the sutures, and all of it would fall apart just as in the other scenario. It all seemed like a no-win situation indeed.

Well, I made my first obstetrical decision that night in New York

City in the Borough of Queens, I decided not to cut anything out, but rather to include all the tissue in my repair.

As it turned out, everything healed up nicely, even without any scarring. It sure wasn't because of my art of suturing, rather the miraculous healing power of the female perineum, perfected through evolution and a million years of childbirth, and well before there were any smart doctors with their scissors, needles, and catgut suture. Through natural selection, the fittest survived and produced offspring with the inbred ability to heal and resist any infection in that vital part of the female anatomy.

After I had completed my three months of OB service I was assigned to ER to "ride shotgun" with the ambulance.

I remember my first ride, sitting high up in the front next to the driver and listening to the wailing sirens and the continuous swearing of the driver at the slow traffic ahead. Finally we stopped in front of a two-story house.

I grabbed my medicine bag and ran upstairs, the driver at my heels. A woman in her fifties opened the door and pointed to her husband who was stretched out on the floor with half his face covered in white cream, he must have been in the middle of shaving.

"Do something, doc, do something!" wailed the woman.

With trembling hands, I opened my medical bag and started to fill a syringe to give him a Coramine injection. Fifty years ago it was used to "stimulate the heart", whatever that meant, but it sure was not good enough to wake the dead.

While I was busying myself with the injection, the ambulance driver took one look and announced:

"It ain't no use, doc. The man is dead."

The woman started to wail:

"Oh my God, oh my God! Is he dead, doc? Is he really dead?"

Well, I'm afraid the driver was right about the diagnosis. I had it in the back of my mind myself, but I wanted to break the bad news slowly and to show the poor woman that I *tried* to do *something* to save the man's life.

If he wouldn't sit up *after* my Coramine injection, then I intended to check his vital signs. If I couldn't find any, only then I would announce:

"I am awfully sorry, Madame. I have done all that is humanly possible, but it was too late. He has passed away."

It was my very first ambulance call.

The driver was an old hand and made the correct diagnosis, called a spade a spade. I had a little indecision and a load of sympathy, a useless emotion under those circumstances.

I made a few other ambulance calls. They were mostly maternity cases. When the woman in active labor did not think she could make it to the hospital on time, someone called an ambulance for her.

We rode out with the sirens blowing: either to deliver the baby at home or to take a chance and try and bring the lady in undelivered. In those cases the driver did not offer his opinion and the decision was mine to make. If I miscalculated and wound up delivering the baby in the ambulance, a messy situation indeed, I had to buy the driver a twelve-pack of Burgermeister or Peels Brothers' Beer for cleaning up the mess in his ambulance.

Well, my previous OB service had given me some insight and I did not have to do a single "in-ambulance delivery".

The fact that I even did not deliver any of them at home either was just a stroke of luck. Once the ambulance reached the hospital ER, my responsibilities had ended.

After the "shotgun rides" I became a "stationary" physician in ER and heaved a big sigh of relief. Those rides were nerve-wracking, being out all by myself in the wilderness without knowing what to expect or do next.

Late morning and early afternoon hours in the ER were relatively quiet. The ambulances came and went without their sirens.

The midsummer heat hung over the paved entrance. A few lazy flies were resting on the stretchers, which were lined up outside in the sun.

I remember one moment in such an idle afternoon when time seemed to stand still. The ambulance had brought in a girl in her teens.

When I entered her curtained-in cubicle, her pallid face managed an embarrassed smile, someone had shot her accidentally, the bullet still buried in her flesh.

I applied the dressing and prepared her for surgery.

I was too young in practice and felt embarrassed examining her heart while her luscious breasts were exposed, pulsating synchronously with her heartbeat. I must have looked at her with admiration and failed to hide it. She had grasped my transgression somehow and kept looking at me with submission and forgiveness in her eyes.

Guilt-ridden, I touched her only with the end of my stethoscope and kept my fingertips away from her skin.

There was no table.

I placed my notepad on the stretcher over her spread-out hair. The white curtains of the cubicle admitted only a soft and shadowless light, which fell upon her blond hair and her fragile complexion. Her eyes followed my pen as I wrote, her lips narrowed with pain.

She followed me with her eyes even after the orderly started to roll her stretcher to surgery.

I never saw her again, but for some reason the memory of her and my sinless transgression has stayed with me over decades.

Another ambulance brought in a youngster with wavy hair.

His blue eyes sparkled and his face was all in smiles. He appeared confused, asking where he was.

His mother hushed him and asked him not to talk.

He was in the euphoric phase that follows a concussion. Soon he became lethargic. His forehead became covered with droplets of cold sweat and the bright colors in his eyes were replaced by confusion.

His mother had turned away, looking at the bare walls and wiping her tears with the corner of her crumpled handkerchief. All was still.

Only high-heeled shoe-steps sounded in the hallway, which was filled with increasing shadows.

The long minutes had become eternity for the now-unconscious youngster.

Those were the lazy hours in the ER.

After the sun had set and early dusk fell upon the city, the sick got sicker and the pregnant women started their twinges of labor.

They came to the ER, seeking refuge from pain and suffering.

During the early hours of night our workload diminished noticeably:

by then the afflicted had taken their sleepers and the pregnant women had gone to bed with their false labor pains, while the neurotic and depressed had lightened their burdens with *Thorazine*, the only tranquilizer available back then.

It was time to take a short break.

Perhaps one could step outside with a cup of coffee. To gaze at the pallid moon and watch the shadows the age-old trees threw on the footpaths.

After midnight, when the bars had closed, a new wave of "customers" arrived. They were shot and stabbed, beat up, or banged up with their cars. Payday had also supplied cash for the services of back-alley abortionists: young women, bleeding and in pain, arrived at the ER through the early morning hours. And we would work without interruption until the city lights had faded and the sky became bright with the new day.

Christmas arrived, and with its white snow and the Yuletide spirit.

Arno had bought a tree and we decorated it with colorful lights while our old box-like TV filled the house with songs of Christmas. An entire shelf in the icebox was filled with bottles of Burgermeister beer, and Estonian Christmas dishes filled the rest.

At the hospital the nurses' stations were decorated with colorful ribbons, cutout angels, and blazing stars.

The chief residents in each department had a bottle of Christmas cheer hidden in the bottom of their desk drawer. With a wink, they invited passing interns over for a shot-glass of the pungent liquid and supplied a peppermint cookie as an hors d'oeuvre.

The tables in the house-staff recreation room were again pushed against the walls and covered with white bed-sheets (borrowed from the Laundry Department).

There were trays full of cold cuts and sweets.

Bottles of different colors and shapes had replaced the water-cooler with "doctored" orange juice, so familiar from the "liver conferences". A maintenance man in a white shirt and bow-tie served as the bartender.

The off-duty house staff wore dark suits with ties. The nurses had exchanged their "touch-me-not" white uniforms for tight dresses. They laughed a lot, smelling of Sak's Fifth Avenue perfume.

Illuminated by the colorful Christmas tree lights, they all danced to the tunes of "Jingle Bells" and "White Christmas".

For a more domestic Christmas party the three of us, Arno, Hazel and I, went to the Estonian House for a dinner of such native dishes as blood sausage, headcheese, and sauerkraut. We sat at the long table and spoke Estonian. Hazel did not understand a word that was spoken, but she laughed along with the crowd. It was a spirited party of my country-men. All were once left homeless, but had found a place in America.

They were success stories waiting to be told.

When still in Hamburg, our group of Estonian male students had founded a new fraternity, Fraternity Ukuensis,[1] which was probably the only one established in exile. Most of its members were then living in the New York area, by a happy coincidence, and we got together once a month at the Estonian House. I went to list the names of my fraternity brothers; almost all of them finished their studies in America (only one member in the New York area had not continued his studies in the US), and were then gainfully employed in their individual fields:

Heinz Ederma, master's degree in Chemistry

Kalju Eik, PhD Agriculture

Richard Pertel, PhD in Chemistry

Medical doctor degrees obtained by: Arvo Ederma, Hillar Leetma, Einar Puström, and Arved Ojamaa.

Doctor of Veterinary medicine: Harry Madissoo

Civil Engineering degrees (MS or BS): Axel Järlik, Hillar Kaasik, Il-mari Kolsi, Arnold Pärnama, and Sven Wichman.

At our fraternity get-togethers we still sang our old *Burschen Lied* in Latin:

> *Gaudeamus igitur,*
> *Juvenes dum sumus;*
> *Post molestam senectutem*
> *Nos habebit humus!*[2]

(A. D. 1781)

On the evening of December 23, 1955, I received a telegram from Dr. Leroy Calkins, head of the Department of OB/Gyn at the University of Kansas Medical Center with the following message: *You have been appointed a resident here, as July 1 1956. Please wire acceptance or rejection.*

This was my first offer of resident training in my chosen field.

I had also applied at the Columbia University Medical Center, among others. Hazel and I both would have liked to stay in New York, and Arno was happy to have companionship in his otherwise empty house. He liked Hazel's laid-back ways.

I was in a pickle now. The Kansas City people were waiting for my answer, ready to pick another applicant from their waiting list in case I did not give them a prompt answer.

I still had some of my penchant for "insidious intrusions" left from the previous decade. I traced down the head of the OB Department at Columbia at his home and inquired about my chances of obtaining resident status for the coming year.

"Well, young man, what's the hurry? We will have our departmental meeting sometime in January and then you'll hear from us."

"Sorry, sir, but I have received an offer from the University of Kansas and they want my yes or no. My wife and I would prefer Columbia if it were possible?"

"Congratulations! Professor Calkins from University of Kansas is a friend of mine and I assure you will be in good hands in Kansas City!" And with that he hung up.

Just imagine. Back then I could call a professor at home to inquire about my residency status!

Those were the good old days.

Today, I wouldn't get past answering machines that gave me Monday morning's office hours!

On the 24 December 1955 I sent the telegram to Kansas City accepting their residency offer.

I was even starting to look forward to life in Kansas City.

We had lived in the East and the West, and would now be in the geographical center of the USA. Besides all that, medical center training would be the best reference when it came time to look for a place to practice. To cheer up Hazel, I promised to let her choose the place where we would settle down after my residency.

As it turned out, that was one of the best decisions I ever made!

Still we did not know a thing about Kansas City.

We were not interested in encyclopedia facts, but wanted to know something about the people we would be living next to. Hazel had met a nurse who was from Kansas City, but all she could tell her was, "the people are friendly enough after you get to know them."

I still had months of internship left.

The winter months were dreary days of wind and snow.

I remember one such day working in the pediatric clinic, giving booster shots and treating children with coughs, colds, and earaches. The same afternoon I was accompanying a student nurse as she was taking a lively kid to x-ray. She couldn't keep the whippersnapper on the cart by herself.

There was a long waiting line at x-ray but lucky for us, Dr. Tofig was in charge of the "traffic". We had barely settled at the far end of the line when I noticed Dr. Tofig's flying windmill hands, he was signaling for us to come to the front of the line. I had to laugh, while Dr. Tofig was explaining to those in the waiting-line who the seriously ill child needed immediate x-raying, our little rascal kept on laughing and punching the poor nurse's ribcage.

Back at the seventh-floor pediatric clinic I found a baby sleeping on my examination table, sitting and wrapped in her mother's balled-up winter coat..

When I was ready to give her an injection, I asked the nurse to give me a hand.

She extended her hand towards me with a laugh, "Here it is, doctor!"

"You know what I mean. Just hold the baby for me!"

While we were bent over the child I wondered if my plea for help was flawed. Perhaps I had said: "Give me *your* hand"?

There was a lot of screaming when a fine needle penetrated the delicate skin, but after a colorful sticker was applied over the aching spot, the baby forgot all about crying and kept looking at her sky-blue "tattoo" featuring the smiling face of the sun.

In the next cubicle sat a middle-aged woman with her four-year-old son. For some reason I still remember her melancholy face:

Michael has bad tonsils.

One cold after another... Her husband has cancer of the colon... They have four small children...

The snow crystals just kept beating against the window, and there were no condolences for me to give.

Back in the healthy children's clinic, a mother with a soft smile and friendly eyes was waiting. She was holding her sleeping child against her breasts. The baby opened her eyes and her mouth was curved for a smile, but she changed her mind and gave a yawn. In the wide-open mouth there were only red gums and no sign of baby teeth yet.

Somehow I remember that day, just as ordinary as any other in the life of an intern at Queens General, almost half a century ago.

I can still see the dreary winter afternoon, with its gray clouds and snow, Dr. Tofig's flying hands, the bundled-up baby sleeping on my treatment table, and the laughing young nurse facing me with her out-stretched hand!

The past has become the present.

[1]Uku – the god of rain, wind, and thunder in Estonian mythology

[2]While we're young, let us rejoice,
  Singing out in gleeful tones;
  After youth's delightful frolics,
  And old age so melancholic,
  The earth will cover our bones.

Chapter 13

Kansas City

The days in Kansas are hot in August.

The afternoon sun hung like a heavy blanket over the city, and covered the ancient trees lining Genessee Street where Hazel and I had rented a furnished apartment covering the entire second floor. It was within walking distance of the university hospital where I was a first-year resident in the Department of OB/Gyn, and Hazel worked as an RN on the Gynecological surgical floor.

For the first six months I was assigned to pathology.

It was as far as one could get from the living female patients I was supposed to become an expert in, but at first I had to start with the study of surgical specimens.

The organs arrived in jars and basins, all carefully labeled with names and numbers, gathering on our specimen table: the breasts, pale and lifeless with hidden affliction, segments of dissected colon with its mesentery, placentas with infarcts, and a garden variety of uterine and ovarian tumors. Throw in a few TUR specimens from old men's prostate glands, and that would cover most of it.

And we, the pathology residents, we were like curious customers at some yard sale, picking and looking at them until the chief resident came and gave each of us his share.

At first one had to weigh and measure the given specimen and give a gross description of it. Then one had to dissect it with care and cut out small representative sections from the different areas of the growth for fixation. After that it would be sliced with a microtome into sections as thin as air, which were then placed on a slide, stained, and "read" under the microscope.

It was the very first time I used a Dictaphone.

Back then they looked exactly like water coolers on wheels with a foot-pedal. It was a most useful contraption, as our hands were too busy dissecting bloody specimens to write things down.

Then we went to see Dr. Bowley, the chief of Surgical Pathology, and together we studied the microscopic world of cancer under the double bi-ocular microscope. The normal tissues were delicate and orderly like a painting of a pastoral landscape. But where cancer cells had invaded, the landscape looked like it had been hit by a tornado or powerful earthquake.

As a rule Dr. Bowley confirmed our preliminary diagnoses, adding or changing a sentence or two. After that we dictated the final reports for our vivacious secretaries to type up so that Dr. Bowley could sign them.

The atmosphere in Surgical Pathology was spirited and full of optimism. We were all young.

The troubles we diagnosed were only pieces of tissue to us, belonging to someone we would never know and whose sorrows we would never be part of. Only the surgeons who came to consult with Dr. Bowley appeared morose with their wrinkled foreheads.

At first the pathology residents looked over my shoulder to give friendly advice, but after one month I was one of them and I could read garden-variety diseases as well as the rest of the gang.

This did not go unnoticed by Dr. Bowley.

The secretaries in the front office let me in on the circulating rumor: Dr. Bowley and the boys wouldn't mind if for some reason I were to change my mind and desert Dr. Calkins' department and become a pathologist instead.

It was true. I had become part of a happy family!

Our long dissection room reminded me of a kitchen where the residents looked like chefs in their white uniforms, sitting behind their fleshy specimens. At one end of the room, behind the open folding doors, sat the secretaries with their typewriters, always ready with a smile for anyone wanting to rest his eyes on a pair of shapely legs under their short dresses.

At the other end, behind the always-open door, Dr. Bowley was bent over his microscope. He was in his late fifties and had practiced family medicine in western Kansas before becoming a pathologist. It wasn't easy to practice on the open prairie with snowstorms in winter, and the scorching heat and tornadoes in summer.

And yes, he had delivered all his babies at home.

He told me about one case in an isolated farmhouse, where the farmer had stood behind him with a loaded shotgun. All the ruckus had started after Dr. Bowley had taken out a razor to give his wife's bottom a shave.

"Don't screw around with your razor, doc! Just deliver the baby or I'll fill you up with buckshot!"

Times have changed.

At that time it was a "must" to shave the parturient bottom, including the pubic hair. Today this practice has fallen to the wayside like the horse and plow. Ladies are delivered nowadays the way they are.

Amazing, isn't it? The prairie farmer was ahead of the times by half a century.

All this had been too much for a sensitive man like Dr. Bowley. He then studied to become a pathologist, and became one of the best.

This all made me waver, should I change my mind and become a pathologist?

For one thing, contrary to Dr. Bowley's department, the junior residents in Dr. Calkins' service were nobodies.

Dr. Hunter, who had trained under him several years ago, told a true story: he had worked in the hospital for several weeks in a row and was in dire need of a pair of new shoes. He went to see Dr. Calkins to get permission to leave the premises to buy a pair. After Dr. Calkins had inspected the soles of his worn-out shoes, he had said: "You go and get yourself a pair of new shoes and report back to me in half an hour." Never mind that Dr. Hunter was married and hadn't seen his young wife outside the hospital dining room for weeks.

In contrast: Dr. Bowley's surgical pathology department closed at five every evening and remained closed over the weekends.

What a life for the residential staff!

He had all of us, including his secretaries, over for Thanksgiving dinner. After the dinner the carpet was rolled up, and the record player geared up for dance music. Everybody swirled around the big room, carefree and content. Dr. Yunis, a curly-haired resident from Mexico, danced with every girl at the party (including Mrs. Bowley), while the old doctor sat in his easy chair and seemed to have the best of times.

Life in the OB department under Dr. Calkins was quite a different ballgame. Its true, the old man had mellowed, but Dr. Hunter's encounter made me wonder what life would be like in that no-nonsense department.

Besides, the first-year OB/Gyn resident's salary was $125 a month, while the pathology residents had an American Cancer Society tax-free grant, and collected a whopping $350.

Hazel's salary was in the $350 range, but it was still a tight squeeze with the car payments, rent, and all the rest. With that extra money as a pathology resident I could even afford the luxury of going to the Katz Drugstore and buying a whole box of Muriel cigars.

Times were tough at first. At KC we did not get paid before six weeks were up, and then they held the first four weeks' salary in an escrow account.

I have already told the story of how I wanted to borrow a lousy hundred bucks from Household Finance for my honeymoon, but they had turned me down. They said I had no collateral, and my "36 Ford, paid up and all, "wasn't worth a nickel." I was embarrassed to no end, and I did not want to go through that kind of rigamarole again any time soon.

I still had the $25 Government Savings Bond that Queen's General had given us interns as a departing gift. I had to cash it in before maturity and got only $18.50 for it. What really kept us afloat was Hazel's final paycheck of $120 from Queens General Hospital.

Well, I was not quite ready to switch to pathology, and took a wait-and-see attitude. Nobody had actually asked me to switch, and the entire hullabaloo had been nothing but talk anyway.

By then my three months of surgical pathology had ended, and for the next three months I was assigned to do autopsies in the pathology-building morgue.

The living people I worked with in that building were all very nice, but the dead ones gave me the willies. My nostalgic frame of mind clashed with the physical aspects of doing autopsies.

I don't mind *reading* about dead people and dying.

In fact, I rather enjoy it. Take for instance Flaubert's gravedigger, who grew potatoes in the empty plots and when the epidemic struck did not know whether to enjoy the deaths or regret the burials. Or Truman Capote's descriptions of the landscape when traveling from Noon City to Scully Landing, where the logs in the swamp looked like water-soaked corpses.

If they *look like* corpses there is literary beauty in the story. If they *are* corpses, all the resemblance to beauty has vanished.

Let me tell you about my first autopsy. Don't worry: I'm not going to disclose any gory details. I am only going to tell you *how I felt* about doing that kind of work.

I was in a cool room in the basement of the Pathology building with a concrete floor, tile-covered walls, and small glass-brick windows.

There were just two of us, the corpse and I.

The body of an elderly lady lay on the autopsy table, wrapped in a white shroud. I had to unwrap it before I could start, but I hesitated for a moment, because I did not know where to start.

I had never undressed a living female, and it seemed sacrilegious to disrobe a dead one.

Should I start by removing the sheet from her face and work down, or move from the feet up?

It seemed to be more civilized to start from her face, and that's what I did. A moment alter she lay naked on the autopsy table.

She had an emaciated body, and her skin had a yellowish tinge. Her pubic bone was prominent, covered with sparse gray hair, and her lack-luster eyes had a distant look.

I started with my autopsy, but had the eerie feeling that she was watching my every move. When I looked up to persuade myself that that wasn't the case, I saw a fly resting on her left eyeball. I have never seen a fly sitting on such a place before. I knew she was dead, but it seemed somehow odd to me that she did not even blink.

I chased the fly with my left hand, but it distracted me from what I was doing. The fly was as determined to return to its resting place as I was determined not to allow it. There was a flyswatter next to me, but I could not whack him by hitting the lady's face.

I gave up the duel, went to find a wet towel to cover her face, and finished my job without further incident.

When I told the pathology residents about my ordeal, they just shook their heads in disbelief. "You mean one fly could get you all derailed like that?"

The days were still hot in the early afternoon in late September.

At a moment when the darkness settled onto the treetops and the streetlights threw only faint shadows on the sidewalks, I was sitting in our second floor balcony. Hazel had gone to bed already, and I was enjoying a moment of solitude.

Then the phone rang.

We did not have any friends to call us at this hour.

The hospital would not call Hazel for extra duty, knowing that she had just worked 16 hours straight, the last eight hours as a Good Samaritan at the bedside of a student nurse struck with encephalitis. Holding down an unconscious but restless patient and doing tracheal suction is not only physically demanding, it is downright dangerous.

Knowing Hazel, she had just gone ahead and done it without any compensation or word of complaint, feeling an obligation toward a future nurse.

Perhaps someone was calling again to talk with the preacher who had lived in the apartment before us.

When I picked up the phone, I was surprised to find that the hospital ER was after me. Dr. Calkins had delivered a still born baby, and requested an immediate autopsy. According to the night supervisor, I was "the pathologist on call".

This was all news to me, and to my knowledge there was no such thing as an "emergency autopsy", especially on a stillborn infant. The pathology residents would have just turned over in bed and continued with their peaceful slumber, but I couldn't ignore a request coming from Professor Calkins himself.

I walked to the hospital Emergency Room to claim the body. There was no other way to transport the little corpse at this hour. Obviously the hospital had no previous experience with emergency autopsies at midnight.

I had to carry the corpse under my arm to the pathology building. It was a clear night with a full moon and a sky full of stars.

The day's heat had been replaced by a pleasant coolness. There was no wind to speak of. The sidewalk ran next to a well-traveled road, and at times I was blinded by the headlights of passing cars. To those drivers I must have looked like a thief carrying valuable loot under my arm.

The limp body wrapped in a white sheet of paper was heavy. *Rigor mortis* had not yet set in, and it bounced up and down like a rubber duck that was synchronized with each of my steps.

When I reached the autopsy building, about one hundred yards from the ER, I found its doors locked. I had forgotten to ask for the key!

I placed the dead baby on the steps just in front of the locked door, and started to walk back to the ER. I was almost there when it suddenly struck me, what if someone was to steal the thing? The white package, so inviting, was clearly visible from the road, and horror stories of body snatchers went through my mind.

I ran back and to my relief found the white package on the front steps in the full moonlight, just where I had left it. I still did not have the keys!

There was no other way to make the trip back to the ER than the two of us together.

I didn't feel like hiding the body under the nearby bushes.

By then I was already sweating from all the running and excitement. My perspiration had melted the paper wrapping and made the corpse at my side mighty slippery.

What if I dropped it? And who would be able to tell what was there before or after the fall!

I decided to hold the dead baby against my chest with both hands, the way they carry live ones. He sure was slippery, and I started to wonder if dead babies could sweat. It is well known that male corpses can grow beard, so why couldn't the body in my arms do some *post mortem* sweating?

There I was, carrying a dead baby in my arms on a summer night. I felt an odd bond between us.

I did not find anything wrong during the autopsy besides meconium stained amniotic fluid in his lungs.

For your information, Dr. Calkins did not inquire about the so-called "emergency autopsy" findings until he received the written report a month later.

He never knew of my ordeal. I kept the night adventure to myself, not wanting to give the pathology residents any extra reasons to question my sanity.

I must have been too aware of non-essentials, the things the others seemed to ignore. My aspiration to become a pathologist with a high salary had become history. I was just too damned sensitive even to become a decent psychiatrist.

There must have been too much chicken blood in my veins.

I realized the only specialization where I would feel at ease would be what I had chosen well before I started carrying corpses around.

I also understood that if I had any hidden talent in my chosen field, it would not have any practical applications in doing autopsies.

My service as a pathology apprentice was not over until 1 January, 1957. Before that date something else transpired to make my return to living patients seem light-years away.

Just before Christmas Dr. Qalfield, the chief resident in pathology, killed himself with a handgun in one of the autopsy rooms. He apparently had been a manic-depressive, an illness for which there was no effective treatment back then.

His fellow residents had the unpleasant duty of lifting him up on the next table and performing the autopsy. They also pulled toothpicks to see who would go and take the sad news to his wife and three small children. And it was Christmas Eve. This episode wrote the last chapter in my ambition to become a pathologist.

I don't remember much else about Christmas 1956, except the invitation Hazel and I received to attend Dr. Calkins' Christmas party with other departmental residents.

It was a formal kind of affair.

We all wore jackets with white shirts and ties, and stood around the gallon-size punch bowl filled with fruit juice. Before we helped ourselves, Mrs. Calkins poured in a whole bottle of white wine "for Christmas cheer", as she put it. We then sipped the red punch, holding our fancy glassware in one hand while the other held a napkin underneath so as not to drip any colored liquid onto our hostess's pale-pink carpet.

Dr. Quint, the second-year resident, had collected five dollars from each of us and presented an electrically powered shoe-shiner to Dr. Calkins as a Christmas present. In return, we received a 50-page booklet he had written a few years earlier, called "Normal Labor". They must have been leftovers collecting dust in some closet.

We all expressed our thanks and delight in receiving such a wonderful gift! Dr. Quint, who was more debonair than the rest of us, carried on a light conversation with Mrs. Calkins while we just stood there, drank our "Christmas Cheer", nibbled at the *hors d'oeuvres*, and made small talk with each other.

Dr. Calkins seemed satisfied with the whole affair, happy that no one bothered him as he stood by himself, enjoying his own drink. Its color was a dead give-away, it hadn't come from our common punch bowl.

After an hour, Dr. Quint thanked Dr. Calkins for the presents, which we were all "sure to treasure for years to come." The hostess was praised for the wonderful drink and tasty *hors d'oeuvres* of cheese and crackers. Then we all put our coats on, wished the professor and his family a "Merry Christmas" and left.

My first stint after the New Year started with service in gynecology, and in the very first week I pulled a blooper that could have cost me my residency.

It was my duty to do physical examinations on private patients the night before they went to surgery, and ask them to sign a surgery permit. Having dealt with autopsies for the last three months and collected signed permits from the next of kin. I walked to one of Dr. Calkins patients, a distinguished-looking black lady, and said in a casual way:, "Would you be so kind as to sign your autopsy permit for tomorrow?"

The old lady jumped up from her bed in horror. I was afraid she was going to have apoplexy then and there and die under my very eyes.

I couldn't have blamed her.

She was scared about her operation in the first place, and now this! I corrected myself and apologized profusely. I explained to her over and over that I was only asking her to sign the *operation* permit. It had nothing to do with autopsies.

It took her a while to calm down. She got out her glasses, read the permit over a few times, and finally signed it.

I sat on pins and needles for the whole week and wondered whether she would complain to Dr. Calkins about the incident. But the chief remained his usual calm and cool self, and after the patient was dismissed safe and sound, I felt like sending her a dozen roses.

I sure would have sent it too, if I had had the resources for such an extravagance.

Dr. Hunter, an associate professor in the Gyn department, was doing a research on vaginal flora and its relationship to developing malignant changes of the uterine cervix. It was known that certain lifestyles predisposed women to those changes.

He had obtained permission to examine incarcerated juvenile females from one of the institutions in central Kansas to secure smears, cultures, and Pap smears from a class of patients different from those seen regularly in private practice.

I was to be his assistant.

That was some change of scenery all right, from the morgue to a penal institution. It was my first time in a prison and the assignment, I would say, was rather extraordinary.

We got all set in the prison infirmary, with our test tubes and culture media and all kinds of solutions and slides piled up on the table.

The female wardens had the inmates line up for the occasion, but the going was slow. There was just one examination table and some of our "patients" were restless.

They made quite indecent comments about our work and us. Some of them kept taking off their undergarments before they were asked. Once they got to take their turns on the examination table, we saw that their lower anatomy often featured tattoos of reptiles and dragons. Some had quotations engraved on their exposed abdomens, and not from Shakespeare either. I remember some of the etchings just above the pubic hairline, the wording borrowed from familiar doormat greetings such as "Welcome" and "Come On In".

It would not be proper for me to comment any further about our findings. We carried the specimen boxes to Dr. Hunter's lab, where the technicians forked for weeks sorting them out. I have to confess I know nothing about the test results. But Dr. Hunter was soon appointed a full professor, and became the head of an OB/Gyn department in one of he Midwestern states.

Besides me there were two other first-year residents, Dr. Fred Korkmas from Texas and Dr. Beverly Robinson from Iowa.

The chief resident was Dr. Goedert, a tall and friendly fellow. He had an unusual combination of characteristics. Besides being a hard worker and a good surgeon, he was the most cheerful fellow in the entire department. He loved his work and used to spend days and nights in the hospital. Only after his wife had joined him for lunch at the university cafeteria wearing a red dress did Dr. Goedert feel obligated to spend the following night at home.

Dr. Steele was one year ahead of me in training. He was a heavy-set man with a serious face and no-nonsense attitude. He sure was a heavy smoker, and when we both happened to be on call the same night, he kept me awake with his coughing spells. He treated his spells by sitting up in bed and smoking another cigarette.

He had been a GP in western Kansas before entering residency training in Kansas City. I had to accompany him on morning rounds, and it was a bore with a capital B. He sat down at every patient's bed to inquire about her bowel movements. Then he pulled down the covers, felt their bellies, and asked about grandmother's asthma back home.

He never seemed to be satisfied with the size of the cone-shaped excision of cervices I made. It was the way we treated pre-malignant lesions. He practically wanted amputation, but I knew better. I had seen plenty of these "cones" in my pathology service, and mine compared favorably with any of them. Getting too aggressive with that sharp-nosed #11 blade scalpel can get you into big trouble. One could easily perforate the narrow portion of the uterine neck and enter the peritoneal cavity. The bleeding which might ensue from this misstep would not show up through the vaginal back, but would rather find its way into the abdominal cavity, and that wouldn't be easy to fix.

Dr. Villareal was a second-year resident from Columbia who arrived in Kansas City with his wife and child. His father allegedly owned a large spread of land with thousands of heads of cattle back in South America. Obviously he was not pressed for money like the rest of us.

He spoke almost flawless English and his Latin charm and bedside manners were irreproachable. Those characteristics did not go unnoticed by the sportive girls from Kansas City. There were rumors that placed him in nearby motels some nights. Whenever anyone raised the question of his whereabouts after the fact, his answer would always be the same: he had been "on call".

Dr. Korkmas was a Texan of Lebanese descent, and still an eligible bachelor. He had his share of female admirers. His patients complained that he was too "rough" with his pelvic exams. Back then there were no sonograms, CAT-scans, or MRI-s and some toughness was inevitable when doing what we used to call "a thorough pelvic exam".

Perhaps Fred was particularly diligent in his scrutiny of hidden pelvic pathologies.

Dr. Beverly Robinson was just called Bev. She was the only female resident among us, and was liked by everyone.

When I happened to be on OB call the same night with Bev, she did not always follow the ground rules of taking turns to deliver the labor patients. At times she let me sleep all night while she carried the entire load by herself. The morning after she looked pretty ragged, her eyeglasses specked with fine droplets of dried blood and amniotic fluid. When I asked her why she did not call me, she looked at me through her spotted eyeglasses and smiled, "Oh, it wasn't bad. I just hated to wake you up! I got a wink of sleep myself in the nurses' locker room."

There were no special facilities for female doctors.

I slept in an air-conditioned room reserved for the residents on call. It had two beds and a private bathroom with showers. She, being of the opposite sex, had to use the nurses' dressing room and I don't know whether there was even a bed to sleep in. At times she tried to catch a wink between deliveries by using a labor room, but only if there happened to be a vacancy.

Then the KCGS[1] dinner meeting came up at the Hotel Muehlenbach. I let Bev go with "I'll watch the store for you."

When Dr. Calkins heard that Bev was going, he pulled out his wallet and gave her a $1 bill to buy herself a drink at the bar.

This itself was most unusual. Dr. Calkins was not foolish with his money. He must have taken a liking to Bev.

When Bev returned, I was busy filling out the required four-page delivery forms. Every stage of labor and delivery had to be recorded in minute detail. From the station of the baby's head in the pelvis to the position of the suture lines. Did the head rotate to the right or left, how many contractions the patient had during descent, how many on the perineum, etc.

It took longer to finish the labor record than to deliver the baby. If you had two patients ready to go and didn't have a chance to make a note about those rotations, you had no choice but to exercise some creativity in filling out those forms. But you had to be careful and not let your imagination run wild: The baby's head would not usually make any gyroscopic movements when still inside the pelvis. The old man knew all the rotations and you might get into trouble if you happened to have too creative a mind.

Well, I was filling out these darned forms when Bev returned from the meeting in a bubbly mood. She even told a joke she had told over a period of three years, and the trouble was that I didn't get it.

Bev got red in the face. She was too embarrassed to repeat it. It was really a clean joke, but could become "tainted" if the listener had a dirty mind. But, repeat it she did, and I laughed after the punchline like I was supposed to. But, I still didn't get it.

You can draw your own conclusion, I was a simpleton, or maybe I just had an "unpolluted" mind.

———

One day, when I was the only doctor in the delivery suite and no one was in labor, a woman was sent from the prenatal clinic with the diagnosis of "Pregnancy at term, in early labor".

After the nurse had helped her undress and supplied her with a paper gown, I came in to check her. I could not hear fetal heart tones not could I palpate the outline of her enlarged uterus. A pelvic examination solved the riddle: her uterus was quite small with an abundance of abdominal fat. She wasn't even pregnant, let alone in labor!

It just so happens that in the regular prenatal clinic the "doctors" were the senior medical students. The resident physician was consulted only if the medical students found something unusual, something they couldn't handle, but this lady had fooled them all. She had stopped menstruating and had morning sickness. They found no reason to consult with the resident physician, and pregnancy tests were almost unheard of back then.

The only pregnancy test available was the so-called *Friedman's Test*, and it was almost as slow and tedious as sending a man to the moon.

First one had to collect the woman's urine, and then inject it into a female rabbit. After 48 hours one would then kill the rabbit to examine the ovaries. If there was evidence of recent ovulation, the person who produced the urine sample was declared pregnant.

It is obvious that those tests were rarely done to diagnose pregnancy, but were used rather to rule out hormone-producing intra-uterine tumors that mimicked pregnancy.

Getting back to our subject: the medical students had taken the patient's word about the baby kicking and when they listened for fetal heart tones, they had mistakenly counted the mother's heartbeat instead.

"How is my labor progressing?"

It was left to me to break the sad news to her:

"Ma'am, you're not in labor because you're not even pregnant."

She did not believe me.

"What do you mean? In the clinic they told me I was in labor and I'd have my baby today!"

"It all has been a big mistake."

"How can it be? I have been attending the clinic for months and I have been reassured that the baby was growing by leaps and bounds. Even this morning, when I started with my labor pains, I was told I'll have my baby today!"

"Well, those doctors at the clinic are young and have to see too many patients in a hurry. They have gone by what you've told them. I am sorry to tell you there is no baby coming."

She broke down and cried a spell.

Her entire world had collapsed. She had repainted the baby's bedroom, had bought the crib and some toys. She had even been preparing for the upcoming wedding! "You see, my boyfriend promised to marry me after I gave him a child."

There was not much I could say. This was not a typical case of *pseudocyesis* – false pregnancy – which is usually diagnosed within the first three months.

She continued to sob, still wrapped in a paper gown, sitting high on that old examination table with a bumpy mattress.

I sat on a low chair and kept looking out the window.

There was no way I could comfort her.

I couldn't claim she was pregnant, not could I make her boyfriend marry her.

Sometimes it isn't easy being a doctor...

I can recall another embarrassing event during my obstetrical service, embarrassing for doctor as well as patient. I might as well tell you about it and ask you try and put yourself in the position of either party.

First, as you might know, back then there were no fetal sonograms and the baby's sex was not known until *after* delivery.

I do not think much of the pictures they give out nowadays showing the tiny fetus, still inside the womb. They now use the sonogram to predict the baby's sex when the mother is only three months pregnant.

It's like opening a Christmas present in July.

Don't get me wrong, I love pictures of babies all right, but *after* they are born. Those all-black-shadowy reproductions of unborn fetuses turn me off. I like the question "boy or girl?" answered *after* the delivery, when the doctor makes the big announcement.

Well, making the big announcement sounds simple enough. But one day I just couldn't tell, *after* I had delivered the baby!

From behind the baby looked like a girl but from the front, one didn't need a post-graduate degree to call it a boy.

My first announcement was "it's a girl," and when a moment later I called it a boy I got the parents all confused, "Hey, doc! Make up your mind, what is it then, a boy or a girl?"

You could well imagine the dilemma that followed:

What should they tell their in-laws, waiting in line with the question "is it a boy or a girl?"

What should I tell the anxious parents?

I don't want to go into all kind of confusing issues of diagnosis and treatment, only to say that the baby was genetically a female. The mother's adrenal glands had been producing an excess of male hormone and making the tiny clitoris grow to the size of a male infant's penis. With proper hormonal treatment and surgical removal of her "false penis", she would grow up as a regular girl.

Think about it: the sonogram would have made a bad situation even worse by calling the girl a boy six months before the actual birth.

December 17, 1957 was an important day for me.

I became a United States citizen. I passed the oral examination about the US Constitution without a problem, but what I had to struggle with beforehand gave me a few sleepless hours.

By now you know the troubles I had with my surname "Ojamaa". No one could spell it, no one could pronounce it. It had become an annoyance being called everything from "Omaha" to "Pajamas". Seeing patients in the University Clinics, it was my practice to start by introducing myself, "I am Dr. Ojamaa." The question then put to me was, "What did you say your name was?" followed by "How do you spell it?" and then even "What kind of name is that?" And the final question, "Wow, where are you from?"

It seemed that the patient was interviewing me and not the other way round. Besides, I didn't enjoy answering these personal questions.

I knew a smart surgical resident, Dr. Kornfield, and I sought out his advice. As you know, when becoming a citizen one can pick any name, and that would become your official name as spelled out on your new Social Security card.

"It is important that doctors have a name the patient can remember easily and pronounce," Kornfield told me. "It is also important that your name starts with an "a". You will be listed in the Yellow Pages in the phonebook alphabetically and if your name starts with a "w", the patient could well be dead before he gets that far.

My family name had already changed once, in 1934. Before that year is was "Bachblum", and back in Estonia we had a heck of a time with that one too. Nobody could pronounce it or spell it. It was a German name and meaning "Brook flower". Well, we changed it to "Ojamaa", meaning "river land". We could not very well take the name of "Brookflower"!

If you ask me how far back in history our old name Bachblum goes, I would say to 1816 or thereabouts. Before that time the peasants had a first name only. That year a new law was passed that everybody had to have a family name too.

The peasants with their families were lined up in front of the local German landowners, the *barons* who just pulled the names out of a hat, so to speak. For instance, a man with many children was given the name *Kindermacher* (Childrenmaker). One of my ancestors must have lived near the Kunda River and had a beautiful daughter, thus "Riverflower". So much for our history.

I decided to take "Ojamaa" as my middle name and take my wife's maiden name "Ashby" as my last name (Hazel had two sisters and no brother). Perhaps, it was too English sounding, but it had the virtues of being easy to remember, easy to pronounce, and easy to spell.

[1]Kansas City Gynecological Society

Chapter 14

TO COLUMBIA AND BACK

As part of my training, starting 1 January, 1958, I was to spend six months in Ellis Fischel Cancer Hospital in Columbia, Missouri, about 130 miles north of Kansas City. Going there, where nobody knew my previous name, it was easy to be Dr. Ashby.

The house staff there was a mixed breed of surgical and urological residents, and physicians from different hospitals in the state. I was the only gynecology resident from the state of Kansas. Because I was now in the state of Missouri, the University of Kansas refused to pay my monthly salary of $125. When Dr. Rhodes, a member of the visiting staff, heard about my ordeal, he thought it a terrible injustice. He called the Missouri Cancer Society and talked them into paying my salary for the coming six months.

There were about six visiting residents. We got room and board and in the evening watched old cowboy movies on TV or played table tennis. Weekdays we assisted in surgery, cared for the post-op patients, and did autopsies on the unfortunate ones.

An operation called a "pelvic sweep" took up to eight hours to perform, with one half-hour break in the middle. A sterile towel was thrown over the incision and the patient was kept under anesthesia as we ate our lunch and used the bathroom.

The named operation was performed on female patients who had persistence or recurrence of their cervical cancer after they had already received the maximum X-ray and/or cobalt therapy. Their vital tissues could not tolerate more of the same.

It was the most dehumanizing and destructive operation I was ever involved in. To me it seemed like performing an autopsy on a living person.

I might as well say what it involved and why it took so long from start to finish. All the pelvic organs had to be removed and that included the rectum, vagina, bladder, uterus with ovaries, and peri-aortic and pelvic lymph nodes. The kidneys were made to drain into a new "bladder" constructed from a loop of small bowel, which was to drain into a plastic bag attached to the abdominal wall, next to another sack collecting the solid waste.

I remember a young woman of twenty-seven who had this kind of operation and when the pathologist examined the surgical specimen, no residual cancer was found. The pelvic mass thought to be cancer, was brought about by leakage of the large bowel due to too aggressive radiation treatments.

I don't want to leave Ellis Fischel Hospital on a sour note.

The clinic days every Tuesday and Thursday brought in folks from the backwoods of Missouri and the Ozarks hill country, where they still brewed ill-legit moonshine and had gun battles with the revenue agents.

If they had doctors over there, they were old-timers, using folksy diagnoses and treatments. To interpret some of the ancient death certificates one sure did not need to know any Latin: they used terms anyone could comprehend, such as: Cause of death: *"Don't know. Went to bed healthy, woke up dead"*; or *"Don't know. Never been fatally ill before"*; or *"Primary cause of death: ax in the head, contributing factor: neighbor's wife."*

On one of those clinic days a bearded man brought in his 80-year-old mother. She did not have much else to complain about except the heartburn brought on by drinking corn liquor. The doctor back in the hill-country had examined her and said it was all due to a tumor or cancer in her belly, and had asked him to take his mother to the cancer hospital in Columbia.

The old lady did not say much and continued chewing her tobacco.

Without much ado we stretched her out on the examination table and pulled her dress up and her pants down in order to feel her abdomen. No question about it: there was a hard mass filling her lower abdomen up to her naval, something with the shape and consistency of a bowling ball. None of us had felt anything like that before.

Well, she was taken to X-ray and after the picture was taken and developed we all looked at it dumbfounded, a large stone filled her abdomen, but one could still identify segments of small bones in its center. Further questioning of the old lady gave us the answer, "It must be at least fifty years ago when I was still a young woman and in the family way. The baby was kicking and everything."

"One day I was raking hay in the field when an awful lightning and thunder struck. It scared me out of my wits and I hid in the haystack. Then the pouring rain came and I started having my labor pains. When the storm was finally over, I had no more pain and walked home, but my baby never came. For awhile I wondered about it , but then I forgot all about it until you fellows started to poke my belly and ask me all these questions."

The medical term for it is: *lithopedian* or, in folksy terms, a "womb stone". An extremely rare occurrence, and almost unheard-of that late in pregnancy. The most amazing thing was that she had carried it in her belly over half of a century, until it had mummified and finally turned into rock.

We assured her that she did not have cancer, and that her inability to tolerate corn liquor was in no way part of her fifty-year-old pregnancy.

When she was rolled out from X-ray, her son was standing there and inquired: "What kind of tumor does my mother have?"

Radiologist Dr. Sala, a smart aleck, answered, "It ain't no tumor, it's your brother."

And on that happy note I'll leave Columbia and join "that old gang of mine" at the Department of Women and Their diseases at KC.

After my six months at Ellis Fishel I had earned my two weeks vacation. Hazel and I drove up to Canada to visit her relatives in Whitby.

Dr. Calkins hadn't given any signs of approval or disapproval of my work, which was usual. But he sure liked Hazel, which I considered unusual. When he made his morning rounds, Hazel had to be found to accompany him because she knew all about his patients without stumbling through their charts. On the first day of my return, Dr. Calkins observed, "About time to be back!" but then added as an afterthought, "I don't care about you, but is *Hazel* back?"

He had a whole bunch of residents and he probably didn't care about our whereabouts, but Hazel was his star nurse. She had all the information about Calkins' patients stored in her head and could shoot out the required information in a fraction of a second.

It did not take long before Hazel was appointed to the position of head nurse on the Gyn surgical floor.

Dr. Tom McGuire was a resident with black-rimmed glasses and a no-nonsense attitude. He was all business, and brave and bright enough to initiate a debate with Dr. Calkins himself.

After Dr. Calkins had retired as the head of the department, a new appointee arrived. He was a most talented young man and a Rhodes Scholar. He knew the answer to every question and could solve any problem, regardless how complicated.

Before his arrival, we called a retropubic operation for stress incontinence a Marshall-Marchetti" operation. After his arrival it became the "Marshall-Marchetti-Krantz" operation. The latter was really the official designation with Dr. Krantz's name belatedly added to the operation. He had done dissecting and tissue staining on the backside of the female pubic bones, and found a previously unknown layer of fascia one could sew the falling bladder to.

One day we had a small group conference.

I do not remember what the subject of discussion was, but I remember Dr. Krantz had reasoned his point of view convincingly and at length. He wanted even the dumbest resident to get the facts straight, for now and forever. However, after someone had mentioned the name of a professor from another university who had an opposing view on the subject, Dr. Krantz surprised us all with his answer, "Don't tell me about *that* guy. He's so stupid he doesn't even know how to masturbate!"

Well. That sure disproved the opposing view conclusively.

During Dr. Calkins' tenure we used to do both midline- and mediolateral episiotomies, depending on the circumstances. Dr. Krantz requested that we do only midline episiotomies so long as he was chairman of the department. When we wondered about women with a short perineum and large baby where laceration of the rectum might occur with a midline cut, he gave us a statistic no one could argue with: he had delivered ten thousand babies with midline episiotomies without a single tear to the rectum.

During his first delivery at KC we were all gathered around to see how well the ML episiotomy really worked.

Unfortunately, the rectal sphincter split.

Stillness hung in the air, broken by Dr. McGuire's count, "Ten-thousand-and-one!"

There were no social hours for the house staff as there had been in New York and its free city called Queens. The unmarried residents and interns used to have parties with the invitation, "We have the girls. You bring your own booze."

Liquor was expensive and one could not spend a month's salary to throw a party. There were, however, plenty of girls willing to meet young physicians at their cocktail parties, hoping it might lead to a more meaningful relationship.

The married couples got together for a home-cooked dinner with a glass of wine. I do not recall ever eating in a restaurant except at the KCGS meetings, where the society picked up the tab.

Mrs. Mary Wagner served the best dinner parties for our residents, at her residence. She was the social secretary and receptionist for Dr. Calkins and had taken the job for a change of scenery. (One can get tired of playing bridge every day of the week.) In her early fifties, she still had a striking figure and the physical appearance of a refined lady. She had gone through three husbands. All of them had started their own business by using Mrs. Wagner's resources, and all these enterprises had failed. After spending a considerable amount of her money with no end in sight, Mrs. Wagner had turned off the money supply and the husbands had departed.

She confessed to being just too gullible and unlucky in picking her lovers.

In later years, when Hazel and I returned to Kansas City for medical seminars, we never failed to invite Mrs. Wagner to have dinner with us at our hotel. At one of those get-togethers I asked if she had heard from the other residents she had been a generous host to in the past.

She took a puff from the cigarette that she was holding in her classy way, blew smoke in the air, and said "no".

Well. People get involved in their endeavors such as busy practices, society meetings, and dinner dates at their country clubs. Perhaps it is unreasonable to expect distinguished doctors to remember wuch small favors as happy hours and dinners at Mrs. Wagner's place way back in KC.

The years in residency training in KCMC were not as colorful or memorable as my internship on the East Coast. The university training involved more teaching, conferences, presenting papers at the departmental meetings, weekly journal reviews, and the like. It was more class-oriented, with high superiors and low interns and, at the very bottom, medical students. The residents were squeezed somewhere in between, with more obligation than authority. You didn't get much of a feeling of belonging, there were just too many chiefs and not enough Indians.

Those were the teenage years in my medical profession. Some episodes, fragmentary and unrelated, are still clear in my memory. Some of the unusual ones I have chosen to describe as they might be seen in the context of medical practice.

The time had come to get my "feet wet" in private practice, somewhere in the American heartland.

Chapter 15

SHEBOYGAN, HERE I COME...

Have you ever heard of a town called Sheboygan?

I hadn't, until four girls from that city sang on the *Arthur Godfrey Show*. They sang about "A Little Dutch Girl in Sheboygan", and the words went:

> *"I warm so easy—so dance me loose,*
> *Dance me loose, dance me loose.*
> *I warm so easy, so dance me loose,*
> *It shines so bright the moon..."*

These singing girls were called the *Chordettes,* and they went to fame and fortune with that catchy tune and many others, including "Mister Sandman" and "Mention My Name in Sheboygan". The girls were real, full of charm and sex appeal. But did this place called Sheboygan exist in real life, or was it just a fairy-tale place?

Well, one evening Vince Meyer from Sheboygan called and straightened me out. The place was not from never-never land, but a real town on the shore of Lake Michigan, inhabited by 48,048 real, but amiable people.

Of course, Vince didn't mention the *Chordettes* and their "Dance Me Loose" song. He was the manager of the Sheboygan Clinic of twelve physicians. Hazel and I were invited to visit their lovely town. In a case of mutual admiration, I was asked to join the clinic as the thirteenth member of the group (that lucky number thirteen again).

This all happened back in the fall of 1959.

I had finished my residency at KUMC and was promoted to instructor in the department, making a whopping $500 a month. As a recent capitalist I had bought a whole box of Murial cigars from the Katz drugstore, a luxury I could only have dreamed about before. A born showoff, I kept it on the coffee table at Gennesee Street. Every time I passed that table, I didn't fail to eye the box of cigars with the "Mona Lisa look-alike" picture on its lid. It gave my ego a lift every time. It really did.

Hazel and I had started asking ourselves where we should settle down.

I was aware that I could easily double or triple my income outside Kansas City. Doctors back then were not a dime a dozen, unlike today, and as a young physician I found myself sought after. I received more invitations to visit potential places of employ than I could manage.

How would anybody know that a young physician was looking for a place to call home after twenty years of wandering? Those hospitals, clinics, and localities who needed a doctor habitually called university hospital heads, asking about the availability of trained physicians.

In our department the calls came to Dr. Calkins' office, and his private secretary and receptionist happened to be nobody other than Mrs. Mary Wagner. She took all those calls, and her recommendation carried more weight than a full page of advertising in the AMA Journal. We had developed a mutual admiration, and she gave out my phone number like lottery tickets.

My phone, dead for four years, lit up like a switchboard. I received calls from several states, including one from Washington D.C. offering me a job at an American oil company hospital in Saudi Arabia.

We had already visited a few places, such as Hill City on a wind-blown prairie and Hannibal on the high banks of the wild Mississippi River, when I received an invitation to visit Dragenton in Utah, a small mining town at the foothills of the high Sierras. The place, so peaceful with its snowcapped mountains, put me under its spell. It reminded me of Shangri-La, a place in the high Tibetan mountains where youth lasted forever and time stood still for centuries.

During our train ride back to Kansas City I couldn't praise the place enough, but I couldn't get a word out of Hazel: whenever I tried to prod some encomia out of her, she seemed to have lost her ability to speak.

———————

I hadn't yet entirely recovered from my "Magic Mountain disease" when the trip to Sheboygan came up in late October. I had been already pre-conditioned by the *Chordettes* with their charm and songs, then it wasn't surprising that both of us found this small town inviting. We had dinner with the Clinic doctors and their wives at the old Foeste Hotel. I remember sitting next to Dr. Hoon, a jovial rotund surgeon who didn't forget to mention the fact that he had trained at the Mayo Clinic. I was impressed. One couldn't get any higher without hitting the clouds.

Dr. Windsor, a young surgeon, inserted a bit of wisdom: "The three most over-rated things are sex, Saturday night, and yes... the Mayo Clinic!"

I had to take his observation seriously. He was an Ivy League graduate himself, from Princeton.

During our flight back to Kansas City, Hazel regained her ability to talk. She made the statement: "I would like to settle down in Sheboygan, more than anywhere else."

Good old Hazel! No snow-capped mountains, open prairies, or high banks of the Missouri River could dissuade her.

We would be heading to Sheboygan, for better or worse!

And so it came to be that we moved to this picturesque town with our cocker spaniel and a few pieces of furniture.

Over four decades have passed since that day and I have to admit, we made the right decision.

To get to Sheboygan in those days you had to take old highway #141 from Milwaukee and travel 50 miles north through tranquil landscapes with prosperous farms, the corn high and the meadows growing green. To your right you got glimpses of the great Lake Michigan, which at times hid itself behind the rolling hills and woods only to appear again, its majestic blueness filling half the horizon. Driving through this dreamy landscape made you feel like every day was Sunday.

And then comes the city, the home of the Bratwurst, Kingsbury beer, and the Stumpf-fiddle. This last looks like a cello with a pogo stick on the bottom and a horn attached. To play it you had to synchronize the pogo stick with fiddling and blowing the horn on the right beat. Liberace used to play Saturday nights at the old Foeste Hotel, but that was before the Stumph-fiddle era.

Sheboygan was also called "Sin City", if I can brag about its colorful past. In the late nineteenth century and up to the 1920s there were Happy Houses on Michigan Avenue and at the riverfront. Some naughtiness perhaps added excitement to everyday, mundane life; who would be there to throw the first stone, anyway? But, this was all history by the time I showed up. As a gynecologist, I think I would have caught wind of such pastimes.

Its more recent designation as the City of "Children, Chairs, Cheese and Churches" would be a better account of its daily life.

My office was located on the second floor at the southeast corner of the old Clinic building, a space previously occupied by Dr. Florence Duckering. She had been the only board-certified obstetrician in town, but sudden illness had forced her to retire at the age of 48.

One of the windows at the corner office looked west onto North 8th Street, the main thoroughfare of the business district. It was like any main street in a small town, most of the buildings dating back to the previous century.

Just across, kitty-corner, was the old Foeste Hotel. And across Ontario Avenue stood the Rex Theater, advertising the current box-office extravaganza *Ben Hur*.

Next to that was the Bock Drug Store, with a narrow stairway leading upstairs to Dr. A.B.C. Bock's office. He had practiced obstetrics and pediatrics since the mid-1930s, and as an eligible bachelor had been popular among his obstetrical patients. The passing years had slowed him down along with his practice, but he was still the master of difficult mid-forceps techniques for delivering babies, procedures that had fallen to the wayside with time and were replaced by Cesarean sections. He was so agile with those forceps that the nurses had just one thing to worry about, to have the seat right under him when he sat down and started to extract the baby, or our good doctor might find himself sitting on the floor, forceps and all.

Then came Rudnick's Brothers Jewelry, established way back in the previous century. The two brothers were first-rate craftsmen who could fix any of your valuable timepieces from grandfather clocks to the tiniest lady's watch, or rebuild or repair your most treasured jewelry. You never needed to worry about leaving your Christmas shopping to the last minute; you could always drop in at Rudnick's and find the perfect gift for the lady of the house.

Next to it was Rupp's, the bar and diner where businessmen congregated in the long windowless bar over lunch hour and where the clinic physicians had their noon meal every Wednesday. Rupp's steak sandwiches were the juiciest in town, and they washed down easy with a cold glass of the local Kingsbury beer.

Further south, past Sears, came Prange's, the classiest store in town, a place where your imagination could run wild over the three floors plus a basement. They sold quality merchandise, from groceries to furniture to ladies wear, and everything in between. On the ground floor were the candy department and WILL CALL with the breakfast counter, where the old folks used to linger with their morning coffee and talk about the good old days.

Prange's motto *"It's not yours "til you like it"* made everything returnable, even the fancy evening dress you wore at the "Heart Ball" on

Saturday night. You could still return it Monday morning for a full refund. Only thing you might want to avoid the *Sheboygan Press* photographer at the event, or you might be featured on the society page wearing that fabulous evening gown you returned.

The window in my office that faced North 8th Street overlooked the Fountain Park with full-grown oak and maple trees. In its center was a two-story sextangular structure. At street level was the park's Public Comfort Station, and above it an open bandstand where old-time oom-pah-bands used to play *Wiener Blut* and beer-barrel polkas on Saturday nights. At times the texts of popular songs were projected onto a screen for public participation, just like the television show *Sing Along with Mitch.*

In the right corner of the park, just across from my window, stood the Civil War Memorial. This was an obelisk that had on its top a soldier who held his rifle and gazed through my office window at the ladies as they undressed behind the screen for their upcoming examinations.

That screen itself was a museum piece. It was only six feet high and didn't fold out any wider than that, thus giving only limited privacy. There was no place for the ladies to hang their garments, and they had to throw slips and other intimate items over its top. Perhaps this was OK in the days of Dr. Florence Duckering, but as a male physician I found the practice distracting. I had a hanging curtain installed and added a clothing stand, where the ladies could hang their clothes.

––––––––––

Just outside my office was Cory's appointment desk.

She was the receptionist, in her mid-20s and always cheerful. It gave me a lift to see a good-looking young woman who could give a hearty laugh in mid-sentence.

She was eager to comfort me when I glanced at the empty pages in my appointment book, "They are coming, Dr. Ashby, they are coming! Look, I just added another new OB to your book!"

She must have recalled the days of Dr. Duckering, when all the pages were filled for weeks to come. Dr. Duckering had retired a few months before I arrived in town and her patients had scattered. Besides family physicians charged $60 for delivery, while my bill came to a high $125.

––––––––––

Cory had been married for a few years and had nothing to show for it. The in-laws had become impatient, and made it a point to stare at her

413

abdominal profile whenever they had the chance.

Well, Cory came down with appendicitis instead.

The surgeon who removed the appendix had taken a good look inside, and declared, "You have an infantile uterus, and you will never get pregnant!"

It was not considerate of Cory to get pregnant even before her appendectomy incision had healed. The floor nurses were all smiles when Cory added her name to my appointment book with the "New OB" designation.

Just across from Cory's desk was Dr. Senty's office. It was comforting to know that free consultation was readily available when I discovered a heart murmur or irregular pulse in any of my OB patients. He was an internist, a truly knowledgeable and compassionate physician.

Further down the hallway were the offices that had belonged to Dr. Harry Heiden, but unoccupied at present. Harry had retired recently in his mid-70s, having practiced medicine in Sheboygan since the First World War.

One day when I was reading the "Green Journal"[1], a tall wiry man with a friendly face entered my office, put out his big hand, and said, "I am Dr. Heiden."

He took a seat next to me, stretched out his long legs, and after a short exchange of niceties he started to talk about his past practice.

At first he had started in pediatrics, but the small town had little use for him and his specialty. The family doctors did all the deliveries, and took care of the babies until they grew up and had their own babies.

Well, Dr. Heiden couldn't make a go of it.

He went back to Milwaukee to learn the ropes of obstetrics to deliver his own babies so he could practice his pediatrics. "That got me started, and pretty soon I was hard at work."

When Dr. Willard Huibregste, a family doctor, heard that story, he gave his short laugh and waved his hand as if chasing flies, "Don't tell me about old Harry!

"Whenever he had a patient in labor he went right over, stretched out on the front porch, and slept until the baby was ready to drop. In winter, when it was too cold on the porch he would lie down across the foot of his labor patient's bed and sleep soundly through all this whooping and hollering. They had to shake him awake to catch the baby!"

414

Later on I queried Dr. Heiden himself about his sleeping habits. He just grinned, "You know those attic apartments with inverting walls and a low ceiling? I'm a tall fellow and at times there wasn't even room for me to stand up and I had to deliver many of my patients down on my knees.

"Naturally I had to rest my kneecaps beforehand."

Going back to Dr. Huibregtse.

Everybody called him "Old Huey", or just plain "Huey". And *did* he have *patients*.

No wonder all the surgeons cozied up to him, looking for referrals, a gallbladder here, an appendectomy there. Add hemorrhoids and hernias, and that was the reason they were all extra-nice to Huey. They listened carefully to what he had to say, and when Huey made a witty remark they all laughed (willingly).

Huey had taken a liking to me. When I was called for consultations, I ran upstairs to his office, taking two steps at a time. You see, he had loads of old female patients with "fallen wombs". But the womb does not fall down alone, it drags the bladder along with it.

This kind of a prolapse could make a lady's life miserable, and at times they didn't even feel like leaving the house. Back then they didn't even have "Depends", and what good would those have done you anyhow!

I was fixing up Huey's patients left and right, and everyone seemed to be happy with the results. One 85-year-old lady stopped me in the street to tell me she was taking cha-cha lessons when before she didn't even dare to go to church.

I remember one patient who was willing to have the corrective surgery performed, but we had some difficulties with terminology. She didn't just want to be "fixed up", she wanted to be "original" again. I mentioned different possibilities of "rejuvenation", but she insisted she only wanted to be "original", or she would take her business elsewhere. I thought: what the heck! I didn't feel like carrying the discussion any further, and agreed with her request, I'd make her "original", nothing more and nothing less.

During the final post-op check she expressed no satisfaction or dissatisfaction with the result. When she was about to leave, I couldn't

415

hold back my curiosity and asked whether she thought she was indeed "original" again.

All she said was, "Yes. My husband thinks so."

The physician and patient used to have a trusting relationship in the old days, maybe even too trusting. With the passing of time the relationship became more like a business transaction.

Let's go back to the year 1936, when Huey had started his practice in Sheboygan. He told me about his first encounter with a type of practice that might have been perhaps not common in earlier surgeons' days. It is kind of sad and funny at the same time, but I'll let you decide.

During the first year Huey was to accompany an established surgeon during his hospital rounds and house calls, in order to "learn the ropes of practice and some bed-side manners."

"One day an urgent call came from Oostburg; an old lady was having bad pains in her belly. We drove right over. The doctor in charge felt a big lump in her abdomen and after he had listened to the bowel sounds, he came to a quick conclusion. 'This is serious! The old lady has a bowel obstruction due to advanced cancer in her belly.'

"To save her bowel from flowing up and killing the patient outright, she was to be operated on immediately. An ambulance was called to take her to St. Nicholas Hospital, and the surgeon performed what he called a 'terminal colostomy' that same afternoon.

"As a result of this operation an incredible thing happened!

"The patient was cured of her cancer, and lived another twenty years with her 'terminal' colostomy. The surgeon's fame and fortune spread well past the county lines."

Then old Huey gave me a knowing smile, "Do you know what the old lady really had? Nothing!

"She was just plain constipated and in need of a good enema."

By now you probably figured out what this abdominal mass was all about, because after a good evacuation there was no mass left in her belly. Needless to say a good soapsuds enema would have performed the same kind of "miracle cure" without the colostomy.

---

[1]The magazine *Gynecology* had a green cover.

Chapter 16

GETTING STARTED

To get started in a new town one needs at least a roof over his head and a bed to sleep in. We didn't have either. Vince Meyer, the clinic manager, came to our rescue; he found us an unfurnished house we could rent on Bluff Avenue, near the Sheboygan Zoo. All we had was a lazy-chair and a TV set, not furniture quite yet.

Vince called the credit manager at Prange's and secured us a line of credit. We outfitted the house with new furniture, and the total bill came to $1,500 with "easy monthly payments". We didn't buy a washer and dryer, but Barbie Schott told Hazel she could use hers until we could afford one.

I was seeing patients in my office and loneliness was the very last thing on *my* mind. But Hazel, who had been working as a nurse for all those years, might have felt isolated in the new town without friends.

Never fear. Soon the first visitors arrived, the Zimmermans and the Osbornes and the Eberts. Marilyn made Hazel feel a load better with her wit, just as Irene did with her easy-going smiles and Florence with her practical hints. I still remember them as they sat on our new couch at 329 Bluff Avenue, carrying on a friendly conversation. They even offered Hazel "taxi service" in case she needed something from the grocery store. You see, it was winter and Hazel couldn't go anywhere without a car.

———————

Things also started to look up at the office.

When checking my appointment book every morning, I found a noticeable change. Where there were only empty pages the day before, there were now names scattered here and there, some even with a "New OB" designation.

Dr. Duckering didn't want to see them until they were three or four months along, or until they felt the baby kicking. Well, if you have more patients than you can handle, you would ask your receptionist to do some screening, too.

Perhaps there was another reason for it?

I became interested in medicine as it was practiced in the 1930s, and nobody I knew could supply that kind of information more factually than Dr. Huibregste. He never joked about it, rather spurted things out in a minute or two as he held a patient's chart in his hand, in the middle of dashing from one office to other.

When I wondered why doctors didn't want to see their pregnant patients before five months, his response was, "Obvious reason, they wanted to be sure they were pregnant and past miscarriage stage." Then, by way of illustration, he went ahead and told me about a case from the 1940s.

A young lady came to the doctor's office, accompanied by her mother. She had missed a few periods and her mother wanted to know why.

Dr. Duckering examined her and announced (in the presence of her mother) that she was pregnant.

According to Huey, after the babysitter's confession all hell broke loose in what had been a loving, close-knit family.

The young lady, declared pregnant, had been babysitting for her sister who was in the hospital having her second child. Before television, those long evening hours could make a husband feel mighty lonely, missing the company of his dear wife. The babysitter wanted only to comfort her lonely brother-in-law, but one thing can lead to another even in the best family, and especially when there is no clear demarcation line between ways of giving comfort.

But this was the *wrong* diagnosis, and an invalid scenario, the young lady *wasn't* pregnant!

Could you imagine the days of happiness the family felt *before* that diagnosis, and the disaster after it.

That story made me extra careful not to shoot before I was sure I had the right ammunition, and then to keep the results confidential with a capital C.

Over the years I had numerous phone calls, such as "you saw my wife (or girlfriend) just an hour ago. Is she pregnant?" The only way to answer those inquiries is to ask the caller in turn: "I don't know who you are talking about. Why don't you ask her?" If he says "she won't tell me," then you know something is cooking and are careful not to put your foot into a potential mess. The best way to settle the matter is to say: "I have seen many patients today and I believe none of them were newly pregnant, and I am not even sure I saw the person you are talking about."

That is sure to bring the conversation to a peaceful end without confrontation. Refusing to answer out of confidentiality might arouse suspicions that you are hiding something.

I asked Cory to give early appointments, as soon as they thought they might be pregnant. For me every new patient was a blessing, and I truly believed that an early visit could benefit the patient and her future offspring. Besides, the women, particularly the young ones, wanted to know at once whether they *were* pregnant rather than waiting for months.

We could even order a quick pregnancy test for confirmation.

The old Freedman test, also called the "Rabbit Test", was history by then, and had been replaced by the "Frog Test". All that was needed for that examination was a few drops of the patient's urine to be installed into the male frog's cloaca.[1] If the lady happened to be pregnant, the frog would ejaculate into his cloaca and fill those urine drops with his sperm. (How the frog might have felt personally about the test is not known, but he sure would be generous in his reaction to a positive result.) A sample of that fluid examined under the microscope would give a quick answer, and if it turned out to be wrong, you could always blame the frog.

It seemed to me that this early appointment approach helped, but I did not want to rely on this approach alone. Sheboygan was a conservative town and patients had the habit of sticking with their own doctor for generations to come. Some of the doctors were up in the years, but no one ever retired. Instead they practiced to "Kingdom come".

Then a new and handsome OB doctor named David Batzner came to town, and opened his practice in the Medical Arts Building.

He was a devout Catholic and attracted most of the patients of the same spiritual calling.

I had no bones to pick with Dave.

He was a nice chap and we talked about some of the non-routine cases. (He liked to call it "picking each others' brains").

One particular instance comes to mind, which caused us both to do some "picking".

We worked side-by-side in a futile attempt to save the life of a patient who wasn't even ours.

I might as well give the full story of what happened.

One day I had finished a delivery at St. Nicholas Hospital and was washing the talcum powder off my hands when I heard the delivery room nurse Mrs. Wuestenhagen on the phone, saying, "Yes. Dr. Ashby is here." And then ending her conversation with "Yes, doctor!" After she had hung up the phone, she turned to me, "Doctor so-and-so is sending in a patient who might have had a convulsion, and he wants *you* to take care of her."

Nobody of sound mind would volunteer to take a patient under those circumstances, which could have been described as "dumping". But for the patient's sake I felt obligated to take her on.

Before I had the chance to change my soiled scrub suit, the patient was wheeled in on a stretcher. She was unconscious and when rolled to the labor room bed she had another *grand mal* seizure.

The information in her case was as follows: The patient was 42 and about eight months pregnant.

That morning she started to have a severe headache, and called her doctor to complain about it. The doctor had ordered Emperin comp. #3 tablets to relieve her symptoms. Her husband was sent to pick up the prescription at Fessler Drug.

But when the husband returned with the tablets he found his wife on the floor, next to her bed. He lifted her back to bed but a moment later she had violent shakes and fell to the floor again. This sequence of events repeated itself a few times until the husband became very concerned and called an ambulance for his wife to be taken to St. Nicholas Hospital.

That was when the call had come in and put me in charge.

Then Dr. Batzner happened to walk in and offered his help.

I won't go into details of the treatment, but with proper medication we were able to stop the convulsions and lower her sky-high PB. No fetal heart tones could be heard on admission and the baby was presumed dead. Dave and I took turns at her bedside, titrating her medication at first and inducing the labor the next day. She delivered a stillborn infant in her bed, with forceps. Trying to transfer her to the delivery room might have precipitated another episode of convulsions.

After a few days she was declared brain-dead and taken off of life support. There was nothing Dave and I could have done to save the mother and her child. Neither of us put in any charges for all the hours we had spent at her bedside. Remaining as good Samaritans was more rewarding to us in this sad case than any dollar bills could provide.

This case of maternal death was the only one I had to attend to in my 30 years of practice. Perhaps God looked kindly upon me after this episode and heard the short prayers I said while scrubbing in for surgery or for delivery. Or some version thereof:

> *"God be merciful to me and to my patient. Guide my hands that no harm will come to this mother and her unborn child. Amen."*

It worked for 30 years, and not only for obstetrical patients, but for all the women I operated upon. This wasn't about skill. I'm not trying to set myself up, but rather to show how merciful the Almighty was to me and to my patients over all these years.

Then something else happened to give my OB practice a real boost.

A physical therapist from New York had moved to town. She had been, among other things, an instructor of the Lamaze method of natural childbirth. In Kansas City we gave a preparatory course for expectant mothers, but in Sheboygan no such course existed. I had been thinking about starting such a class, but so far had no instructor. She was a godsend to get things rolling in the right direction, and I thought such a class would quickly become popular with mothers-to-be. I was right.

She was happy to take the assignment and meet the expectant mothers in town. A dozen air mattresses were secured, and the exercise classes got started in the Clinic conference room Thursday evenings. At first there were only six or seven participants, but within a month all the mattresses were filled and soon there were more students in the Lamaze class than we had mattresses. They had to start taking turns.

I could have ordered more mattresses, but the exercise room was getting too crowded and St. Nicholas Hospital was happy to take over the class with all its obligations. That, of course, would open it to all the pregnant patients in the community, but I didn't mind. I had started something that ended up making delivery safer and more rewarding for many patients across town.

That was good for a start, but I didn't intend to stop there.

I wanted the young mothers to know what was best for them and their babies. Labor was painful enough, but knowing what to expect would help them become participants in the process. I wanted my OB patients to be well informed on all aspects of pregnancy, and to that end I supplied each patient with a complimentary booklet on "Natural Childbirth", which I signed and had stamped "with compliments of the Sheboygan Clinic". In addition, I put together a mimeographed compendium of do's and don'ts; a proper diet during pregnancy with tables of food-values rich in protein and vitamin C, and additional calcium and iron. I even included a chapter about sex during pregnancy. Back then even the word "sex" was taboo, and many young women knew very little about it and were too shy to ask. Today all this information is public knowledge and readily available from multiple sources. In the early 1960s, rather strangely, it was not even discussed.

Another thing that I stressed to my patients was that they should call me at home if they had an urgent problem such as pain or bleeding.

I never installed any answering machines to give them canned messages.

Most patients were considerate and called only when they felt it was urgent. At times they were looking for reassurance, but there were times when they minimized their symptoms. Over the phone you couldn't always tell the difference. It was better to get out of bed and see her in the ER, or I wouldn't be able to sleep without knowing whether a condition was serious or not.

Everybody knows the "take two aspirins and call me in the morning" joke. I know one doctor who gave such guidance over the phone, only his patient didn't call back next morning because he was dead by then. I knew that patient-to-be, he was my friend.

Of course there were some nights when a call didn't excite me very much. As a rule an itch in the private parts didn't make me rush to the ER, because it never proved fatal. That was the time to use the weatherworn instruction "take two aspirins, etc…"

I might not have sounded friendly to those callers who found they were out of birth control pills at midnight, knowing very well that their prescription had run out a month ago.

If I lost such a patient I hadn't lost much.

They didn't even save any money by skipping their yearly exam and only contacting me to get their prescriptions renewed. The pharmaceutical salesmen had left me so many samples that I gave every patient at least a six-month supply of pills (worth $60 back then) and charged only ten dollars for the visit, and that included the Pap smear.

I thought I was considerate, and I expected reciprocal treatment from my patients.

I remember one Thanksgiving evening.

We had just sat down for dinner when the phone rang. It was a patient who had had her baby ten days before, and she was bleeding. She didn't believe the bleeding was excessive, but I could sense from her voice that she was frightened. When I met her in the ER she was pale as a ghost and had no blood pressure or pulse, only her heart was still beating at a rapid rate.

An emergency hysterectomy was performed without delay. We quickly opened her abdomen, and stopped the hemorrhage by clamping the main blood vessels leading to the bleeding uterus. After her vital signs were stabilized, first with blood-volume expanders followed by pre-warmed blood transfusions, only then it was safe to go and finish the operation. Any undue manipulation when the patient was still in shock might have precipitated cardiac arrest. When I left her, her vital signs were stable with good urinary output. In her case, any reassurances over the phone would have had tragic consequences.

Back at home I ate my cold turkey alone and felt the tender happiness of true thanksgiving. She wouldn't miss her uterus, since her family was complete. And besides, I had "tied her tubes" after her delivery some two weeks before.

The old-time male doctors strictly regulated the sterilization operation generally known as "tying the tubes", and these became part of the hospital by-laws:

> The sterilization operation can be performed only if both the patient and her husband request the named operation and she (the patient) meets the following criteria:
>
> She must either (1) be 35 years of age and have at least three children, (2) be 30 years old with four children, or (3) be 25 and have five children. Any deviation from that norm will require consultation with the husband and written recommendations from two consulting physicians giving good reason for deviating from these regulations.

Meanwhile Dr. Gary Quinn had joined me in OB/Gyn practice at the clinic. He was a good Irishman, and a Catholic like Dr. Batzner, and both of them refused to perform such an operation on religious grounds.

As a Lutheran I had no restrictions, and I spent many of my lunch hours doing the procedure in question.

The urologist did the vas ligations on their male patients. It was an office procedure and no outside consultation was required and men were the ones who decided whether their "cords" would be cut or not. It was no one else's business and no one else had jurisdiction over his "private parts". This operation did not become very popular among men, they wanted to keep their ability to make a woman pregnant, or they might lose their identity as a virile male!

One had to give the men credit, though. They were generous enough to give their wives permission to undergo their own sterilizations.

Although these antiquated and perhaps chauvinistic rules were in the books, I had to find ways to get around them. There were enough open-minded doctors who were willing to put their "John Hancock" down for the sterilization operation without even reading the consultation note. They knew that I wouldn't perform such an operation indiscriminately. All I had to say was: "I need your signature for a 'tubal ligation' permit", and that did it.

I lost all esteem in the eyes of Sister Callista, the OB supervisor at St. Nicholas Hospital, but my obligation was to my patients only and they had the right to make such a decision for themselves.

As far as abortions were concerned, I performed one in my 30 years of practice, on a 25-year-old lady with polycystic kidney disease. It was the opinion of two consulting internists that she would die well before the viability of her offspring. The operation was done in early pregnancy and she died within a year of uremia.

Kidney transplants, even dialysis, was unknown then.

I must have gotten lost somewhere.

Oh yes, I was talking about supplying my obstetrical patients with books and pamphlets.

News of my attention to detail spread and I started to have OB patients who wanted to transfer to my service after they had already seen their family doctor. Those cases were exceptional and in general the family doctors took good care of their patients. I don't want to give the impression that I was the only doctor who knew how to deliver a baby. All I wanted to do was give my patients confidence that I could give good care if and when complications set in during their pregnancy or delivery. With this in mind, I gave Cory the liberty to register any patient who requested an appointment.

Such an open-ended practice can get one into trouble.

I should know because my open-door policy brought about some problems once.

It was one of those Friday evenings when we still had office hours until nine in the evening. I saw a patient who had been under the care of a lady physician in town. She had had problems with her previous pregnancy and decided to seek the care of an obstetrician.

This all sounded reasonable, and I told her that I would take her case.

As I got into her history in more detail, I learned that she had given birth to a stillborn baby because of Rh incompatibility. The dictum back then was "once a stillbirth due to Rh factor, always a stillbirth". In short, there wasn't much else I could do but deliver her another dead baby.

Then she added as an afterthought: "I'd better tell you that my husband is a very jealous man! He threatened to shoot any male physician that I see."

Well, delivering another stillborn infant for her had cooled my enthusiasm, but her husband's attitude had put me on the spot, so to speak. I had already accepted her as my patient and could not well back out now. I wanted to know more about her husband, "He must have some emotional problems! Is he under the care of a psychiatrist?"

"Oh yes. He is seeing Dr. Houfek at the First Federal Bank building."

"Does your husband know you came to see me?"

"I'm not sure. He might have seen the appointment slip the receptionist gave me."

"Well. Perhaps it is best not to tell him about today's visit. I want to talk to Dr. Houfek first to learn more about your husband's condition. We'll get the blood tests today, including the Rh antibody titer, and I'll see you again in two weeks."

I saw Dr. Houfek the next day at the hospital, and explained my problem to him and wanted to learn more about the man he was treating.

425

Dr. Houfek didn't beat around the bush, "I'm not afraid of my patients in general, but he is number one on *my* list. Just the other day we were having a peaceful session in my office when without any warning he took a heavy ashtray from the table and threw it at me. I ducked quickly and he missed me, but the ashtray left a big dent in the wall just behind my head."

That was not quite the information I was looking for. I had faced greater dangers in the past, and this possible ordeal didn't worry me too much. But before I left my office in the evening, I started to look around first, just to be on the safe side.

To make a long story short, my patient's antibody titer had hit the roof. The intrauterine change transfusions were not performed back then, and I'm not sure how much difference that would have made in her case anyhow. One month later her baby died, and the only thing for me to do was wait for the onset of labor.

Meanwhile Dr. Houfek had several sessions with her husband and informed him about the facts that his wife had been seeing a male specialist, and that the baby would be stillborn again. He had accepted the facts and had promised to behave, but only if he was allowed to be with his wife throughout the labor and delivery. Otherwise he might get all crazy and wouldn't know what he would do next.

In the 60s neither hospital allowed the husband to enter the delivery suite, as if it were some kind of sanctuary. I discussed the situation with the St. Nicholas Hospital sisters, and particularly with Sister Callista, who was in charge of the labor and delivery floor.

We worked out a plan in advance.

The patient would be delivered in one of the labor rooms. Her husband would not be separated from his wife, but her bed would be arranged in such a way that her husband would be boxed in the corner. To get at me he would have to jump over the bed, but by then I would be long gone through the open labor-room door. Dr. Houfek had alerted the police department and two detectives were in the doctors' dressing room as a precautionary measure. They had frisked him before he was allowed to enter the labor suite.

Everything went along without any problem.

The husband was most docile in his corner, holding his wife's hand. The baby was stillborn as expected, showing advanced stages of *hydrops fetalis.*[2]

426

This was the first time a husband was permitted to be with his wife during labor and delivery. It took more than a decade before the rules changed and the couples were allowed to be together during the important episode in their married life, the birth of their child.

[1]common chamber into which open the hindgut, bladder, and genital tracts
[2]excessive accumulation of fluids in fetal tissues

Chapter 17

HAPPY DAYS

I finally had a place I could call home.

Hazel was from a small town in Canada and I was raised on a farm. We just loved the unhurried lifestyle that only a small town could provide.

What a change from all the bustle of cities like San Francisco and New York, even Kansas City, where we had lived a vagabond life. Settled in Sheboygan, we had bought a house in a quiet neighborhood and found pride living in our own home. What a change from the days when all I had were the hands in my pockets and the wind on my back.

The days, weeks, and years seemed to melt together into everyday tasks. I had established a good practice, and enjoyed every moment of it.

I had three offices and the two best OB nurses, full of enthusiasm and their own individual charm. Pregnant women and particularly the young ones could identify with Nancy and Jackie, as both of them had given birth to their own children. They could share their feelings more meaningfully with expectant mothers than I ever could, never having had labor pains myself. Both of them radiated enthusiasm and excitement, and I must add, it was highly "infectious" to the patients and even to an aging doctor.

They did not become my nurses by coincidence or by chance. No sir!

I had picked them out all by myself.

Both of them happened to be delivery room nurses first, and I had the chance to admire the way they handled their labor patients.

I remember when one of my young patients, frightened and restless, was not progressing in labor.

The next shift brought Jackie to the scene.

She went to the patient's room, bent over with her head next to the patient's, and stayed in this awkward, and may I say, rather unladylike, position as she started to mumble something to her. I do not know what Jackie was saying, but the patient quieted down, quit "fighting" the labor, and in half an hour was ready for delivery.

To me it seemed a miracle.

I must admit that I am a pretty good salesman, and it didn't take me long to convince Jackie to quit her hospital job and become my office nurse instead.

At St. Nicholas Hospital was another nurse who gave exceptional care to her patients in labor. Nancy had an uncanny ability for establishing instant rapport with the labor patients, and her empathy made them trust her implicitly. They submitted to Nancy's tutoring, leaving all the worry on her shoulders. No wonder she would sometimes stay with her patients even past her hours of duty. Her dexterity was also exceptional. If there was no vein to start an intravenous infusion, then Nancy was called.

Needless to say she became my office nurse, too, but continued to work as a part-time delivery-room nurse at night. When my patients, who had met Nancy in the office, happened to be admitted in labor during Nancy's shift, they felt like it was Christmas all over again. And when new mothers came for their six-week check-ups, they brought her flowers and "I love my nurse" coffee mugs.

At times I picked up the office phone and heard a happy voice at the other end, "Oh, Dr. Ashby! I don't want to talk to you! Could I talk to Nancy?"

It pleased me, of course, that Nancy was *numero uno* in taking some of the load off my shoulders. I thought it a blessing that she was my nurse, and not a competing obstetrician in town.

Oh, let's not forget Linda. She was the nurse who filled in in times of need.

At first she was just one of the new nurses in the delivery room at Memorial Hospital, but what made her stand out from the rest was her uncanny ability to pick up things quickly. When I told her something, she knew it, and the next time she even reminded me if I deviated from the norm.

Linda was one of those "see, do, teach" kinds. She was perhaps more determined than the rest of us, but if you have a smart nurse who happens to be enterprising, it's far better that she works for you and not for your competitor!

What about the aging doctor?

Whenever I fished at home for both compassion and encouragement by bringing up the subject of being "in labor" up to 300 times a year, Hazel would cool my inquiring, "You'll get the same flowers as everybody else!"

She couldn't complain, though. For our tenth wedding anniversary I took the whole afternoon off to play golf with her!

To get things done on time, I used to walk with a quick step.

Dr. Willis made a remark once, claiming that I left only a blur behind me. Mrs. Apel, one of my devoted patients, wrote in her thank-you note that I was the fastest walking doctor she had ever seen.

Well, if you feel good and things are going your way, what's the use of loitering around? The sooner I got there, the less time somebody had to wait.

I was happy with my own practice, but the so-called "clinic calls" in the '60s were most annoying. If you were "on call" that meant you had to treat anything under the sun from nosebleeds and earaches to car accidents. The hospitals did not have any emergency room doctors back then, and if someone walked in and you were on hospital call, you'd better rush over and treat anything under the sun.

For me it was like having my internship all over again.

It was no use calling any old-time surgeons to handle a case. All the ice from the North Pole would doubtless melt before you would get them out of bed in the middle of the night.

When orthopedic surgeon Dr. Peter Brown joined the Clinic, it was a great blessing as far as I was concerned.

Peter was a first-class gentleman. I could call Peter any time, and he would say "Don't worry about it, I'll go and take care of it!"

One Sunday a kid twisted his ankle when playing baseball and could hardly walk. I had to go to the hospital, look at the X-ray, and treat him accordingly.

I could tell a leg-bone from an arm-bone, but anything beyond that was a Chinese puzzle to me.

The twisted ankle happened on a beautiful spring Sunday. The birds were singing, and lilacs were in full blossom. How could I get anybody to help me on a day like this?

With a heavy heart I called Peter Brown.

His wife, Roma, answered. She was always so nice to hear over the phone with her continental English, "This is *Rouma*. Peter is fixing the roof."

I told Roma about my problem. Could she ask Peter if he would go and see a kid with a busted ankle at St. Nicholas Hospital?

"Please wait. I'll go and ask!"

Then I could hear Roma shouting the message to Peter, who was still on the roof.

I couldn't hear Peter's answer, but Roma was back at the phone, "Peter said he'd take care of it. It will take him a minute or two to get down and clean up!"

I tried to imitate the way she said "Roma" "Thank you, *Rouma.*"

She laughed at my counterfeit English, and hung up.

———————

One evening I received an urgent message, "Hey doc, hurry over! My baby just swallowed a dime and is choking." He gave the address and promised to leave the porch light on.

I was still new in town, and ended up in the city dump. The smoke and smoldering flames convinced me that I was off the track. I had to back out and it took me a while to find the house with the porch light on.

A middle-aged man was rushing out to meet my car as I drove in, "Forget it, doc! There's no need to come in. He already coughed up the dime!"

He must have stood on that porch for a while waiting for me, knowing that if I didn't enter the house, the house call wouldn't transpire and there couldn't be any charge!

We ended up on a friendly note. He saved himself the house-call money and I saved my blood pressure from going through the roof, since I didn't have the slightest idea anyway of how to get a dime out of a baby.

———————

There was another call I remember so well. It was the very first and last time I did some baby-sitting.

It was a cloudy morning with a cold wind.

It had rained all night, and there were pools of water with autumn leaves scattered on the wet pavement. A man with a cracked voice had just called me at five in the morning to tell me about his ordeal. He had a fever and cough and had been confined to bed for a week because of weakness. And he had no family doctor to call.

I found the house.

The door wasn't locked, and I went right in. What I saw made me pause for a moment.

There was a large frying pan in the middle of the living room carpet with a child's shoe in it, half-buried in the hardened grease. Two young girls ages perhaps three and four and dirty from head to toe, were playing hide-and-seek and chasing each other merrily around the pan. Back in a small windowless room was a man about forty in a narrow bed propped up by pillows. He was sucking for air, his lungs were filled with rales and he had a high fever. He belonged in the hospital for sure, but what about the girls?

"Where is your wife to take care of the children?"

"She left me."

"Don't you have any friends or relatives to take the girls?"

"I have nobody."

That put me on the spot, and I didn't know what to do next.

There must have been some social agencies in town, but I had no idea how to reach them. I called Dr. Senty instead.

He told me to send the patient to the hospital and when I wondered about the children, he said, "Can't you stay with the girls for a half an hour or so until I find someone to take them?'

There was nothing else I could do, and the idea of babysitting kind of appealed to me.

I sat on a corner of the couch, my medical bag between my legs, and watched the girls as they continued to run and laugh. At times they stopped and looked at me, their big eyes all turned serious for a moment.

They were the most beautiful carefree little girls. Their dirty faces added to their charm.

Even today I wonder whatever happened to them. They must be past their prime by now, but in my memory they will remain children forever.

Their father turned out to have acute leukemia with superimposed pneumonia, and there wasn't much hope for him.

Since I'm on the subject of house calls, I'll add one more as it contrasts with the others. House calls were common in the early 60s, and I used to see a number of my own patients in their homes.

I remember one call like it was only yesterday, certainly not 40 years ago.

It must have been close to midnight when the phone rang.

It was a man's voice, rather coarse, telling me about his daughter-in-law and some kind of female problem she had. She had had her first baby perhaps ten days ago, and had been home less than a week. He couldn't give more details, only that the couple lived upstairs and his son had come down and asked him to call the doctor, Dr. Ashby, who had delivered the baby. The young couple didn't have a phone upstairs, and that was the reason he had made the call.

The place was way outside the town, somewhere in the back woods. He told me that he was running a bar downstairs. It was closed at this hour, but he promised to leave on the *Schlitz* beer sign, which could be easily seen from the road. There was no way I could miss it.

It was a windless night in early fall.

The cloudless sky was filled with stars. I drove out in my '57 Chevy with my black bag next to me in the front seat.

At first there were isolated farmhouses with their high silos, ghost-like against the moonless sky. Then came the woods, the tree branches meeting across the road, their leaves red and yellow at the headlights. I was beginning to think I'd gotten the directions wrong when the *Schlitz* sign came to view behind the bend. Its glow threw eerie shadows on the forest, the road, and the tavern.

There were no cars on the graveled parking place in the front.

When I pulled up a bearded and stocky man, perhaps in his late 40s, came to show me in.

"My son and wife are upstairs. Let's go up and see them, but you'd better go first."

When we reached the upper steps of the narrow unlit stairway, the door opened and what I saw startled me.

A naked woman was running around the room.

One could not even tell she had a baby a fortnight ago: her abdomen was well shaped without any stretch marks, and she had feminine hips and slender legs and waistline. She did not have the Lady Godiva's long hair to cover part of her lush anatomy, which was all-visible in a well lit room.

When she noticed me standing at the doorway, she stopped running and looked at me in amazement, and then realized that she had no clothes on. She grabbed a bed sheet, wrapped it around her and said with a friendly voice, like a greeting, "Dr. Ashby! What are *you* doing here?"

I was all set to ask her why she was running around without clothes, but then realized that it was her apartment and if she wished to be naked, that was her free choice. There was no dress code under those circumstances!

I was the intruder and her question to me was reasonable and entirely justified.

Instead of answering, I asked how she was *feeling.*

"Just fine!" was her short answer.

I turned to her husband, who was standing halfway behind the open door, and asked him if there was anything he was concerned about.

"Not any more," was his brief response.

I apologized for the intrusion, and wished the young couple good night.

When I went down that narrow stairway, I noticed that the bartender was all shook up. I didn't blame him; the view was extraordinary, and he was not used to the kind of "shock treatment" his shapely daughter-in-law had just given him.

Downstairs, he drew a mug of cold *Schlitz* for each of us. We spoke about the weather, the crops, and the Green Bay Packers with their new coach, Vince Lombardi.

Driving home I was in a festive mood. Of all the house calls I made in the 60's, this midnight call was the most extraordinary.

What had happened? I have no idea. If the young lady had a short episode of "split personality" and thought herself the 11th century Lady Godiva, my brief visit had effected a cure and brought her back to the 20th century.

Chapter 18

THE DAY I REMEMBER

It is early morning and I am on my way to Memorial Hospital, listening to T. Perry Jones's Morning Prayer on the local radio station. Exactly at seven Bob comes on with his "good morning to all you listeners in WHBL land..." He then goes on to talk about all the bargains one can find at "Ebenreiter Lumber" and "Peg's Pantry", where they are all *"on the job again!"*

By this time I have negotiated the only stoplight between home and the hospital, and parked in the semicircular drive in front of Memorial.

It's early and the front lobby is deserted.

The first door on my left in the hallway leading to the elevator is Mrs. Olson's office, still closed at this hour. She is the hospital administrator, usually sitting behind her small desk and typing some kind of report. She doesn't have a secretary, and if you have something on your mind, just step in, sit in that vacant chair next to her, and tell her your gripes, no appointment needed!

She will then stop whatever she is doing, cross her forearms while propping her elbows on the desk, and give you a friendly smile. She lives next door to the hospital in a red brick house with white window frames, and takes the incoming calls or complaints, day or night. (One shouldn't have much to gripe about when the charge for a semi-private room is only $14 a day.)

Opposite her office is the doctor's lounge, with morning newspapers. The freshly brewed coffee is next to the record room, where each doctor has his own designated spot for unfinished charts. Adjacent to it is a long table with a Dictaphone and a chair.

In the middle of the room is Marge's desk. She is the assistant administrator and the head of the medical records department. Marge is a slender woman in her early forties with a pair of good-looking legs every doctor could see when pouring his morning cup of coffee.

She is trying to charm the doctors into completing their records.

This, however, is no easy task because there are some egos involved; the height of a doctor's stack of unfinished charts was a measure of his importance and the size of his practice.

Marge's charms were of no use in clearing one particular pile.

The doctor had passed away, leaving behind quite a stack. Some of these charts didn't have a single notation from the doctor, not to mention the fact that they were missing histories and physical exam information. Only the nurses' notes proved that a lost soul had been a patient here sometime or other. Whatever happened to that patient, it was hard to tell from the unclaimed files... whether he had been taken out through the service elevator by two men in raven—colored suits, or had left the premises under his own power.

Reading the nurses' notes would throw some light on the mystery.

No wonder Marge was using any available technique, including her fading sex appeal, to try to attract doctors to the records room. Some of the "high-stack" doctors were old geezers, and if they happened to kick the bucket she would be stuck with another pile of unfinished records. Marge didn't want to go through that kind of rigmarole again any time soon.

All this goes through my mind as I stop in the doctor's lounge to flip on my light. I see the waiting newspapers, still folded up on the coffee tables, and the freshly brewed coffee next to the record room.

No sight of Marge or any doctor yet at this early hour.

The elevator takes me to surgery on the fifth floor. It's a long walk down the hallway to the operating rooms, so it's always nice that the large windows on my right give a panoramic view of Lake Michigan in its vast blueness.

I had "snuck in" a quick surgery before the regular 8:00 a.m. starting time. Carol knows that I will be finished well before that, and the operating room will be ready for the scheduled case at eight.

I always admire how quickly the surgery crew could clean the room between cases. It takes only a minute or two to remove the soiled laparotomy pads and sponges, the green drapes, surgical table covers and all the instruments and mop the floor at the end. I call them "circulating nurses" in the true sense of the word, with Pat the busiest bee in the bunch. They never bump into each other or even get in each other's way while crisscrossing the room.

They wear caps and masks but I recognize each of their eyes and voices, some of them having been my patients sometime or other.

And there is Linda (not to be confused with the OB nurse Linda), the surgical tech who is my scrub-nurse in the morning mini-laparotomy case.

She is young and full of enthusiastic charm.

Linda has all the "rat-tail" sponges lined up and anticipates my moves by offering first the scalpel and sponges, then the retractor, then the narrow and long laparotomy pads and finally the needed instruments.

She hands me a straight Kelley and I want a curved one, "Linda, could you bend those for me?"

It's an old joke from the Fred Hiddie days. When the scrub nurses handed Dr. Hiddie a straight clamp and Fred wanted a curved one, he threw the clamp over his shoulder to the floor behind him and yelled at the nurse: "What happened to the *curved* clamp?!" It was a brave nurse indeed who answered him with, "I am bending it for you, sir!"

That's where the joke originated, but Linda is too young to know about Fred and answers in all seriousness: "I wish I could!" And she means it, too!

With Linda's expert help I was finished in a jiffy.

Sponge and instrument counts were correct, and by the time the patient is taken to recovery, the full crew has cleared the room well before Otto is supposed to start hammering nails into someone's busted hip joint at eight.

There is no way I can leave Dr. Otto Stewart without praising his professional skills, since he pinned Taka's broken leg! Taka was a red-tailed hawk who was hit by a car and brought to my first son to be nursed back to health. He had a busted eye and broken leg. Otto pinned the leg under fluoroscopy wearing no protective gloves, which would have been cumbersome in manipulating the broken ends of a pencil lead -size bone.

If you ever happen to see a one-eyed red tailed hawk sitting atop a telephone pole out on the rural west side of Sheboygan, that's the one Otto fixed up!

My next stop is at the third floor to see my *post-partum* patients.

Mary, the head nurse, greets me with a mysterious smile. Mrs. Olson, the administrator has sent up a piece of cake with a candle. We sit in a narrow long room next to the nurses' station. It's called a kitchen, but is a far cry from a true kitchen with its metal counters and ice-cube makers. Mary lights the candle with a smile, "Happy Birthday, Dr. Ashby", and then pours a cup of coffee for each of us.

I place the candle on an upside-down coffee cup, and the white candle burns with a yellow light as we drink our morning coffee.

Mary is about 40, a well-shaped woman with pleasant face and motherly charm. She is such a caring nurse, telling me about the worries she has been facing on the floor.

When I am finished with the cake, I look up and say, "Good old Mary! You worry too much!"

She drops her hands on her lap and looks out the window over the young birch trees and at the narrow ribbon of lake glittering in the morning sun.

Then we make rounds.

A patient who had a Caesarean section the day before is already busy putting on her lipstick. Half-finished but still holding her lipstick, she takes her eyes from the compact mirror and inquires, "Will I get something to eat today?"

Without waiting for an answer, she returns to her stretched-out lips, oblivious to the rest of us. Mary asks her to wait and pulls up her hospital gown so I can listen to her lungs. Then she removes the abdominal dressing and I sit at the patient's bedside and palpate gently around the incision and listen to her abdomen.

Mary just stands there, holding the charts against her chest, as I announce, "Full liquids today. May take shower."

In the next room is a young mother sitting up in bed.

She is eating her breakfast, breastfeeding her baby, talking on the telephone and smoking, all at the same time!

When we enter the room, she hangs up the phone and puts her fork on her plate while the baby continues to suck at her swollen breasts, "Hey, doc! How about letting me go home tomorrow? My insurance company won't pay if I stay any longer."

"It's ok with me. Talk to your pediatrician about checking out your baby on time."

Mary and I walk back to the nurses' station. She hands me the charts one by one as I make my notations.

When I stand up to leave, she looks up and says again, "Happy Birthday!"

"Thank you, Mary. Be a good girl and don't worry about little things!"

She gives me a departing smile.

Next I take the elevator to the second floor to see one of my post-op patients.

She is doing well and will be dismissed today. I have given her instructions already, only adding a note of caution, "No relationship with your husband for four weeks, and nothing passionate before your six-week check-up."

Her jaw drops while she keeps her lips closed, as if she is trying to suppress a smile. I am not sure she will follow my instructions.

A flash in her eyes makes we warn her, "…Watch it!"

When I come down it's already nine o'clock.

When downstairs I suddenly remembered Dr. Ira Bemis in Ward 2K, admitted to the hospital two days before with chest pains.

When I had visited him that morning, he was sitting up in bed and didn't seem to be in any distress as he told me what had happened, "I was having my usual office hours last night when I started feeling chest pain. At first I ignored it and continued to work. After a while the pain got so bad I couldn't go on. I asked my nurse to give me a quarter grain of morphine intravenously, and finished seeing all my patients.

"It was well past midnight when I finally sat down to write a note. You see, I'd promised a bit of land I owned at the lake to one of my sons. I put it all down on a piece of paper and asked my nurse to witness it. After that I asked my maintenance-man to drive me to the hospital."

That conversation being two days ago, I felt I should go to him again and see how he was doing.

I found his hospital room empty. The mattress was bare and the floor recently mopped.

I got hold of a nurse at the end of the hallway, "What happened to Dr. Bemis?" I asked.

"Didn't you know? He passed away last night!"

I felt deep sorrow. Back then they didn't have any Intensive Care Units, cardiac catheterizations, coronary stents, or by-pass operations. There was only bed-rest and sedation, administered with tons of reassurance.

This wasn't enough for Dr. Bemis.

Ira was one of the few doctors outside the Clinic whom I felt close to. He was a very heavy-set man, recognized even by the laundry department, who classified the scrub suits as small, medium, large, and

"Dr. Bemis".

I still remember the night I first met him.

I had spent most of that night in the hospital and had finally delivered one of my patients after a long labor. I was truly tired, physically and mentally. Before leaving I dropped in the nursery for a moment to check the baby I had just delivered when a cheerful voice came from the back of the room where the nurse was re-wrapping someone's screaming "bundle of joy":

"Oh, Dr. Ashby! Do you know Dr. Bemis has been looking for you?"

My first thought was to dash downstairs, flip off my light, and disappear into the night, but I knew I couldn't do it. I have this cowardly nature, which makes me feel guilty when I try to flee from my obligations.

I found Dr. Bemis and listened to his problem, "I have this young girl who's been in long labor. I tried to deliver her with forceps, but couldn't. Perhaps you want to put on the "hooks"[1] and give it a try, or should we go ahead and do a Caesarean right off the bat?"

His cheerful disposition contrasted with mine. I looked at Dr. Bemis's physical size and wondered how much traction this man had applied to the baby's head before he gave up…

"Oh. No! No more forceps! We'd better get the surgical crew in instead!"

I knew it would be a difficult case. After the prolonged labor and "failed forceps", the birth canal wouldn't be sterile. The traction with forceps had most likely glued the baby's head into the bony pelvis. Dislodging it through the uterine incision from above would be difficult. The tissues were likely thin after long labor and would tear like wet cigarette paper with engorged blood vessels next to it. Trying to extract the baby's head without ripping onto those "big mamas" would be tricky.

I gave the nurse my pre-op orders, "Call the supervisor and ask her to get the surgical crew in here stat! Get the lab on the phone and ask them to cross-match two units of blood, just in case. Notify the pediatrician "on call" and start the second intravenous line with 5% Lactate Ringers, use #16 needle. Insert the Foley catheter and ask the pharmacy to send up two grams of Cephobid[2]".

And to Dr. Bemis, "Let's go see your patient, and then we'll talk to her husband in the waiting room."

In half an hour we were scrubbed in.

I had said my short prayer and after the anesthetist said "GO", we were in business.

Here speed (and skill) comes into play; it is desirable to deliver the baby within two minutes of that "GO" signal. At the start the mother would be under only slight anesthesia but temporarily paralyzed with curare[3] so she wouldn't move. Curare has a large molecule and doesn't cross the placental barrier, having no effect on the baby. A large dose of Pentothal off the bat would make the baby sleepy at birth. The patient could be fully anesthetized only after the umbilical cord had been clamped.

As you can see, speed is of the essence during a Caesarean section.

On the other hand, the surgeon can't act like a bull in a china shop with all those vital tissues, the urethras, bladder, bowel, and those big veins, less than an inch away from your operating field.

But everything turned out well. I ended my operating note with, "The baby and mother both left surgery in good condition."

My prayer had done its wonders again: I was able to extract the baby's head from the pelvis without additional injury to the uterus or to the engorged veins, which were lying like coiled snakes on either side of the womb.

That was the night Dr. Bemis and I met.

During his 40 years of practice, Dr. Bemis had become a part of the country itself. His office hours were usually from nine in the evening until beyond midnight, and any time in between. Sometimes a knock at the window at two in the morning would get him up to see a late, or perhaps we should call it an early, patient. The farmers couldn't squander daylight hours with doctor's appointments!

He didn't send out bills. The folks paid all their other bills first and the doctor's last, but they paid. During the Great Depression money was hard to come by, and they brought him chickens and eggs. Or the patients, knowing Dr. Bemis just loved homemade bread still warm from the oven, would ask him over after they'd done some baking.

Those were just some of the things I'd learned from Ira over the few years I knew him.

For a little community called Batavia, it was the end of an era.

Without Dr. Bemis, life wouldn't be the same. No other doctor would ever settle in the village. The clinic would open a branch in the nearest town with their central processing units, computerized billing, and animated answering service.

It all would be a strange New World for the people of Batavia.

It looks like I got lost again with my reminiscence.

I drove to the office and opened my mail. At first this consisted mostly of drug company circulars, requests of record transfers, and the like. Then I came across a handwritten pink perfumed envelope, an old-fashioned love letter. It didn't make any sense for me to receive such an emotion-filled confession. Dr. Jochimsen, our psychiatrist, happened to be walking past my office, "Hey, Earl, could you step in for a minute!"

With a coy smile and perhaps even a touch of pride I got to the point, handing the perfumed letter over to him, "You see, Earl, I got this unusual letter and I don't even remember the person who sent it to me!"

It took Earl less than a minute to read part of it, then he dropped it on my desk and looked at me with a smile, "Now don't get all excited! For your information, this woman even wrote love letters to Dr. Florence Duckering!"

He stood up, serious again.

"If you don't mind, I'll take it with me and put it in her chart."

"Go ahead!"

With some faint misgivings, I watched Earl carry my perfumed letter away down the hallway. I must confess, it was the only one of its kind I'd received ever thirty years of practice, and it had turned out to be fake.

I realized how happy my practice really was. I didn't see sick and dying patients as a rule. Most of them were young and pregnant. I enjoyed seeing their babies growing in utero and I enjoyed delivering them. There was always so much excitement, some anxiety combined with hopeful expectation, because pregnancy is the only human condition where pain and suffering are not due to any disease and the suffering endured is rewarded with a new life.

It is natural for a patient to want her own doctor to deliver the baby.

Take Julie for instance.

She works in the office and comes in with a pile of records for me to put in the charges for rendered services. I like her friendly but sometimes domineering attitude. She only becomes domineering when trying to protect my own interests, "How come you charge less than your partners? Is your work inferior? That's what the patients think when they compare their bills."

She's right. "Ok, Julie, put in the standard charge."

That makes her happy.

"I do not want my doctor to be cheap!"

Julie is herself expecting, and says, "Don't go to Florida again in October. I don't want anybody else!"

"If I were to charge less and be a 'cheap doctor', would that make you switch to somebody who charges more?"

"Don't change the subject! I want you to be there, and don't give me that mysterious smile!"

Good old Julie. She is so cute in that red sweater, which matches her youthful cheeks:

"Don't worry, I'll be there."

That makes Julie happy, and why not? I would love to deliver that first child for her. Perhaps I should go in November instead?

My charges are still flexible.

One of the ladies I'd been seeing for years worked at Montgomery-Ward. The store had just closed and she was out of a job. Her insurance company had promised to pay the doctor's surgery bill in full, but wound up paying only half.

"Don't worry, Lisa! Tell the business office that you've spoken to me and there shouldn't be any additional charges. If they give you a hard time, you call me back."

She was obviously relieved: "Thank you, Dr. Ashby!"

I know firsthand how hard it can be when you find yourself unable to pay all the bills. I could say with all honesty that I never turned down such requests in my thirty years, justified or not.

When there is a free moment, I step into Ruth's business office.

She is an attractive lady with a young face and prematurely gray hair. This gives her such a distinguished look as she sits at her desk among all her machinery, clicking and ticking and spitting out reports.

Ruth is in a good mood nine days a week and I owe her a lot.

One day I mentioned to Vince, our Clinic manager, that my checking account was all messed up. I had enough money in there, but my bills weren't being paid on time. I just couldn't handle such a disaster!

Vince talked to Ruth, and she straightened out my omissions and transgressions. She even filed the paid bills in a separate folder, and wrote the dates and check numbers on them. I've never seen such bookkeeping in all my life. This in itself was a good reason to go and see Ruth every morning to find out if I would need Chapter 11 protection.

She pushes her chair from the desk and gives me a knowing smile. She knows that my question is only an excuse to drop in, "Don't worry! I'll let you know well ahead of time!"

She stresses the word "worry".

Perhaps my question is a bit bogus, but I could always use reassurance. It's a good way to start a new day.

What else had happened in my social life during my first decade in Sheboygan?

Well, I had joined the Pine Hills Country Club back in 1965. Dr. Bernie Marsho was my sponsor, and back then it cost only $500 to join.

In Sheboygan I'd also developed an interest in photography. I bought an expensive camera and set up a darkroom at home to develop my own colored enlargements up to 16 x 20.

Ladies Home Tournament was coming up, and I wanted to use my fancy camera and take some pictures for the Pine Hills ladies.

I just walked into the clubhouse, although this was a "no-no" for a male member on such a day. The ladies were having lunch, and the dining room was filled with distinguished foursomes, but first I had to get past Dolores who happened to be standing at the entrance and asking me in a friendly way, "Dr. Ashby! What are you doing here?"

A good question.

"I am a freelance photographer and want to take pictures of all the wonderful ladies here."

"All right, but then you have to take my picture first."

Good old Dolores! ("Old" just being an expression!) She is fun to talk to, because you never know how she might challenge you with a question, or a smart answer to a question of your own.

The ladies didn't seem to mind my intrusion.

They posed willingly for the picture taking, and were happy to stay sitting behind their tables with dishes, wine glasses, and elegant cutlery.

A ladies "Hole-in-One" party was coming up and I was asked to be their official photographer for the occasion.

I think this was all Alice's doing.

If you don't know Alice, you must be from the planet Mars.

She owns and manages "Johnsonville Sausage" with her husband Ralph. She lives next to me in a fancy house I call "Alice's Palace", and she drives a Mercedes-Benz with the license plate "Brats 1".

If you tell me that Alice is meek, then we're talking about two different Alices.

Alice and I are good friends, and it must have been her salesmanship (sales-ladyship) that got me the "job" as the "Hole-in-One" photographer.

It is not a paying job, but it has its benefits.

I am to sit at a long table with the honorees, all of whom have accomplished the impossible by hitting a golf ball some 160 yards out and getting it into the cup with a single stroke.

I am the only male guest among 100 women, the best company I've ever been part of. I am to sit next to Alice and she sure takes good care of me.

When I go to take pictures of the tables of foursomes, Alice sends my steak back to the kitchen to be kept warm, and she asks the waiter to top-off my wineglass.

That isn't the end of the benefits, not by a long shot.

I have the honored title of "The Official Guest-Photographer of the Pine Hills Ladies 'Hole-in-One' Club". The length of my title compares favorably to that of the Prince of Wales.

And it is just as high an honor.

[1]slang expression for obstetrical forceps
[2]an antibiotic
[3]extract from various plants that produces muscle paralysis during surgery (Old Indian "arrow poison")

Chapter 19

GOING BACK

I am on a Boeing 737 enroute to Tallinn.

The first leg of the flight, from Chicago to Stockholm, took eight hours. Only one more hour and I'll be back in Estonia, the country I fled fifty years ago.

Drizzly rain was falling at take-off time in Stockholm, but now there is nothing but the sun, blue skies, and aquamarine waters of the Baltic Sea.

Estonia is free again, after 50 years of Russian occupation!

When the first streak of land emerges from the distant horizon, I become glued to the plane window with a pounding heart. There it is, my Estonia, the country whose freedom I fought for in my youth. Now I realize the hopeless folly it all was, a few thousand Estonian fighters with rifles were trying to hold back Stalin's armored divisions. Millions of people have perished since, either fallen in battle or died in Siberian labor camps near the Arctic Circle. Other millions have fled from the Red Tide in Eastern Europe. Independent countries like Romania, Czechoslovakia, Hungary, Poland, and the Baltic States had fallen prey to it. The Russians even took Karelja, the part of Finland with the most fertile soil.

I think of the long-forgotten verse from Friedrich Schiller, as quoted by Mrs. Grace back in Zahna half a century earlier:

> *Ein ruheloser Marsch war unser Leben*
> *Und wie des Windes Sausen heimatlos,*
> *Durchstürmte wie die kriegsbewegte Erde'.*

> *Our life was a restless roam*
> *Like the howl of homeless wind,*
> *Storming through the war-torn land.*

Memories of sad departures have been my bedfellows for years with repeated dreams of fleeing, always fleeing. I see the faces of my fallen comrades in front and behind me, skiing again in a long row in the drifting, endless snow.

And they used to call me the "lucky one" as I sat in front of the hot coal-stove, burning the names of my fallen comrades in birch-wood crosses. They were right, I must be the only one left from that crowd of old fighters.

The plane is circling low now, giving a birds-eye view of the countryside. There are clumps of woods here and there, and farm fields left to lie fallow, the plots of tilled land are only occasional, with dilapidated collective farm buildings from the Russian era. And there is Tallinn, the capital of Estonia, a thousand-year-old city with its medieval towers and churches.

After a smooth landing a stairway is rolled next to the plane, and we all descend under our own power to the baggage claim. All the passengers seem to be Estonians; mostly old people coming to visit the country they were forced to leave in their youth. We are the fortunate ones, escaping from the Russians' labor camps and deportations!

After my passport is stamped I find myself in a small waiting room crowded with people. Suddenly my sister Asta is running to me and we hug each other. I have seen her in photos, of course, but I am still struck by her chubby waistline and the weak-tea color of her once-blond hair. Her husband Boris stands next to her, a tall, balding and most kind man with stooping shoulders and big hands. There is also Lia, my niece. I saw her last when she was sixteen and danced at my confirmation party back in the summer of '43. The years have undone much of her beauty, but she still has lively eyes and a bubbly spirit. Her husband's name is Erich.

There are more handshakes and hugs, a few tears. They take my suitcases and my carrying bag, and we head toward the exit.

A fresh wind is blowing in from the sea.

The smell of decaying seaweed and the cry of the seagull bring back memories of days past. So much has changed, but much remains eternally the same, like the sea and the gulls. They were there when I left as a young man, and they are here again to greet me when I return, wiser and advanced in years.

My sister and her husband live in Kadriorg, four or five miles from the airport. It is a park-like setting close to the sea. Asta and Boris have a living room, bedroom, kitchen and bathroom. There are bookcases with many books, and paintings on the walls. Outside behind the large old-fashioned windows are full-grown linden trees, their green leaves shield the afternoon sun.

Asta is four years older than I, but she is quite agile and shows me around the apartment, pointing out items she still has from our old home in Kullenga; there is the old Singer sewing machine with the foot pedal, the one my godmother Priida used when she sewed me the outfit with bows and buttons to wear in first grade. I sure stood out like a sore thumb from the other kids.

And there is that old mirror in its carved wood frame!

I used to sit in front of it at the age of six, dressed in a dark-colored winter coat with a white handkerchief tied in the front, reading the family bible in a clear and loud voice and pretending to be Eberhard, the old minister from Väike-Maarja.

I sit in front of the magic mirror once more, but now I see only an old man's face looking back at me; there's no sign of the child who once sat there and pretended to be an ordained minister.

Then we all sit down at the long table and eat, drink, and talk for hours on end.

It is almost midnight when I go to bed. It's still light outside: Tallinn is north enough that after the sun has set in June, the afterglow lasts until dawn the next day.

I sleep soundly in the room with the old sewing machine and ancient mirror, relics from my childhood.

I had arranged a get-together for the class of '39.

There are four girls: Õie, Hilja, Ellen, and Lydia. I am the only male. Õie and Lydia had spent years in Siberia. Hilja escaped to Sweden before the Russians came, and visits her home country every summer.

Ellen had been a dentist in Tallinn, is now retired, and lives in her old home in Väike-Maarja with her cat.

We get together at Õie's place, a rundown house in the woods, only a few miles from Väike-Maarja. Her father was a captain in the Estonian defense forces and died years ago in Siberian labor camps. Õie lives in this old house with dark oak furniture, faded tapestries, and framed pictures of her long-dead relatives hanging on the walls.

We eat our dinner, drink some wine, and reminisce about days gone by.

Lydia Vaiksalu (now Tagamets) has her story of living in exile.

I am amazed how matter-of-factly she can reminisce. After so many years of sadness and gloom, she must have been able to save her sanity only by crawling into a protective shell and leaving her emotions dormant for years.

The Russians, as you know, reoccupied Estonia in the fall of 1944.

I had lived with my mother on our farm. I had two brothers, and both of them fought the Russians like you. We never learned the fate of my older brother, which itself wasn't unusual as many were killed by the Russians and buried in common graves. My younger brother was teaching school at the time of his arrest, which was only two weeks into the occupation.

My mother and I worried about our own safety as every day we heard about arrests of people we knew. I used to sleep nights at our neighbors, but had to come home during the daytime to help my mother take care of the farm animals.

It was on 25 March, 1949 when the Russian soldiers arrived with horses and sleighs. They carried rifles and told us we were under arrest. My seven-year-old niece happened to be visiting us, and was arrested and sent to Siberia with us. We were given one hour to gather our belongings such as warm clothes, blankets, and pillows, and all the food items to eat during the long journey such as pork, potatoes, and a sack of flour. We packed our pots and pans, dishes, and some cutlery. The Russian soldiers helped load the things on the sleigh and we were on our way to Väike-Maarja, perhaps two or three miles from our place. There was already a large crowd, mostly women with children, all arrested from neighborhood farms. One young woman had been hiding under a load of hay in the barn, but the Russians had found her by using pitchforks. She was still bleeding from the stab-wound in her calf, covered with rag bandages. She considered herself the lucky one: most of the time the Russians didn't bother with pitchforks, they just "raked" all the hay supplies in the barn with their automatic guns and laughed.

"Yobtvoiu mat![1] That'll teach them...!"

We were all loaded into military trucks and driven to Rakvere, where a freight train was waiting for us. The freight car doors were opened and the soldiers threw in all our belongings.

There were 46 persons in our cattle-car: 10 men, 25 women, and 11 children, all of them less than 8 years old. (The youngest child was only 9 months.) We had a small stove in the middle of the cattle-car and 6-7 empty buckets for our toilet needs. The doors were bolted shut, and the train took off.

The mood was most depressing: women and children were crying, the men were swearing. It was pitch-dark at night, during the daylight hours only dim light came in through two small windows that were close to the ceiling and covered with steel bars.

The train trip to Siberia took two weeks with frequent stops. Men had to empty the buckets with solid and liquid waste at the stations and get some coal for the oven, accompanied by guards. At times when the excrement buckets were full, a sudden movement of the train made the liquid contents splash all over the wagon floor.

Occasionally they gave us a slice of bread with soup. It was mostly water with shreds of cabbage and foul-smelling meat.

When the train reached deep into Russia, we were allowed to step out for a few moments of fresh air at the train stops. It was the first time I saw how long the cattle train really was I could hardly see the end of it. The wagons were all filled with Estonians, mostly women and children. (Their husbands had been arrested earlier.) Two locomotives were pulling the long train.

From Novosibirsk our train left the main Siberian tracks to Iskitim, and from there 20 miles by sleigh to an isolated state kolkhoz. The land was flat and there was nothing but crusty snow and cold wind. There were no trees anywhere, only mud huts here and there with stovepipes for chimneys, some of them smoking.

The sight was most depressing. Nobody spoke. There was nothing to say. There were no more tears left for crying. One woman in our sleigh had a heart attack and died. Two of her children, aged ten and twelve, stayed with their dead mother ten miles until we got to an isolated kolkhoz. There the dead woman was removed and her two children were sent to an orphanage.

We were told that all of us were sentenced to life in exile and whoever tried to escape would be sent to a prison camp for 25 years. We had to acknowledge that this information was given to us by signing on the dotted line. After that our passports were confiscated: the exiles had no rights beyond work at that desolate country kolkhoz.

We all had sent applications to Moscow, claiming to be innocent and arrested without any known cause. The applications were returned to us, stamped "DENIED". Stalin died in 1953 and we applied again, this time to the new chairman Khrushchev. After a year or two children up to age sixteen were allowed to return, and that included our niece who was sent to Siberia at the age of seven only because she happened to be at our house at the time of arrest. It took numerous applications until we all were allowed to return to Estonia after eight years of exile. We were able to claim our house and all the furniture, only because one of our relatives had moved in with her child after we were deported. But the land and cattle were gone for good.

Õie has a similar story, except she had married a Russian in hopes of escaping from lifelong exile. No such luck, but she left the husband behind when she was allowed to return after eight years. She doesn't want to talk about the marriage in more detail, but admits having had no children.

My own odyssey has a silver lining. Just think about it, without the Russians and the war, I wouldn't ever have gone to America, the "land of the free and home of the brave".

We were once classmates in a young and prosperous country, but now are living in different worlds. I could well imagine what would have happened if I had stayed...

After Lydia finishes her story, nobody speaks for a while.

The dusk falls over us and over the table with leftover food and half-filled glasses of wine, There is meager light through the dark curtains, but we still can see the heavy-framed photographs of long-dead people looking down on us from the surrounding walls. Beyond the windows and their peeling paint, the crickets are singing their distant song.

The following day I go to visit Väike-Maarja High School,[2] sixty years after my graduation. My favorite teacher back then was Miss Helmi Eller, who had died recently in Stockholm at the age of 95. I had established a scholarship in her name at my old high school. The old school building is no more, replaced by the Russian-style structure of cement slabs.

The principal is a blond lady of about forty. She meets me at the entrance and leads me to her office, filled with soft light coming through the windows with white curtains. There is a computer with printer and a fax machine next to her large desk. Against the opposite wall is a built-in couch, and in front of it flowers on an oval-shaped coffee table. Then the Estonian language teachers, all four of them women, come to meet me.

In my professional work I have dealt with the female gender all my life, and I felt most content in their company.

We sit on that long couch while we drink coffee and talk in Estonian, the language I haven't conversed in for a generation, but all its excitement comes quickly back to me. I feel like a schoolboy sitting in the principal's office, among the amiable lady teachers.

I am led into a small classroom filled with senior students. I sit down at the first bench and all the junior girls sing for me. They are so close I could reach out and touch them.

Then Mrs. Eelmaa, the principal, introduces me to the class and asks me to say a few words to the students.

Words of nostalgia and contentment, I am deeply moved to stand up and after so many years make my first (and perhaps last) speech in Estonian.

Eller, my old Estonian teacher, would have been proud of me as I surprise myself with my fluent recollection of events from my school days. It all comes back to me as I cite Estonian poetry and old algebra axioms, word for word.

Everybody seems to be with me in my reminiscences. I try to be careful and end it on time.

The principal presents me with a book called "The Cultural History of Väike-Maarja". Its first page is filled with the children's written-in mementos. I feel charmed by a keepsake note:

"Estonia and Ojamaa are *über alles,"* signed "Algis and the women of Estonia".

There is one more place for me to visit, my old homestead.

It is only six miles from Väike-Maarja and my brother-in-law Juhan Maasi offers to take me there.

I was hesitant at first, perhaps I wanted to remember it the way it was that foggy evening before Christmas, in the year 1943, the evening I left it for good.

The road took us past Kullenga, where once the endless fields of rye were blossoming and the voluntary firemen were sitting on the hillside, passing around a bottle of government brew with their horses grazing nearby.

I see but empty fields with melancholy thistles waiving in the afternoon breeze.

We have to turn left towards Kadila, where the gravel road is fraught with potholes filled by recent rain showers.

After a mile we come to a dirt road, and there, a few hundred yards on our left, are the house and barn, still standing. The trees my father had planted in the 20s have grown high, throwing their shadows over the dusty farmyard where sweet-scented camellias once grew.

The barns are still standing, but the roof has collapsed in places and the bare rafters are pointing toward the sky. The hay barn is gone, the lumber perhaps used to heat the house over the cold winters.

No one is home except for a dog tied to the barn, and his ferocity shatters the tranquility of a quiet afternoon.

The large pond behind our barn is overgrown with cattails and water lilies, exposing only a few square yards of open water. The old farm road leading to our neighbor's house is overgrown with grass and weeds; no horse-drawn vehicle or foot-traveler has used it for generations.

The neighbor's house, barely a stone's throw from our pond, is gone, and I can't see anything but endless fields of grass. I find traces of an old dirt road leading to where the house used to be. The path is really nonexistent, and I walk it more from memory than from any hints of ruts left by cartwheels.

I sit down on the rubble, recalling the old-time boasting among neighbors in a by-gone era, who had the wildest horses, the tallest corn, or who got most rye or wheat per acre. There was a lot of put-on and bragging, and our neighbor Kaarel was better than anyone at this.

In the mid-30s we had a radio installed, with the antenna sticking out from the roof. That rubbed Kaarel the wrong way because he couldn't buy one for himself, if he couldn't be the first, then he was against it.

The summer after our radio arrived was a dry one, and Kaarel made a claim one day when he was at the Kullenga creamery delivering milk from his cows, "Do you know why we haven't had rain this summer? Those damned radio waves from Julius' antenna have driven away all the rain clouds!"

But Kaarel, not to be outdone, went out and bought himself the swankiest gramophone money could buy. The following Saturday night we blasted polka music at him through the open window, while all of us danced in our large kitchen: mom with dad and I with my sister, while our small nippy dog Tipsi circled between us and added his bark to the beat. After the ruckus had quieted down, Karrel cranked up his gramophone and played back to us, *Mets mühiseb. Ja kägu kukub raal.* [3]

I walk back slowly along the same overgrown path that I had wandered as a child, when the corn was so high and the dust so soft between my toes.

Low clouds have risen over the ancient River Hill, covering the sun.

Wind and rain clouds are at my back, and the tall grass comes up to my knees, waving me farewell.

I walk toward my old home and the waiting car.

[1] "mother f----r"
[2] See *Capful of Wind"*, Chapter 5
[3] Woods murmur while cuckoo sings.

EPILOGUE

To borrow a phrase from T.S. Eliot's *Four Quartets,* "In my end is my beginning."

With age, there arises a certain need to speak about the past. To talk about the past as it "really was", but to give that reality all the color of an epic novel, and all the vivid charm and wisdom of a fairy tale.

How to end a story that is all told out, yet the lifelong colleague to a person who is still moving?

How to acknowledge the pains of my long life without spoiling the joys, how to be faithful to the joys without trivializing the griefs?

As we get older, we become our own stories...

They say you can't go home again.

It's true, the old man who looked into the old mirror with the carved wood frame wasn't the boy who had peered into it 60 years earlier.

The buildings that were once my home were overgrown with weeds. And then there were the fading photographs, the home and people that had been sacrificed, forever lost.

But I *did* go home again. As so often, the huge changes in the buildings, people, and roads that I knew didn't mask the few things that have remained the same. Instead, they made me see them all the more.

I really saw several Estonian homes that June. One of them I found more alive than ever. It wasn't in the buildings, but in the soil, trees, air, and sky. And in the people, especially the young folk. The young students and teachers I met in my old high school gave me a new and positive outlook in my old young country.

As an old man, and still a romantic despite all the wonders, horrors, and silliness I've witnessed in my many years, I want to end by quoting something Frank Harris wrote right around the time I was born.

Harris was editor of the *London Evening News,* an obsessively successful "ladies man" who towered over his conquests, and an autobiographer who was exhausting and delightful.

He ended the second book of *My Life and Loves* (1922) with a tired look on life, including these wise words, "Man's life is like a fireworks wheel, starting with low noise,

Dancing around and around.

Throwing off sparks and radiating energy.

Then gradually slowing, sparks fading, radiance dying –

Burned out amber..."

Exactly when does, did, the failing amber replace the noise, the dancing, the sparks? Fortunately, or unfortunately, I cannot pretend to know the answer.

And that might be another way of saying: I've been lucky.

Made in the USA
San Bernardino, CA
24 April 2015